SOUTHEAST ASIAN AFFAIRS 2013

The **Institute of Southeast Asian Studies (ISEAS)** was established as an autonomous organization in 1968. It is a regional centre dedicated to the study of socio-political, security and economic trends and developments in Southeast Asia and its wider geostrategic and economic environment. The Institute's research programmes are the Regional Economic Studies (RES, including ASEAN and APEC), Regional Strategic and Political Studies (RSPS), and Regional Social and Cultural Studies (RSCS).

ISEAS Publishing, an established academic press, has issued more than 2,000 books and journals. It is the largest scholarly publisher of research about Southeast Asia from within the region. ISEAS Publishing works with many other academic and trade publishers and distributors to disseminate important research and analyses from and about Southeast Asia to the rest of the world.

SOUTHEAST ASIAN AFFAIRS 2013

Edited by
Daljit Singh

ISEAS
INSTITUTE OF SOUTHEAST ASIAN STUDIES
Singapore

First published in Singapore in 2013 by
ISEAS Publishing
Institute of Southeast Asian Studies
30 Heng Mui Keng Terrace
Pasir Panjang
Singapore 119614
E-mail: publish@iseas.edu.sg
Website: http://bookshop.iseas.edu.sg

ISEAS Library Cataloguing-in-Publication Data

Southeast Asian affairs.
1974–
Annual
1. Southeast Asia — Periodicals.
I. Institute of Southeast Asian Studies.
DS501 S72A

ISSN 0377-5437
ISBN 978-981-4459-54-9 (soft cover)
ISBN 978-981-4459-55-6 (hard cover)
ISBN 978-981-4459-56-3 (e-book PDF)

Typeset by International Typesetters Pte Ltd
Printed in Singapore by Mainland Press Pte Ltd

Contents

Foreword vii
Tan Chin Tiong

Southeast Asian Affairs: Forty Years of Research and Analysis ix
Donald E. Weatherbee

Introduction xi
Daljit Singh

THE REGION
Divided or Together? Southeast Asia in 2012 3
Bridget Welsh

Southeast Asian Economies: Building the Base for Stronger, Better Distributed Growth 17
Manu Bhaskaran

Southeast Asia in America's Rebalance to the Asia-Pacific 40
Satu P. Limaye

Chinese Perspectives on the U.S. Role in Southeast Asia 51
Zhu Feng

BRUNEI DARUSSALAM
Brunei Darussalam in 2012: Towards a *Zikir* Nation 63
Hajah Sainah Haji Saim

CAMBODIA
Cambodia in 2012: Towards Developmental Authoritarianism? 73
Kheang Un

Cambodia's Border Conflict with Thailand 87
Pou Sothirak

INDONESIA
Indonesian Politics in 2012: Graft, Intolerance, and Hope of Change in the Late Yudhoyono Period 103
Greg Fealy

Resource Nationalism and Constitutional Jihad 121
Ahmad D. Habir

LAOS

Laos in 2012: In the Name of Democracy 137
Holly High

MALAYSIA

Malaysia in 2012: Promises of Reform; Promises Met? 155
Graham K. Brown

Shades of Citizenship: Betwixt the Civic and the Ethnic 168
Lee Hock Guan

MYANMAR

Myanmar in 2012: *mhyaw ta lin lin* or Great Expectations 191
Robert H. Taylor

Myanmar's 2012 By-Elections: The Return of NLD 204
Tin Maung Maung Than

THE PHILIPPINES

The Philippines under Aquino III, Year 2: A Ponderous Slog Continues 223
Patricio N. Abinales

The Philippines in the South China Sea: Out of Time, Out of Options? 240
Maria Ortuoste

SINGAPORE

Singapore in 2012: A Year of Scandals, Attempted Political Engagement, and Socio-economic Anxieties 257
Narayanan Ganesan

Singapore's Population Conundrum: The Great Balancing Act 2 274
Yap Mui Teng

THAILAND

Thailand in 2012: A Year of Truth, Reconciliation, and Continued Divide 287
Chairat Charoensin-o-larn

TIMOR-LESTE

Timor-Leste in 2012: The Harsh Reality of Independence 307
Damien Kingsbury

VIETNAM

Vietnam in 2012: A Rent-Seeking State on the Verge of a Crisis 325
Alexander L. Vuving

Navigating the Crisis: The VCP's Efforts to Restructure the Economy and Fight Corruption 348
Le Hong Hiep

Foreword

I have great pleasure in presenting this fortieth edition of *Southeast Asian Affairs*. Over these past four decades, this annual review of the region has become an indispensable source of information and analysis for all those interested in Southeast Asian developments. It is designed to be easily readable so that it can be of value to both specialists and non-specialists.

In 2012 Southeast Asia showed impressive economic resilience in the face of weak demand in the developed economies and risks posed by financial stresses in the eurozone. It was geopolitics which perhaps drew more attention — and concern. New leaders took over the reins of power in China, Japan, South Korea, and North Korea. President Obama was re-elected for a second term. The U.S. "rebalancing" to Asia, announced in late 2011, raised considerable interest, and in some quarters, concern. There were signs that the Sino-American relationship would see more strategic competition notwithstanding the many cooperative aspects to it. Disputes in the East China Sea aroused fears of a clash between China and Japan through miscalculation. Tensions in the South China Sea continued, with no early prospect of a legally binding Code of Conduct. Within Southeast Asia, Myanmar continued on the path of reform but faced huge challenges in translating good intentions into policy and implementation that would better the lives of ordinary people and ensure domestic stability.

I would like to thank the authors and the editor, as well as others in ISEAS who have helped to make this publication possible. The chapters in the volume contain a wide variety of views and perspectives. The authors alone are responsible for the facts and opinions expressed in their contributions. Needless to say, their interpretations do not necessarily reflect the views of the Institute.

Tan Chin Tiong
Director
Institute of Southeast Asian Studies
April 2013

SOUTHEAST ASIAN AFFAIRS
Forty Years of Research and Analysis

In March 1974, Professor Kernial Singh Sandhu, Director of the Institute of Southeast Asian Studies (ISEAS), launched a major new publishing initiative, the Institute's annual *Southeast Asian Affairs*. The appearance of *Southeast Asian Affairs 1974* was the first of its kind: an annual review devoted to the international relations, politics, and economies of the region and its nation-states. The project was part of the ISEAS mandate to be a leader in research on the problems of stability and security, economic development, and political and social change in Southeast Asia.

The comprehensiveness of coverage in the annual series expanded as ASEAN itself expanded from its original five members to today's ten. The collected volumes of *Southeast Asian Affairs* have become a compendium documenting the dynamic evolution of regional and national developments in Southeast Asia from the end of the "second" Vietnam War to the alarms and struggles of today. Over the years, the editors of *Southeast Asian Affairs* have drawn on the talents and expertise not only of ISEAS' own professional research staff and visiting fellows, but also have reached out to tap leading scholars and analysts elsewhere in Southeast and East Asia, Australia and New Zealand, North America, and Europe. A full list of contributors over forty years reads like a kind of who's who in Southeast Asian Studies.

When asked to contribute this special introduction to the current *Southeast Asian Affairs*, I went back to look again at the first number in the series. I was struck by how many of the themes raised some forty years ago resonate today. It is not a matter of *plus ça change, plus c'est la même chose*. It is that persistent problems and structural issues continue to be in play. For example, in 1974 three general levels of political threat were identified. The first level was international, where in the region there was a sense of anxiety and insecurity with respect to the future roles of the great powers in the regional international order. Special mention was made of China's forceful expulsion of Vietnam from the Paracel Islands and claims to the Spratlys. The second, regional, level consisted of unsettled territorial claims, described as "smouldering embers that could give rise to future fires". The fires burned over the years. At the third, domestic, level, attention was given to separatism, struggles for autonomy, and ethnic and religious tensions; all threatening national and regional stability; and they still do.

Looking at the regional economies, *Southeast Asian Affairs 1974* underlined the continued dependency of Southeast Asia on the state of the global economy. Then, the issue was an energy crisis. The authors also looked at the indicators of real economic development but worried about growing income inequalities. The conclusions were generally upbeat, buoyed by the tremendous economic development potentials in Southeast Asia. In retrospect, it is fair to say that *Southeast Asian Affairs 2013* bears out the economic optimism of the previous generation. Arguably, ASEAN's greatest real achievements have come on its economic playing fields.

The anxieties in the broad patterns of ASEAN's international political and security environments laid out in *Southeast Asian Affairs 1974* give a historical dimension to the contemporary anxieties felt in the region. All of the categories of threat at the three levels — international, regional, and domestic — that informed the first number of *Southeast Asian Affairs* exist today. Steady forward steps towards economic integration within the region and between the region and its trading partners have not been matched in the political and security fields. The conflicting interests in the South China Sea threaten to undo ASEAN itself, let alone its vision of community. Bangkok and Phnom Penh are waiting for the International Court of Justice (ICJ) to drop the other shoe in the Preah Vihear dispute. Significant ethnic and religious conflict persists at different levels of violence and humanitarian suffering in Indonesia, Myanmar, Thailand, and the Philippines, to mention only the more prominent among the many unresolved political and security problems. Overarching them all are the uncertainties about China's ultimate ambitions in the region and America's willingness and capability to give real substance to the rhetoric of the so-called "pivot" or "rebalance."

Regardless of specific events and outcomes in political, economic, and social developments in Southeast Asia's future, we can expect that future numbers of *Southeast Asian Affairs* will continue to provide the expert analysis that has marked the publication since its founding. It has become an important contributor to the knowledge base of contemporary Southeast Asia.

Donald E. Weatherbee
Visiting Professorial Fellow, Institute of Southeast Asian Studies, Singapore
Russell Distinguished Professor Emeritus, University of South Carolina, United States

Introduction

The Region

Great power rivalry has returned to Southeast Asia over the past few years after a hiatus of over two decades — and, with it, traditional security as another salient concern. The Asia- Pacific region, of which Southeast Asia is part, is now marked by tensions involving a nuclear-armed North Korea, near-confrontations between China and Japan in the East China Sea, and incidents between some Southeast Asian states and China in the South China Sea which have also produced strains in the Association of Southeast Asian Nations (ASEAN).

The year 2012 featured considerable media and elite attention to the U.S. "rebalance" to Asia, which had been announced in part to alleviate the anxieties of allies and friends about an overbearing China. It thus had the support, public or tacit, of most Southeast Asian states as a hedge or balance against China. Beijing tended to portray the U.S. rebalance as a stepped-up effort to contain China. Beijing seemed determined to demonstrate that it would not be unnerved — indeed its posture in the South China Sea and the East China Sea remained uncompromising. It was over the Senkaku/Diaoyu islands in the East China Sea that major power tensions appeared to reach dangerous levels after the purchase in September 2012 of three of the islands by the Japanese government from private owners, to which China reacted strongly. Incidents that occurred included the scrambling of Japanese fighter bombers in response to the flight of Chinese maritime patrol aircraft near the islands and the alleged locking by a Chinese naval ship of its fire control radar on a Japanese warship. In the absence of channels for crisis communication and management between the two militaries and strong nationalistic fervour in both countries, the danger of an outbreak of conflict in which the United States could also be drawn in was real.

While the East China Sea disputes were separate from those in the South China Sea between China and four Southeast Asian countries, they were by no means unconnected. Big power tensions in one part of East Asia are bound to have spillover effects to other parts where the same big powers have important interests. The maritime space off the East Asian littoral through which vital trade routes of Japan, China, and South Korea pass is a continuum from Northeast Asia, through Southeast Asian waters and into the Indian Ocean. Japan certainly takes this view and sees the troubles in both the East China Sea and the South China Sea coming from a single source, that is China's assertiveness. It has made known that peace and stability in these waters is a national interest of Japan and has sought to increase security links with and assistance in capacity building to Southeast Asian countries, including the donation of ten new patrol boats to the Philippines Coast Guard.

In the South China Sea itself, China was not alone in its intransigence. However, given the fact that China is a big power amidst much smaller and weaker countries, its actions, unsurprisingly, drew much more attention and scrutiny. With its geographical proximity to Southeast Asia, its rising economic and military power, its assertiveness, and its willingness to use economic weapons against countries perceived to be not respecting its interests, China increasingly loomed large in the foreign policy calculations of Southeast Asian states.

Intra-state politics and security in Southeast Asia saw no major surprises in 2012. Governments continued to wrestle with the familiar challenges of governance, development, regime legitimacy, or rebellious/restive minorities, often differentiated from the majority by ethnicity or religion. A bright light of the year was the framework agreement reached between the Philippine government and the Moro Islamic Liberation Front (MILF) to end the MILF insurgency, even if there were some uncertainties about its implementation. Islamic extremism and terrorism remained a threat in a number of countries, especially Indonesia and the Philippines. Indonesia, a self-proclaimed tolerant and "moderate" Muslim country, continued to see harassment of and violence against religious minorities that were condoned by the authorities. Myanmar remained saddled with the same problems which it has faced for some years: ethnic minorities, violence between Rohingyas and Myanmar Buddhists, and, above all, economic development. The high expectations of its people that democracy would improve their lives had not been fulfilled. It will be a difficult and long haul, given the weaknesses of the relevant state institutions and lack of trained and skilled people.

Some unease remained in Malaysia and Thailand about possible leadership transitions. In Malaysia this was caused by uncertainty about the outcome of the next general election that was expected to take place in 2012, but did not, and would instead take place in the first half of 2013. In Thailand, the roots of disquiet lay not only in the continuing polarization between the political forces aligned with the traditional establishment and the pro-Thaksin ones, but also over the possible repercussions on the political order of the demise of the country's revered but ailing King, whenever that occurs. In Indonesia, the next presidential and parliamentary elections were already casting their shadow on the country's politics, even though they are due only in 2014.

The economic performance of Southeast Asia in 2012 was commendable, with regional economies showing surprising resilience in the face of weak demand in the developed world and financial troubles of the eurozone — a testimony to sound macroeconomic policies and reforms carried out in recent years. However huge disparities in development and incomes remained between the four newer members of ASEAN and the older six, a gap which will take a long time to narrow significantly. Even among the older members, significant poverty levels still exist in Indonesia and the Philippines despite recent good economic growth rates.

The regional section of this volume has four chapters. In the first chapter, "Divided or Together? Southeast Asia in 2012", Bridget Welsh discusses the schisms in ASEAN, highlighted by the Association's failure, for the first time in its history, to issue a joint communique at the end of its Annual Ministerial Meeting. She covers the divisions over the South China Sea issue, the divergent responses to China, the differences over human rights brought out by the introduction of the ASEAN Human Rights Declaration, and the tensions over economic integration and free trade agreements. She also deals with the persistent internal conflicts from Myanmar to Papua in Indonesia. In the sphere of domestic politics, she observes a greater tendency on the part of states to resort to short-term populist strategies to address society's grievances and demands. She concludes by acknowledging that, at another level, there are also forces "pushing the region toward shared goals of prosperity, stability, and empowerment" and a persistent but quiet building of regional architecture.

In his economic survey of Southeast Asia, Manu Bhaskaran observes that in 2012 Southeast Asian economies stood up well to the deceleration of global demand, the financial stresses arising from ultra-easy monetary conditions in the developed world, and frequent bouts of financial turbulence in the eurozone — in the process showing a degree of resilience that few had expected. Economic growth held up, supported by domestic demand. The resilience was due to structural factors and is, therefore, likely to be sustained. Bhaskaran sees some positive forces emerging in Southeast Asia that will help boost the region's growth prospects and economic resilience. They include more synergies from economic integration, and prospects of more foreign direct investment as investors seek to diversify investment to other locations in the region besides China.

In "Southeast Asia in America's Rebalance to the Asia-Pacific", Satu Limaye argues that the importance accorded to Southeast Asia in the rebalance is one of the two distinctive features of the U.S. overall strategy, the other being the inclusion of India. He sees a structural process of institutionalization of U.S.-Southeast Asia relations as being underway in which the United States seeks to strengthen alliances, deepen relationships with emerging partners, engage with regional multilateral institutions, expand trade and investments, and advance democracy and human rights. It would be a mistake to regard this process as only a function of the U.S.-China relationship. He goes on to discuss U.S. policy in each of these areas, cautioning that achievements will not be smooth or swift, and that both Southeast Asia and the United States will need to work on them patiently and persistently to mutual benefit.

In the next chapter, Zhu Feng presents a Chinese perspective on the U.S. rebalancing. There is a tendency in China to see the rebalancing as the latest U.S. effort to keep China encircled and contained. According to Zhu, the rebalancing deepens the perceived security dilemma between the United States and China, increases strategic distrust, and makes escalation of geostrategic tensions more likely, though in itself it is unlikely to lead to a new Cold War. But rebalancing will not make China soften its position on maritime disputes. Zhu is of the view that rather than opt for a balance of power strategy, Southeast Asian countries should enhance cooperation with China to settle the South China Sea disputes and show sensitivity to China's deep sense of insecurity. He acknowledges that the United States has important interests in Southeast Asia and deep-seated bonds with the region, but reminds that Southeast Asia is not a U.S. backyard and China, which now wields a bigger economic clout in Southeast Asia, also has its interests. Zhu is also implicitly critical of China's assertiveness in the South China Sea since 2009 which lost it much political capital in the region. It is time, he says, for Beijing to ponder why, despite its rapid rise and its economic clout, it is still unable to command the level of respect it deserves in the region.

The Countries of the Region

The eleven country reviews and seven country-specific thematic chapters look into developments in individual Southeast Asian countries.

In "Brunei Darussalam in 2012: Towards a *Zikir* Nation", Hajah Sainah Haji Saim records some of the incremental achievements towards realizing the country's Vision (Wawasan) 2035, which combines modernity and material progress with spiritual and religious values. Steps were taken to make the civil service more efficient, attract foreign investments, improve education and skills, and develop infrastructure. In parallel, there was more stress on Islamic values and observance of Islamic practices. Islamic Religious Knowledge and Malay Islamic Monarchy subjects were made compulsory in secondary schools. As the new ASEAN Chair, the country was also preparing to hold the various high-level ASEAN meetings in 2013.

In his review of Cambodia in 2012, Kheang Un notes further consolidation of power by Prime Minister Hun Sen and his Cambodian People's Party during a year which saw the passing away of the country's revered former King, Norodom Sihanouk. Hun Sen used the country's rising economy (it grew by over 6 per cent in 2012) and regional and global linkages to open up new economic opportunities, attract foreign investments, and build infrastructure. In defiance of the West's criticisms, a defiance facilitated by China's economic and political support, space for civil and political liberties and for opposition politics was constricted. The government also adopted some measures against corruption which has become an intrinsic part of the country's patronage system. In foreign relations, the highlight of the year was Cambodia's chairmanship of ASEAN, and in particular the unprecedented failure of the ASEAN ministerial meeting in July to issue a communique, which many attributed to China's strong influence on Cambodia.

In the theme chapter on Cambodia, Pou Sothirak examines the Thailand-Cambodia border dispute, discussing the various approaches so far taken to resolve it and why they have achieved little progress. Although the border has been more quiet recently, Sothirak is not optimistic about a solution because the dispute has become entrenched in the nationalism and domestic politics of the two sides, making a compromise solution difficult.

In the next chapter, Greg Fealy sees political developments in Indonesia in 2012 as generally consistent with past patterns, including the internal party squabbles and prevalence of corruption. Corruption scandals damaged President Yudhoyono's Democrat Party, diminishing his ability to influence the presidential elections in 2014 and 2019 by fielding candidates from his family network. A major break from past patterns was the election victory of Joko Widodo, popularly known as Jokowi, as governor of Jakarta over a better financed and better connected (to the political and business elites) incumbent who had the support of several political parties. Fealy is of the view that each of the three "established" candidates for the 2014 presidential election — Prabowo, Megawati, and Bakrie — has his or her problems, though Prabowo was the front-runner. This could increase the chances of the emergence of a more popular independent candidate, but it was not clear who that could be. Fealy notes the continuing intolerance of and violence towards minorities and restrictions against freedom of religious expression which are being condoned or even openly supported by local and national politicians — in sharp contradiction to the country's self-proclaimed "moderate" and "pluralist" Islamic status. The Ahmadiyah and the Christians continued to be targeted, but the most significant development of 2012 was violence against the Shi'a minority. While many of the anti-Shi'a groups have doctrinal objections to Shi'ism, many also receive funding from Saudi and other Middle East sources that encourage anti-Shi'a action.

In the second chapter on Indonesia, Ahmad Habir discusses resource nationalism in the context of Indonesian politics and global trends, using the oil and gas industry as a case study. Some groups, including certain Islamic political parties, succeeded in getting an important 2001 oil and gas law reviewed by the Constitutional Court, as a result of which the regulatory authority for oil and gas, BP Migas, was disbanded. But, to the dismay of those behind the move, the government shifted BP Migas' regulatory functions to the Ministry of Energy and Mineral Resources, pending the preparation of a new oil and gas law. Until then the tussle between those the author describes as the "traditional resource nationalists" and those who favour more state involvement in order to enhance the international competitiveness of the resource industries would remain unresolved.

In her review of Laos, Holly High draws attention to the existence of considerable debate and airing of public grievances, much of it conducted in a form that suggests that critics were only asking the government to adhere to its own laws and declarations. Though there are of course limits to how far the critics can go, the debates show convincingly that ordinary people are dissatisfied with corruption and inequality. She cites, among other things, a more activist National Assembly which seeks to be the voice of the people and debates in cyberspace and the media. There are also the effects of internationally influenced changes to Laos' legal framework, for instance the changes required for accession to the World Trade Organization. To quote High: "[a] pattern has been building up for several years now ... despite continual setbacks and repercussions ... where, rather than debate being censured and impossible in public, it is not only tolerated, but called for, publicized and responded to. There are unspoken parameters to what counts as acceptable criticism, but significantly these parameters are themselves being subjected to debate." High has the sense that there is a tense internal battle taking place among leaders and elites in which some support more open forums for debate while others are opposed.

On Malaysia, Graham Brown describes the year 2012 as "one of held breath, with the country awaiting an election that never came". He discusses Prime Minister Najib Tun Razak's promise of reforms, regarded by many as necessary for the long-term survival of the ruling Barisan Nasional coalition even though they would endanger the short-term interests of many in the dominant United Malays National Organization (UMNO). For Najib, winning popular support through reform was a matter of personal political survival. Brown cites the assessment of the reforms by the *Economist* magazine as "just enough to alienate his own party and too little to convince the centre ground". The longer term reforms were stalled or superceded by short-term measures adopted to win elections. Contestations over the use of the word Allah and over the possible implementation of *hudud* continued to feature prominently in the socio-political landscape — with the *hudud* issue further widening the factional divides within the opposition coalition in which Anwar, the glue that has held together the uneasy partnership between the Pan-Malaysian Islamic Party (PAS) and the Democratic Action Party (DAP), and his confidantes seeming increasingly out of touch with the grasssroots of his party. The economy grew around 5 per cent. However, the government deficit also grew due to extensive subsidies in the lead-up to the announcement of an electioneering budget.

In the second chapter on Malaysia, Lee Hock Guan shows how the citizenship form in Malaysia remains bounded in colonial constructions. British colonial rulers used a mixture of *jus sanguinis* (right of blood) and *jus soli* (right of the soil) principles to classify colonial subjects into different classes of membership that have access to differential rights and privileges. After the Japanese Occupation, the British plan to introduce a civic citizenship was jettisoned because of strong Malay resistence to it. Consequently, because UMNO advocated an ethnic citizenship to grant the Malays special rights by virtue of their indigenous position, both civic and ethnic elements of citizenship were contradictorily included in the Merdeka (Independence) Constitution. As a result, Lee argues, since independence, the different ethnic groups have interpreted differently the meanings of the constitutional provisions regarding the equality of rights of citizenship and Malay special position and privileges.

In his review of Myanmar, Robert Taylor regards 2012 as the year of great, but unfulfilled expectations. Despite the welcome freedom of the press and open government created by the newly civilianized political order, old problems remained and a few new ones had been created. The much-hyped economic potential of Myanmar had resulted in little aid or investment in new economic sectors and hence few new jobs. Governance in the new constitutional order was proving difficult to manage as the executive, legislative and judicial branches all attempted to define their roles, though, to the surprise of many, the legislature was exercising its powers to "check and balance". President Thein Sein undertook initiatives to end armed conflict and reach negotiated peace settlements with the ethnic minorities, but achieved only limited success. Armed conflict remained isolated in the Kachin state and a small part of neighbouring Shan state. Conflict between the Rohingyas and Myanmar Buddhists erupted again, as it has in every decade since the 1930s. In foreign relations, President Thein Sein reiterated in his United Nations speech the position of every government since the 1950s: the pursuit of "independent and active" non-aligned foreign policy. Taylor ends on a hopeful note: the international climate in which the country operates has clearly changed for the better and the support that the Thein Sein administration receives from foreign governments and international agencies as well as domestically bodes well for the future.

In "Myanmar's 2012 By-Elections: The Return of the NLD", Tin Maung Maung examines the by-elections held on 1 April 2012, viewing them as a landmark event in the political transition from military rule to an elected government. The elections not only brought back the National League for Democracy (NLD) and its leader Daw Aung San Suu Kyi into the political mainstream but also led to the easing of Western sanctions. The NLD, which had boycotted the 2010 general elections, won forty-three out of forty-four contested seats in the legislature. Daw Aung San Suu Kyi, who won a seat in the Lower House, became an active participant in the political process whose legitimacy she had questioned earlier. The by-election seems to have transformed the Nobel Laureate, who had been a democracy icon for over two decades, into a practical politician.

In the review of the Philippines, Patricio Abinales argues that the 7 per cent economic growth in 2012 tended to mask troubling trends like the decline of foreign direct investments, expansion of the illicit economy, rising poverty levels, and huge inequalities in income. President Benigno Aquino III's personal approval ratings remained high, but in the public's eyes the legitimacy of the state and its institutions remained dubious, with continuing misgivings about their capacity to deal effectively with poverty and other fundamental economic problems. Filipinos were not expecting any dramatic change for the better. "The prevailing sentiment", observes Abinales, "is that they can live with what they have — provided that the outlet to go abroad and find jobs with better pay remains open". Finally, Abinales credits Aquino with two significant achievements during the year: the signing of the framework agreement between the government and the MILF and the passing of the Reproductive Health Bill by Congress in the face of fierce opposition from the Catholic Church. The latter will allow women access to birth control pills and promote condom use.

In "The Philippines in the South China Sea: Out of Time, Out of Options?", Maria Ortuoste weighs Philippine options in the South China Sea including ASEAN multilateralism, U.S. commitment and assistance, and having a credible Philippine defence capability. She sees limitations in each recourse in a regional environment marked by a stronger and less cooperative China, lingering doubts about the longer term sustainability of the U.S. security presence, and faltering ASEAN multilateralism. Ortuoste discusses Philippines-China relations in the context of rising nationalism in both countries, and outlines the economic pressures China applied against Manila during the Scarborough Shoal stand-off.

On Singapore in 2012, Narayanan Ganesan highlights the by-election held in the single-member Hougang ward, called after the stepping down of the incumbent opposition Worker's Party (WP) Member of Parliament because of a sex scandal. The WP retained the seat with only a small erosion of its popular support. Ganesan discusses the skyrocketing property prices, the cost of living, persistently high inflation, and the growing number of foreigners working in Singapore — issues that have caused much discontent among Singaporeans. Low-wage earners in Singapore faced pressures on their wages due to a large intake of low-paid foreign workers. He observes that unless the People's Action Party (PAP) government acts to alleviate these grievances, there is a danger that its post-independence social contract with its citizenry could unravel.

In "Singapore's Population Conundrum: The Great Balancing Act 2", Yap Mui Teng discusses the inter-related issues of ultra-low fertility, rapid ageing, and immigration. Over the past decade, the Total Fertility Rate (TFR) has fallen below 1.3 births per woman in spite of policy measures to promote marriage and childbearing. An increased influx of foreigners to meet the labour shortage has caused unprecedented unhappiness among Singaporeans who have complained about over-crowding and competition for jobs and other resources. While remedial measures are being undertaken to address the population's concerns, the longer term conundrum remains: Will a slower workforce growth affect economic growth in the future, or can the slower workforce growth be offset by increases in productivity? Is slower growth desirable for the country, or can the country accept a more rapid workforce growth (and ultimately a larger population and a larger foreign population) without lowering the quality of life and social relations?

After half a decade of political volatility, 2012 was another year of uncertainty and instability for Thailand, according to Chairat Charoensin-o-larn. Parliamentary bills for reconciliation and constitutional amendment proposed by the democratically elected Yingluck government were prevented from being adopted by strong-arm tactics and dubious constitutional means by the Yellow Shirts People's Alliance for Democracy and institutions and parties aligned with the traditional elite. They feared that, if passed into law, the bills would pave the way for the exoneration of former Premier Thaksin. There was also disillusion among some Red Shirts that both Thaksin and the Yingluk government were prepared to compromise with the traditional elite to advance their own interests. The report of the Truth for Reconciliation Commission of Thailand, issued in September 2012, instead of reconciling, re-opened old wounds. Chairat sees reconciliation and truth as tools used by the two sides to attain their political objectives. He observes that the conflict has gone beyond the point accommodation, "as each side waits for the right moment to wage total war to destroy the other". Violence in the south, which escalated from July, only added to the political uncertainties. On the economic front, the government's populist policies contributed to rising public debt and decline in exports, when what is needed is structural reform to make the Thai economy more competitive.

In his review of Timor-Leste, Damien Kingsbury sees the country in early stage of its development and consolidating its young democracy. The economy grew strongly, but almost entirely as the result of government spending based on the use of the country's US$11 billion petroleum fund. While Dili had some of the features of a boom town, much of the rest of Timor-Leste languished. The country's human development indicators showed improvement, if of very low levels, but for many Timorese little had changed over the ten years of independence. The real question hovering over Timor-Leste's future, according to Kingsbury was whether, with the ending of the current U.N. mission and the withdrawal of peacekeepers, its newfound sense of stability could be sustained through its coming challenges.

In "Vietnam in 2012: A Rent-Seeking State on the Verge of a Crisis", Alexander Vuving argues that the state, ruled by the Vietnam Communist Party (VCP), has evolved into a rent-seeking state that is now nearing a crisis point. The rescue of the clogged economy through needed structural reforms is thwarted by rent-seeking and by leadership divisions. There is a widening gap between the rulers and the ruled as a result of various popular grievances, especially over official corruption and land seizures. In foreign relations, by 2012 Vietnam's leaders, according to Vuving, "were no longer uncertain about China's determination to control the South China Sea, yet their response to this unambiguous threat remained ambivalent." The ambiguity reflected the China dilemma of the VCP state: while China presented a clear threat to Vietnam's perceived territorial integrity, it was also regarded as important for the VCP regime survival. Gathering international support for Vietnam's cause in the South China Sea was the main feature of Vietnam's foreign policy as the country continued to seek strategic partnerships with global and regional players. During the year Vietnam had to put up with aggressive acts by China in the South China Sea that led to four anti-China public protests which were contained and discouraged by the authorities.

In the second chapter on Vietnam, Le Hong Hiep analyses efforts of the VCP to buttress its declining performance-based legitimacy by restructuring the economy and intensifying the fight against corruption. The results so far still leave much to be desired. The central issue in economic restructuring is reform of state-owned enterprises (SOEs). They are responsible for inefficient public investments, account for a large part of the bad debts of banks, and are fertile grounds for corruption and waste. But they are resistant to radical reform because they are viewed by the Party as an essential foundation for progress towards socialism and because they have become an integral part of VCP power structure. The fight against corruption too needs SOE reform; further, it needs measures like an independent judicial system and freer media which would be seen as threatening the Party's survival. As Hiep points out, weak and ineffective efforts to fight corruption will harm the party while strong efforts that are effective will also undermine its monopoly of power.

Acknowledgements

This issue of *Southeast Asian Affairs* is the fortieth in the series that began in 1974. I thank Professor Donald Weatherbee for writing his commemorative thoughts on this anniversary which precede this Introduction. With his characteristic style and historical sweep, they succinctly capture the value of this series and salient points of a journey of forty years. Given his long association with ISEAS and *Southeast Asian Affairs* dating back to the 1970s, he was just the right person to make these observations. ISEAS was honoured to have him as a Visiting Professorial Fellow for three months in early 2013.

I would like to thank all the writers for their contributions. I thank Reema Bhagwan Jagtiani for her cheery and efficient editorial assistance and Rahilah Yusuf of ISEAS Publishing for her patience and understanding and for the long hours spent copy-editing the manuscript. Ms Betty Tan, was, as always, an efficient and dedicated secretary to the project. Finally, we appreciate the support of ISEAS Director Tan Chin Tiong, Deputy Director Ooi Kee Beng, and Head of ISEAS Publishing Mrs Triena Ong.

Daljit Singh
Editor
Southeast Asian Affairs 2013

The Region

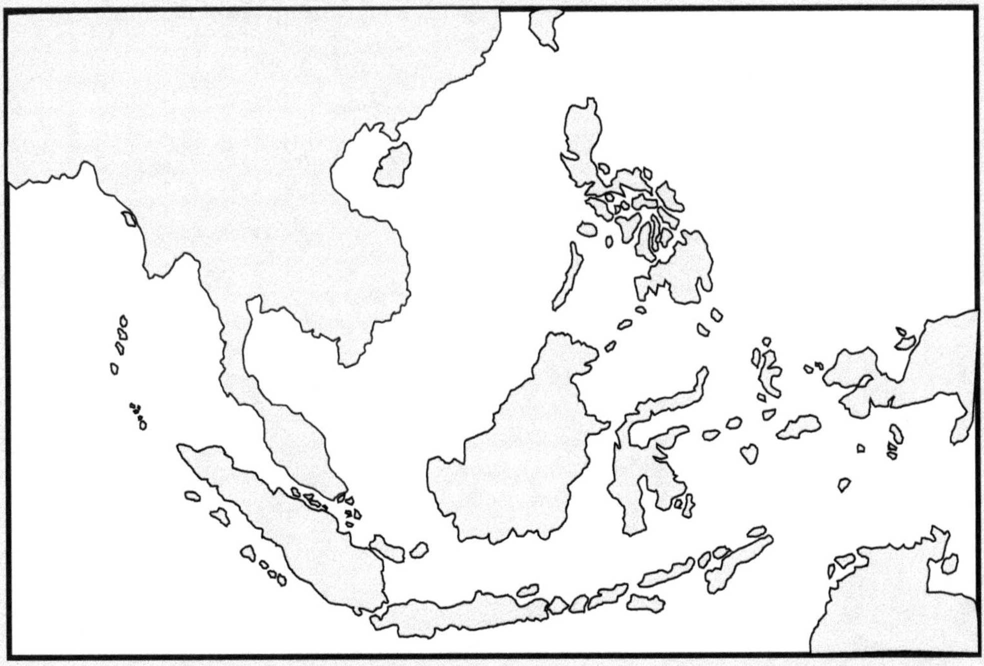

DIVIDED OR TOGETHER? Southeast Asia in 2012

Bridget Welsh

The year 2012 has brought to the fore the difficult realities of a region adapting to a more competitive global environment. With intensifying great power rivalry in the region, continued global economic uncertainty and legitimacy challenges of Southeast Asian leaders, the strains of maintaining consensus within ASEAN, promoting shared economic opportunities and maintaining stability while meeting governance demands have become more prominent. While regional politics in the past year illustrated some of the serious obstacles the region as a whole faces in working collaboratively, developments also highlighted new initiatives that are being introduced to promote the welfare of Southeast Asians.

ASEAN under Strain: Cambodia's Dismal Chairmanship

From a regionwide lens, the dominant story of the year was ASEAN. In this forty-fifth year of ASEAN's founding, this was perhaps one anniversary best forgotten. The failure of the organization to sign a basic communiqué in the July meeting in Phnom Penh and the limited traction on the code of conduct agreement with China over the contentious South China Sea issue at the East Asia Summit in November showcased the divisions among member states rather than a strengthening regional architecture. The core members of the group, led by Indonesia, had to pick up the pieces to save the organization's face and minimize the blame game that resulted from the annual July meeting. Diplomatic efforts by Indonesia led to the publication of "ASEAN"s Six Point Principles on the South China Sea" in the meeting's aftermath, but the

Bridget Welsh is Associate Professor in the School of Social Sciences at the Singapore Management University.

damage was already done. After the years during which ASEAN developed stronger regional ties and excelled itself on the international stage under the chairmanships of Indonesia and Vietnam, 2012 was a wake-up call of the hurdles ahead for ASEAN under comparatively weaker chairs of the region's smaller countries. Under Cambodia's chairmanship, the dominant mode was one of limited consensus, showcasing division rather than unity.

The primary source of division reflects divergent views of the role of China in the region. From 2008, China has become more assertive in its territorial claims in the South China Sea. Two months before the ASEAN meeting in July a stand-off between China and the Philippines occurred over the Scarborough Shoal. This continued to flare up after the meeting and was reinforced by other measures. China released the "nine-dash map" claiming the South China Sea, including this map in Chinese national passports. Then it formally appointed administrative responsibility over the Paracel Islands, Macclesfield Bank, and Spratly Islands to the newly created prefecture of Sansha. It also widened its presence in the area in escorting trawlers and, importantly, established a military garrison in the Sansha prefecture with the responsibility to cover two square miles of water.[1] China's presence has extended economically as well, including stepping up efforts to control oil and gas production. In June 2012, nine offshore blocks were put up by the China National Offshore Oil Company (CNOOC), many overlapping with claims by Vietnam.[2] China has further focused more investment in the region, especially in its neighbours. China's investment, for example, in Cambodia is reported to be US$2 billion, twice the combined value today of all the investment of ASEAN countries in Cambodia and ten times that of the United States.[3] Differences between the South China Sea claimant Philippines and strong China-ally and this year's ASEAN chair Cambodia in particular were quite pronounced, limiting the ability of member states to reach common ground. The year passed without the passage of a code of conduct after the ten-year period allocated to address this matter expired.

Part of this was due to developments outside of Southeast Asia. Both China and the United States consciously opted for a more competitive dynamic in their relations with the region. The United States set the course by deepening its "pivot" approach to Asia, renamed "rebalancing" at the June Shangri-La Dialogue.[4] The United States increased their number of high-level visits and adopted a more assertive position on security with its allies and friends, including the Philippines and Vietnam. There was also a rise in the number of naval patrols and a deepening of military cooperation. The United

States also increased financial support, for example, offering US$50 million for the Lower Mekong Initiative and significantly increasing aid to Myanmar.[5] China on its part also ratcheted up its involvement in the region, and reacted to the U.S. interventions which openly challenged its increasing presence in the region. China's mode continued to be one focused on bilateral ties, as China increased international aid and loans to individual countries and made its presence felt with high-level visits. Rather than lead, ASEAN was forced to react to ongoing great power rivalries. Cambodia, arguably China's closest ally in the region, brought to the fore the underlying divisions over China.

Diversity over a Rising Dragon

The difficulties at the elite level over China, however, are not as marked among Southeast Asian publics. The third wave of the Asia Barometer Survey data of national surveys conducted in East Asia from 2010 to 2012 highlights that there is a more positive view of China's rising influence among general publics. While the survey results suggests that the United States continues to have significant soft power, considerably more than China, the views of ordinary Southeast Asians reveal more accommodative views of China's role in the region.

Table 1 highlights some of the differences in ordinary views.[6] Publics in the region overwhelmingly see China's role positively; in every country surveyed a majority views China positively. The region as a whole is divided over who has the most power, with Singaporeans and Vietnamese selecting China as the most powerful, and the Filipinos, Indonesians, Malaysians, and

TABLE 1
Southeast Asian Views of China and the United States

Country	*China Most Powerful*	*U.S. Most Powerful*	*China Role Positive*	*China as Model*	*U.S. as Model*
Cambodia	26%	58%	71%	20.3%	43.8%
Indonesia	23%	41%	71%	13.5%	25.9%
Malaysia	35%	44%	59%	13.9%	8.0%
Philippines	17%	66%	73%	7.3%	69.1%
Singapore	60%	28%	81%	14.1%	22.9%
Thailand	42%	44%	67%	16.2%	15.5%
Vietnam	69%	16%	55%	9.4%	22.0%

Source: Asia Barometer Surveys, 2010–12.

ironically, in light of Cambodia's stance at ASEAN meetings, Cambodians opting for the United States. The Thais are evenly split.

The soft power of China and the United States, measured by those who opted to follow either China or the United States as their country's respective model, favours the United States, with its strongest advocate being the Philippines. Only in Malaysia and Thailand, countries with large Chinese diasporas and minimal security conflicts with China, did a plurality of citizens opt for China as a model to follow. Many of the countries in the region chose themselves as a model, and in some cases, such as Malaysia, chose Japan. In the comparison between the great power rivals, however, U.S. soft power remains dominant, despite China's rising influence.

These findings suggest that not only are there differences among Southeast Asians over China and the United States in the region, there are differences between publics and their elites. This is most pronounced in Cambodia, where citizens offered considerably higher assessments of U.S. power compared to that of China. The results also highlight that fact that being forced to choose between the United States or China will split the region further. Southeast Asia may be divided over how they perceive great powers, but most would prefer not to have to choose. The year 2012 illustrated clearly that when pressed on matters over great powers, division rather than consensus will emerge.

Lowest Common Denominator on Human Rights

Consensus for the sake of consensus, however, may also have its drawbacks. Another important highlight of 2012 involved the signing of the ASEAN Human Rights Declaration (AHRD). Views differed significantly over AHRD with Human Rights Watch calling it a "full blown train wreck" and regional leaders hailing it as a "landmark legacy for our children".[7] Others were more measured, such as Indonesia's Foreign Minister Marty Natalegawa who called it an important "benchmark"[8] and yet others labeling it the ASEAN "Magna Carta".[9]

The AHRD includes forty different articles that outline principles and goals that extended from civil and political liberties and economic, social and cultural rights to the broader goals for ASEAN in protecting these rights.[10] From any account this document is historic in that it represents the first time ASEAN and many of its member states openly and collectively affirmed a commitment to human rights. A number of important rights were included in the AHRD, notably education, freedom from arbitrary arrest and security, and some measures addressed transnational issues such as human trafficking. Minimally, the attention to human rights reflects the ongoing effort to strengthen the regional architecture and to include more attention of the organization to the welfare of ordinary citizens.

This document was not without its problems. There are many loopholes for states that effectively remove the obligation of states to protect rights. These include the right of any government in the region to suspend human rights for real or claimed grounds of "national security, public order, public health, public safety and public morality". Member states were also given considerable leeway in applying these standards with the adoption of the phrase that human rights "must be considered in the regional and national context". Rights were furthermore to be balanced with "duties", denying the universality of rights as inalienable. These qualifications on the scope of freedoms in the AHRD reflect the intense debate among member states over the Declaration. The main sticking point was Article 7, involving the word "particularities".[11] At issue was the scope to regional and national contexts to limit the applicability of rights. Some countries preferred to emphasize their "particular" circumstances, while others wanted a more universal standard. By limiting rights to a specific context, this was de facto also limiting the scope of rights in the document. The word "particularities" was ultimately removed, but the limited scope of rights remained. In the final analysis, those in favour of allowing states to curb freedoms won out.

It is thus not surprising that the AHRD received considerable criticism for not meeting international standards. There was opposition to the idea that rights are not universal, but rather are regional and country specific. The U.N. Office of the High Commissioner of Human Rights (OHCHR) Navi Pillay led the charge, pointing out how the document was below basic international norms.[12] She also pointed to weaknesses in engaging cross-border issues such as statelessness. There was also blatant exclusion of free speech[13] and protection of gender rights.[14] Pillay was joined by sixty-four non-governmental organizations under the rubric of the International Federation for Human Rights who criticized the AHRD for flying "in the face of the international consensus on human rights principles that have been in place for more than six decades".[15]

The AHRD reflects the lowest common denominator position in ASEAN on rights. As the region has been transforming, there are underlying tensions that go beyond security and extend to rights and democracy. There are also tensions between rigid commitments to sovereignty with simultaneous pressures from regional integration and transnational forces. The consensus that was reached was one that revealed some of these tensions, with more authoritarian states in the region unwilling to adopt more liberal and inclusive approaches towards rights, and yet others leading the way in bringing ASEAN onto the international stage as a regional grouping in the developing world that leads the way for others to follow.

Economic Integration or Competition: Regional Trade Agreements

Division was also the theme that emerged over trade, as there is emerging competition over economic cooperation and integration. This was showcased at the East Asia Summit in December where ASEAN officially launched the Regional Comprehensive Economic Partnership (RCEP) in which China is the dominant economic powerhouse. RCEP is a free trade agreement (FTA) that includes ASEAN and its trading partners, namely Australia, New Zealand, China, South Korea, and India, all of which have free trade agreements with ASEAN.[16] RCEP has the potential to build an Asian FTA that would rival every other region in the world. When completed RCEP will span sixteen countries and include a combined market of 3 billion people with a combined GDP of USD$19.8 trillion.[17] This is estimated to be 28.5 per cent of world trade.

This framework is being pitted against the U.S.-led Trans-Pacific Partnership (TPP). TPP in contrast is dominated by the United States and focuses on enforcing World Trade Organization standards in the wake of the collapse of the Doha round. Unlike RCEP, this initiative has a leader to push for its passage. The TPP aims at reducing trade barriers for 700 million people with combined GDP of US$26 trillion.[18] The TPP excludes China and India, and a number of ASEAN states do not qualify, such as Myanmar and Cambodia. The agreement, however, includes South American countries such as Chile and links Asia with the Americas. This agreement reflects the multilateral approach of the Obama administration towards trade, but also highlights some of the inherent challenges in signing an agreement with the United States. Ultimately there are problems of reaching consensus on standards and balancing interests between international requirements and domestic realities. Problem areas include conflicting intellectual property rights regimes, the neutrality of state-owned enterprises, government procurement, and labour and environmental standards.

Many of the countries in ASEAN, including those that have signed on to the TPP initiative such as Malaysia and Vietnam, are divided on pursuing this strategy.

This is an important third arena of underlying division in ASEAN, the strategy to adopt towards free trade and economic integration. Should the approach be through region-focused integration, or be more global and transnational in scope? Should the path be one grouped as a loose framework, as envisioned by RCEP, or one based on a foundation of standards? These questions are not likely to be answered easily or consistently. Many in ASEAN would like both options, such as Singapore, others such as Myanmar are inclined towards neither, at least at this stage of its economic opening. The differences in ASEAN over economic integration are similar to those over rights and security in that at their heart they involve the protection of national interests, as perceived by those in power. Of the three arenas, the process of trade liberalization is perhaps the most contentious domestically, as it pits sectors against each other and pressures state-owned enterprises to open up and become more competitive. In 2012, the conflicts over trade were framed as part of the regional great power rivalry, RCEP versus TPP, but in fact the reality is that divisions over trade and economic integration are much broader and go well beyond the issue of which globally promoted trade framework to adopt.

Periphery Pressures and Terrorist Transformations

The year 2012 also witnessed divisions of a different kind within individual countries in Southeast Asia. The most prominent headlines on conflict involved violence on the peripheries of Myanmar, Thailand, Indonesia, and the Philippines.

Myanmar dominated the headlines internationally, as it continued its process of political liberalization over the year. In June, however, the reports were less favourable, as news centred on the sectarian riots in the Rakhine (Arakan) state between Muslims and Buddhists. The fighting was reported to be started by the alleged rape of a Rakhine woman by a Muslim man, and extended to attacks on villagers from both communities, especially Muslims. The majority of the Muslims in the Rakhine state are Rohingyas, who are believed to originally come from Bangladesh and often lack citizenship rights. They face serious prejudice in a periphery region that has ongoing tensions over land and high levels of poverty. The riots extended for nearly three weeks, despite the declaration of an emergency on 10 June. In October fighting restarted, with additional casualties and damage in the northern part of the Rakhine state. The total loss of lives is estimated to be more than 150 people, with 100,000 people displaced. By year's end, the Muslim majority communities remained displaced, with some putting their lives as risk and boarding vessels with the hope of international asylum in neighbouring countries.

The violence revealed some of the inherent challenges Myanmar faces in its political liberalization. Religious tensions were heightened with blatant anti-Muslim mobilization and sentiments expressed in a now more open Myanmar. The ineffectiveness of the police force became clear as the government had to bring in the military as peacekeepers. Humanitarian groups, including the United Nations High Commission for Refugees (UNHCR), faced problems protecting refugees. In July, 10 UNHCR personnel were arrested and three were charged for "stimulating" the riots.[19] Concerns over how to balance humanitarian relief amidst persistent sectarian tensions continued throughout the year, as organizations such as Doctors without Borders reported in November harassment of Muslims and threats to their treatment of Muslims.

This periphery conflict became internationalized early on. Many Muslim nations called for the protection of their community, and in August the Organization of Islamic Cooperation (OIC) sent in a fact-finding mission buttressed by US$50 million of humanitarian relief promised by Saudi Arabia. In October the Myanmar government reversed its decision to allow the OIC to open an office. President Thein Sein also rejected calls for ASEAN to intervene, although the organization pledged support for conflict resolution.[20] This issue opened up another divide in ASEAN — division between Muslim member states and Myanmar.[21] Leaders in Malaysia and Indonesia faced public pressure to respond to what was being reported on social media sites as "genocide" — although with false photos and exaggeration. Indonesia appointed former vice-president Jusuf Kalla as a special envoy to Myanmar on the matter. Concerns of a similar nature were also echoed by human rights organizations, who drew attention to ongoing abuses.[22] Despite international pressure, the situation in the Rakhine state remains tense with large numbers of displaced people.[23]

The persistence of conflict on the periphery was also an issue in southern Thailand. This conflict is now over a decade old. International Crisis Group reports 5,473 deaths from January 2004 through November 2012 with an end to the violence not in sight.[24] The nature of the violence has taken a worrying sharp ethnic turn, with most of those killed civilians and many of those targeted due to their religion and occupation. One group that has been especially hit has been Buddhist teachers in the south.[25] After the 31 March bombings in Hat Yai and Yala provinces, attention has been riveted on the systematic execution of teachers in November and December. Calls are increasing for a different approach towards peace, with increasing calls for international intervention.

The lack of coherent domestic strategy could be seen in Papua as well, as almost daily killings have become the norm. In May and June conditions worsened with increasing militarization. On 14 June deputy head of the West Papua National Committee (KNPB) pro-independence organization, Mako Tabuni, was killed by police. Papua has a long-standing conflict that has its roots into the 1960s, but current developments, including failed efforts to promote and protect special autonomy have exacerbated tensions.[26] This year marks the fiftieth anniversary of many of the early independence efforts, bringing international attention to the conflict and raising expectations. Efforts to reduce violence have largely failed to date, with more pressure being placed on the Susilo Bambang Yudhoyono administration to promote meaningful conflict resolution.

It is in the Philippines, however, where a bright spot for peripheral conflicts shined. In October, the Moro Islamic Liberation Front (MILF) and the Philippine government signed the Bangsamoro framework agreement. This deal was brokered by the Malaysian government and holds the promise of peace between parties who have been fighting for decades. It is essentially a path for sustaining peace and includes nine different sections ranging from land and revenue issues to new administrative bodies.[27] While it is too early to say whether this framework will last, the document is a breakthrough in stemming violence and offers a road map for broader peace. The two main challenges will be long-standing issues, a commitment to the promises made especially on the part of the Philippine government, and avoiding the emergence of splinter groups among the rebels that will resort to violence to promote their interests, often motivated by greed.

Violent conflict remains a serious problem in the region, as does terrorism. The year fortunately did not feature bombings. Terrorist threats, however, actively continued in 2012 with authorities uncovering and foiling several attacks. For example, in October, Indonesian authorities thwarted a coordinated attack on the U.S. and Australian embassies as well as the U.S. consulate in Surabaya and the office of mining company Freeport.[28] Earlier in the year there were several attacks and foiled bomb attempts in Poso between August and November, leading to arrests.[29] Successful policing has minimized the loss of life across the region, but the challenge of minimizing violence remains real.

Regional terrorist organizations have diversified and regrouped.[30] Increasingly their focus is government law enforcement personnel, especially the police.

ASEAN as an organization has recognized the importance of reducing conflict in these uncertain times. In November it launched the ASEAN Institute for Peace and Reconciliation (AIPR) led by Indonesia. This Institute aims to promote conflict resolution. It faces an uphill task given the persistence and increases in violence over the year. Nevertheless, this common purpose stands out amidst the many divisions in the region.

Rise of Populism: Domestic Legitimacy Building

The shared goal of addressing division is perhaps one of the striking features of Southeast Asia of 2012. Since the 1997 Asian financial crisis Southeast Asian countries have faced rising inequalities. While most of the region has recovered from this crisis and even weathered the subsequent 2008 U.S.-induced financial crisis, they have not been able to stem the widening divide within Southeast Asian societies. Growth has largely not been accompanied by rising equality, as wages levels have remained stagnant for large shares of Southeast Asians. What has deepened in 2012 has been the increasing use of populist strategies to address these inequalities.

The broad pattern has been an evolution in the region's politics away from patronage to populism, a pattern than involves a breakdown of personal face-to-face ties towards greater dependence on the state and government coffers for services and benefits. As governments in the region have faced more domestic demands, including pressures from the expansion of social media, more have turned to short-term populist measures to appease citizens and shore up their electoral fortunes.

Leading this populist effort has been Thailand. Beginning in 2006 under the leadership of Thaksin Shinawarta, Thailand began a series of initiatives such as the 1 million baht programme to villages. These distributions underscored Thaksin's political support in the rural areas. His sister, Yingluck Shinawarta, has continued with this policy pattern. What distinguishes the initiatives in the past year has been a move away from a focus on lower income groups, replicated in the subsidy policies in Malaysia and Indonesia, towards middle class groups and more urbanites. Today, the measures on the table include housing loans, car loans, transportation subsidies and in places like Malaysia even subsidized smart phones. This pattern of governance is becoming more common, especially in countries where electorates have become more demanding and leaders are facing more intense contests for power. In Malaysia Najib Tun Razak's populist pre-election primer of 2012 has extended to raising salaries for civil servants, a record-breaking cash transfer programme known as Bantuan Rakyat 1Malaysia (BR1M), or the 1Malaysia People's Assistance Programme, and a variety of politically targeted handouts to the government's traditional political base, from taxi drivers to teachers.

This expansion of populist measures raises questions about the nature of development in the region. The move is one from long-term to short-term measures. Many of the initiatives are aimed at having an immediate "feel-good" effect. For recipients, the money is often spent so fast that its effect is short-lived with limited impact on the economic inequalities in society. There is clearly a real impact on budgets, with rising deficits due to the spending. Thailand's rice policy is illustrative.[31] Yet, at the same time, governments are putting money into economies, driving consumption, and importantly in countries where the focus has been on housing and education, reallocating funds directly to citizens for investments in human capital and public welfare. It is too early to determine whether the populist initiatives will yield substantive gains for citizens. Ironically, however, politics has moved from hierarchical networks towards greater equality, as people's needs have reasserted their prominence reminiscent of the goals of early Southeast Asian leaders. Populism may be a product of divisions in society, and even foster different divides between citizens and governments, it is nevertheless putting people first in many of the countries of Southeast Asia.

Regional Resilience: Beyond Surin Pitsuwan

It is thus fitting to close the discussion of 2012 with recognition of the togetherness of the region. Now with over 600 million people and comprising the ninth largest economy in the world with a US$2.1 trillion combined GDP, Southeast Asia is facing difficult challenges on security, rights, economic integration, terrorism, and peripheral conflicts.[32] At the same time there are forces pushing the region towards shared goals of prosperity, stability, and empowerment.

The year marked the end of the tenure of one of the leading architects of this common vision, former ASEAN Secretary-General Surin Pitsuwan. An idealist who advocated a stronger regional architecture, he left his post with ASEAN stronger as an institution. The everyday forces of dialogue and cooperation are more resilient than ever, as ASEAN conducted over 1,000 meetings in 2012 alone. Those that received the most attention were those where division dominated, but the overwhelming majority featured cooperation. Pitsuwan's greatest touted success in office would arguably be the interlocutor role that ASEAN played in Myanmar after the 2008 Cyclone Nargis, and 2012 continued to feature the gains of these interventions as political liberalization deepened, despite the violence in Rakhine state. Less overt, but perhaps as important, has been the move to prioritize the needs and interests of ordinary citizens in the region. This underlying democratic force that is moving ASEAN away from an elite talk shop towards a more broad-based regional organization for its citizens promises greater vibrancy and inclusion. The norm will likely be one of division, but there are strengthening institutions and measures in place to engage these differences, even if these are still evolving. The move towards the ASEAN Charter is part of this evolution. Pitsuwan has turned over leadership of ASEAN to Le Luong Minh, the former deputy foreign minister of Vietnam as the new Secretary-General of ASEAN. It is fitting perhaps that the transition involves passing the baton of leadership to the countries that were brought into ASEAN after 1995, as this shows that despite divisions there are indeed underlying bonds promoting the region's resilience.

Notes

Special thanks to Ang Wei Zheng for assistance with research for this article and to Steven Wong for critical insights into regional developments. The errors are my own.

1. Carlyle Thayer, "Behind the Scenes of ASEAN's Breakdown;", *Asia Times*, 27 July 2012.
2. Randy Fabi and Chen Aizhu, "Analysis: China Unveils Oil Offensive in South China Sea Squabble", Reuters, 1 August 2012.
3. Mark MacDonald, "Indecision and Infighting: That's the ASEAN Way", *Los Angeles Times*, 20 November 2012.
4. Donald K. Emmerson, "Challenging ASEAN: The American Pivot in Southeast Asia", *East Asia Forum*, 1 January 2013.
5. Nicole Gauette, "Clinton Announces $50 Million for Lower Mekong River Projects", Bloomberg, 13 July 2012.
6. See Yun-han Chu, Liu Kang and Min-Hua Huang, "How East Asians View the Rise of China", Paper presented at a workshop for the Institute of Advanced Studies of Humanities and Social Sciences and Asia Barometer Survey, National Taiwan University, October 2012, and Bridget Welsh and Alex Chang, "Follow the Leader: Soft Power of China and the U.S. Compared", for a conference at Brookings Institute in collaboration with the Program for East Asia Democratic Studies, Institute for

the Advanced Studies of the Humanities and Social Sciences, National Taiwan University, and Institute of Arts and Humanities, Shanghai Jiao Tong University in spring 2013.

7. "ASEAN Human Rights Pact under Fire", *Gold Coast Bulletin*, 19 November 2012.
8. Ibid.
9. Kevin H.R. Villaneuva, "How West Was Won: ASEAN Magna Carta", *Philippine Daily Enquirer*, 18 November 2012.
10. <http://www.asean.org/news/asean-statement-communiques/item/asean-human-rights-declaration>.
11. Villaneuva, "How West Was Won".
12. "UN Experts Raise Concerns over 'Landmark' Southeast Asian Human Rights Declaration", M2Presswire, 16 November 2012.
13. Geoffrey Cain, "The ASEAN Human Rights Declaration: Light on Free Speech", *New Mandala*, 22 November 2012.
14. Purple Romero, "When Will Asean Protect Gender Rights?", AFP, 6 April 2012.
15. Stuart Grudgings and Manuel Mogato, "SE Asia to Adopt Human Rights Platform; Condemned by Activists", Reuters, 17 November 2012.
16. Sanchita Basu Das, "RCEP and TPP: Comparisons and Concerns", *ISEAS Perspective*, 7 January 2013.
17. "Roundup: Obama Visit, Human Rights, Trade take Center Stage at ASEAN", Xinhua News Agency, 20 November 2012.
18. Sanchita Basu Das and Hnin Wint Nyunt Hman, "The Trans-Pacific Partnership (TPP): Economic and Strategic Implications for the Asia-Pacific", *ISEAS Perspective*, 23 July 2012.
19. Gwen Robinson, "UN Aid Workers Face Myanmar Riot Charges", *Financial Times*, 15 July 2012.
20. "ASEAN Countries Pledge Support for Conflict Resolution in Myanmar", AFP, 18 August 2012.
21. Bridget Welsh, "ASEAN's New Myanmar Challenge", *ASEAN Monthly Commentary*, August 2012.
22. Human Rights Watch, "'The Government Could Have Stopped This': Sectarian Violence and Ensuing Abuses in Burma's Arakan State", August 2012 <http://www.hrw.org/sites/default/files/reports/burma0812webwcover_0.pdf>.
23. International Crisis Group, "Myanmar: Storm Clouds on the Horizon", Asia Report No. 238, 12 November 2012.
24. International Crisis Group, "Thailand: The Evolving Conflict in the South", Asia Report No. 241, 11 December 2012, p. 4.
25. Human Rights Watch, "Thailand: Rebels Escalate Killings of Teachers", 17 December 2012 <http://www.hrw.org/news/2012/12/17/thailand-rebels-escalate-killings-teachers>.

26. International Crisis Group, "Indonesia: Dynamics of Violence in Papua", Asia Report No. 232, 9 August 2012.
27. International Crisis Group, "The Philippines: Breakthrough in Mindanao", Asia Report No. 240, 5 December 2012.
28. "Indonesian Police Kill Alleged Militant in Raid", AP, 3 November 2012.
29. "Suspect Militant Killed in Police Raid in Poso", *Jakarta Globe*, 3 November 2012 <http://www.thejakartaglobe.com/news/suspected-militant-killed-during-police-raid-in-poso/554013>.
30. International Crisis Group, "How Indonesian Extremists Regroup", Asia Report No. 228, 16 July 2012.
31. "Thai Rice Subsidy Program Short of Money", Reuters, 7 February 2013.
32. Sanchita Basu Das and Termsak Chalermpalanupap, "Can ASEAN Keep Aiming for New Goals Without Having Reached Old Ones?", *ISEAS Perspective*, 17 December 2012.

SOUTHEAST ASIAN ECONOMIES
Building the Base for Stronger, Better Distributed Growth

Manu Bhaskaran

This chapter will review recent trends in the economies of Southeast Asia. It will first study cyclical trends in economic variables across the region such as economic growth, inflation, the external accounts, and currency stability. It will then highlight and assess emerging trends in the region which will help drive future patterns of economic activity.

Recent Economic Trends: Region in Good Shape

A Challenging Global Environment

Most Southeast Asian economies remain highly integrated with the global economy. Economic growth and other dimensions of the regional economies are therefore substantially affected by global developments. The year 2012 was marked by significant headwinds and challenges emanating from the global environment.

First, global demand for the region's exports grew weakly as the major global economies endured another year of challenges. Financial and other stresses also emanated from the major economies. The eurozone economies continued to suffer the consequences of the sovereign debt crisis: fiscal austerity depressed demand while business and consumer confidence was dampened. The United States was in better shape but there too economic growth was mediocre, with a material deceleration in capital spending by the business sector that grew wary over the risks of political impasse over key budgetary decisions. China saw a clear trend of slowing growth through the year which was only beginning to reverse in the

MANU BHASKARAN is Chief Executive Officer of Centennial Asia Advisors Pte Ltd, Singapore.

third quarter. Japan saw a rebound from the effects of the triple disasters of March 2011, but the recovery lost momentum as the year progressed.

Second, repeated bouts of monetary easing have created a global financial system that is flush with liquidity and where interest rates are at unusually low levels. This has been compounded by a highly uncertain business and financial environment as a result of the eurozone sovereign crisis, the worries over imbalances in the Chinese economy and uncertainty over the elections in the United States. As a result, flows of portfolio capital have been extremely volatile, with risk appetites rising and falling unpredictably through the year and resulting in destabilizing capital flows that rendered management of the region's currencies and external accounts difficult.

Third, as a result of a weaker global economy, commodity prices in general have fallen. In particular, prices of economically sensitive commodities such as rubber, thermal and coking coal, and base metals have fallen. Prices of food-related crops which are important to the region, such as crude palm oil, have also fallen, hurting incomes for rural households in much of the region.

Fourth, energy prices have, however, remained higher than expected. Although prices have eased, the multiple political flashpoints in the Middle East have kept the risk premium in oil prices at a high level. Thus, even as global economic activity moderated, oil prices did not fall as much as they should have.

Fifth, political events had material effects on regional economies. Tensions over territorial disputes in the South China Sea and East China Sea intensified in 2012. There were signs that Japanese manufacturers have become keener to relocate some production out of China to locations in Southeast Asia as a result. Business spending on capital equipment in the United States was hurt by uncertainty over the U.S. presidential elections and concerns over the political impasse over fiscal policy — this hurt regional exports of information technology goods. Multiple crises in the Middle East supported the price of oil, which did not fall as much as the weakening of global demand should have caused. This kept energy prices in the region at a relatively high level, hurting those countries in particular which continued to provide large fuel subsidies to consumers.

Overview of Recent Trends

Table 1 provides a quick overview of the past year for the economies which provide sufficient and timely data. A number of patterns stand out.

TABLE 1
Overview of Economic Trends in Southeast Asia in 2012

Country	*GDP Growth*	*Inflation*	*Current Account*	*Currency*	*Policy Stance*
Indonesia	Strong	Decelerated	Deficit emerged	Stable	Easing
Malaysia	Strong	Decelerated	Surplus falling	Stable	Easing
Philippines	Strong	Decelerating	Stable	Stable	Easing
Singapore	Weakening	High relative to history	Large surplus	Appreciating	Tightening
Thailand	Up from low base	Slight deceleration	Steady improvement	Stable	Easing
Vietnam	Decelerating	Rising after modest deceleration	Weakening	Stabilizing	Easing

Note: High frequency data is not available for several countries, hence their absence from this table.
Source: Collated by Centennial Asia Advisors.

First, economic growth in the region mostly held up despite the global headwinds. Figures 1 to 4 and Table 2 show that economic growth in 2012

FIGURE 1
Indonesian Growth at High Steady Rates

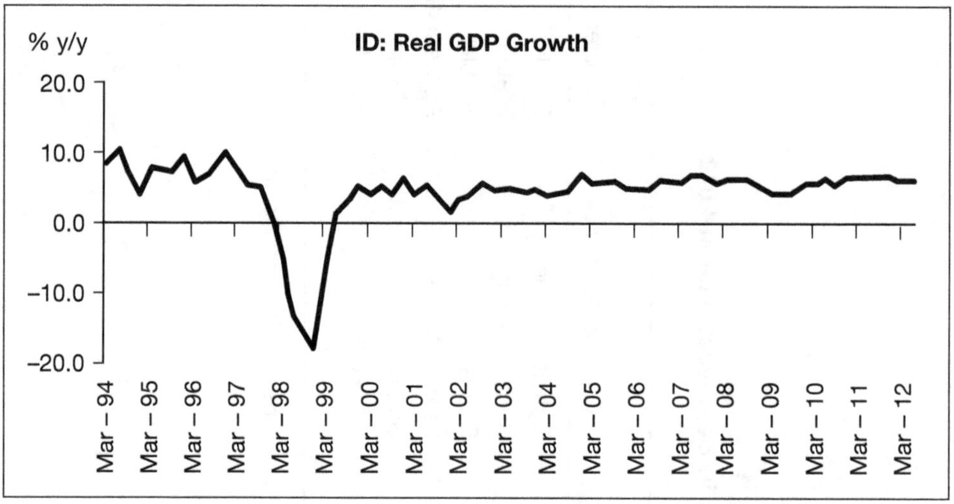

Source: Calculated by Centennial Asia Advisors using CEIC Database.

FIGURE 2
Philippines Enjoyed an Acceleration

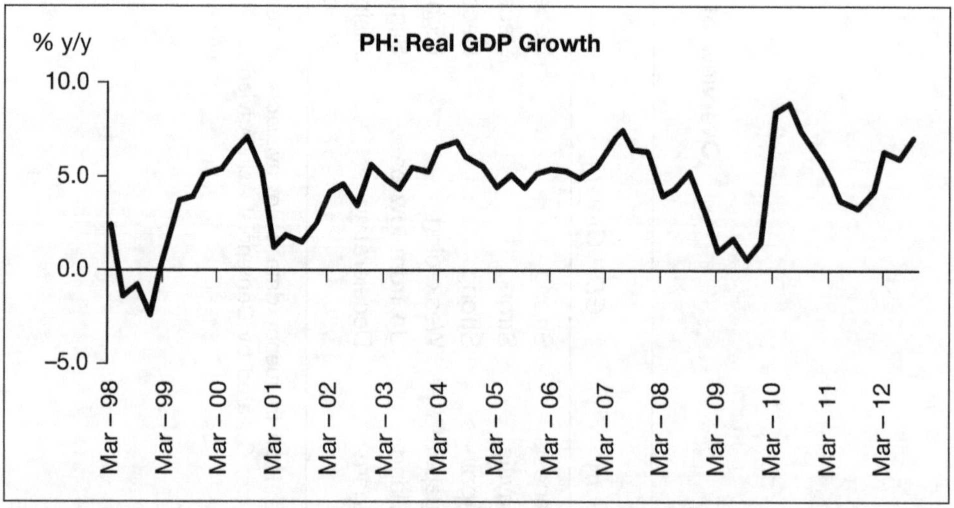

Source: Calculated by Centennial Asia Advisors using CEIC Database.

FIGURE 3
Malaysia Held Up Well

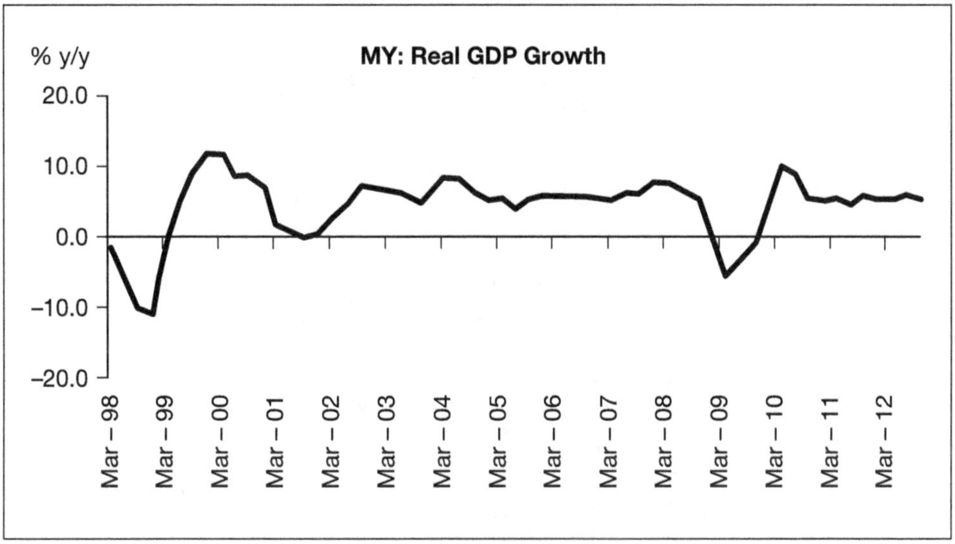

Source: Calculated by Centennial Asia Advisors using CEIC Database.

FIGURE 4
Singapore Bucked the Trend

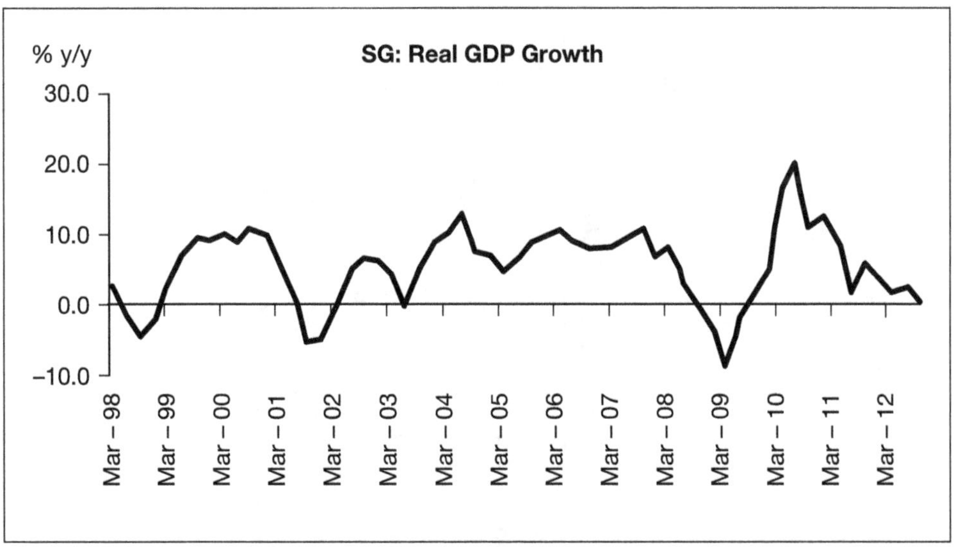

Source: Calculated by Centennial Asia Advisors using CEIC Database.

TABLE 2
GDP Growth Performance in Southeast Asia

	Dec 09	*Mar 10*	*Jun 10*	*Sep 10*	*Dec 10*	*Mar 11*	*Jun 11*	*Sep 11*	*Dec 11*	*Mar 12*	*Jun 12*	*Sep 12*
Singapore	5.3	16.5	19.8	10.6	12.5	9.1	1.2	6.0	3.6	1.6	2.5	0.3
Malaysia	4.5	10.1	9.0	5.2	4.8	5.0	4.3	5.7	5.2	5.1	5.6	5.2
Thailand	5.9	12.0	9.2	6.6	3.8	3.2	2.7	3.7	–8.9	0.4	4.4	NA
Philippines	1.4	8.4	8.9	7.3	6.1	4.9	3.6	3.2	4.0	6.3	5.9	7.1
Vietnam	7.7	5.9	6.3	7.4	7.2	5.4	5.7	6.1	6.1	4.1	4.7	5.4
Indonesia	5.6	5.9	6.3	5.8	6.8	6.4	6.5	6.5	6.5	6.3	6.4	6.2
Brunei	2.4	3.9	6.6	3.0	–1.9	2.8	2.3	2.5	1.3	0.7	1.0	NA

Source: Calculated by Centennial Asia Advisors using CEIC Database.

TABLE 3
Export Growth Trends

Country	*Average Export Growth Jan–Sep 12*	*Export Growth 11*
Indonesia	–1.4	30.3
Malaysia	3.9	9.3
Philippines	1.3	–4.9
Singapore	2.3	7.7
Thailand	–2.3	15.8
Vietnam	23.5	–7.1

Source: Calculated by Centennial Asia Advisors using CEIC Database.

remained relatively strong for most of the region. Singapore, however, decelerated significantly — not surprising given that it is the most heavily exposed economy to global demand, especially demand from the United States, Europe, and Japan.

Across the region, export growth decelerated sharply (Table 3), with only Vietnam and the Philippines enjoying stronger export growth in January–September 2012 compared to 2011.

Second, domestic demand clearly supported growth across the region. As Figures 5 to 8 show, taking Malaysia and Thailand as examples, domestic spending by consumers and businesses helped to support overall economic growth in the region. Encouragingly, the region saw domestic investment pick up momentum, despite the concerns over global growth. Malaysia, for example, enjoyed the highest ratio of private investment to GDP since the financial crisis of the 1990s, suggesting that there has been a structural improvement in the investment environment.

Personal consumption spending has also supported domestic demand. Years of rising commodity prices have bolstered rural household incomes and provided them with a buffer of high savings, which allowed them to sustain spending even as commodity prices eased through 2012. Policy changes have also helped. In a number of economies, minimum wages have either been introduced (as in Malaysia) or raised significantly (as in Thailand). However, as the year progressed, there were some signs that consumer spending may weaken in future: the rate of growth of rural household incomes has weakened. In Thailand, for instance, farm income growth decelerated sharply as the year progressed.

FIGURE 5
Malaysian Investment Rate

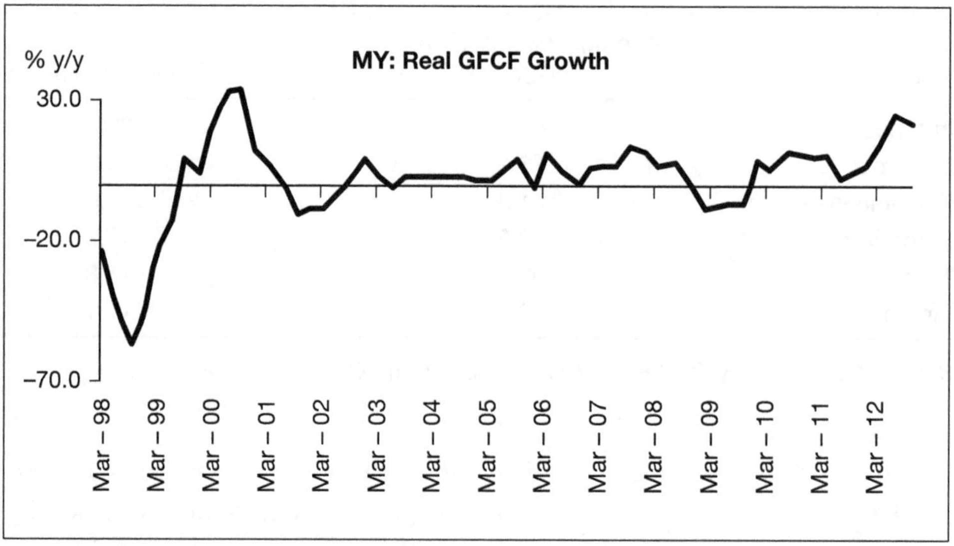

Note: GFCF — Gross Fixed Capital Formation.
Source: Calculated by Centennial Asia Advisors using CEIC Database.

FIGURE 6
Thailand's Investment Rate

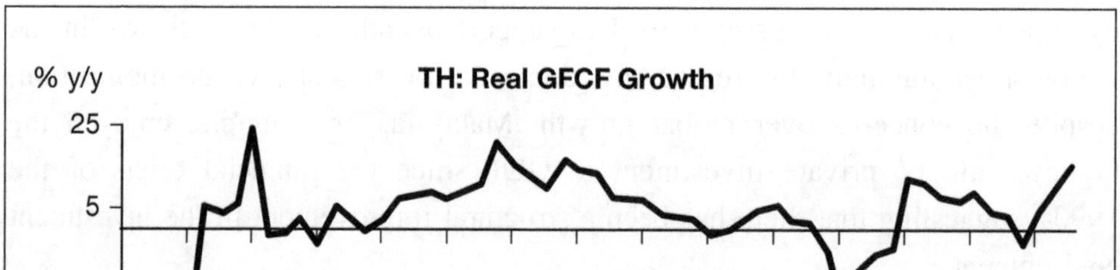

Note: GFCF — Gross Fixed Capital Formation.
Source: Calculated by Centennial Asia Advisors using CEIC Database.

FIGURE 7
Malaysian Consumer Spending

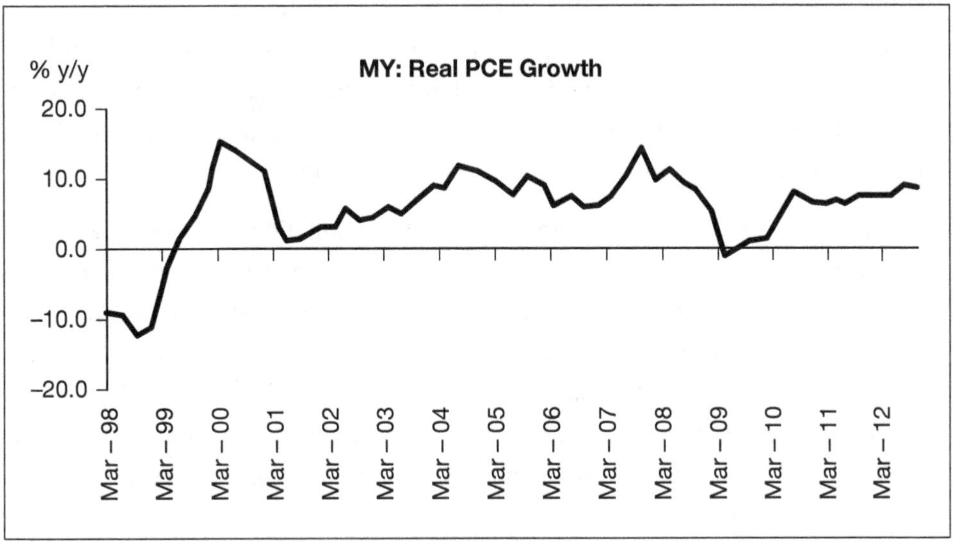

Note: PCE — Personal Consumption Expenditure.
Source: Calculated by Centennial Asia Advisors using CEIC Database.

FIGURE 8
Thailand's Consumer Spending

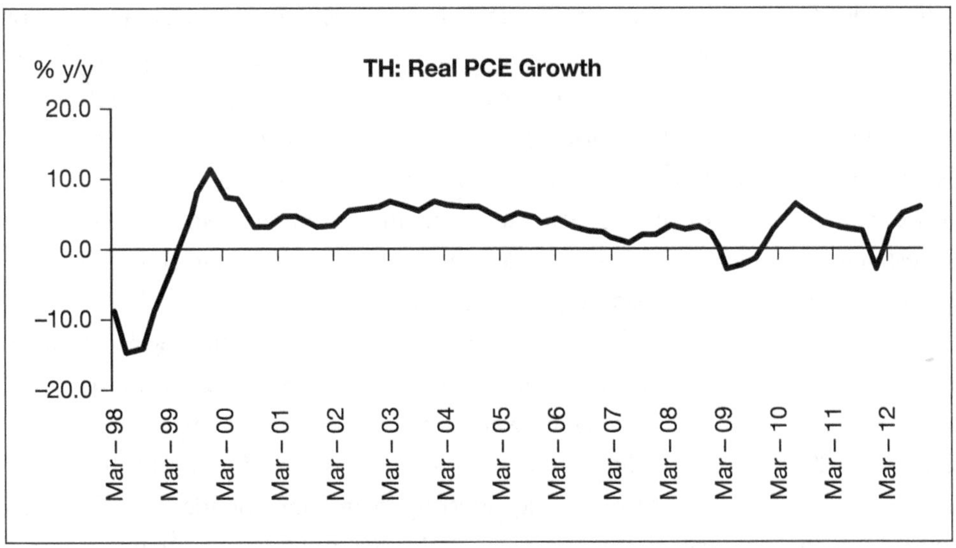

Note: PCE — Personal Consumption Expenditure.
Source: Calculated by Centennial Asia Advisors using CEIC Database.

Third, economic stability has generally been well managed in the region. In general, inflation has been much better managed in the region in recent years. Table 4 depicts recent trends in consumer price inflation across the region. In most cases, headline inflation has remained low and core inflation has been held in check. This suggests that central banks have generally managed the challenges to monetary management from volatile capital flows and unusually low global interest rates well. A number of trends are worth noting:

- Singapore which has an enviable record of low inflation has seen its inflation rate rise — unusually for Singapore, its inflation rate in recent months has been higher than that of its trading partners. Labour costs, rentals and costs related to private transportation have all risen significantly in the past year. The central bank has responded with tighter monetary policy in the form of an appreciating exchange rate. However, as the economy slows and as the policy tightening impacts the economy, inflation is likely to come down, as seen in the latest inflation data.
- Vietnam has succeeded in bringing inflation down in 2012 but the latest data suggest that inflationary pressures remain stubborn as inflation edged up again as the year progressed.

In terms of external stability, the region continued to enjoy broadly stable external accounts, as seen in Table 5 which shows trends in current account balances over 2010–12. In general, current account balances are falling, with Indonesia's current account balance now in deficit. However, this is not necessarily a source of concern. First, it is quite normal for developing economies to run current account deficits since investment rates will tend to be high while domestic savings may not be sufficient in a less developed economy. Second, what is driving the weakening in current account balances is typically not excessively loose monetary policy but a structural rise in investment. So long as these investments are productive, and so long as the current account deficits remain small, the risk to external stability will remain low.

Clearly, foreign exchange markets remained confident in the region. Table 6 presents trends in local currency changes against the U.S. dollar in the past two years. Typically, regional currencies were appreciating against the U.S. dollar in 2010 and 2011. In 2012, this trend has reversed but only modestly. Southeast Asian currencies remain broadly stable, attesting to growing confidence in financial markets in the regional outlook as well as the rising credibility of the region's central banks.

TABLE 4
Inflation Trends in Southeast Asia: Quarterly Changes Year-on-Year

	Mar 10	*Jun 10*	*Sep 10*	*Dec 10*	*Mar 11*	*Jun 11*	*Sep 11*	*Dec 11*	*Mar 12*	*Jun 12*	*Sep 12*
Singapore	0.9	3.1	3.4	4.0	5.2	4.7	5.5	5.5	4.9	5.26	4.2
Malaysia	1.3	1.6	1.9	2.0	2.8	3.3	3.4	3.2	2.3	1.72	1.3
Thailand	3.7	3.2	3.3	2.9	3.0	4.1	4.1	4.0	3.4	2.52	2.9
Philippines	3.9	3.8	3.9	3.576	4.5	4.9	4.7	4.6	3.1	2.94	3.5
Vietnam	8.5	8.9	8.4	10.8	12.8	19.4	22.5	19.8	15.9	8.59	5.6
Indonesia	3.6	4.4	6.2	6.3	6.8	5.9	4.7	4.1	3.7	4.50	4.5
Brunei	0.4	0.2	0.2	0.6	1.6	2.1	2.4	2.0	0.6	0.22	0.5
Cambodia	7.0	4.1	1.7	3.3	3.6	63.7	6.7	5.3	5.5	2.91	NA
Laos	4.6	4.8	7.6	6.8	6.8	9.5	6.6	7.4	6.1	3.90	3.3
Myanmar	6.5	8.7	7.3	8.31	8.6	7.1	3.5	1.2	–0.5	–1.50	NA

Source: Collated by Centennial Asia Advisors using CEIC Database.

TABLE 5
Quarterly Current Account Balances
(US$ million)

	Mar 10	*Jun 10*	*Sep 10*	*Dec 10*	*Mar 11*	*Jun 11*	*Sep 11*	*Dec 11*	*Mar 12*	*Jun 12*	*Sep 12*
Singapore	9,753	14,048	15,904	16,060	14,317	13,666	15,819	13,265	10,580	10,477	11,703
Malaysia	8,681	4,578	6,416	7,634	7,990	7,612	9,086	7,106	5,910	3,084	3,048
Thailand	4,134	603	1,018	4,269	4,568	–53	927	447	1,424	–2,389	2,747
Philippines	1,672	1,757	3,365	2,128	902	1,906	2,304	1,876	844	2,831	
Indonesia	1,891	1,342	1,043	870	2,947	265	766	–2,301	–3,126	–7,688	–5,336
Brunei	1,397	1,121	1,411	2,113	1,961	1,851	2,295				
Cambodia	–157	–258	–272	–86	–150	–380	–24	–158	–31		
Laos	–38	33	34	48	19	–127	–10	–7			

Source: Collated by Centennial Asia Advisors using CEIC Database.

TABLE 6
Currency Fluctuations in Southeast Asia
(Percentage Change vs U.S. Dollar over the year, negative sign implies local currency appreciation)

	Mar 10	*Jun 10*	*Sep 10*	*Dec 10*	*Mar 11*	*Jun 11*	*Sep 11*	*Dec 11*	*Mar 12*	*Jun 12*	*Sep 12*
Singapore	–7.3	–5.5	–5.8	–6.6	–9.0	–10.9	–9.5	–1.2	–1.0	2.0	1.6
Malaysia	–7.1	–8.7	–10.3	–8.4	–9.6	–6.9	–4.2	1.1	0.4	3.1	3.3
Thailand	–6.9	–6.8	–6.9	–10.0	–7.2	–6.5	–4.6	3.4	1.4	3.3	4.0
Philippines	–3.6	–5.0	–6.0	–6.7	–4.8	–5.0	–5.6	–0.4	–1.7	–1.1	–2.0
Vietnam	7.4	9.5	10.4	9.0	9.6	11.5	10.1	9.7	4.2	0.8	1.0
Indonesia	–20.3	–13.5	–10.0	–5.4	–3.9	–5.8	–4.3	0.4	2.2	8.3	10.4
Brunei	–7.2	–5.6	–5.7	–6.5	–8.9	–10.9	–9.7	–1.2	–1.1	2.0	1.7
Cambodia	1.7	2.0	1.7	–0.9	–3.3	–3.9	–3.3	–1.6	–0.2	–0.1	NA
Laos	–0.5	–2.8	–3.6	–5.1	–4.9	–3.2	–2.3	–0.4	–0.6	–0.3	0.0
Myanmar	–3.2	2.1	3.2	2.3	–1.2	–6.9	–4.9	–0.3	1.4	NA	NA

Source: Collated by Centennial Asia Advisors using CEIC Database.

Fourth, a detailed analysis of economic resilience in the region shows that the region's robust performance in the face of external challenges is deeply rooted. Southeast Asian economies are inextricably linked to the global economy through trade, financial, commodity price, and other channels. They are thus vulnerable to the ups and downs of the global economy. What is important, is therefore, not so much how vulnerable they are, which is unavoidable, but each economy's capacity to absorb the shocks and stresses which emanate from the global economy and rebound from any downturn.

Figure 9 presents a measure of economic resilience which brings together the various determinants of resilience — how diversified the economies are, how strong balance sheets are, the strength of financial sectors, and the capacity of policy to respond quickly and effectively to external challenges. The figure shows the resilience performance of key Southeast Asian economies for which sufficient data is available against other Asian economies:

- The trends are very positive, showing a substantial improvement in economic resilience in the region since the Asian financial crisis of the late 1990s. The only country where economic resilience has declined is Vietnam.
- Recent years have shown continuing improvement in economic resilience. However, resilience has edged down marginally in Malaysia and Thailand.

FIGURE 9
Improving Economic Resilience in Southeast Asia

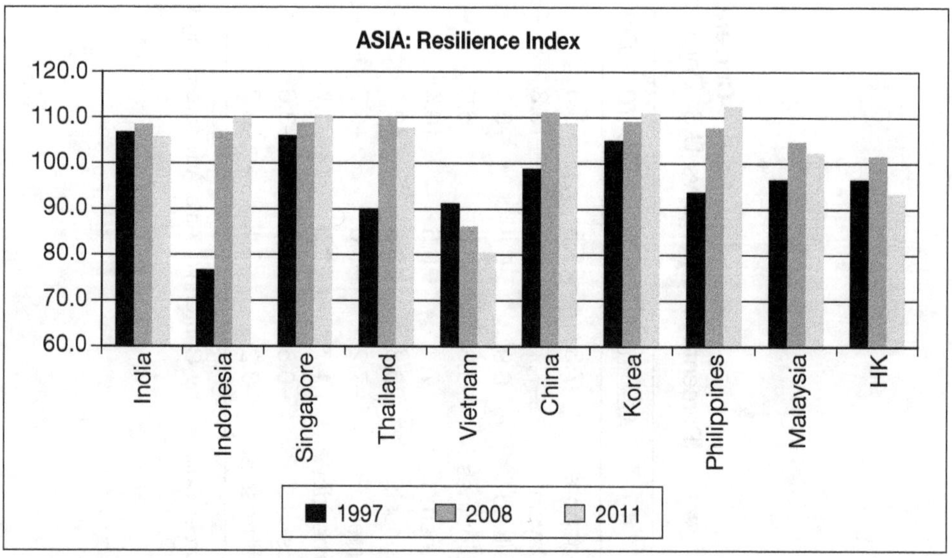

Source: Prepared by Centennial Group.

Table 7 shows a more detailed assessment of resilience trends across the region.

TABLE 7
Analysis of Economic Resilience in Southeast Asia

	2000	*2011*	*Comments*
Cambodia	108.2	98.7	***Significant deterioration*** in resilience score, placing it at the second lowest in ASEAN. Major factors: • Governance: Sharp fall in the legal area. • Bank soundness also saw a sharp fall. • However, export resilience improved markedly.
Indonesia	80.5	110.4	***Substantial improvement*** • Big improvement in monetary policy credibility. • Bank soundness has also soared as a result of a stronger capital base, better asset quality and reduced risks to bank income generation. • Governance, external resilience have improved.
Malaysia	90.3	102.3	***Substantial improvement*** • Bank soundness improved with asset quality. • Export diversity, export independence, external debt and foreign reserves strengthened. • Improvements in government effectiveness and in monetary policy credibility were offset by a deterioration in fiscal policy soundness.
Philippines	91.7	112.4	***Substantial improvement*** • Significant improvement in measures of policy effectiveness as fiscal and monetary policy credibility improved. • Financial resilience improved markedly as a result of a sharp improvement in asset quality. • Exports are more diversified; reserves and import cover have risen; private sector debt fell. Counter-cyclical remittances from abroad have helped stabilize the currency and build up a healthy stock of international reserves. • Governance scores have however fallen a tad primarily due to a mark down in the legal sector.

TABLE 7 *(Cont'd)*

	2000	*2011*	*Comments*
Singapore	108.3	110.7	*Retains its position as one of the most resilient economies in Asia* despite its high dependence on the external sector. • Financial resilience improved with asset quality. • Export diversity has improved but external resilience has been held back by one of the lowest scores in the region for export independence. However, its extraordinarily strong reserves position helps offset this. • Governance, capacity for strong pro-active and credible fiscal and monetary policies contribute to Singapore's overall strong resilience.
Thailand	92.9	108	*Remarkable increase in the overall resilience score index score since 2000.* • Fiscal policy effectiveness up while monetary policy credibility remains high. • Financial resilience has improved markedly as a result of better asset quality, stronger capital bases of banks and reduced risks to banks' income generation capacity.
Vietnam	89.7	81.2	*Worrying decline in resilience* • Lowest resilience score in ASEAN. • Policy effectiveness is a source of weakness: fiscal and monetary policy soundness have both diminished. High and volatile inflation rates create high inflation expectations as well as volatile expectations of currency depreciation which weaken its external resilience as well. • Aggressive private sector external debt a worry. • Reserves buffer is low.

Source: Centennial Group.

Underlying Drivers of Longer Term Economic Trends Emerging

This section takes a step back to survey some of the longer term trends in the region. We look at the changing and expanding nature of economic integration; the greater emphasis of government policies on social safety nets; and encouraging trends in regional investment.

Expanding Economic Integration Beginning to Release Synergies

Economic integration is proceeding at many levels within Southeast Asia. If these trends hold, the region will see a substantial rise in flows of trade in goods, capital, tourists and labour which will expand economic and business opportunities in the region.

First, the ASEAN-wide economic integration initiatives are making progress. This is evident in the ASEAN Economic Community (AEC), which is now set to be in place by the end of 2015. The ASEAN Secretariat monitors each country's compliance rate with that country's obligations under the AEC process in a Scorecard. Averaging the results of the first two AEC scorecards gets ASEAN a compliance rate of 67.5 per cent for the obligations in the period 2008–09 and 2010–11. Table 8 outlines more details of the progress of each main component of the AEC Blueprint in these periods. While it is a concern that the compliance rate has fallen from the first period's assessment when 73.6 per cent of targets were met, there is still considerable progress being made.

TABLE 8
Compliance Rate for Obligations Under AEC Blueprint

Component	*Target Achievement Rate after Phase 1 (%)*	*Target Achievement Rate after Phase 1 and 2 (%)*
Single Market and Production Base	82	65.9
Competitive Economic Region	50	67.9
Equitable Economic Development	100	66.7
Integration with Global Economy	100	85.7
Overall	73.6	67.5

Source: AEC Scorecard 1 and 2.

While some concern has been expressed at the slow pace of implementation of the measures needed to implement the AEC, enough progress is being made to stimulate increased flows of trade, capital and people. The real test in any economic integration effort is whether it changes the behaviour — production/business location, capital allocation, and business strategy — of economic agents. While it is early days yet, this is beginning to happen in ASEAN. Private businesses in some sectors are showing through their investments and acquisitions that they increasingly see ASEAN as an economic bloc. In the aviation sector, AirAsia, the region's biggest low-cost carrier, has relocated its chief executive officer to Jakarta, where the ASEAN Secretariat is headquartered as it expands throughout the region. Leading private sector business leaders including the chief executive officers of CIMB Bank, Bangkok Bank, AirAsia, and the Ayala Group have jointly launched the ASEAN Business Club (ABC) in order to engage in ASEAN community-building efforts.

In another sign that companies are taking the cue from economic integration, cross-border mergers and acquisitions and joint ventures within ASEAN are also increasing. Banks and telecommunications companies from the two most developed economies in ASEAN, Singapore and Malaysia, have invested across the region. Thailand's Siam Cement, is planning to invest up to 75 per cent of its 2012–16 capital spending in ASEAN countries. In addition, companies outside ASEAN are also beginning to treat the region as an economic bloc. Shin Shin-Etsu Chemical, Japan's leading chemical producer, has invested US$64 million to build two chemical plants in Vietnam with the hope of serving a large base of customers in ASEAN as a whole.

Second, new forms of integration are taking shape, giving integration further impetus. At one level, the region has sub-regional economic integration efforts such as the Greater Mekong Subregion which has progressed to the point where a web of roads and transport linkages backed by improvements in the behind-the-border issues has created conditions for a greater flow of goods and peoples.

At another level, there is economic integration of a more partial kind such as the Iskandar Region in Malaysia bordering on Singapore, which is increasingly being integrated with the Singapore economy. The year 2012 saw substantial progress within Iskandar as major projects began operation. Theme parks such as Legoland and the Hello Kitty Park have opened with revenues growing much faster than initially expected. Several large education projects such as universities and schools have also started operating. Moreover, with business costs in Singapore escalating and placing pressure on the profitability of small and medium enterprises (SMEs) there, several Singapore SMEs are relocating manufacturing and other activities to Iskandar.

As Iskandar achieves critical mass and demonstrates the efficacy of such smaller scale cross-border economic engagement, there is a greater likelihood that it will serve as a model for more such integration efforts across ASEAN.

A Rising Investment/GDP Ratio

One major reason for slower growth in ASEAN economies after the 1997–98 financial crisis was the fall in the share of investment in GDP (Table 9). The ensuing loss of confidence, banks' unwillingness to lend and companies' desire to rebuild balance sheets rather than expand capacity coincided with the rise of a more competitive China to weaken the incentive to invest in the region. Without a significant rise in efficiency a lower investment share of GDP meant a lower rate of economic growth.

There is now some evidence in 2012 that investment rates are set to rise, potentially raising the underlying economic growth rate in the region. Table 9 shows a pick up in the investment share of GDP in 2012 to the highest rates in almost a decade for several countries. Figures 5 and 6 show how Malaysia and Thailand are enjoying the strongest growth rates in investment in years.

There are some powerful forces driving this revival of investment:

- First, Southeast Asia's share of global flows of foreign direct investment (FDI) has risen and is almost back to the pre-1997 levels — before the rise of China and the Asian financial crisis which set the region back (Figure 10). A good part of this revival in Southeast Asia is due to the recovery in Indonesia's share, which at 1.2 per cent in 2011 is the highest since 1996 and close to the average Indonesia share in the 1990–96 period of high growth (Figure 11). Singapore continues to pull in a large part of Southeast Asia's share of global FDI flows.

TABLE 9
Share of Investment in GDP

Country	*1980*	*1990*	*2000*	*2006*	*2011*	*1–3Q12*
Indonesia	20.9	28.3	19.9	24.1	32.0	32.6
Malaysia	31.1	33.0	25.6	22.0	22.1	25.7
Philippines	27.2	23.1	21.2	20.1	19.1	20.3
Singapore	45.0	35.1	33.2	21.2	22.4	25.2
Thailand	27.8	40.4	22.0	28.1	26.3	28.8
Vietnam	NA	14.0	28.7	34.4	34.9	NA

Source: Collated by Centennial using CEIC Database.

FIGURE 10
Southeast Asia Share of Global FDI Rising Again

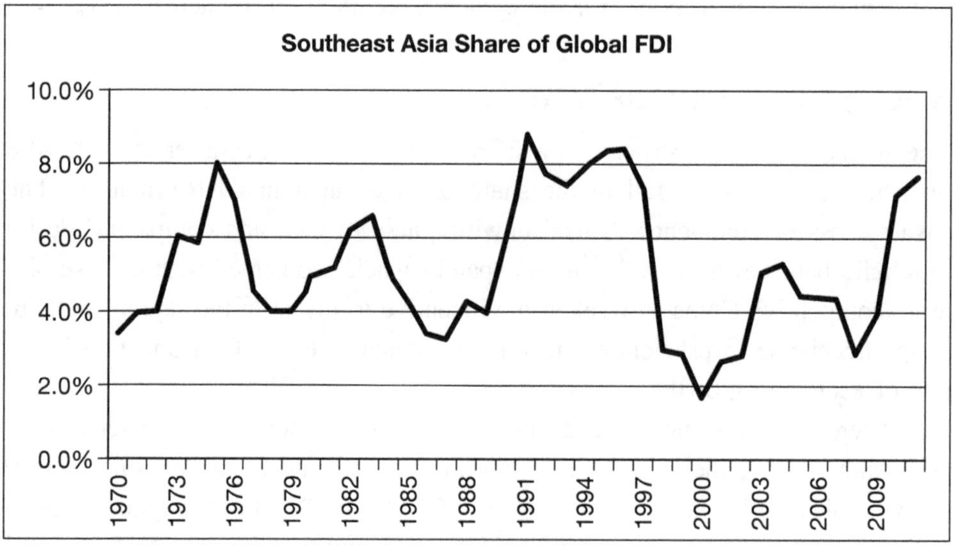

Source: Calculated by Centennial Asia Advisors using CEIC Database.

FIGURE 11
... Powered by Indonesia's Improvement

Source: Calculated by Centennial Asia Advisors using CEIC Database.

- Second, the region has been under-investing in infrastructure for many years. As the infrastructure constraint began to bite, governments have started to push infrastructure spending more aggressively. As a consequence, spending on roads, mass transit and power generation capacity in particular has been ramped up in 2012. For example, massive urban transport infrastructure programmes are underway in Thailand, Malaysia, and Singapore.
- Third, higher investment also reflects a recovery in private investment. In Malaysia, for instance, the private investment share of GDP has risen to a post-crisis high.

Increased Consciousness of Social Welfare

A final trend of interest is the rebalancing of policy towards a greater emphasis on social welfare and national priorities rather than the previous emphasis on economic growth and price stability. The past year has seen countries as diverse as Indonesia, Thailand, Malaysia, and Singapore introduce shifts in policy in line with this trend.

First, there is a greater use of minimum wages as a policy tool. A minimum wage was introduced in Malaysia while minimum wages in Thailand and Indonesia have been raised significantly. At one level, this reflects a growing sense among policy-makers that minimum wage policies are not as harmful as once thought and that a well-structured minimum wage could be positive on balance for the economy. At another level, these policy changes arise from policy-makers' realization that more needs to be done to address the plight of low income workers and to reverse the growing trend of rising income inequality.

Second, there is also an expanding consciousness among policy-makers of the need to more directly demonstrate their commitment to protecting citizens' or national interests. It is in Indonesia where we have seen much of this new trend. For example, Indonesia has moved to press companies to add more value domestically to natural resources so that more of the benefits of Indonesia's vast natural resources are retained domestically. Indonesia has also responded to worker unrest by tightening labour laws to restrict the use of contract workers (who typically have fewer social and legal protections than normal workers). Some of these policies have aroused some concern among businesses of their cost and other implications.

However, it is not just in Indonesia but also in countries long known for their pro-business stance where such policy shifts are also evident:

- In Thailand, the government of Yingluck Shinawatra has implemented its 2011 election promise to support rice farmers by buying rice at much higher prices than before. Other forms of support for consumer spending were also implemented, such as financial support for first-time home buyers.
- In Singapore, whose policy framework has consistently been based on free and open markets including one of the most highly open labour markets in the world, there has been a clear shift in policy approaches. The government is now rigorously curtailing the growth of the foreign worker population.
- Malaysia has stepped up cash handouts to poorer families. Subsidies of various kinds rose in 2012 to RM31.5 billion from RM25.9 billion in 2011.

In these countries, though, policy-makers have made efforts to ensure that the concerns of the business sector were addressed as much as possible. In Singapore, for example, more efforts are underway to provide support to SMEs to enable them to adjust to the labour shortages and rising wage costs resulting from the policy change.

Conclusion: ASEAN Is in Good Shape

The above discussion leads to the following conclusions.

First, the cyclical performance of Southeast Asian economies has been commendable. Economic growth in the region has weathered the deceleration in global demand reasonably well in 2011 while maintaining inflation at reasonably low rates. External positions remained fairly robust as well, although there were signs that current account surpluses were falling. This record was achieved in spite of the financial stresses arising from ultra-easy monetary conditions in developed countries and frequent episodes of financial turmoil in the eurozone.

Second, this improved cyclical performance is testimony to structural improvements in the regional economies and is therefore sustainable. Of particular note is the growing economic resilience of most of the region's economies. The analysis of resilience above shows how the improvements were due to progress in structural factors, such as the conduct of monetary and fiscal policies, the levels of external debt, the strength of balance sheets in banks and the corporate sector, and the diversification of the export bases of the regional economies.

Finally, recent trends are also building the economic base for stronger and better distributed economic growth in the future. The trends we identify above show that economic growth in future can benefit from rising synergies from regional integration and a rise in the investment rate. In addition, political leaders and policy-makers are becoming more sensitive to the need to translate economic growth into welfare gains for the common man.

SOUTHEAST ASIA IN AMERICA'S REBALANCE TO THE ASIA-PACIFIC

Satu P. Limaye

Introduction

President Barack Obama's mid-November 2012 post-re-election travel to Myanmar, Cambodia, and Thailand, including attendance at the East Asia Summit (EAS) and United States-ASEAN Leaders Meeting, marks three important "firsts" for a sitting American president: the first bilateral visits to Myanmar and Cambodia, the first *mainland* Southeast Asia-only trip, and the first Southeast Asia-only trip. Even more significant is the growing structural importance being accorded to all of Southeast Asia in the context of a broader American rebalance or "pivot" to the Asia-Pacific region. The emphasis on Southeast Asia in the U.S. rebalance to Asia arguably constitutes the most distinctive element of the overall strategy — next only to the inclusion of India. The opportunities and constraints for U.S.-Southeast Asia relations in the immediate years ahead can best be appreciated by understanding how the rebalance strategy implicates Southeast Asia, and how Southeast Asia is critical to its success.

Southeast Asia's Place in America's Rebalance to the Asia-Pacific

Secretary of State Hillary Clinton's November 2011 article "America's Pacific Century"[1] is the single most comprehensive and detailed public articulation of the Obama Administration's Asia rebalance policy. In it, she is forthright that American objectives are to "sustain leadership", "secure interests", and "advance values". In other words, quite reasonably, American policy objectives

SATU P. LIMAYE is Director, East West Center in Washington D.C. and Senior Advisor, Center for Naval Analyses, United States.

vis-à-vis Asia are not fundamentally different than in any other region — or, for that matter, nearly every functional issue. The instruments identified to help achieve these objectives are sixfold: strengthening bilateral security alliances, deepening working relationships with emerging partners, engaging with regional multilateral institutions, expanding trade and investment, forging a broad-based military presence, and advancing democracy and human rights. This list of instruments is noteworthy in the regional context not because they are unique to the Asia-Pacific region, but because they are all increasingly, intensely, and deeply salient there. It is in the Asia-Pacific where five of seven American treaty allies reside including two in Southeast Asia and one very close strategic partner — Singapore; where rising powers such as China, India, and Indonesia, as well as Vietnam and a transitioning Myanmar, provide possible new partners; where new multilateral institutions are trying to take root; where resilient and growing economies are altering the global landscape of production and supply chains and hence trade, investment, and finance; where unresolved territorial and historical disputes pose challenges requiring a recalibrated military presence; and where the opportunity to improve democracy and human rights is compelling.

What is crucial about the rebalance to Asia is not the novelty of American objectives or instruments, but the region's growing centrality to advancing and applying American foreign policy and security objectives and instruments in cooperation with allies, friends and partners. To the objectives and instruments of the rebalance strategy may be added two other contextual aspects of the policy: the "new geography" of America's strategy, and the effort at reprioritization away from Southwest Asia and towards the Asia-Pacific region. The objectives, instruments, and premises of America's rebalance to the Asia-Pacific all directly implicate and depend on greater interactions with Southeast Asia.

The first premise of the rebalance strategy is that with the end of U.S. combat operations in Iraq and the planned drawdown of forces in Afghanistan, the United States will be able to pay even more attention to the Asia-Pacific region. Southeast Asians among others complain that America is over- and even unproductively-engaged in the broader Middle East. Clashes between Hamas and Israel during President Obama's Southeast Asia visit in November (causing the diversion of Secretary Clinton to the region for crisis management) highlighted how that region could intrude into America's Asia rebalance. But what is abundantly clear from the last four years is that ongoing American involvement in Southwest Asia and the Middle East has *not* constrained American attention to Asia or to Southeast Asia.

The more difficult challenge for U.S.-Southeast Asia relations is not a United States distracted by Middle East disruptions but by differences about issues relating to the region. Whether on Palestinian statehood or Iranian energy purchases, the United States and Southeast Asia are likely to need more rather than less mutual engagement about the Middle East and North Africa — particularly as Southeast Asia's own diplomatic, economic and other interests increase there. And this dialogue needs to be reframed as an opportunity for expanding and consolidating relations, not distracting or disrupting them — even as domestic sensitivities in Southeast Asia will pose constraints to a consonance of views. One inadvertent "downside" about the articulation of the premise that America can rebalance to Asia because it can shift away from wars in Iraq and Afghanistan, is that it has led observers to mistakenly interpret that the United States intends to turn primarily its military capabilities towards the Asia-Pacific. Many thoughtful Americans, including policy-makers, wish to see a rebalance to Asia that is well calibrated with the range of American military, economic, normative, and public diplomacy tools.

The second premise of the rebalance strategy is America's wider and maritime-focused geographical conception of Asia — sometimes referred to as the "Indo-Pacific". The geographical conception itself is not new. The George W. Bush administration released a *Quadrennial Defense Review* (QDR) in 2001 (10 September to be precise) using the phrase "East Asian littoral running from the Sea of Japan to the Bay of Bengal" to indicate a focus beyond Northeast Asia and encompassing the maritime littoral up to India. These formulations highlight the two "new" approaches of America's rebalance Asia strategy — greater salience of Southeast Asia and the inclusion of India.

Southeast Asia and "Adapting Alliances"

The primary policy instrument of the American rebalance to Asia is alliances. Secretary Clinton declared that U.S. treaty alliances are the "fulcrum for our strategic turn to the Asia-Pacific". For the last decade "alliance adaptation" has been focused on Japan and the Republic of Korea due to base realignment initiatives in the context of force reposturing. But today, driven by changed security realities, shifting domestic politics in regional countries, the demand of regional governments and now the U.S. rebalance strategy, adaptation is being applied to American alliances in Southeast Asia (Thailand and the Philippines and "strategic partner" Singapore) consistent with the "three core principles" identified to guide alliance adaption; namely, political consensus on alliance objectives, making alliances nimble enough to address new challenges and opportunities and guaranteeing the capabilities to make alliances "operationally and materially capable of deterring provocation from the full spectrum of state and non-state actors".

While the scale, scope and interoperability of alliance adaption in Northeast Asia are larger and deeper, alliance reform with Thailand and the Philippines provides long-overdue corrections and new directions. A case in point is the newly announced 2012 Joint Vision Statement for the Thai-U.S. Defence Alliance issued during U.S. Defence Secretary Leon Panetta's November 2012 visit to Bangkok. The new vision statement makes no mention of fighting communism, which was at the heart of the 1962 Rusk-Thanat communiqué that forms the basis for the U.S.-Thai alliance, and instead focuses on partnership for regional security in Southeast Asia, supporting stability in the Asia-Pacific region and beyond, bilateral and multilateral interoperability and readiness, and relationship building, coordination and collaboration. Much work remains to translate these guidelines into actual exercises, training, capacity-building, and even military acquisitions.

Similarly, in the case of the Republic of the Philippines, with the removal of large U.S. bases in that country, the alliance relationship moved to focus on counter-terrorism after the 9/11 attacks. With new priorities and challenges emerging, efforts are again underway to adapt this alliance in ways that are mutually acceptable. The fact that the United States and the Philippines held their first-ever 2 + 2 meeting (of Foreign and Defence Secretaries on each side) in January 2012 is the start of this process. Eventually, the alliance is likely to involve greater rotational throughput of American military forces, expanded and recalibrated training and exercises, and the provision of capabilities suitable for the Philippines' own greater focus on maritime needs. These efforts at adapting post-1945, post-Cold War and post-9/11 alliances in Southeast Asia are symbolic of the profound applicability of this element of America's rebalance strategy to the subregion.

Southeast Asia and Forging a Broad-based Military Presence

Related to "adapting alliances" is adapting American military presence to the requirements of a new security environment. Again, Southeast Asia lies at the core of these efforts. As Secretary Clinton's article states, "We are modernizing our basing arrangements with traditional allies in Northeast Asia — and our commitment on this is rock solid — while enhancing our presence in Southeast Asia and into the Indian Ocean." And even more specifically, "We are also looking at how we can increase our operational access in Southeast Asia and the Indian Ocean region and deepen our contacts with allies and partners." To some extent the emphasis on Southeast Asia among security interests such as freedom of navigation, counter-proliferation, and military transparency is derivative: The United States needs cooperation with Southeast Asia to achieve these goals. Thailand's decision to join the Proliferation Security Initiative (PSI) is a case in point. But also important is that on its own terms Southeast Asia offers new opportunities for partnerships and is sending a strong demand signal for a U.S. presence. In the current climate for U.S. defence resources, it is highly unlikely that the United States will seek major new bases or facilities in Southeast Asia. But as American military leaders and civilian defence officials have repeatedly stated, Southeast is likely to see, as Chairman of the Joint Chiefs of Staff General Martin Dempsey put it on a visit to the Philippines, "three mores — more attention, more engagement and more quality".[2]

Southeast Asia and Emerging Partnerships

More dramatic than the steady, careful work required to adapt alliances and to forge a broader military presence are new and revitalized relationships in Southeast Asia. President Obama's first-ever visits to Myanmar and Cambodia (and Secretary of State Clinton's visit to Laos — the first by a U.S. Secretary of State in fifty-seven years) epitomized the policy of reaching out to countries with which the United States has been either not engaged or under-engaged for nearly a generation. America's "return" to *all of mainland* Southeast Asia is a singular feature of the rebalance and one that gets lost in the dramatic opening of relations with Myanmar. New relationships are not just for mainland Southeast Asia, however. Jakarta and Washington, for example, have a new mechanism for enhancing bilateral relations in the form of the Comprehensive Partnership. The U.S. relationship with Vietnam is also trending upward following a painstaking process of normalization.

Given the diversity of countries involved and the complex nature of issues the United States has with each of them, no one should expect quick or unambiguous outcomes. Complicated democratic and non-democratic politics in many of these countries, historical sensitivities about relations with the

United States, and natural differences of perspectives, interests and values will constrain some of these newly emerging partnerships. But an irreversible process of engaging in new relationships between the United States and Southeast Asia has begun and is likely to achieve a continuity and forward trajectory over the coming years.

Southeast Asia and Asia-Pacific Multilateralism

Another key feature of America's rebalance towards the Asia-Pacific is active membership in all regional multilateral organizations. To apply President Obama's phrase about overall U.S. commitment to the Asia-Pacific to regional multilateralism, the United States is "all in". Southeast Asia's place in this aspect of the rebalance is critical because the United States has recognized "ASEAN as a fulcrum for the region's emerging regional architecture".[3] Indeed, the Obama administration's signing of ASEAN's Treaty of Amity and Cooperation (TAC) soon after taking office was a prerequisite for U.S. membership in the region's widest leader-level meeting — the EAS. But several difficulties lie ahead for the United States and Southeast Asia regarding multilateral organizations.

First, the conditions surrounding the multilateral project have become worse over the past year with continuing and intensifying territorial and maritime disputes across the region, an unprecedented lack of consensus among ASEAN member states, and tensions in U.S.-China relations. Second, though multilateral organizations are mechanisms for the United States to "institutionalize engagement" in the Asia-Pacific, they are not the only mechanisms. The United States is also institutionalizing its role through alliances, new partnerships and non-institutional, non-ASEAN-led forms of multilateralism such as mini-laterals, forums such as the Six-Party Talks and functional efforts ranging from the PSI to the Asian Maritime Forum. So the institutionalization benefit to the United States afforded by ASEAN-led multilateralism would be insufficient to justify major commitments if this multilateralism is ineffective. Third, while the United States is unlikely to retreat from its commitment to participate in the various regional organizations the United States has now joined, the robust level of its commitments will require desirable outcomes to be sustainable. Fourth, regional organization/institution-building is not the same as regional order-building that includes norms, rules, and values. There is long, hard work ahead on creating shared norms, rules, and values. It is imperative for the United States to strengthen multilateralism in the region to contribute to deterrence, dissuasion, and reassurance: deter countries from "acting out" unilaterally, dissuading countries from thinking they can supplant U.S. leadership and smaller country interests, and reassuring American friends and allies that the United States has a commitment to the region. Fifth, an underlying "tectonic" competition between a pan-Asian and trans-Pacific regional project is continuing and will impact the utility and viability of regional organizations. And finally, the United States and Southeast Asia will have to work hard to make organizations effective by turning dialogue into results, calibrate different topics of priority, and decide how to streamline (both in terms of hierarchy/representation and functional differentiation/issue selection) overlapping organizations. The decision to institutionalize the annual U.S.-ASEAN Leaders Meeting as a Summit is a useful mechanism to coordinate improvements on regional multilateralism.

Southeast Asia and Expanding Trade and Investment

There has been much criticism that the U.S. rebalance to Asia is "over-militarized" and does not take into account the changing economic dynamics in the region, such as shifting patterns of trade and investment and the successful negotiation of free trade arrangements. These complaints go hand in hand with other exaggerated economic narratives that China is supplanting the United States as the economic partner for Asia, that intra-Asian integration is weakening trans-Pacific links and the United States is partner of choice for security while China is the partner of choice for trade and investment. As evident in the course of recent tensions in the region, the picture painted by some of an Asia willing to set aside historical and territorial disputes in the interests of economic growth is growing ever fuzzier. Indeed, the use, particularly by China, of trade and investment punishments in the context of these disputes is notable.

The United States has taken important steps to expand trade and investment in the region. The successful conclusion of the Korea-U.S. Free Trade Agreement (KORUS) and the launch and ongoing negotiations for a Trans-Pacific Partnership (TPP) are just two examples. Again, Southeast Asia is a critical part of these efforts. It is a fact that currently only Brunei, Malaysia, Singapore, and Vietnam from Southeast Asia are party to TPP negotiations though interest has been expressed by Thailand. However, it should be noted that the United States is working on many paths to enhance ASEAN-wide economic strength and expanded U.S.-ASEAN economic ties. Normalization of relations with Burma will help end Burma's isolation from U.S. region-wide economic efforts and U.S. assistance for Laos' entry into the World Trade Organization

(WTO) is a step on the path to bridging the development divide among ASEAN members. The United States also provides economic and technical assistance for ASEAN's own plans at economic integration. During President Obama's November 2012 Leaders Meeting with ASEAN, the two sides announced the launch of the U.S.-ASEAN Expanded Economic Engagement (E3) Initiative. The immediate goal of this effort is to expand trade and investment. Longer term, and more importantly, the goal of the effort is to "lay the groundwork for ASEAN countries to prepare to join high-standard trade agreements, such as the Trans-Pacific Partnership (TPP)".[4] Indeed, if and when all ASEAN member countries are in a position to meet the high standards of a TPP-like agreement, the prospect of a U.S.-ASEAN FTA could also materialize.

Southeast Asia remains a vital opportunity for commerce. It is the largest destination of American foreign direct investment (FDI) in Asia and usually among the top five Asian sources of FDI into the United States, usually among the top few trade partners, and the source of nearly 50,000 foreign students at U.S. universities generating about US$1 billion of contributions to the U.S. economy.[5]

Southeast Asia and Advancing Human Rights and Democracy

A final element of the U.S. rebalance strategy towards the Asia-Pacific is the insistence on advancing democracy and human rights. Southeast Asia is a "special" focus for this element of U.S. strategy as the recent visit of President Obama showed. There was criticism in the United States and elsewhere that the President's visit to Myanmar was too early of a "reward" for an incomplete transition away from military rule. The President was also criticized for having a short bilateral meeting with Prime Minister Hun Sen of Cambodia whose actions on democracy and human rights have been severely criticized. The U.S. approaches to Southeast Asia will continue to stress democracy and human rights, and diaspora communities from Southeast Asia in the United States are likely to play a particularly important role in influencing U.S. policy on such issues, but U.S. strategy currently privileges engagement over isolation. Cynics will read this as politico-security interests trumping real commitment to human rights and democracy. They would be wrong. Of course, policy implementation will always calibrate multiple, overlapping interests. But should there be a reversal or steep decline in human rights and democracy in Southeast Asia, the United States will react. Moreover, even now, human rights and democracy concerns continue to constrain specific engagement ranging from military interactions to faster, further progress in overall bilateral relations with key regional countries. This should indicate that the United States remains committed to advancing human rights and democracy even when other compulsions such as enhancing emerging partnerships are at stake.

Southeast Asia in America's Rebalance to the Asia-Pacific: Conclusions

The United States has been profoundly engaged in Southeast Asia over the past decade and especially after the Obama administration took office in January 2009. The United States has signed the TAC, appointed a resident ambassador to ASEAN, acknowledged ASEAN as a fulcrum of multilateralism, attended the EAS, pursued the TPP, begun the process of normalizing relations with Myanmar, and delivered principled and clear statements on territorial disputes in the South China Sea — *all before the formal articulation of the "pivot"/ rebalance to the Asia-Pacific strategy*. President Obama's visit to the region in November 2012 put mainland Southeast Asia on the U.S. "mental map" after a generation. Given the remarkable dynamism in U.S.-Southeast Asia relations, natural questions include: What next? What challenges remain? What successes have been achieved?

Among the challenges ahead, sustaining a high level of attention to U.S.-Southeast Asia relations will be key. And the reason for this has little to do with resources and more with policy and personnel. Speaking earlier this year about the U.S.-India relationship, Secretary Clinton said "Well, today there is less need for dramatic breakthroughs that marked earlier phases in our relationship, but more need for steady, focused cooperation aimed at working through our differences and advancing the interests and values we share. This kind of daily, weekly, monthly collaboration may not always be glamorous, but it is strategically significant. And that is, after all, what this dialogue is all about."[6] To some extent, the dramatic and glamorous work in U.S.-Southeast Asia relations is accomplished; now comes the work of making substantive progress on a robust series of initiatives. Also challenging will be the constellation of political leaders and officials responsible for relations both in the United States and in Southeast Asia. Inevitably many will change, and it remains to be seen if new leaders and officials have the same energy and commitment to ties. Finally, events will intrude that will compete for time and energy to push forward U.S.-Southeast Asia ties.

A major positive in U.S.-Southeast Asia relations is what I have called the "Goldilocks Balances". Relations are balanced across issues ranging from defence to diplomacy and energy to economics (for example, unlike earlier, the Cold War or the "global war on terror" or GWOT does not dominate the agenda). Both sides must take care not to let China become the new single issue that drives relations with each other. Relations are also balanced between the supply and demand for U.S. presence and role in the region even though persistent fine-tuning is required; and finally the United States is balancing constructive ties with China with reassurance to allies, partners and friends across the region. The United States is pursuing neither a "China first" nor "Allies first" strategy but an "Asia First" one — this makes particularly good sense in Southeast Asia.

Too many caricatures of the U.S. rebalance paint it as containment of China. Of course, U.S. strategy is *about* China, but it is not only *at* China. Given China's critical importance to the United States and to all Asian countries, it would be strikingly odd if U.S. policy was not crafted to react to China's rise. It is well to recall that in the first two or so years of the Obama administration's first term many in the region expressed alarm about Washington and Beijing moving towards a "G2". Current U.S. rebalance policy in the region seeks neither a "G2" with China or a Cold War 2 (CW2). There is regional demand for continued U.S. leadership (and ample ability in the United States to supply it) precisely because China's rise is affecting the balance of power but not the balance of order. U.S. primacy is a public good — especially when regional countries are uncertain about China's willingness or capacity to provide such a public good and due to concerns about what China's conception of order would look like (for example, "New Security Concept" or "9-dash line"). In this context, there remains a strong demand signal for the supply of U.S.-backed order and reassurance. Of course, there are limits to that demand signal. No country in Asia, or anywhere else, wants to make stark choices between the United States and China or get "entrapped" in demands that are not in their immediate interests or domestically sustainable. U.S. primacy provides Asia the space to have confident and productive dealings with China and carry out nation and state-building activities. Neither the United States nor China have asked the region to make an exclusive choice. That is a straw man — or a "fallacy of choice". The region has already made a choice — and that choice is that it wants U.S. ability to ensure order so that that the region can have constructive and mutual benefits from relations with China.

All in all then, Southeast Asia has a singular place in America's rebalance to Asia. As the global and regional environment evolves, and as Southeast Asian states grow their economies and increase their abilities to play important roles, U.S. interactions with regional countries are sure to increase further to mutual benefit.

Notes

The views expressed in this article are entirely personal.

1. Secretary of State Hillary Clinton, "America's Pacific Century", *Foreign Policy*, <http://www.foreignpolicy.com/articles/2011/10/11/americas_pacific_century>. The other important statement about America's rebalance to Asia is President Barack Obama's speech to the Australian parliament <http://www.whitehouse.gov/the-press-office/2011/11/17/remarks-president-obama-australian-parliament>.
2. Cheryl Pellerin, "Dempsey: Asia-Pacific is of Global Strategic Import", *American Forces Press Service*, 7 June 2012 <http://www.defense.gov/news/newsarticle.aspx?id=116665>.
3. Secretary of State Hillary Clinton, "America's Engagement in the Asia-Pacific", speech to the East West Center, Honolulu, 28 October 2010 <http://www.state.gov/secretary/rm/2010/10/150141.htm>.
4. Key Facts on U.S.-ASEAN Expanded Economic Engagement Initiative <http://iipdigital.usembassy.gov/st/english/texttrans/2012/11/20121119138863.html#axzz2FWM6TWFp>.
5. See East West Center, *ASEAN Matters for America/America Matters for ASEAN*, at <www.AsiaMattersforAmerica.org>.
6. Transcript of statement by U.S. Secretary of State Hillary Rodham Clinton and EAM S.M Krishna After Their Meeting, 13 June 2012 <http://www.mea.gov.in/outoging-visit detail.htm?19739/Transcript+of+statement+by+US+Secretary+of+State+Hillary+Rodham+Clinton+And+EAM+SM+Krishna+After+Their+Meeting>.

CHINESE PERSPECTIVES ON THE U.S. ROLE IN SOUTHEAST ASIA

Zhu Feng

The United States is a long-term stakeholder in the Asia-Pacific. China recognizes that the United States is an irreplaceable "security anchor" in the entire region. Basically the U.S. role of "balancer" against any uncertainties in Southeast Asia — indispensible and tenacious — is an integral part of stability, peace, and prosperity at the regional level. Simultaneously Beijing understands the significance of close bonds between the United States and the ASEAN region — Southeast Asia needs the United States to counter-balance a rising China.

Yet, in China's perception the Obama administration's "rebalancing" moves portend a worrying trajectory for the Sino-American strategic relationship. Diplomatically, in China's perception, the Obama administration has continually sought to keep China cornered and subdued with regard to the South China Sea issue by aligning with Vietnam, opening new military facilities in the Philippines, and excluding China from the Trans-Pacific Partnership (TPP). From a military perspective, the United States has sought to increase its preparedness through the Air-Sea Battle concept, a response to China's anti-access and area denial (A2/AD) strategy, and moves like selling advanced F-16 C/D jetfighters to Indonesia and establishing a new military base in Darwin, Australia.

The ramifications of Beijing-Washington relations extend far beyond their immediate bilateral terrain, and will clearly decide the landscape of the Asia-Pacific region in a much broader sense. Any balance of power system will not automatically promote the highly valuable regional economic vigour which has now spread throughout the Asia-Pacific. Enduring economic growth at the very least reduces security concerns even if it does not produce security. China, contributing substantially to regional economic prosperity, will not be alone

ZHU FENG is Professor and Deputy Director at the School of International Studies, Peking University, China.

in independently seeking answers to some crucial questions such as how both powers can hedge against each other strategically while providing economic and trading benefits to the region. China-U.S. relations and their repercussions on the region must be supportive of regional economic prosperity. Otherwise, both countries will lose their appeal. The growing complexity of Sino-U.S. relations, if not well-managed, has the potential to destabilize Southeast Asia.

Strategic Distrust Could Increase, But Cold War Is Unlikely

The United States has been a long-term ally, friend, and key trading partner to Southeast Asia. America's strong desire for a steady presence in the region has existed since the end of World War II. For that presence and influence, the United States fought the Vietnam War in the 1960s and earlier formed the Southeast Asian Treaty Organization to counter communist expansion. Even in the post-Cold War era and with the closure of some American military bases in the region, Washington has never underestimated the strategic significance of Southeast Asia as a key location on the geostrategic chessboard of the Asia-Pacific. Historic links, traditional allies, and the long-standing acceptance of the United States amid the ASEAN member countries provide a solid basis for U.S.-ASEAN relations. Beijing has been keenly aware of such congruence between the United States and Southeast Asia, and the Chinese would be unlikely to mistakenly see Southeast Asia as a "boxing ring" between Beijing and Washington.

Nevertheless Southeast Asia is not the backyard of the United States, and China-ASEAN relations have changed greatly since the early 1990s. Beijing's rapid economic growth and its geographic proximity facilitate economic and social interconnection based on mutual benefit. In fact China's rise coincides explicitly and happily with the surging tide of regional economic integration. The consequence is that Beijing has outperformed the United States in economic clout in the region in recent years. But China's massive economic outreach to the Southeast Asia does not suggest that the region is increasingly compelled to choose a new side. Southeast Asia, as a whole, never accommodated to China's rise, and instead has raised its concerns about the pull of China's influence. Relying on the United States to be a strong "balancer" vis-à-vis China while also pushing for ASEAN as a counter-weight and a proactive regional player between the two giants has been the primary choice of the region. Given its "good neighbour" policy towards ASEAN, China does not merely aim to compete for geopolitical influence with the United States, but also wants to strengthen the economic glue to bind China and Southeast Asia together. Prior to 2009, Beijing had been enjoying its growing diplomatic and political space in Southeast Asia because ASEAN was more friendly to China, and consequently, it was less likely that the region would assist the United States to "encircle" China.

However, China has proven to be a premature power since 2009. It is unaware of the negative impact of its "assertiveness" in the territorial disputes in the South China Sea and simultaneously of the implications of America's strategic turnaround — "pivoting Asia". The fallout from ASEAN's strategic bewilderment at China's apparent unreliability and the U.S. strategic posture against China makes the South China Sea a tense and heated area, at least diplomatically. Territorial disputes over small shoals, islets, and rocks in the South China Sea have gone beyond contending sovereign claimants, with great power rivalry looming large.

The Sino-American relationship of today includes a new aspect never before seen since normalization of ties between the two countries in 1979 — power competition over geopolitical and geo-economic influence in East Asia. This power competition is redefining the U.S. strategic ties with ASEAN, and highlighting its new strategic imperative to prevent China's geopolitical rise in the region. Secretary Clinton's historic visit to Myanmar at the beginning of December 2011 and President Obama's parachuting to Myanmar in December 2012 are telling evidence. Beijing is fearful that its commercial ties with Myanmar will be put at risk in the face of the U.S. offensive and that Washington's strong push for Burmese political liberalization might ignite a new "Color Revolution" on China's periphery.

The most damaging aspect of the Obama administration's "Rebalancing" moves in the Asia-Pacific is not the fundamental change to Beijing-Washington relations, but the deepening of the perceived "security dilemma". What matters more is not the frayed ties, but growing strategic distrust between the two capitals. There is an increasing likelihood of escalating geostrategic tension between the two countries. It also causes the sceptics to wonder if ASEAN would be able to "hold the centre". But neither the United States nor China has the intention to slide into a new "Cold War", and for sure, Southeast Asia intrinsically opposes great power rivalry between Beijing and Washington. Obviously China remains a robust partner to Southeast Asia despite the lingering territorial disputes. America's "rebalancing" might complicate Chinese security calculations, but not necessarily undermine Chinese diplomatic and economic association with Southeast Asia.

American Factor between China and ASEAN

Beijing has been vigilant about the adverse consequence of Obama's "rebalancing" for China's role in East Asia. On 6 December 2012, Chinese President Hu Jintao unambiguously asserted that China should accelerate the transformation of its naval force structure and promote combat readiness.[1] His remarks are likely not only an attempt to placate his Chinese domestic audience, but also the start of counter-measures against the United States. In order to mitigate security concerns of both countries, the United States should clearly explain to what extent it will respect China's legitimate interests without losing its primacy, and Beijing should work to increase strategic trust between China and its neighbours as well as with the United States.

Two important points may require clarification. First, many commentators tend to conveniently adopt the line of argument that China's growing territorial assertiveness may also be a consequence of pressure from nationalists within the PLA-Navy. Other factors that have been mentioned as possibly leading to an increase in Chinese territorial activism in the coming years include leadership succession in the Communist Party in 2012 and improving cross-Straits relations under a KMT government in Taiwan. However, such analyses ignore the mass sentiment in China that it has been bullied and humiliated by the United States and some of its allies, like the use of spy planes near China's border and coastlines, the bombing of Chinese embassy in the former Yugoslavia, and harassments of its ships in open seas. America's public assurance to Japan that the Diaoyu Islands are covered by U.S.-Japan security alliance is likely to further fan that sentiment though it is not the United States' desire to be involved in some territorial disputes where China is a party. Another point that the analyses ignore is how China is likely to respond in the near, medium, and longer term to the U.S. resistance and hostility to the rise of China as perceived by the Chinese public, and to the actions of some of its allies trying to take short-term advantage of the situation. It is insecurity that inspires Beijing to flex its muscles.

Since November 2011, the White House, Pentagon, and American officials have attempted to deny that the rebalancing strategy is designed to "contain" China, or that it is meant only to target China. The motives behind the U.S. rebalancing are indeed multiple. It is unfair to conclude that the "rebalancing" only targets China. But it is safer to contend that America's new anxiety about China is one of most significant reasons motivating the the United States to retool its strategic posture in the Asia-Pacific.[2] By definition, "rebalancing" is the combination of geographic rebalancing and capability rebalancing. As one

American authority has argued, "strategic rebalancing should therefore not be considered a new product of the Obama administration alone, but rather a long-term effort to sustain U.S. access and presence in the world's most vital region that should and will survive administrations to come".[3]

The United States worries that China's potential acquisition of A2/AD or "anti-access/area denial" capabilities will jeopardize its military assets in the region that have been deployed from afar. The South China Sea has clearly become a new focal point of U.S. concern that China's naval build-up and military presence at the Spratly Islands, if it takes place, would lead to the southward movement of Beijing's strategic presence, and perhaps threaten the "freedom of navigation" by the U.S. Pacific Fleet. Another problematic factor in the eyes of Americans is the lack of transparency surrounding who really controls China's armed forces: the People's Liberation Army (PLA) is not formally part of the state, it is responsible to the Communist Party of China (CPC), and is run by the party's Central Military Commission, not the Ministry of Defence. Even though party and government stand close in China, it is common knowledge that the party is even less transparent and accountable than the government. Hence, China watchers in the United States are even more sceptical about the true ambitions of the people who control Chinese guns and ships.

However, it is difficult to say if America's "rebalancing" would significantly weaken China's traditional claims in territorial disputes in the South China Sea. In fact the tougher response from the United States has not led to more flexibility on China's part.

Southeast Asia needs to enhance its understanding of China's growing sense of insecurity at present. Beijing in fact sees itself as being under siege by American allies, strategic partners and defence cooperators. The fact that the United States has important allies and security partners in Japan, India, Korea, the Philippines, Thailand, and Singapore as well as allied forces of Australia and New Zealand reduces the chance of Beijing becoming so emboldened as to confront the United States, unless China is provoked over territorial disputes in the South China Sea and the East China Sea. The rebalancing moves do not seem to have prevented China from adhering to its claims and instead have raised awareness in China about the need to fortify the claims. The growing Chinese concern is evidenced in the establishment of Shansha City and Shansha Garrison in the disputed Paracel Islands and the Spratly Islands area, and can be seen even more clearly in China's less conciliatory attitude on the Diaoyu/Senkaku Islands, an unsolved territorial dispute between Beijing and Tokyo.

The United States has strongly urged China to compromise in multilateral talks with its ASEAN counterparts to find a solution in the South China Sea disputes. But Beijing's strong preference is to work through bilateral talks. The diplomatic tit-for-tat over this even caused the division of the ASEAN countries at the ASEAN Regional Forum (ARF) ministerial meeting at Cambodia in July 2012.

For most Chinese, it remains unclear if the United States would really favour a "proxy war" with China to create more "troubles" for it in order to pre-emptively weaken it as a potential "peer competitor". Some of China's neighbours today might be tempted to think like Winston Churchill who believed that it was in his country's best interests at the end of World War II to make the United States a rival of the Soviet Union. They might seek to ensure that it was in their best interests to make the United States a rival to their neighbour China. Ominously there are signs which suggest that the United States may take that line. According to two senior American military officers, "U.S. forces made adjustments designed to maximize their ability to project power to 'hot spots' where armed conflict could threaten allies and friends. The goal was to reassure allies and others concerning the safety and stability of an increasingly interconnected system of global trade and security."[4]

Therefore Beijing is quite aware of the effect of a "small power trick" in the territorial disputes — contending claimants tending to use American back-up to force China to back off from its sovereign claims in the South China Sea. For China, the rampant domestic nationalistic sentiment is hard to resist, unless the new Chinese leadership, centred on Xi Jinping, shows more determination to seek a settlement rather than stay stuck in the impasse. Given Xi's domestic preoccupations, it is unlikely that Beijing's policy on the South China Sea will tend to be more "assertive". Xi vowed that the disputes in the South China Sea should be dealt with through "political resolution" when he attended the Nanning China-ASEAN Forum in September 2012. It is a positive sign that Chinese new leadership wants to see the South China Sea issue becoming "less disruptive".

How ASEAN Affects Sino-U.S. Competition

The chance of a direct military confrontation in the near future between the United States and China remains low. In preparing for the worst case scenario, the Pentagon is simply doing its job. What the United States has been doing with the rebalancing strategy in the Asia-Pacific region is to hedge, a concept which has caused a bitter and hot debate among Chinese strategists. "Hedging" is jargon used in the financial world. A typical example is to buy both a stock (hoping its value goes up) and its option (you make money when the stock's value goes down). To "hedge" is to seek the best outcome while also preparing for the worst, or building a counter-force to balance another country's power.

The Chinese often consider hedging actions taken by other countries as signs of hostility. At the same time, the Chinese do not seem to understand how to hedge in response to China's external challenges. Despite this, the mainstream Chinese view is more inclined to see "rebalancing" as an updated version of hedging strategy — dubbed "hope for the best, and prepare for the worst".

Based on this reality, America's rebalancing moves do not provide a major imperative for China to change its policy course. Beijing will continue to be an inward-looking, conservative, and developmental state. There is little likelihood that China would try any coercive diplomacy to seek a quick resolution of the South China Sea territorial disputes in China's favour. Preserving the status quo serves China's interests best. The most important question is how China will ultimately weigh the American factor in its interests and security calculus on a number of issues, and how far the United States is prepared to advance its new policy on geostrategic issues at China's expense.

Chinese foreign policy is pragmatic and risk-averse, and thus it is unlikely that China will want to start a stand-off with the United States, or challenge the U.S. predominance by attacking any ASEAN member, notwithstanding domestic nationalism. In the light of this, Sino-U.S. relations are likely to be more complicated than worrisome, and remain manageable on the whole. Southeast Asia should enhance its understanding of the unique character of China's domestic transition, avoid overstating China's "assertiveness", and try "soft push" tactics. In this way, Southeast Asia will be better able to influence China's policy.

The United States and China have become strategic competitors, but they are certainly not doomed to be enemies. In this new stage of U.S.-China strategic competition, both countries must avoiding falling into the trap of perceiving one another as enemies. This is the key to preventing U.S.-China relations from leading to turbulence or even the creation of geopolitical divisions in East Asia.

United States-China relations are, by nature, structural relations in the international system. These relations are not complex simply because they are between a "dominating power" and a "rising power", but rather because of their competing political ideas, beliefs and interests, which lead to the ambiguous and contentious nature of U.S.-China relations. The United States and China's strategic intentions towards one another are plagued by doubts, which is hardly surprising. However, they should not view one another as enemies. It would be a great strategic error for a rising great power to perceive the dominating great power in the existing international system as its enemy. It would be an even more fatal mistake if the dominant great power were to "force" the rising power into the role of an enemy. In the 1990s, when there were high tensions between the United States and China over Taiwan and the human rights issue, the Chinese often warned the United States that if it views China as its enemy, then China would become just that. Chinese people now need to ask themselves the same question: if we view the United States as our enemy, then the United States might well turn into China's enemy, and is this the kind of enemy that China wants? The idea raised by Chinese leaders of a mutually beneficial partnership between China and the United States should become China's underlying theme in its policy towards the United States. Moreover, this shows the significance of developing and implementing "new type of great power relations" between China and the United States.

Strategic competition between the United States and China is unique because the powerful government departments in the two countries, such as the military, the intelligence service and the domestic security departments carry out their duties with the "worst possible scenario" in mind. However, this does not in any way mean that the governments and people of the two countries need to be hostile to one another. To a large extent, international relations mirror social relations. In social life, it is very common for there to be competition between different people. If there are competing interests at stake, then there will of course be suspicion and struggle between the parties involved, and the two will inevitably be on their guard. However, if competitors develop into enemies, this will not only lead to fierce competition and intensify conflict between those involved, but even more importantly, it will narrow down one's own options.

The competition in U.S.-China relations, which exerts great influence over the entire East Asian region, is in itself the result of changes in the power and interests of the United States and China. However, the real danger of the strategic competition between the two countries lies in the continuation of the belief that the United States and China are enemies. If we do not effectively manage the risks of conflict between the two nations over the series of maritime border and territorial disputes in East Asia, then we cannot rule out the possibility that the United States and China will become embroiled in a direct military conflict.

Conclusion

How can ASEAN better influence China, and how can China change itself from within? These questions may well be the central ones. Avoiding a new Cold War is a common goal for the United States and China, as well as the rest of the region. To a large extent, this depends on whether America's "balancing China" policy — namely, a policy of hedging against the power aspirations of China — is also accompanied by a policy of actively influencing and positively encouraging China to innovate itself. For that purpose, ASEAN should help prevent any prospect of the militarization of Sino-U.S. relations in the years to come. Thus the central response ASEAN should choose is not to maintain the delicate balance between facilitating the United States to balance China while avoiding being sidelined by great powers. Instead, ASEAN could take the approach of solidifying collaboration with Beijing to settle the South China Sea issue. Obviously "balancing China" is an option, but not an optimal one. Of course, for the suggested approach to work, it would also depend on whether China itself can clearly reset its foreign and security policy towards the United States as well as towards the region.

China's rise has brought economic development and prosperity to the East Asian region, and it has become nearly every East Asian country's largest trading partner. As long as China is sincere in its desire for a peaceful rise and in its desire to enhance its image as a major power through a win-win strategy; a strategy simply based around balancing China will lose its lustre. For its part, Beijing's optimal option in blocking the U.S. "rebalancing" is not just to build its power, but also to strengthen China's influence by building its capacity to help sustain the "regional commons". The contestation between Beijing and Washington in the end is less about muscle flexing, but more about sustainable, inclusive, and acceptable influences. The more mindful Chinese government can be of this factor the greater its regional clout will be, and the more productive the regional order will become. So it is time for Beijing to reconsider the question why a rising China is still unable to command the level of respect it deserves, and why China, whose economic contribution to the region surpasses that of the United States, is losing its strategic clout.

Notes

1. "Hu Jintao asks PLA for better preparation for military conflict", *The People's Daily*, 7 December 2012.

2. Mark E. Manyin et al., "Pivot to Asian-Pacific: The Obama Administration's Rebalancing towards Asia", Congressional Research Service R42448, 28 March 2012.
3. Thomas Fargo, "The Military Side of Strategic Rebalancing", *Asia Policy* 14 (July 2012): 29.
4. General North A. Schwartz and Admiral Jonathan W. Greenert, "Air-Sea Battle: Promoting Stability in an Era of Uncertainty", *The American Interest*, 20 February 2012 <http://www.the-american-interest.com/article.cfm?piece=1212>.

Brunei Darussalam

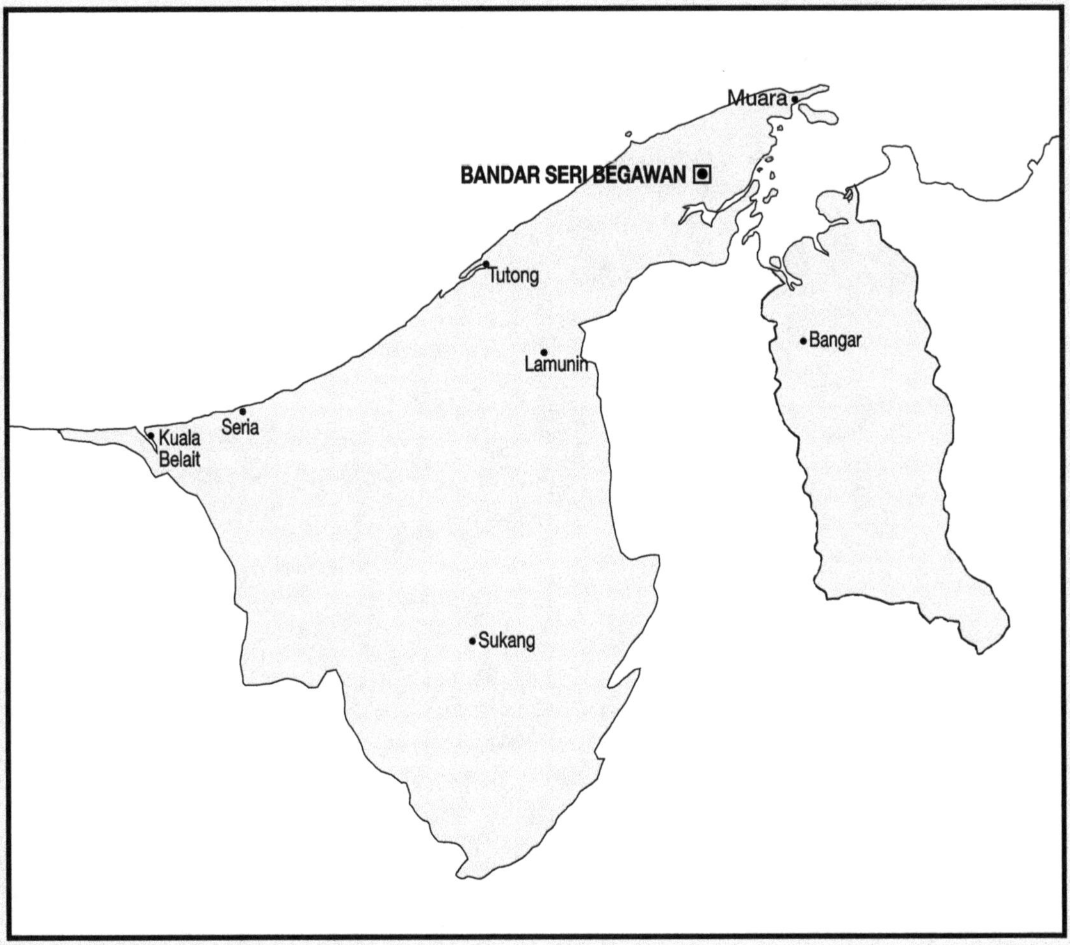

BRUNEI DARUSSALAM IN 2012
Towards a *Zikir* Nation

Hajah Sainah Haji Saim

Brunei Darussalam's preoccupation with an array of issues was evident throughout 2012. While none of the issues were distinctively pressing, they prompted leaders to engage the nation towards realizing Wawasan (Vision) 2035, the vision for Brunei Darussalam national development by 2035. Incremental achievements have gradually progressed towards the vision. As a hereditary monarchy, and with the absence of a contested and confrontational political environment, Brunei Darussalam's national emphasis is on economic, social, and spiritual goals that can be pursued congenially.

Governing the State

Brunei Darussalam is an MIB (Melayu Islam Beraja or Malay Islamic Monarchy) state. The Malay Islamic Monarchy concept is the core of the national solidarity that ensures harmony, security, stability and well-being of the nation. It is the responsibility of Brunei Darussalam citizens to uphold and to ensure continuity of the values of the Muslim Brunei Malays as well to adhere to and preserve the Monarchical System.

In facing domestic challenges and the turbulent global trends, while upholding the MIB, efforts to better manage and modernize the government are necessary, in particular to make the Civil Service more resilient, dynamic and relevant to accord with the aspirations of the Sultan of Brunei Darussalam. In accordance with his wish is to make the Sultanate a *Zikir* nation, His Majesty has called for the fulfillment of spiritual obligations while dealing with worldly challenges. (A *Zikir* nation is one that upholds Allah's laws, has good moral

HAJAH SAINAH HAJI SAIM is Senior Lecturer, Public Policy and Administration, Faculty of Business, Economics and Policy Studies, Universiti Brunei Darussalam.

values among its citizens as well as in its approach to other countries.) The monarch reinforced his commitment to develop the country into a true nation of *Zikir* in his *titah* to mark the new Islamic year, 1433 Hijrah. The country has since increased its diligence in upholding Islamic practices. This call is to uphold the image of the nation as an Islamic country through alignment with the *syariah* or Islamic law and to prevent errant Muslims from skipping the obligatory prayers. Following the *titah*, the Brunei Ministry of Home Affairs instructed all business premises and offices, centres of entertainments, recreation and sports including cineplexes and playgrounds, foodstalls, markets and other business establishments to close on Fridays from 12.00 noon to 2.00 p.m., effective 2 November 2012, bringing to a halt, the country's entire commercial activities for two hours every Friday.

Upholding the Law

Syariah Criminal Law will govern most of Brunei's court cases in the very near future and talks are being conducted by the State Mufti's department to make the people understand better what Syariah Criminal Law is. Both the Civil Courts and the Syariah Court will soon run in parallel in the country without affecting one or the other.

The year also saw the establishment of the International Property Office (PRO) that will help boost innovation efforts and consolidation. First and foremost, beginning in January 2012, the Patent Order 2011 was enforced to safeguard and protect copyright as well as to promote, among others, investments in research and innovation. The Business Licensing System was established to restore business licences. The Income Tax Act was amended to lower the corporate tax rate to 20 per cent. Further institutional progress was seen, to protect the security of businesses and consumers and laws were introduced relating to Money Laundering in Criminal Assets Recovery Order 2012. The Consumers Protection (Fair Trading) Order 2011 was enforced to create fair transactions to safeguard consumer interests. These measures will hopefully generate growth of the private sector and in turn growth of employment opportunities.

Strengthening Security and Defence

Brunei Darussalam and the Philippines convened their Joint Defence Working Committee on 11 April 2012. Meeting in Brunei Darussalam, defence officials from both countries updated each other on their nations' respective priorities, such as strengthening the Navy and conducting maritime exercises with partners, the maritime security situation in the West Philippine Sea and the Mindanao peace process. The defence officials also reviewed the bilateral defence cooperation of the two countries and explored means to further enhance their partnership in areas such as education and training, maritime training activities and intelligence exchanges. The Joint Defence Working Committee provides policy direction and supervises the implementation of bilateral defence cooperation between the Philippines and Brunei Darussalam.

The Network of ASEAN Defence and Security Institutions (NADI) emphasized that ASEAN unity is important in ensuring that it continues to play a central role in the regional security architecture. A two-day workshop convened by NADI on the Future Trajectory of ASEAN Cooperation with its Dialogue Partners in ASEAN Defence Ministers Meeting (ADMM) Plus and East Asia Summit (EAS) was successfully concluded in the Rizqun, an international hotel in Gadong in October. Chaired and hosted by the Sultan Haji Hassanal Bolkiah Institute of Defence and Strategic Studies (SHHBIDSS), and attended by delegates from ASEAN member states, the workshop was held to discuss current strategic relations and developments pertaining to ASEAN and their implications for the regional security environment.

It also focused on cooperation in ASEAN under the Political and Security Community pillar and discussed the challenges facing the regional organization, especially those relating to ASEAN centrality. It then examined the current state and prospects of ASEAN cooperation with its Dialogue Partners and made recommendations on how ASEAN could manage its relations with the Plus countries to preserve ASEAN centrality. The following areas would need continuing emphasis and attention: the shifting dynamics of strategic relations; the internal consolidation of ASEAN, including improving existing cooperation, focusing on priorities, and on quality rather than quantity; and ASEAN's role as a stabilizing force in the conduct of the relations between its members and the Plus countries. NADI also plans to hold a number of workshops in 2013 including on Strengthening Strategic Security Cooperation in ASEAN, Cyber-security and Security and Development. SHHBIDSS, as the upcoming NADI Chair, will be hosting the 6th NADI meeting in March 2013.

United States-Brunei Darussalam relations in defence training continued positively. The latest in the series of yearly CARAT (Cooperation Afloat Readiness and Training) exercises between the U.S. and Brunei Darussalam Navy were held in November 2012. The defence establishments of the two countries have built up excellent links through joint exercises, training and other cooperative arrangements.

Discussions during Singapore Prime Minister Lee Hsien Loong's visit to Brunei Darussalam focused on regional developments, including Brunei's preparations for its ASEAN chairmanship. Lee noted that the bilateral defence relationship was one of the hallmarks of Singapore-Brunei Darussalam ties. The Singapore Armed Forces continue to train in Brunei Darussalam.

Singapore and Brunei Darussalam reaffirmed the importance of facilitating trade, investment and tourism between the two countries, with the upcoming forty-fifth anniversary of the Currency Interchangeability Agreement. The Monetary Authority of Singapore and the Monetary Authority of Brunei Darussalam have been working together on currency matters.

Steering the Economy

With the global economic situation remaining uncertain, Brunei Darussalam was able to record economic growth of about 1.6 per cent. With this growth, combined with fiscal consolidation efforts, the country will be able to continue economic expansion into 2013.

During the year 2012 and earlier, efforts focused on strengthening institutions, especially those directly related to the generation of economic activity. As these efforts continue, the Brunei Darussalam government has set up an investment holding company under the Finance Minister (Minister for Finance Corporation) named Darussalam Assets Sdn Bhd or Darussalam Assets Private Limited. This company was established with the purpose of holding and actively managing the investments of the government in government-linked companies (GLCs). The company is intended to play a strategic role in the investment activities of the government in order to achieve development and economic diversification and provide employment opportunities for the people.

This arrangement allows for more effective ownership and management of government-linked companies based on commercial principles with a strong corporate governance practices. In line with the national goal, Brunei Darussalam will be "pro-business" and "pro-investment".

Foreign direct investment (FDI) in oil and gas has been encouraging. Apart from the upstream industries, downstream industries also booked promising progress. In addition to the liquefied natural gas (LNG) and methanol production, the government has been considering several opportunities in the downstream oil and gas industry. Progress in this field is expected to generate employment opportunities for the next generation of Bruneians. Statistics show that only 40 per cent of jobs in this sector are filled by locals. The Department of Energy and the Prime Minister's Department have already implemented a number of joint initiatives with Brunei Shell Petroleum and other stakeholders.

Renovating Education

Brunei Darussalam's vision 2035 envisages the country's eventual recognition globally for the "accomplishment of its well-educated and highly-skilled people" and quality of life. The new national education system for the twenty-first century or abbreviated as SPN21 has made progress despite some hiccups. The first batch of SPN21 students are now at pre-university level.

At the same time, the Ministry of Education has been assessing the status of technical and vocational education to meet the needs of industry and jobs for local school leavers. More scholarships in Technical and Vocational Education and Human Resource Capacity Building Scheme have been provided to improve the skills of those who will serve in the private sector. The first polytechnic was established during the year to cater for this need.

Efforts have continued in line with creating the *Zikir* nation, to equip school children with the right skills, such as reading, writing and arithmetic, and true religious knowledge as the cultural base of the nation. The Primary School Assessment or Peperiksaan Sekolah Rendah (PSR) has been improved to ensure school children master the basic skills. Islamic Religious Knowledge and Malay Islamic Monarchy subjects have been made compulsory at all levels. The Compulsory Religious Education Act (2012) was introduced during the year and implemented on 1 January 2013.

Cultivating a *Zikir* nation also entails improving the environment. To promote a green Brunei Darussalam, the country has embarked on a campaign to keep weekends free of plastic bags. Shoppers have to bring their own recycled bags for shopping. As many as fourteen retailers have participated in the scheme.

The year also saw the launching of the second and third pilot projects of the Brunei Darussalam national service programme. Locally dubbed as the Program Khidmat Bakti Negara (PKBN), the first pilot scheme of three months was launched in December 2011. The programme is handled by the Ministry of Culture, Youth and Sports. It has four components, namely: self-resilience, physical and discipline training, community service and work attachment, and entrepreneurship. The programme is expected to mould children between the ages of 16 and 22 years, upon completion of their Brunei-Cambridge General Certificate of Education Ordinary and Advanced levels, into well-prepared and equipped citizens of the future generation. A proposed 40-hectare site in Batu Apoi, Temburong, will cost an estimated B$23.5 million, and it is expected to be completed by 2014.

The PKBN also seeks to produce a future generation with a range of capabilities to represent the country in the international sports arena. For example, the London Olympics will hold a special place in the memory of Bruneians since Brunei Darussalam made history at the 2012 London Olympics by sending three athletes — Maziah Mahusin, Ak Hafiy Tajuddin Pg Rositi, and Anderson Lim Chee Wei — to compete.

Developing Infrastructure

An increased number of National Development Plan (NDP) projects were implemented during 2012. In the first year of the tenth NDP, the government provided additional funds to finance projects in progress, which include infrastructure projects such as bridges that will link with Lumapas, Tutong, and Temburong District. The issue of traffic congestion is also given priority and it will be addressed in a comprehensive manner.

Brunei Darussalam's International Airport's new arrival and departure terminals are expected to be completed in October 2013, in time for the East Asia Summit and ASEAN's other summits with major dialogue partners which will be held in Brunei Darussalam.

The Ministry of Communications also introduced a demerit system for traffic offences. Close circuit television cameras have been installed in many locations in the country for this purpose and for security reason. A motor-car driver will be given 24 merit points each year and points will be deducted from this for any traffic violation. This system will be fully functional in April 2013.

Another development is the replacement of post-paid electric meter to prepaid meter in residential houses in the country. The cost is borne by the government. The change is expected to enhance public awareness of their electricity usage. Effective 1 January 2012, electricity tariffs for public housing were revised — with 1 cent per kwh for the first 600 kwh usage, 8 cents per kwh for the usage of 601 kwh up to 2,000 kwh, 10 cents for usage of 2,001 kwh up to 4,000 kwh, and 12 cents per kwh for usage above 4,000 kwh.

Strengthening International Standing through ASEAN Chairmanship

The ASEAN region continues to be among the world's fastest growing economies. It ranks as the tenth largest economy in the world, with a population of over 600 million and an average economic growth of 5 per cent annually.

Brunei Darussalam, as the ASEAN chair in 2013, has pledged to continue strengthening ASEAN's central role by encouraging consensus without compromising members' legitimate national interests, nor disregarding the legitimate interests of its external partners. Brunei Darussalam has stated that pursuing a code of conduct (COC) in the South China Sea will be the main priority for the ten-nation bloc in 2013. Brunei Darussalam as the chair will be expected to contribute to community building and a new architecture of cooperation for Southeast Asia. The meetings to be held during 2013 will include the ASEAN Summit Meetings of the Heads of Government of the member states of ASEAN, the East Asia Summit Meeting, the ASEAN Plus Three Summit, and the ASEAN-U.S., ASEAN-Japan, ASEAN-China, ASEAN-India, and ASEAN-Korea Summits.

Internationally, Brunei Darussalam, as a sovereign nation, has been steadfast on issues of religion and sovereignty. The country will not condone any slight to its religion or sovereignty. This includes any act insulting Islam or the Prophet Muhammad, in whatever form, as happened, for example, through the issuance of the film *Dilim Muslim* and, most recently a movie titled *The Innocent Prophet*. Both were seen as provocative to the religion.

A Sad Episode

A sad episode during the year was a military helicopter crash during training session in the local jungle. Many of the soldiers killed were among the best graduates in different fields newly recruited by the military.

References

Brunei Times (several issues)

Borneo Bulletion (several issues)

Borneo Post <http://www.theborneopost.com/2012/10/31/spore-fully-supports-bruneis-leadership-of-asean-in-2013/#ixzz2AqNOJbiU>.

Titah KDYMM Paduka Seri Baginda Sultan dan Yang Di-Pertuan Negara Brunei Darussalam <www.pmo.gov.bn>.

Cambodia

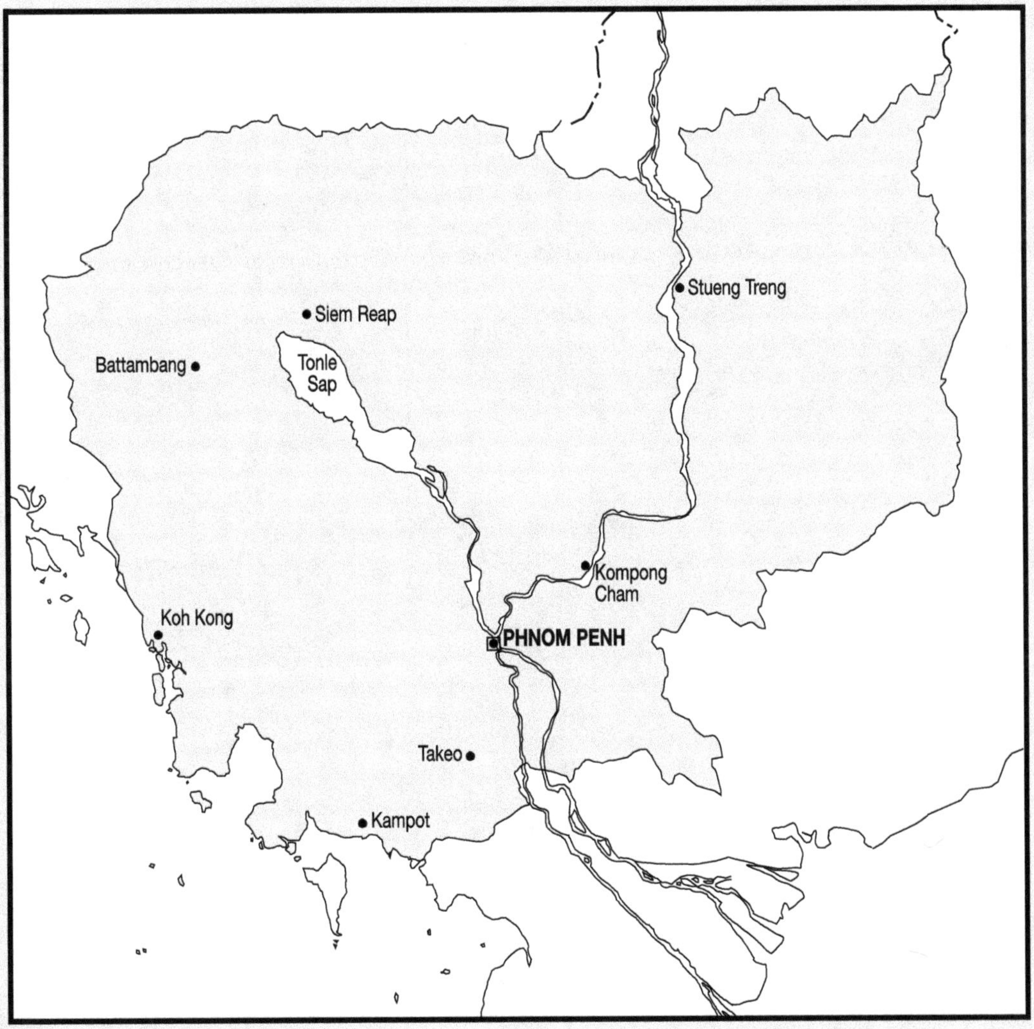
Stueng Treng
Siem Reap
Battambang
Tonle Sap
Kompong Cham
Koh Kong
PHNOM PENH
Takeo
Kampot

CAMBODIA IN 2012
Towards Developmental Authoritarianism?

Kheang Un

A number of major events occurred in 2012 signalling Cambodia's movement deeper into an era of transformation in the spheres of politics, economics, and international affairs. The country's economy continued to be strong, growing at around 6.6 per cent. Cambodia received international attention as it assumed the rotating chairmanship of the Association of Southeast Asian Nations (ASEAN). Cambodia's politics witnessed deeper consolidation of power by Prime Minister Hun Sen and his party, the Cambodian People's Party (CPP). This chapter addresses these changes, juxtaposing views of the regime's opponents and proponents around four themes: Hun Sen's power consolidation, decentralization and the reconfiguring of opposition parties, socio-economic development, and foreign relations.

Deeper Consolidation of Power by Hun Sen/CPP

In October, Cambodia mourned the death of its revered former king, Norodom Sihanouk, who had been closely intertwined with modern Cambodian history for over six decades. Cambodians remembered the former king as the champion of Cambodia's independence from France in 1954 and a stabilizing force and icon of morality in the fragile post-conflict Cambodia of the 1990s and early 2000s. The death of the former king and the declining health and power of CPP's nominal party president — Chea Sim — has left Prime Minister Hun Sen as the towering figure in contemporary Cambodia.

KHEANG UN is Assistant Professor of Political Science at Northern Illinois University, United States.

With sustainable economic growth based on an ideology of developmental authoritarianism, the government implemented key reforms while restricting civil and political liberties. After almost two decades of resistance to domestic and international demands, it began to address the issues of corruption and impunity, which had long been seen as endemic and damaging to the country's sustainable and inclusive growth. The year saw a number of high-profile arrests and prosecutions of government officials including senior police and military officials, judges, and court clerks. Arguably, these actions have tamed corrupt practices among government officials because they realize that someone else is now watching over their shoulders. This phenomenon will not, however, significantly reduce rent-seeking because power in Cambodia is structured, exercised, and legitimized via patronage. Electoral victory and political legitimacy is based on personal gifts by CPP's leaders — particularly those of Prime Minister Hun Sen — made possible by the financial contributions of state officials and businessmen/women. As most income of these officials and business tycoons is acquired through rents, the government's approach to corruption did not end the practice; rather it transformed corruption into a centralized neo-patrimonial form that combines a modern bureaucracy and personalized patron-client relationships within a traditional system of patrimonialism, without clear distinction between the public and private realms.

Although patronage politics often inflicts social costs such as inequality and monopolies, it can in some instances produce aggregate positive benefits such as political stability, improvement of public services and increased inflow of foreign investment. Cambodia has shifted from decentralized patronage conditions wherein elites were vulnerable and, therefore, focused on a short-term scramble for resources, into a centralized, confident neo-patrimonial regime whose elites believe that they have a stake within the society. That confidence is reflected in continuing elite engagement in coordinated long-term investment in banking, real estate, natural resource extraction, and agriculture.

Another trajectory of power consolidation by the CPP and Prime Minister Hun Sen is the appointment of the children of current CPP leaders to responsible ministerial positions, a practice that creates a new class of princelings. Some of these appointees were trained in Western universities and presumably are qualified for the positions they hold. Another prominent feature is the increasingly active political engagement by CPP's "youth groups" whose members were recruited from various government institutions and universities to engage in rural development under the leadership of the children of the CPP's current leaders. The youth groups are structured in a similar fashion to the current CPP, consisting of multiple groups under the umbrella of Prime Minister Hun Sen's sons and other CPP senior leaders' sons. This younger generation has intensified their contacts with the Cambodian public, particularly in rural areas, using tactics similar to those used by their parents, i.e., personalized base politics. The extent to which this younger generation is able to move the country forward in a legal and rational fashion is contingent upon the willingness and ability of their parents to move the country away, in a meaningful way, from the current form of governance based on personalized politics.

The suppression of opposition parties by Hun Sen/CPP emerged from two factors: the first is their culture of non-tolerance of any opposition; second is their belief in the success of their leadership. Given political stability, sustained economic growth, and continuing improvement of physical infrastructure, the ruling party has projected itself beyond its initial claim as liberator of the country from the Khmer Rouge regime to include claims to be the guarantor of peace, driver of national development and defender of national sovereignty. Furthermore, the CPP brought prestige to the nation, an endeavour unfulfilled by previous Cambodian leaders; Hun Sen made this assertion at the end of the ASEAN Summit:

> I would like to take this opportunity to respect the soul of the late King Father ... to be informed that his children have been doing a good job in fulfilling some of the work that was not fulfilled by His Majesty ... I also apologize that I cannot control myself from letting my tears fall because what the King Father wanted was to have a prestigious nation. The nation [now] has prestige at the time when His Majesty has passed away.[1]

The ruling party, therefore, views its critics as lacking gratitude.

Decentralization and Reconfiguration of Opposition Parties

The year 2012 marked the third local elections for commune councils designed to bring accountability, transparency, and responsibility to local government. As expected, the CPP commanded overwhelming victory with over 8,292 council seats, allowing the party to control 1,592 communes (or 97 per cent of the total communes). The Sam Rainsy Party (SRP) and the Human Rights Party (HRP) came in distant second and third, capturing only 2,155 seats and 800 seats respectively.[2]

A number of factors contributed to the CPP's victory. The first is the presence of the CPP's working groups funded by the party's leaders, government officials, and big businesses. These working groups form a symbiotic relationship with voters by bringing resources made available through rent-seeking to local areas, thereby allowing the CPP to provide more than token gifts to include construction of rural roads, schools, and temples. By combining funds from communes, local government–local people partnerships (in the case of Phnom Penh) and party working groups, communes have been able to enhance local services including local road maintenance and construction both in rural and urban areas. In urban areas, 69 per cent of survey respondents thought that commune councils used their funds to improve infrastructure including roads and drainages systems. In rural areas, 79 per cent of people believed that their local councils used funds to construct roads, irrigation, and schools.[3]

Given the country's history of poverty, popular alienation, and poor public service delivery, the combined use of commune funds and CPP's patronage resources has increased the perception that the CPP presides over a service state. The CPP's patronage politics is sustained by rent-seeking associated with extraction of resources — particularly land — and other state services. Consequently, in resource-rich areas, local communities continued to see local leaders as agents of predatory elites exploiting their communities' resources. As the artery of their livelihood was blocked, people in these resource-rich areas cast their votes for the SRP and the HRP.

Another factor that contributes to the opposition parties' poor electoral performance is an unequal playing field. The CPP/Cambodian state uses its power to deny opposition parties access to broadcast media and to harass and prosecute opposition leaders. The 2012 local election occurred without the presence of Sam Rainsy, the popular leader of SRP who had been in self-imposed exile since 2009, escaping an eleven-year sentence following a court conviction for inciting illegal protest, disinformation and destruction of public property for having removed a temporary Cambodian-Vietnamese border marker.

Facing seemingly insurmountable challenges, the opposition parties — SRP and HRP — after years of division and uncoordinated struggle against the CPP, finally merged into the Cambodia National Rescue Party (CNRP) in July. Prime Minister Hun Sen described the CNRP as a "storm in a clay pot".[4] Such characterization reflected the reality of Cambodia's politics because even though the merger might strengthen the opposition, CNRP's ability to meaningfully challenge the CPP remains extremely limited. The majority of Cambodian voters have accepted the country's electoral authoritarian regime under the CPP's hegemony because they know they stand to gain something when they vote for the CPP. The small middle class is content with sustained economic growth and preoccupied with cash, cars, condominiums and, increasingly, credit. Rural voters, though aware of the inequalities, tolerate them partly due to their belief in fate and largely because of their improved well-being — which is impressive, given the background of Cambodia's recent tragic history. Although it can be argued that the CPP has held rural voters perversely accountable in exchange for gifts and local infrastructure projects,[5] rural voters have also felt a sense of empowerment as they can manipulate the CPP's working groups for additional resources in exchange for their votes.[6] The reliance of critics on international leverage on the CPP government for keeping some democratic space has been weakened by China's increasing presence and largess in Cambodia (a topic further discussed below).

The CPP has cannily marginalized or neutralized protests for justice in resource governance and distribution and in wages and working conditions. Protests by victims of land grabbing are isolated cases that might attract sympathy but not open support from the Cambodian general public. At the current level of social, economic, and political development, most Cambodians do not possess broad consciousness over the potential effects of land concessions because this phenomenon does not negatively affect them directly or immediately. This absence of shared consciousness or concern allows the government to nip in the bud any sign of potential social mobilization including arresting human rights and citizen activists and using force against those protesting land grabs and evictions as in Kratie in April. Furthermore, as the discussion below illustrates, Prime Minister Hun Sen's personally driven "leopard strategy" has assured many farmers of tenure for their land.

The government has demonstrated its commitment to resolve the grievances of garment workers. Such attention is associated with the garment sector's linkages to the globalized world populated by consumers with increasing consciousness of workers' rights. As exports of garment products are tied to good labour practices and the Cambodian government's performance-based legitimacy, Cambodian garment workers were able to demand better salaries and working conditions. Hence, the Cambodian government has actively participated in a semi-corporatist mechanism involving the garment industry, the International Labour Organization and the Ministry of Labour and Vocational Training to promote good labour practices as a condition for preferential status for exports from Cambodia.

Following demonstrations and strikes, workers saw their salaries increased by US$7 per month, raising their monthly income to US$73.[7] The Cambodian government's ability to satisfy workers' wage demands has distanced some worker unions from the SRP, the founder of the first garment worker union in the early 1990s.

As sustainable economic growth, political stability, and peace awarded the ruling CPP legitimacy, opposition parties have focused on the issues of Vietnamese encroachment on Cambodian territory, illegal Vietnamese immigrants, corruption and a weak judiciary. Anecdotal evidence suggested that many Cambodians are resentful of the large presence of Vietnamese immigrants in Cambodia and the country's alleged loss of territory to Vietnam. Undoubtedly, given a decade of Vietnamese occupation of Cambodia and the current close relationship between the CPP and the Communist Party of Vietnam, Prime Minister Hun Sen takes any allegation of Vietnamese encroachment on Cambodian territory personally. To defend the Cambodian-Vietnamese border agreement and to prove that Cambodia lost no land to Vietnam, Prime Minister Hun Sen offered a five and a half hour speech at the National Assembly in August. Contrary to the opposition parties' claims that Cambodia has lost its territory to Vietnam, the Prime Minister showed that, using modern survey technology, Cambodian territory within the existing boundaries is actually larger than its current official size of 181,035 square kilometres. The Prime Minister subsequently authorized the exploration of the possibility of a constitutional amendment to change Cambodia's current territorial size. The constitutional amendment aims to close once and for all any claim of Vietnamese encroachment on Cambodian territory as the government would have not only legal but constitutional grounds for prosecution of any individual making such claims.[8]

Socio-Economic Developments

Over the past ten years, Cambodia's economy has experienced continued growth accompanied by improving socio-economic indicators. One indicator of such improvement is the steep decline in the infant mortality rate from 117 deaths per 1,000 live births in 1990 to 102 in 2000, and 43 in 2011.[9] Cambodia's economic performance in 2012 remained strong with projected growth of 6.6 per cent propelled by the garment industry and tourism. The garment sector employs 400,000 people and contributes US$4 billion to the country's economy of US$13 billion.[10] Over the past two decades, experts have been concerned over the lack of diversification within the Cambodian economy. However, over the past few years, signs of diversification have emerged following foreign investment in automobile assembly and other light manufacturing in Cambodia's special economic zones. One of the sources of capital is Japanese firms which increased their investments from $75 million in 2011 to $300 million in 2012.[11] However, continuing sustainable economic growth depends on the government's ability to address the challenge of a skilled labour shortage and Cambodian workers' low productivity which stands at 35–45 per cent of the regional efficiency level.[12]

Land conflicts remained critical in 2012 perpetuated by three interrelated issues which reached serious proportions over the past decade. First, population growth has placed pressure on the availability of land previously under cultivation, resulting in land atomization and forcing people to search for new land. Second, peace and improved infrastructure have enabled people to move further into previously uncultivated land or state land. Third, Cambodia's economic liberalization, compounded by rising global demand for agricultural produce, particularly from China, has led to increased foreign investment in agriculture. Realizing the potential of large-scale agriculture in generating employment and economic growth, the government has, through economic land concessions, awarded approximately two million hectares of land to foreign and local firms. Ambiguous land policies and, more importantly, weak implementation of laws due to corruption, cronyism, and patronage, led to rising conflicts between villagers and land concessionaires.[13] Since 2003, 420,000 people had been affected by land concessions.[14] Land conflicts have resulted in displacements, deaths, and imprisonments of human rights and community activists.

A corrupt and politically dependent judiciary has meant that just resolution to land conflicts was an allusion for the poor.[15] The Cambodian Human Rights and Development Association reported that between 2009 and 2012, among 623 cases of land conflicts roughly 10 per cent went to the courts.[16] As their livelihoods were under threat due to investors' encroachments on their land, some villagers travelled to Phnom Penh to file petitions to Prime Minister Hun Sen and his wife. Other victims formed their own networks for self-defence and monitoring. In Kratie province, villagers organized protests against eviction from land the government awarded to Casotin — a rubber plantation company. Labelling them as "anarchists" attempting to create a secessionist region, the government used heavy force to crack down on the movement resulting in the death of one girl.[17] In other areas affected by land concessions and illegal logging, villagers organized watch groups — the largest of which is the Prey Lang Network which claimed to have 200,000 members spanning across four provinces: Kratie, Preah Vihear, Steung Treng, and Kampong Thom. However, active members constituted a much smaller number.[18]

The impact of non-governmental and community-based organizations such as the Prey Lang Network is limited due to a number of factors. First, for international legitimacy, the Cambodian government allows the existence and operation of civil society organizations. However, it does not tolerate any sign of social mobilization that could potentially — even slightly — undermine its power. For instance, in its crackdown of protesters in Kratie province earlier in 2012, the government publicly accused, arrested and tried some human rights workers and activists for inciting protests that endangered national order and security.[19] The most prominent case involved Mom Sonando, owner of the last independent radio station — Beehive Radio — who was tried, convicted, and sentenced to twenty years in prison.[20] Second, weak rule of law and impunity from arrest and punishment undermined the work of environmental activists as in the case of Chut Wutty who was gunned down in April while investigating illegal logging in Koh Kong province.[21] Third, isolated protests in many parts of the country have had limited impact on comprehensive policy reform given the absence of broad social consciousness over the plight of landless people and the victims of land grabbing. Of the 21 per cent of all Cambodians who believed that Cambodia was headed in the wrong direction, only 19 per cent cited land grabbing as the issue.[22]

Prime Minister Hun Sen appeared determined on many occasions to resolve land issues. He warned of a possible peasant revolution emerging out of land conflicts and threatened to punish his officials who engaged in illegal land transactions. So far there has been a gap between his words and deeds — an outcome of Cambodia's neo-patrimonial politics sustained by rent-seeking and informal rule. The government's neo-patrimonial form of governance and allocation of land has deprived some people of their livelihood and drawn condemnation from domestic and international human rights groups.[23] Prime Minister Hun Sen has recently again proclaimed his commitment to resolve land conflicts through what he termed the "leopard strategy".

The leopard strategy aims to address the impact of economic land concessions on existing villagers living within land concessions by ensuring that no existing villager will lose his land. Villagers found within concessions will receive land titles if their lands are not tied to any litigation. At the end of the day, land economic concessions will resemble the leopard's skin wherein small-holders/existing users would be found living within the concession areas. In May 2012, Prime Minister Hun Sen issued directive No. 1 in which 1,100 students funded by the prime minister's personal funds were sent to various provinces to survey land for farmers living in economic land concessions spread across over 1.8 million hectares of land.[24] By the end of the year, Prime Minister Hun Sen had given out hundreds of titles to farmers as a result of this work.[25]

The extent to which the leopard strategy will lead to long-term strengthening of institutions governing land ownership and distribution remains to be seen. The mobilization of youth underscores the persistent weakness of existing state institutions and the prime minister's frustration with such weaknesses. However, such mobilization also reflects the ongoing power centralization, a process that potentially hinders any effort at strengthening state institutions. Concerning youth volunteers, In Chhun Lim, Minister of Land Management, states, "It really helps the authorities when youth go out dressed in military uniforms as a symbolic and effective force, showing the power of Techo [Prime Minister's] youth".[26] Furthermore, Prime Minister Hun Sen also declared that there would be no more land concessions as long as he is in power and imposed a tax of US$5 per hectare for land concessions. However, since the announcement of the moratorium, the government has approved an additional thirty-two land concessions based on the justification that the government's approval of these concessions predated the moratorium.[27] Given the absence of transparent governance of natural resources and inter-institutional constraints on the executive branch, rent-seeking involving land concessions remains a concern.

Cambodia's Foreign Relations

Never before in its recent history has Cambodia affected regional politics in the way it did in 2012. First, Cambodia remained an important ally for former Thai Prime Minister Thaksin Sinawatra, allowing Thaksin to use Cambodia as a location for maintaining contact with his supporters in Thailand. In April, the Cambodian government arranged logistics and security support in Siem Reap province for Thaksin to address 30,000 Red Shirt supporters.

Cambodia gained international spotlight in 2012 when it assumed the rotating chairmanship of ASEAN. It was the first time in Cambodia's history that leaders of the world powers, including U.S. President Barack Obama, gathered in its capital for the East Asia and ASEAN Summits. Cambodia's chairmanship was controversial because of China's alleged influence over Cambodia. China and several ASEAN members have overlapping claims in the South China Sea where the major contention is between China, Vietnam and the Philippines. At the earlier ASEAN Ministerial Meeting (AMM) in July, Vietnam and the Philippines insisted on including language critical of China's posture in the South China Sea (i.e., regarding the Paracel Islands and the Spratly Islands). Cambodia's objection to these demands by Vietnam and the Philippines prevented the AMM from issuing its traditional concluding Chairman's Statement. Even Japan, which had in the past restrained from making public criticism of Cambodia, joined Vietnam and the Philippines in criticizing Cambodia's bias towards China in its capacity as chair of ASEAN.[28] The allegation of China's influence over Cambodia surfaced again at the November ASEAN Summit when the Filipino delegation accused the Cambodian government of abusing its role as ASEAN's chairman by declaring that all ASEAN members unanimously endorsed non-internationalization of territorial conflicts in the South China Sea when in fact the Philippines had never made such an endorsement.

The South China Sea has great strategic interest to China in terms of navigation and natural resources such as oil, natural gas, and maritime products. Facing overlapping claims with many members of ASEAN, China favours bilateral negotiations over multilateral negotiations as the latter could potentially restrict China's room for manoeuvres. To avoid facing a unified ASEAN, China has used its soft power — diplomatic protocols, trade and investment, and economic assistance — to attract support from sympathetic ASEAN members, noticeably Myanmar, Laos, and Cambodia.

Since 1997, China has offered over US$10 billion in loans and grants to Cambodia[29] compared to a total of around US$12 billion from Cambodia's other development partners. In 2012, top Chinese dignitaries who visited Cambodia included President Hu Jintao and Premier Wen Jiabao; these visits were followed by promises of additional aid and trade.[30] In September, as Japan, Vietnam, and the Philippines accused Cambodia of toeing China's line, the Chinese government offered US$523 million in loans and grants to Cambodia for assisting China to maintain "friendly relations with ASEAN".[31]

The general belief among observers of Cambodia and ASEAN members — noticeably Vietnam and the Philippines — was that China used its leverage on the Cambodian government to influence ASEAN's agenda. The Cambodian government denied the allegations.[32] The Cambodian government does desire a more politically and economically integrated ASEAN. However, at present, given the absence of any significant economic assistance from ASEAN, Chinese aid is critical not only for Cambodian economic development but also for the CPP's legitimacy to rule. Thus far, China's loans and grants have helped fund over 2,000 kilometres of roads and bridges in Cambodia.[33] Infrastructural projects financed largely by China's loans and grants have earned the CPP much legitimacy in the eyes of the Cambodian people as has been consistently reflected in national surveys. In December 2011, 81 per cent of Cambodians believed that their country was headed in the right direction, of which 72 per cent mentioned road construction as a reason.[34] Furthermore, China has offered not only economic assistance but also an economic model for Cambodia — a model that focuses on economic development with limited political liberties. With reference to increasing Chinese influence in Cambodia, Secretary of State Hillary Clinton warned of Cambodia's overdependence on China. Such a warning has no resonance with the Cambodian government because strong ties with China permit Cambodia to avoid its dependence on aid from Western governments and multilateral institutions, such as the World Bank and the International Monetary Fund who link aid to the protection of human rights and promotion of democracy.

The United States has maintained good relations with Cambodia. Economically, the United States has been a critical market for Cambodia's garment exports. The total U.S. assistance to Cambodia from 1992 to 2012 was US$800 million.[35] For the Cambodian government, good relations with the United States are crucial for Cambodia's international legitimacy. For opposition parties and human rights and democracy NGOs, the United States' involvement in Cambodia is critical to their survival. As democratic space has been severely constricted, local and international human rights organizations, and opposition parties lobbied the U.S. government to pressure Prime Minister Hun Sen to address the key issues of land grabbing, free and fair elections, and human rights. As a result of lobbying efforts by Cambodian and international human rights groups, President Obama reportedly confronted Prime Minister Hun Sen over his government's poor human rights record and absence of free and fair elections and cited them as "impediments to the United States and Cambodia developing a deeper bilateral relationship".[36] The Cambodian government might make some token gestures, as it has done in the past, such as the release of jailed activists; however, meaningful democratic reform emerging from U.S. leverage will be limited due to two fundamental reasons. First, Cambodia has cooperated with the United States on critical areas such as drug trafficking, counter-terrorism, and human trafficking. Second, Cambodia possesses a geopolitical position that is critical to the United States' strategic "pivot" in the Asia Pacific. Therefore, it is unlikely that the United States will adopt any harsh measures against the Cambodian government for fear that Cambodia fall even deeper into China's orbit.

Conclusion

Arguably, 2012 marked the beginning of a new era for Cambodia as it moved towards developmental authoritarianism in several critical respects. The passing away of former King Norodom Sihanouk and the declining health of the CPP's President Chea Sim entrenched Prime Minister Hun Sen as the paramount leader of Cambodia. Economically, Cambodia has integrated into global and regional economies, producing a healthy growth of over 6 per cent. The improved economic conditions are credited by Cambodians directly to the leadership of Prime Minister Hun Sen. The trend, as evidenced by developments in 2012, is an ongoing consolidation of power by Prime Minister Hun Sen. The rise of China and its close relations with Cambodia as evidenced by China's regional integration and the huge rise in its economic assistance helps Cambodia to withstand pressure for democratic deepening. The prime minister cannily used Cambodia's rising economy on the one hand and constricted space for civil and political liberty on the other to broaden the country's economic opportunities. The overall assessment of Cambodia's progress depends on one's viewpoint; from a human rights-based perspective, Cambodia has regressed; however, from a purely development-based approach, Cambodia has advanced — which has earned Prime Minister Hun Sen increased legitimacy to continue his rule.

Notes

Information for this chapter was collected mainly during the period when the author served as a Fulbright Fellow in Cambodia.

1. Naren Kuch and Simon Lewis, "Hun Sen Sheds a Tear at Close of Asean Summit", *Cambodia Daily*, 21 November 2012, pp. 1 and 2.
2. Mengleng Eang and Abby Seiff, "Official Results Confirm CPP Election Sweep", *Cambodia Daily*, 25 March 2012, p. 22.
3. International Republican Institute, Survey of Cambodian Public Opinion, 30 November–25 December 2011 <http://www.iri.org/news-events-press-center/news/iri-releases-survey-cambodian-public-opinion-0>.

4. "New Party No Problem: PM HS", *Phnom Penh Post*, 9 August 2012, p. 4.
5. Kheang Un, "Patronage Politics and Hybrid Democracy: Political Change in Cambodia, 1993–2003", *Asian Perspective* 29, no. 2 (2005): 203–30.
6. The author's field notes, January 2012.
7. Narim Khuon and Dene-Hern Chen, "Manufacturers Raise Garment Workers' Pay", *Cambodia Daily*, 12 July 2012, pp. 1 and 24.
8. Radio Free Asia <http://www.rfa.org/khmer/indepth/hunsen_react_to_border_report-09252012085219.html>.
9. Laurence Crothers, "Cambodia Records Significant Reduction in Child Mortality", *Cambodia Daily*, 12 September 2012, p. 19.
10. "Cambodia's Economy: Not a Complete Stich-up", *Economist*, 29 September 2012, p. 44.
11. Stuart Grudings and Prak Chan Thul, "Cambodia Economy Hurts by Land Eviction", *Cambodia Daily*, 14 November 2012, pp. 1 and 2.
12. Don Weinland, "ADB Says Good Staff a Priority", *Phnom Penh Post*, 12 April 2012, pp. 1 and 7.
13. K. Un and S. So, "Land Rights in Cambodia: How Neopatrimonial Politics Restricts Land Policy Reform", *Pacific Affairs* 84, no. 2 (Summer 2011): 289–308.
14. Kate Bartlett, "Land Evictions Cause Mass Protests and Arrests to Escalate", *Cambodia Daily*, 24 May 2012, p. 21.
15. On the judiciary, see Kheang Un, "The Judicial System and Democratization in Post-Conflict Cambodia", in *Beyond Democracy in Cambodia: Political Reconstruction in a Post-conflict Society*, edited by Kim Ojendal and Mona Lilja (Copenhagen: NIAS, 2009), pp. 70–100.
16. Naren Kuch, "Mired in Land Disputes, Villagers Found No Remedy in Courts", *Cambodia Daily*, 1–2 September 2012, p. 12.
17. Narim Khuon and Abby Seiff, "Kratie Village Sealed Adter Girl's Killing", *Cambodia Daily*, 18 May 2012, pp. 1 and 22.
18. Ngin Chanrith and Willemijn Verkoren, "Community-Based Network and Common Resource Protection", Paper presented at Workshop on Global Land Rush and Democratic Governance in Host Countries, sponsored by Cambodia Research Group, University of Amsterdam, Phnom Penh, 4–5 April 2012.
19. Naren Kuch and Abby Seiff, "Rights Worker Leave Cambodia; Court Questioning Postponed", *Cambodia Daily*, 24 August 2012, p. 18.
20. Peter Zsombor and Khuon Narim, "Sonando Jailed for 20 Years; Sentence Denounced", *Cambodia Daily*, 2 October 2012, pp. 1 and 2.
21. Soeuthrith Saing and Abby Seiff, "Forest Activist Chut Wutty Shot Dead", *Cambodia Daily*, 27 April 2012, p. 1.
22. International Republican Institute, "Survey of Cambodian Public Opinion".
23. Surya P. Subeti, Report of the Special Rapporteur on the Situation of Human Rights in Cambodia, The United Nations Human Rights Council, 16 July 2012 <http://

cambodia.ohchr.org/WebDOCs/DocReports/3-SG-RA-Reports/A-HRC-21-63_en.pdf>.

24. Savuthy Khy and Kuch Naren, "Hun Sen Lauds Land Project, Lashes Media", *Cambodia Daily*, 25 June 2012, pp. 1 and 23.
25. Peter Zsombor and Phorn Bopha, "Policing, Free Expression Raised at Donor Meeting", *Cambodia Daily*, 27 September 2012, pp. 2 and 18.
26. Narim Khuon, "Two Thousand More Students to Measure Land", *Cambodia Daily*, 19 October 2012, p. 18.
27. Peter Zsombor and Aum Pheap, "32 Land Concessions Approved Since Moratorium", *Cambodia Daily*, 19 November 2012.
28. Simon Lewis, "Japan Adds to Criticism of Cambodia's Role as ASEAN Chair", *Cambodia Daily*, 9 September 2012, p 16.
29. "Chinese Checkers", *The Economist*, 21 July 2012, pp. 35–36.
30. Bopha Phorn and Abby Seiff, "Chinese Promises Billions More in Aid and Trade", *Cambodia Daily*, 2 April 2012, pp. 1 and 2.
31. Peter Zsombor and Khuon Narim, "China Gives 523 m, Thanks Cambodia for ASEAN Help", *Cambodia Daily*, 4 September 2012, pp. 1 and 2.
32. Simon Lewis, "Hun Sen Denies China's Influence Over Cambodia", *Cambodia Daily*, 5 April 2012, pp. 1 and 2.
33. "China Aid to Cambodia Helps Cement Ties", *Wall Street Journal*, reprinted in *Cambodia Daily*, 19 November 2012, p. 21.
34. International Republican Institute, "Survey of Cambodian Public Opinion".
35. USAID Cambodia <http://cambodia.usaid.gov>.
36. "What Obama Said to Hun Sen", *Cambodia Daily*, 21 November 2012, p. 17.

CAMBODIA'S BORDER CONFLICT WITH THAILAND

Pou Sothirak

Introduction

This chapter examines the border dispute between Cambodia and Thailand, which has been entrenched by the legacy of the past and the nationalism of the present. The dispute has led to a border conflict — a direct result of the domestic politics in both countries.[1]

On the Thai side, the dispute was ignited by a charge of treason by the Democrat Party and the royalist People Alliance for Democracy (PAD), also known as the "Yellow Shirts", against successive pro-Thaksin governments for losing Thai territory to Cambodia.[2] As a result, there were street protests in Bangkok between the rival protagonists, setting a series of military confrontations between the two countries in motion. On its part, Cambodia has regarded the Thai military build-up at the border as a direct national security threat and has embarked on mobilizing national support for the exercise of its legitimate right to defend its sovereignty from what it considers deliberate acts of aggression by Thailand.

The border dispute stirred up widespread nationalistic sentiment and invoked bitter hostility on both sides. Military stand-offs flared up, intermittently, to the brink of war, damaging not only the bilateral relations, but also threatening the unity of the Association of Southeast Asian Nations (ASEAN) and affecting the regional body's capacity to form a community by 2015.[3]

Pou Sothirak was a Visiting Senior Research Fellow at the Institute of Southeast Asian Studies (ISEAS), Singapore in 2012 and is now an Associate Fellow at ISEAS. He is a former Ambassador of Cambodia to Japan.

This chapter describes the dispute against a backdrop of historical animosity and nationalistic tensions between Cambodia and Thailand. It starts with a background section dealing with the origins of the border dispute and its evolution from the early 1900s up to the present day. The main section of this chapter depicts the different approaches each country has taken to manage the dispute and the conditions under which a possible resolution could materialize. The final section deals with factors that have shaped and influenced the different positions taken by both Cambodia and Thailand.

Scope of the Dispute

The boundary dispute between Cambodia and Thailand concerns the shared land border which separates both countries and stretches approximately 499 miles.[4] Although the land border dispute centres on the unfinished process of demarcating the borderline by the Joint Border Commission (JBC),[5] the most contentious area is a piece of land, of about 4.6 square kilometres, surrounding the Temple of Preah Vihear. Accordingly, both countries maintain:

- Cambodia only recognizes the Annex I Map, drawn up by France under the 1904 and 1907 Franco-Siamese Treaties, which indicates a clear boundary line between the two countries.[6]
- Thailand relies on a unilaterally produced map, unveiled at the World Heritage Session in Christchurch, New Zealand in 2007, which shows the area of land claimed by Thailand.[7]

Background

The origins of the border dispute between Cambodia and Thailand can be traced back to more than a century. The border dispute should be understood in two phases: the period between the early 1900s and a 1962 ruling by the International Court of Justice (ICJ), and the period between the 2006 military coup in Thailand and the present day.

In the earlier phase of the dispute, the border tension culminated in arbitration at the ICJ, which ruled in 1962 that, "the Temple of Preah Vihear is situated in territory under the sovereignty of Cambodia".[8] The ICJ came to its decision after reviewing the 1904 Convention and the 1907 boundary treaty between France (then ruler of Cambodia) and Siam (Thailand), and the work of the mixed Franco-Siamese Commission for the delimitation of the border, including maps prepared by the same commission.[9]

The whole work of delimitation in the sector of Dangrek, in which Preah Vihear is situated, had been accomplished by the end of January 1907; thus establishing the exact borderline around that area.[10] Thereafter, a series of eleven maps, including the Annex I Map covering the border adjacent to the Temple of Preah Vihear, were completed by late autumn 1907, demarcating a large part of the frontier between French Indochina and Siam. These maps were printed by a well-known French cartographical company called H. Barrère and were communicated to the Siamese government in 1908. An examination of the Annex I Map reveals that the whole of the Preah Vihear promontory, with the temple area, is within Cambodia.

The Mixed Commission had installed seventy-three border poles along the frontier in 1908–09. With regard to the Annex I Map, the ICJ found that the Siamese authorities had received and accepted it. The Siamese authorities did not raise any objections to the Annex I Map among themselves, or to France or Cambodia until negotiations[11] in Bangkok in 1958. Thailand had claimed that the map is not consistent with the text of the 1904 Convention which suggested that the border be demarcated using the watershed principle. However, the ICJ ruling opined:

> The real question, therefore, which is the essential one in this case, is whether the Parties did adopt the Annex I map, and the line indicated on it, as representing the outcome of the work of delimitation of the frontier in the region of Preah Vihear, thereby conferring on it a binding character.[12]

Therefore, Thailand's insistence on rejecting the maps produced by the 1904 Franco-Siamese Convention had no traction at the ICJ hearing as the Siamese authorities had failed to take any corrective action to protest the boundary demarcations set by the Mixed Commissions despite having many opportunities to do so. Moreover, if Thailand intended to go on with the rhetoric of not recognizing the French-made 1:200,000-scale Thai-Cambodian border map, it would risk damaging its international image further.[13]

The resurgence of the border dispute between Thailand and Cambodia in 2008 is closely linked to Thai domestic politics — following the dramatic military coup that brought Thaksin down from power in 2006. Nationalistic calls for the use of military force to protect sovereignty arose within Thailand. Border clashes erupted in July 2008, after the World Heritage Committee's decision to put the Temple of Preah Vihear on the UNESCO World Heritage List.

After heavy fighting in February and April 2011, which resulted in many casualties, damage to property, and the displacement of tens of thousands of civilians, the United Nations Security Council (UNSC) and the ICJ called on both Thailand and Cambodia to withdraw their troops, to refrain from actions that may exacerbate the already tense situation, and to resolve the dispute peacefully through dialogue with the help of ASEAN. Despite a statement[14] by the UNSC in February 2011 and an order from the ICJ for a provisional measure in July 2011,[15] ASEAN's observer and monitoring operations in relation to the dispute have yet to commence.[16]

Even so, border tensions between the two countries have been easing substantially since the pro-Thaksin Pheu Thai Party won a landslide victory in the general election in Thailand on 3 July 2011 and the subsequent nomination of Yingluck Shinawatra, who is the sister of former Prime Minister Thaksin, in August that year. This positive turn was further buttressed by a high-level visit by the newly elected Thai Defence Minister, Yuthasak Sasiprapha, to Phnom Penh on 23 September 2011, during which the defence ministers of both countries agreed to comply with the 2011 ICJ provisional measure to withdraw troops from the disputed area surrounding the Preah Vihear. In addition, during the Eighth General Border Committee (GBC)[17] meeting in Phnom Penh on 21 December 2011, both countries agreed to set up a Joint Working Group (JWG) to draw up a plan for the complete and simultaneous withdrawal of military personnel from the provisional demilitarized zone. Thailand agreed to host the first meeting.[18]

However, the stark contrast in the approaches taken by the two countries in their efforts to settle the border conflict is indicative of more difficult challenges ahead; a quick resolution to this conflict remains elusive.

For Thailand, until national reconciliation can be achieved among its top leaders and politicians, the piece of land adjacent to the Preah Vihear will remain a useful ploy for the anti-Thaksin camp to stoke the fire of nationalism under the rhetoric of having "lost territory" to Cambodia. Unless there is improvement in the political situation inside Thailand, no solution can be achieved.[19]

For Cambodia, national pride is at stake. With Thailand's unwillingness to settle the dispute through available bilateral and regional mechanisms, multilateral channels appear to be the way forward.

The border dispute has reached a stalemate, with both sides continuing to hold on tightly to their respective territorial claims. Unless both can genuinely compromise, the dispute will remain an obstacle to the normalization of their bilateral relations.

Bilateral Approach to the Border Issue

There is a bilateral mechanism sanctioned by a Memorandum of Understanding (MOU), signed by both countries in June 2000.[20] The MOU establishes a JBC to carry out a joint survey and demarcation of the land boundary all along the Thai-Cambodian border in accordance with important documents such as the Franco-Siamese Convention signed in Paris on 13 February 1904, the Treaty between His Majesty the King of Siam and the President of the French Republic signed in Bangkok on 23 March 1907, the Protocol on the delimitation of boundaries that is annexed to the 1907 Treaty, maps prepared by the Mixed Commission, as well as other documents related to the application of Franco-Siamese Convention of 1904 and the Treaty of 1907.

Since then, several meetings of the JBC were held with an attempt to complete the survey and demarcation work according to the MOU. However, the JBC has not been able to completely demarcate the Thai-Cambodian border due to the terrain and the difficulties related to locating the seventy-three boundary posts left by Siam and France over 100 years ago.[21]

In addition to these technical difficulties, there are more serious factors obstructing the bilateral efforts related to the border demarcation process which reflect the mistrust felt on both sides:

- In July 2008, Cambodia claimed that Thailand had provoked a war by sending troops into the disputed area around the Temple and Thailand in turn accused Cambodia of meddling in its internal affairs when the Cambodian Prime Minister Hun Sen appointed Thaksin as economic adviser to the Cambodian government on 24 October 2009. The squabble deepened when Thaksin visited Phnom Penh in November 2009 to give a lecture on the global economic crisis. Enraged by this turn of events, Thailand recalled its ambassador to Cambodia, prompting Cambodia to do the same. Former Prime Minister Abhisit Vejjajiva then warned of a border closure between the two countries.[22] Meanwhile, Hun Sen claimed that Cambodia's actions were well within the political rights of any sovereign state, and not an interference in the internal affairs of Thailand.[23]
- Since Thaksin was ousted from power in 2006 in a military coup, the work of the JBC was held back by the political turmoil in Thailand, preventing it from carrying on with the unfinished task of border demarcation. Moreover, Abhisit's government failed to earn the trust and confidence of its Cambodian counterparts as it kept sending mixed signals that suggested that it would employ both diplomatic and military means to settle the dispute[24] — thus undermining bilateral relations.

- Since the 2006 military coup until the recent general election in 2011, Thai foreign policy towards Cambodia has been marred by the PAD's stance. This ultranationalist non-state actor has been lobbying the Thai government to warn Cambodia that it is ready to annul the MOU and consider military means to safeguard Thai sovereignty.[25] The Thai military, meanwhile, affirmed that the armed forces are prepared to carry out the government's instruction, whenever required, to push out Cambodians from the area surrounding the Preah Vihear.[26]

All these developments created unfavourable conditions for bilateral negotiations on the border issue to proceed in good faith. They also triggered a recourse to military action which led to repeated armed clashes between the two countries. As a result, the Cambodian government declared that the bilateral avenues had failed and called for a multilateral solution to the conflict.[27]

Multilateral Approach

When violent border clashes reoccurred in February 2011, the Prime Minister of Cambodia sent a letter to the President of the UNSC in New York, requesting an urgent meeting to stop Thai aggression.[28] On 14 February 2011, a statement by then UNSC President, Maria Luiza Ribeiro Viotti of Brazil, highlighted the UN's grave concerns and called on both sides to display maximum restraint. UNSC members urged both sides to establish a permanent ceasefire and to resolve the situation peacefully through dialogue. They also reiterated UN support for ASEAN's active role in this matter and encouraged both Cambodia and Thailand to cooperate with ASEAN.[29]

Indonesia, as the chair of ASEAN in 2011, hosted an informal meeting of ASEAN Foreign Ministers in Jakarta on 22 February 2011 to try to contain the dispute. Indonesia was prepared to send observers with a mandate to assist and support Cambodia and Thailand to implement their commitment to avoid further armed clashes and to resume their bilateral negotiations as soon as possible.

On 28 April 2011, Cambodia filed an application requesting a reinterpretation of the judgement rendered on 15 June 1962 by the ICJ,[30] together with an urgent request for an order for provisional measures.[31] While the ICJ has yet to give its ruling on the Cambodian request on reinterpretation, it ordered a provisional measure on 18 July 2011.[32] The Court instructed both sides to withdraw their troops from a temporary demilitarized zone, refrain from any armed activity directed at that zone, and allow Indonesian observers to have access to the site.[33]

The Cambodian government resorted to multilateral approaches to settle the border dispute when it realized that the bilateral process was ineffective, cumbersome, and had been exhausted without any gain. Several factors help to explain this decision:

- There is a long-standing concern on the Cambodian side that one day Thailand might use military means to re-take the Preah Vihear. This anxiety has existed since the time of Field Marshal Sarit Thanarat's military dictatorship in the late 1950s when the Thai military occupied the Preah Vihear Temple. Thailand, with the backing of many right-wing nationalists, has neither fully accepted the 1962 ICJ ruling nor Cambodian sovereignty over the temple.[34] This lingering Cambodian anxiety resurfaced when the leaders of the PAD proposed a list of actions to be taken by the Democrat-led Thai government, including the use of force to settle the Preah Vihear dispute, at a rally near the Government House in Bangkok in early August 2008.[35]
- The Cambodian government was frustrated with the Thai Democrat Party administration's handling of the issue concerning the Preah Vihear, and, in particular, the inconsistency of the Thai government with regard to the listing of the Temple of Preah Vihear as a World Heritage Site. A major source of irritation was Thailand's about-turn — after its initial support for Cambodia's listing, Thailand made an about-turn and mounted campaigns to oppose the listing. Thailand was willing to go as far as to withdraw its membership from the World Heritage Convention (WHC) because the WHC did not consider its request to postpone the Preah Vihear Temple's inscription plan, one that the Thai government maintained could lead to the loss of Thai territory. However, a Thai academic argues that there was no solid evidence supporting Thailand's claim that the management plan intrudes on the 4.6-square-kilometre piece of land. Indeed this is the reason why Thailand failed to gain support from most member nations of the WHC.[36]
- As mentioned above, the Cambodian government was losing trust in the Thai government's management of its foreign affairs. For example, the Democrat Party-led government had allowed the PAD to exert relentless pressure to send Thai troops into the Temple of Preah Vihear. It had also threatened to revoke an agreement between the two countries to explore oil and gas

reserves in the Gulf of Thailand, withdrew aid from a project to upgrade a highway, and declared that all ties between the two countries would be up for review.

- There were concerns that the border clashes would escalate into an even bigger armed conflict affecting peace and stability between the two countries and the region as a whole.

Possible Solution to the Border Conflict

With the question of ownership centred on the area surrounding the Temple of Preah Vihear, there has been a show of military strength on both sides of the border, provoking furious spats between Thailand and Cambodia. Each time a clash occurred, both sides blamed each other for initiating it. Amidst ongoing tension, Thailand has continuously expressed its preference for bilateral negotiations while Cambodia has opted for multilateral options and was able to internationalize the matter.

The bilateral approach, which has recently been reimplemented, still faces challenges. The negotiation process depends on the domestic politics of Thailand and the ability of the Thai government to convince Cambodia of the merits of this method given the unsuccessful outcomes of bilateral negotiations in the past. The success of the bilateral negotiation depends primarily on the ability of the JBC to resume its task under the framework of the MOU, without further military intervention or hindrance from any non-state actor.

The regional approach — Cambodia's request to allow the chair of ASEAN (Indonesia at the time) to provide good office, conciliation and mediation — was a slow-moving process even though both nations had given Indonesia the green light to commence the process of mediation. A proposition by Indonesia known as the package of solutions[37] was unveiled in May 2011. This includes Terms of Reference (TOR) for both parties to resolve the conflict and steps to support bilateral negotiations with an appropriate Indonesian observer team to monitor the ceasefire. While Cambodia is ready to employ bilateral instruments, it has insisted that ASEAN act as a referee for negotiations with Thailand. As such, Cambodia has agreed to Jakarta's proposed TOR for monitoring the border but Thailand, especially the Thai military, has not firmly endorsed the TOR. The Thai government, under Yingluck, has only recently been more open to a regional approach. For this approach to work successfully, both sides must overcome their expressed reservations and agree swiftly to allow the JBC to complete its work without preconditions and to avoid delaying any ASEAN intervention. Without goodwill and concessions made by both sides, ASEAN, which is not equipped with any enforcement measures, can do little to move the conflict towards its successful end.

The multilateral approach, also initiated by Cambodia, has yet to prevail. Given Thailand's reluctance in accepting Indonesian observers, the Cambodian government has instead sought a speedy decision by the ICJ in the hope that it will help resolve the border crisis. The second ICJ ruling is expected to be out in April 2013.[38] While both sides are discussing how to pull troops out of the disputed area in line with the ICJ's injunction for a demilitarized zone, there is reason to believe that Thailand may opt to delay the withdrawal of its troops until the ICJ delivers its ruling.[39] If the ICJ rules in Cambodia's favour, Thailand may find it difficult to adhere to the ruling due to pressure from nationalist sentiments inside the country. But neglecting the court ruling would seriously damage its international standing. It is not certain what will happen if a party refuses to comply with an ICJ judgement. Nevertheless, the winning party should have recourse to the UNSC for appropriate enforcement. If Cambodia wins its case and Thailand refuses to heed the decision of the ICJ, Cambodia should have the option to request the UNSC to deploy a peacekeeping mission to the Thai-Cambodian border to resolve the conflict.

Conclusion

The border dispute between Cambodia and Thailand remained dormant from 1962 until July 2008 when the Temple of Preah Vihear was listed as a World Heritage Site. Notably this coincided with political disorder within Thailand that was further inflamed by ultranationalist factions.

This tension has damaged bilateral relations between the two countries and has threatened peace and stability in the Southeast Asian region. Both countries have tried to settle their competing claims through existing bilateral mechanisms, such as the MOU. However, such bilateral negotiations could not make headway in the face of the antagonistic nationalistic forces that had been unleashed and that favoured military means to defend territorial sovereignty.

The Cambodian position has been clear with regard to the border conflict with Thailand. It does not believe that the Thai government is sincere in the bilateral process as it considered using military force to pressure the Cambodian government into accepting a solution that was more favourable to the Thai side. As bilateral discussions with Thailand were exhausted without any substantial result and with tensions at the border escalating, the Cambodian government turned its attention towards multilateral efforts. Cambodia was able to persuade regional and international communities to help mediate the situation.

For Thailand, its position is rather complex, overshadowed by domestic political turmoil and violence from 2006 right up till mid-2010. Although Thailand was clear in insisting on bilateral mechanisms to resolve the border dispute, it failed to create a conducive environment to convince Cambodia on the merits of this approach. Complications emerged mainly from the ultranationalist PAD and the Thai army, both seeking to play a strong role in Thai politics. They exerted relentless pressure on the Thai government to adopt a tough stance towards Cambodia. For its own political gain, the Thai government dragged its feet in the bilateral process and rejected any settlement options proposed by the international community.

So far, both countries have resorted to the JWG, established in December 2011, to discuss the terms and conditions required in the implementation of the provisional measure ordered by the ICJ in 2011. The troop withdrawal did take place in July 2012.[40] It remains unclear as to how "demilitarized" the demilitarized zone will remain due to the absence of ASEAN observers. The JBC, which resumed negotiations in Bangkok in February 2012, has heralded hope that diplomacy might prevail after all in the search for a durable resolution.

Although the situation at the border has improved, the various approaches — bilateral, regional, or multilateral — and the selection of a preferred settlement mechanism will remain a difficult choice. The dispute may drag on for many years as long as the respective governments of Cambodia and Thailand remain unable to subdue the forces of nationalism and unwilling to compromise with each other.

To achieve a lasting resolution to the border tension, it is important that both countries sincerely engage in a process of building mutual trust and confidence. This requires them to remove military threats from the border area, engage in sincere dialogue, and allow for regional and international diplomatic efforts to take effect.

If no effective solution is found, the border dispute between Cambodia and Thailand could undoubtedly deteriorate further. This will put severe strain on their bilateral relations and create an unwelcome security threat which could destabilize the region and in turn damage the reputation of ASEAN, of which the two conflicting parties are members.

Notes

1. See Thitinan Pongsudhirak, "Domestic Determinants of the Thai–Cambodian Dispute", *East Asia Forum*, 18 May 2011 <http://www.eastasiaforum.org/2011/05/18/domestic-determinants-of-the-thai-cambodian-dispute/> (accessed 2 April 2012).
2. See Pavin Chachavalpongpun, "Embedding Embittered History: Unending Conflicts in Thai-Cambodian Relations", *Asian Affairs* XLIII, no. 1 (March 2012): 90 <http://camwatchblogs.blogspot.com/2012/04/embedding-embittered-history-unending.html> (accessed 2 April 2012).
3. See Arlina Arshad, "ASEAN Integration Message Lost on Thai-Cambodia Border", Agence France-Presse, 5 August 2011 <http://www.abs-cbnnews.com/-depth/05/08/11/asean-integration-message-lost-thai-cambodia-border> (accessed 3 April 2012).
4. For details of boundary between Cambodia and Thailand, see "International Boundary Study: Cambodia–Thailand Boundary", No. 40, Department of State, 23 November 1966 <http://www.law.fsu.edu/library/collection/limitsinseas/ibs040.pdf> (accessed 5 April 2012).
5. The JBC was established by a Memorandum of Understanding signed by both countries on 14 June 2000 to carry out a joint survey and demarcation of the land boundary all along the Cambodian-Thai border.
6. See map "Area of the Temple of Preah Vihear in the Dangrek range of mountains (extrapolation from the map recognized by the International Court of Justice, 15 June 1962)", the Temple of Preah Vihear, Inscribed on the World Heritage List of UNESCO since 2008, edited by the Office of the Council of Ministers, Phnom Penh, May 2010, p. 7.
7. See map "Recent map for the same area unilaterally prepared and presented by the Kingdom of Thailand in Christchurch, NZ during the 31st session of the WHC (2007). The yellow colored area indicates the claim by Thailand", the Temple of Preah Vihear, Inscribed on the World Heritage List of UNESCO Since 2008, edited by the Office of the Council of Ministers, Phnom Penh, May 2010, p. 8 (right-hand side).
8. Summary of Judgment Case Concerning the Temple of Preah Vihear (Merits), Judgment of 15 June 1962 <http://www.icj-cij.org/docket/files/45/4873.pdf> (accessed 10 December 2012).
9. For details of the works done by the Mixed Commissions, see the Report of Judgments, Advisory Opinions and Orders on the Case Concerning the Temple of Preah Vihear (Cambodia v. Thailand) Merits, Judgment of 15 June 1962, International Court of Justice, pp. 17–27 <http://www.icj-cij.org/docket/files/45/4871.pdf> (accessed 6 April 2012).
10. Ibid, p. 16.

11. Ibid. p. 25.
12. Ibid, p. 22.
13. See Supalak Ganjanakhundee, "Nationalists Risk Making Us a Laughing Stock", *The Nation*, 19 August 2010 <http://www.nationmultimedia.com/home/2010/08/19/politics/Nationalists-risk-making-us-a-laughing-stock-30136167.html> (accessed 5 April 2012).
14. Security Council Press Statement on Cambodia-Thailand Border Situation, 14 February 2012 <http://www.un.org/News/Press/docs/2011/sc10174.doc.htm> (accessed 25 April 2012).
15. For details, see the ICJ's Summary of the Order of 18 July 2011, dated 18 July 2011 <http://www.icj-cij.org/docket/files/151/16584.pdf> (accessed 27 April 2012).
16. ASEAN issued a statement to welcome and support the reiteration of Thailand and Cambodia's strong commitment to the principle contained in ASEAN's Treaty of Amity and Cooperation (TAC).
17. See Joint Statement of the 8th Meeting of the General Border Committee between the Kingdom of Cambodia and the Kingdom of Thailand, Phnom Penh, 21 December 2011.
18. See "Cambodia, Thailand Agree to Form Joint Working Group for Troop Withdrawal Plan", *Xinhua*, 21 December 2011 <http://news.xinhuanet.com/english/world/2011-12/21/c_131320006.htm> (accessed 5 April 2012).
19. See "Thai Professor Sees Politics as Crux of Border Problem", *Voice of America* <http://www.voanews.com/khmer-english/news/Thai-Professor-Sees-Politics-as-Crux-of-Border-Problem-118765559.html> (accessed 10 April 2012).
20. For details of the MOU, see Norbert Klein, "Memorandum on Cambodian-Thai Border Issues", *The Mirror* 5, no. 701 (24 January 2011) <http://www.cambodiamirror.org/2011/01/24/memorandum-on-cambodian-thai-border-issues-monday-24-1-2011/> (accessed 10 April 2012).
21. See "Cambodia and Thailand Continue Border Talks", *MCOT* <http://enews.mcot.net/view.php?id=7217&t=3> (accessed 10 April 2012).
22. See "Thailand-Cambodia word war continues", Global Voice Online, 15 November 2009 <http://elitestv.com/pub/2009/11/thailand-cambodia-word-war continues?utm_source=feedburner&utm_medium=feed&utm_campaign=feed%3A+ElitesTV+%28Elites+TV%29> (accessed 6 August 2012).
23. See Supalak Ganjanakhundee, "Hun Sen to appoint Thaksin as his advisor", Center for Mekong Study, Mekong Review, 24 October 2009 <http://indochinapublishing.com/index.php?module=content&submodule=view&category=2&code=an24100912250163> (accessed 6 August 2012).
24. See "Cambodian PM Warns of 'Bloodshed' over Thai Border", CNN, 9 August 2010 <http://ireport.cnn.com/docs/DOC-480221?ref=feeds%2Flatest> (accessed 11 April 2012).

25. See Sebastian Strangio, "Border Spat Set to Drag On", *Phnom Penh Post*, 10 August 2010 <http://khmerization.blogspot.com/2010/08/border-spat-set-to-drag-on.html> (accessed 17 April 2012).
26. See "Army Awaits Government Command on Border Dispute", *Thai-ASEAN News Network*, 10 August 2010 <http://khmerization.blogspot.com/2010/08/army-awaits-govt-command-on-border.html> (accessed 17 April 2012).
27. See Cheang Sokha and Sebastian Strangio, "Hun Sen Takes Firm Stand on Border Dispute with Thailand", *Phnom Penh Post*, 10 August 2010 <http://khmerization.blogspot.com/2010/08/hun-sen-takes-firm-stand-on-border.html> (accessed 17 April 2012).
28. For details, see letter from Prime Minister Hun Sen to H.E. Maria Luiza Ribeiro Viotti, President of the United Nations Security Council dated 6 February 2011.
29. See Security Council Press Statement on Cambodia-Thailand Border Situation, 14 February 2012 <http://www.un.org/News/Press/docs/2011/sc10174.doc.htm> (accessed 25 April 2012).
30. For details, see Application of the Kingdom of Cambodia to the ICJ, "Request for Interpretation of the Judgment of 15 June 1962 in the case concerning the Temple of Preah Vihear (Cambodia v. Thailand)", 28 April 2011 <http://www3.icj-cij.org/docket/files/151/16470.pdf> (accessed 27 April 2012).
31. For details, see Request by the Kingdom of Cambodia for the Indication of Provisional Measures submitted to the ICJ on 28 April 2011 <http://www3.icj-cij.org/docket/files/151/16472.pdf> (accessed 27 April 2012).
32. For details, see ICJ Order, "Request for Interpretation of the Judgment of 15 June 1962 in the Case Concerning the Temple of Phreah Vihear" (Cambodia v. Thailand), General List No. 151, 18 July 2011 <http://www.icj-cij.org/docket/files/151/16564.pdf> (accessed 4 July 2012).
33. For details, see the ICJ's Summary of the Order of 18 July 2011, dated 18 July 2011 <http://www.icj-cij.org/docket/files/151/16584.pdf> (accessed 27 April 2012).
34. See Tom Fawthrop, "Who does the Preah Vihear Temple Belong to?", Aljazeera, 4 June 2011 <http://www.aljazeera.com/indepth/features/2011/05/2011531124449228802.html> (accessed 15 April 2012).
35. "Sondhi Limthongkul's Solution to the Preah Vihear Dispute", *Prachatai*, 2 August 2008 <http://www.prachatai.com/english/node/732> (accessed 17 April 2012).
36. "Suwit on the Defensive over WHC", *Bangkok Post* <http://www.bangkokpost.com/news/local/244471/suwit-on-th-defensive-over-whc> (accessed 23 April 2012).
37. See Mustaqim Adamrah and Dina Indrasafitri, "Indonesia Hosts Another Round of Thai, Cambodia Border Talks", *Jakarta Post*, 19 May 2011 <http://ki-media.

blogspot.sg/2011/05/ri-hosts-another-round-of-thai-cambodia.html> (accessed 3 July 2012).

38. See "World Court to Hold Preah Vihear Hearing", *Cambodia Daily*, 7 November 2012.
39. See "Talks Begin on Troop Withdrawal from Preah Vihear Disputed Area", *Bangkok Post*, 3 April 2012 <http://www.bangkokpost.com/print/287166/> (accessed 6 April 2012).
40. See Kuch Naren and Zsombor Peter, "Troops Pack Their Bags and Withdraw From Preah Vihear", *Cambodia Daily*, 19 July 2012.

Indonesia

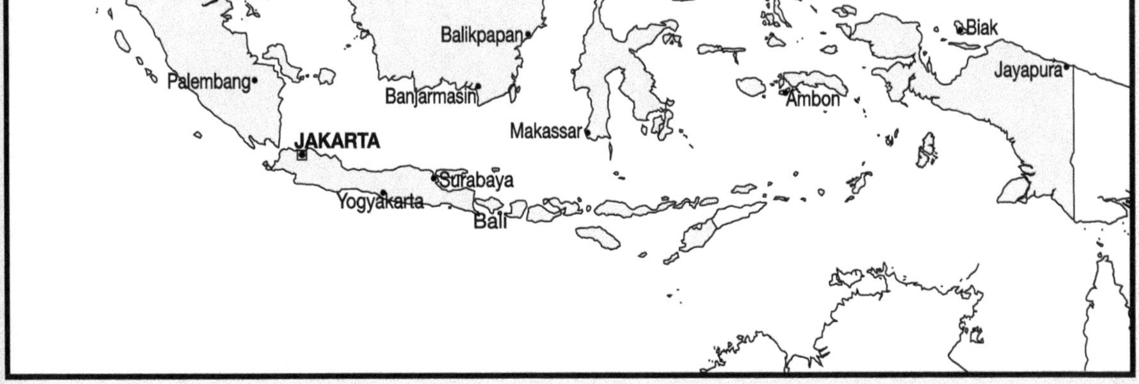
Banda Aceh
Medan
Batam
Palembang
JAKARTA
Yogyakarta
Surabaya
Bali
Balikpapan
Banjarmasin
Makassar
Manado
Ambon
Biak
Jayapura

INDONESIAN POLITICS IN 2012
Graft, Intolerance, and Hope of Change in the Late Yudhoyono Period

Greg Fealy

Much of the commentary on Indonesian politics in recent few years has focused on the struggle between those pressing for continuing reform and those seeking to halt or reverse it. Pro-reform forces include the media, civil society groups, intellectuals and, to some extent, the public; counter reform forces are generally characterized as elite interests, such as the executive, parliament, major parties, senior public servants and powerful corporate groups and business people, who have an interest in reducing public scrutiny and accountability, particularly as it affects their ability to use high office to generate money for political campaigns, personal enrichment and patronage opportunities.

The majority of commentators have argued that the rapid democratization following Soeharto's downfall in 1998 has now stalled and in some important areas has been sliding backwards.[1] They cite two types of phenomena to support their contention. The first is overtly political and refers to such democratically regressive initiatives as the government's attempts to eliminate direct election of governors and restrict the election of district heads, parliament's efforts to reduce the independence and effectiveness of the Corruption Eradication Commission (KPK), the legislating of greater powers for the military and intelligence services, and a new bill on mass organizations that limits freedom of association. The second type of development that is described as contrary to democratization is the rise of religious intolerance. This can take the form of harassment and vilification of, as well as physical violence towards, minorities, and also discriminatory

GREG FEALY is Associate Professor of Indonesian politics at the College of Asia and the Pacific, The Australian National University, Canberra.

actions by the state that restrict freedom of religious expression. Much of this intolerance originates at the community level but is often tacitly condoned or even openly supported by local and national politicians and leads to restrictive laws and regulations on the grounds of maintaining public order and harmony. Pro-reform groups are typically outspoken in their criticism of political rights and transparency issues, but many of these same groups are tepid or silent in their response to sectarian issues.

The events of 2012 provide new material with which to assess the pro- versus contra-reform struggle. In the political field, some developments remained utterly consistent with patterns established over the past decade, particularly relating to prevalence of corruption, internal party ructions, and pragmatism trumping any ideological considerations in decision-making. But one event, the Jakarta gubernatorial elections, in a manner completely unexpected at the beginning of the year, shook the political establishment and its impact is likely to be felt in the 2014 presidential elections and many of the regional head elections in coming years. The Jakarta election demonstrated that a sizeable portion of the electorate is disillusioned with the "politics as usual" approach of major parties and has a renewed appetite for political change. Whereas the pro-reform forces had previously been seen as falling back in the face of increasingly powerful forces of conservatism, 2012 provided the prospect of resurgence as sections of the electorate embraced a new style of leader with different agendas for change. On the other hand, the past year was notable for the deepening of sectarian inclinations, both within general society and local and national politics.

Politics as Usual

Corruption dominated the media coverage of politics in 2012, much as it has every year since Indonesia embarked on its *reformasi* process in 1998. In particular, it was the continuing fallout from the Muhammad Nazaruddin case, which first came to public attention in early 2011, which provided the most sensational headlines. In April 2012, Nazaruddin, a parliamentarian and former treasurer for President Susilo Bambang Yudhoyono's Democrat Party (PD), was found guilty by a Jakarta court and sentenced to four years ten months' jail, with a US$20,000 fine, for his role in the corrupt allocation of contracts to build athletes' dormitories for the 2011 Southeast Asian Games in Pekanbaru. Nazaruddin appealed the severity of the sentence to the Supreme Court, only to have the judges impose a seven-year jail term and US$30,000 fine.[2] But more dramatic were the string of allegations that Nazaruddin made against other politicians, including fellow PD parliamentarian Angelina Sondakh, Youth and Sports Minister Andi Mallarangeng and PD chair Anas Urbaningrum. What followed was a procession of high-profile KPK investigations and prosecutions.

Sondakh, a former beauty queen and darling of the media was accused by Nazaruddin of being a key figure in arranging bribes for both the Games dormitory and the construction of a sports stadium in Hambalang, West Java. She was arrested by the KPK in April 2012 on charges of corruptly taking more than US$1 million and eventually found guilty in January 2013, receiving a four-and-a-half-year jail sentence.[3] Next to fall was Andi Mallarangeng. He was named a suspect by the KPK in December 2012 in the Games and Hambalang scandals. He denied any wrongdoing but promptly resigned from the ministry after consulting with the president.[4] Anas was also under intense investigation by the KPK during late 2012, and in early 2013, the media reported KPK sources as saying he would soon be charged.[5]

These corruption scandals and subsequent in-fighting between pro-Anas forces and Yudhoyono loyalists have proved disastrous for PD. In late 2010 and early 2011, opinion polling showed PD's support in the upper 20 per cent range, well ahead of any other party. But by late 2012, its approval rating had slumped to below 10 per cent, making it the third-ranked party. In a bid to arrest its decline, Yudhoyono, in his position of head of PD's Supreme Council, took over responsibility for the running of the party from Anas, though he did not seek to remove the latter as general chairman.[6] Yudhoyono's son, Edhie Baskoro ("Ibas"), who served as party secretary-general, resigned his seat in parliament in order to assist his father in restoring the party's fortunes. PD's slide threatens Yudhoyono's succession plans. He had hoped that PD would retain its leading party status, thus providing him with a strong base from which to influence not only the 2014 presidential election but also that of 2019. His dynastic inclinations were evident from his relentless advancement of Ibas, despite his son's lack of political aptitude, and his rapid promotion of brother-in-law Pramono Edhie Wibowo, to lieutenant general and Army commander. Many commentators speculate that Yudhoyono would like his eldest son, Agus Harimurti, an army officer and by many accounts a person of high leadership ability, to be a presidential candidate in 2019. But these plans hinge upon PD having political clout. Yudhoyono's prospects of restoring PD's high standing are slim. Although the president's own popularity helped to lift support for PD, the exposure of corruption and animosities with the party had alienated voters. In reality, the party exists primarily as a vehicle for Yudhoyono and his family, and it has little ideological or policy coherence. With its two most able younger leaders — Anas and Andi — tainted by corruption scandals and Yudhoyono nearing the end of his term, PD is unlikely to bounce back.

Other major parties are also facing problems, though not of the magnitude of PD. GOLKAR is divided over nominating its chair, Aburizal Bakrie, for the presidency, though in the wake of PD's sliding fortunes, most polls now have the party leading the field. Megawati Sukarnoputri's Indonesian Democratic Party of Struggle (PDI-P) is cohesive and ranking second to GOLKAR but it is awaiting Megawati's decision on whether she will again seek the presidency, give her blessing to her daughter Puan Maharani to do so, or switch her support to a non-PDI-P candidate. All of the Islamic parties are languishing in the polls with most observers predicting that the "Islamic vote" at the next election will be well below the 29 per cent figure recorded at the 2009 election — which was the lowest figure in a democratic election in Indonesia.

The Jokowi Phenomenon

The political highlight of 2012 was the election of Joko Widodo, almost universally known as "Jokowi", as governor of Jakarta. There are many reasons why his election stunned pundits and experienced politicians alike. To begin with, the Jakarta governorship is arguably the second most important elected position in Indonesia after the presidency. Not only is Jakarta the administrative and economic capital, its politics also command national attention. Traditionally, the Jakarta governorship has been the preserve of "establishment" politicians — those who are wealthy, well connected to the vast commercial interests and social networks that shape decision-making, steeped in the arcane and often highly corrupt operations of the city's administration, and supported by powerful elements in the national government. The incumbent governor, Fauzi Bowo, enjoyed the support of Yudhoyono and PD. His predecessor, a former general, had the backing of then President Megawati Sukarnoputri. At the beginning of the campaign, Fauzi was widely expected to win. He had the support of the largest number of parties, abundant funds and an expert team of campaign advisors. He had carefully cultivated major Islamic and social groups, particularly from within the "indigenous" Betawi community. By contrast, Jokowi, who was the mayor of the Central Java city of Surakarta, was a left-field candidate. He had few existing connections in Jakarta, his campaign was only modestly financed, and he had taken the politically daring step of appointing a running mate who was not only Chinese but Christian — regarded by many commentators as double black marks in an electorate like Jakarta's. And yet, Jokowi managed to beat not only Fauzi but also four other sets of candidates to secure his victory. To understand the significance of Jokowi's win, a closer examination of the dynamics of the campaign is necessary.

Fauzi Bowo had deep roots in Jakarta elite politics. A German-trained town-planner, he spent most of his career working in the Jakarta administration and building a political base, which included holding senior positions in the regime party, GOLKAR, during the late Soeharto period. He became deputy governor in 2004 and then won the governorship by a large margin in 2009. In that election he enjoyed the support of all but one of the major parties. During his five years as governor, he had drawn strong criticism for perceived failures in addressing the city's chronic traffic, flooding, and infrastructure problems. Despite his questionable record, he was nonetheless seen, in early 2012, as almost unbeatable for a second term, given the support of the president and major parties as well as his substantial war chest. Most other major parties chose established figures as their nominees. GOLKAR, for example, recruited the governor of Lampung province in south Sumatra as their candidate, and the Islamic party PKS put forward its former president. In all, the campaign appeared to be shaping up as another conventional race between lacklustre but well-funded candidates.

The nomination of Jokowi quickly changed the dynamics of the contest. Jokowi had been a successful businessman working mainly in furniture manufacturing and export before becoming the mayor of Surakarta in 2005. He developed a reputation as a problem-solving administrator with a knack for communication with grassroots communities. The key figure behind Jokowi's nomination as Jakarta governor was Prabowo Subianto, a former general, presidential aspirant and chairman-founder of the Greater Indonesia Party (Gerindra), which had gained 5 per cent of the national vote in 2009. Prabowo sensed that Jokowi had the potential to arouse the interest of a disaffected Jakarta electorate. Prabowo then persuaded Megawati that PDI-P should support Jokowi rather than run its own candidate. The combined Gerindra-PDI-P support gave Jokowi his initial momentum. Prabowo was also pivotal in the selection of Ahok as Jokowi's running mate. Prabowo claimed that Ahok had been selected because of his competence and experience, as well as a statement of ethnic and religious pluralism. However, there were hard-headed political calculations as well. Prabowo's relations with the Chinese and Christian groups had soured since the late 1990s, when he was widely seen to have vilified and perhaps instigated attacks on these communities. In his bid for the presidency in 2014, he is desperate to secure Chinese and Christian support, or at least neutralize their opposition to him. The championing of Ahok symbolized Prabowo's inclusive and pluralist agenda.[7]

From the outset, Jokowi's campaign was unconventional. He and Ahok adopted the distinctive and eye-catching garb of matching red and white check shirts, which immediately set them apart from the other candidates who opted for more standard election attire, such as traditional ethnic or religious garb, safari suits, batik shirts, the black felt cap (*peci*) or casual business shirts and slacks. This design quickly became the emblem of their campaign. Their strategy on the hustings was also different. Jokowi ran a grassroots, man-of-the-people campaign, with frequent visits to poorer areas and policy statements focused on addressing social deprivation and inequalities. Of all the candidates, Jokowi seemed to have the most ready rapport with "ordinary" people, and television news bulletins often captured him eating at a humble roadside stall talking to locals or visiting crumbling infrastructure managed by the Jakarta government. More than a few observers noted similarities between Jokowi and Barack Obama. Apart from a certain physical resemblance — both are somewhat lanky, with longish faces and toothy smiles — they also shared an easy-going spontaneity and humour when meeting voters. This placed Jokowi in stark contrast to Fauzi, who tended to be stiff and given to lecturing his audiences.

Jokowi and Ahok had another advantage in the gubernatorial race: both had strong records of achievement in local government. Jokowi had been a highly successful mayor of Surakarta, where he was credited with developing infrastructure, preserving the city's heritage, promoting tourism and addressed socio-economic problems. He was nominated for World's Best Mayor award, of which much was made in his gubernatorial campaign, eventually coming in third.[8] (Much less attention was given to the fact that Fauzi had also been nominated for this award several years earlier, coming tenth.) Ahok, a geologist and businessman, had been the head of Bangka-Belitung district in Sumatra, 2005–06, where he had attracted national attention for his reforms and for being a rare instance of a popularly elected Chinese regional leader. These backgrounds enabled Jokowi and Ahok to promote themselves as clean, "can-do" candidates who offered hope for solving Jakarta's daunting and seemingly intractable transport, environmental, and social problems.

The first round of the election in July delivered a shock victory to Jokowi over Fauzi, 43 per cent to 33 per cent, with none of the other four pairs of candidates gaining more than 11 per cent of the vote. While pre-election surveys had shown Jokowi closing on his rival, few pundits predicted his win. The campaign for the run-off election proved far more rancorous than what had preceded it, with Fauzi's supporters, in particular, launching personal attacks on Jokowi and especially Ahok. The popular Islamic singer and preacher, Rhoma Irama, warned Muslims that their faith forbade them from voting for a non-Muslim leader.[9] His view was supported by numerous conservative Muslim groups and leaders but rejected by the National Council of Islamic Scholars (MUI), which declared that Islamic law placed no bar on Muslims electing non-Muslims.[10] Ahok was also racially abused at a number of public rallies and subject to denigratory SMSes. The use of ethnic or religious slurs against political rivals is not uncommon in Indonesia's often rough-house regional elections, but it was unusual to have this type of campaiging conducted in the glare of national media attention. Jokowi and Ahok responded equably to the controversy and avoided counter-attacks on their critics. When the second round voting took place on 20 September, Jokowi defeated Fauzi easily, 54 per cent to 46 per cent.[11]

The fallout of Jokowi's victory for national politics was significant. Above all else, Jokowi's success was testimony to the electorate's desire both for change and administrative competence. There was widespread disillusionment with Fauzi Bowo, both with his style of governance and his lack of achievements. He was seen as an uninspiring product of an incompetent and unresponsive city administration. Voters were desperate for new leadership that could begin to make the capital more liveable and less inequitable. The Jakarta election showed that conventional political strategies relying on big money and establishment figures were now vulnerable to independent candidates who could connect with electors and draw favourable media attention. Jokowi's campaign style is already being copied in other regional elections, most particularly, that of West Java, where the PDI-P gubernatorial candidate, Rieke Diah Pitaloka and her anti-corruption NGO leader running mate Teten Masduki, have donned red-check shirts and launched grassroots-focused activities.[12] Yudhoyono has also begun regular unannounced Jokowi-style visits to poor communities, going to great lengths to be seen to be engaging directly with *wong cilik* ("the little people").

The Jakarta election also brought into sharper focus the declining influence of political parties upon voting behaviour. By the second round of the election, Fauzi Bowo was supported by six of the eight largest parties in the Jakarta legislature that between them commanded over two-thirds of the votes in the chamber. Despite the financial and membership resources of these parties, a significant number of their supporters voted against their preferred candidate. This marginalization of parties has been a growing trend in Indonesian politics. Surveys shows that only 20 per cent of voters now regard themselves as closely affiliated to any one party.[13] But the Jakarta election provided the most dramatic manifestation of this trend. The Prosperous Justice Party (PKS), for example, received almost 25 per cent of the vote in the 2004 legislative election, making it the largest single party. In 2009, this fell to 18 per cent and the PKS gubernatorial candidate in 2012, Hidayat Nur Wahid, only received 11 per cent of the vote, despite his being the party's most popular national figure. PKS's decision to back Fauzi in the second round also back-fired, with many of the sub-districts that had once voted for the party now giving their support to Jokowi. PD, which had been the largest party in Jakarta after the 2009 election, had a similarly disheartening gubernatorial election.

The 2014 Presidential Election

The impact of the Jakarta election on the preparations for the 2014 presidential election is considerable, particularly with growing possibility of an independent candidate emerging who could quickly overtake more established candidates. For most of 2012, public opinion surveys consistently showed that there are three front-runners: Gerindra's Prabowo; former president and PDI-P chair Megawati; and the GOLKAR chair and business magnate, Aburizal Bakrie. Prabowo has been the most popular with support levels spanning percentages from the high teens to the low forties.[14] Megawati's support has been steady in the 15–18 per cent range and Bakrie has hovered in the low teens. None of the other commonly mentioned candidates, including Yudhoyono's wife, Ani, former vice-president, Jusuf Kalla and ex-general Wiranto, poll above 8 per cent.[15]

Although well ahead of the rest of the field, each of the three leading candidates face significant obstacles in winning the presidency. Prabowo, though by far the most articulate and politically astute of the front-runners, has a number of major problems. The first is his image as an autocratic, volatile, even ruthless figure who might endanger Indonesia's democratic reforms by seeking to concentrate power in his own hands. This perception of him is due partly to the lingering taint of his involvement in serious human rights abuses when he was a military officer, though many younger voters seem only dimly aware of this, and partly to his well-documented attempt in 1998 to coerce newly installed President Habibie to promote him to Armed Forces commander. Second, he is viewed askance by much of the international community because of his human rights record and, if elected president, may not be welcome in many Western nations. Third, is the fear in business circles that Prabowo would be a predatory president who would use high office to advance his own and his family's commercial interests. Many of Indonesia's wealthiest entrepreneurs are quietly prepared to fund rival candidates in order to keep Prabowo out of the presidential palace. The strength of this "Anyone But Prabowo" sentiment looms as his greatest challenge. Megawati, though enduringly popular among her PDI-P support base, has little prospect of attracting voters from other constituencies. Bakrie faces a number of hurdles: he is not from the politically dominant Javanese ethnic group and thus will struggle to win a majority; he is seen as avaricious and prone to using political power for commercial gain; and last of all, his public standing has been tarnished by his perceived failure to promptly and fully compensate victims of the massive mud lake created in East Java by a botched drilling operation by one of his companies.

More broadly, all three candidates are well into their sixties and have been public figures for many decades. This has led to much bemoaning in the media and political circles of the lack of political regeneration in Indonesia. As mentioned above, two younger politicians seen as presidential material — Andi Mallarangeng and Anas Urbaningrum — are both discredited by corruption allegations, and their longer term prospects will hang on the outcome of their respective cases. Various other parties have spoken dutifully of nominating their chairman or other senior leaders, but it is an indictment of the weak cadreization culture in the party system that none is presently taken seriously as a presidential candidate.

These circumstances of a disillusioned or uncertain electorate and lacklustre or problematic candidates are favourable to the emergence of independent candidates who might quickly gather momentum and eclipse their rivals. Yudhoyono, himself, set the precedent in 2004 for a humble-start-to-handsome-win trajectory. At the beginning of that year he had public support of less than 5 per cent and yet by July, he topped the first round of the presidential election with 37 per cent, eventually gaining 61 per cent in the final round in September. Hence, the search is underway for a prospective candidate, probably independent, who could capture the public's imagination in the manner that Yudhoyono did and attract support from parties seeking to maximize their chances of securing positions in government.

For much of 2012, pundits and the media focused on a number of possible "independent" candidates. One of the most frequently mentioned was the Chief Justice of the Constitutional Court, Mahfud MD, who is due to stand down in April 2013. A former law academic, PKB politician and Defence Minister, Mahfud is widely respected and held to have done well as Chief Justice, but his popularity as presidential candidate remains in single digits. The high-profile State Enterprises Minister, Dahlan Iksan, has made no secret of his willingness to be a candidate, but his outspoken and controversial style has not endeared him to the very party leaders upon whose support his nomination would hang; he also has health issues. Anies Baswedan, the U.S.-trained rector of the Paramadina

University in Jakarta, is another prospect, but he is little known in rural areas and among poorer voters.

Late in the year, however, a number of credible polls, not all of them made public, recorded a dramatic rise in Jokowi's ratings as a presidential candidate. Initially political strategists dismissed the results as a temporary blip due to Jokowi's "honeymoon" status after his Jakarta election; most argued that Jokowi would need to wait till 2019 when voters could judge his record as governor. But as his support has continued to rise in early 2013, with some polls placing him ahead of Prabowo, party leaders are beginning to ponder the possibility of his nomination, particularly if he provided the best option of thwarting Prabowo. While there are still some eighteen months to the presidential election, the volatility of the electorate, and voters' seeming receptivity to political regeneration means that the Jokowi scenario should not be lightly discounted.[16]

Despite Jokowi's highly favourable media coverage, there are reasons to regard his possible nomination with some caution. To begin with, Prabowo and the formidable political machine behind him enabled Jokowi's rise to the Jakarta governorship. While there has been no suggestion so far of Jokowi doing favours for Prabowo or his family, Prabowo could nonetheless be expected to strenuously oppose any Jokowi bid for the presidency. Secondly, Jokowi's record in his short time as Jakarta governor is, at best, mixed. Though he has quickly pushed through a number of popular health and welfare measures for poor Jakartans and has embarked on a purge of underperforming senior officials, his comments and decisions on the more complex transportation and flood-control measures suggest that he is yet to master the detail of these issues. To become a credible presidential candidate, where the policy issues are broader again, would pose immense challenges to Jokowi.

Targeting the Shi'a

The success of Jokowi and his Chinese Christian running mate, Ahok, in the Jakarta elections drew much favourable comment from admirers of Indonesian diversity. The attempts of Ahok's detractors to use race and religion ultimately failed, suggesting that, at least in the capital city, much of the electorate held inclusive values. But other aspects of Indonesia's inter-religious affairs are less commendable. Indeed, in 2012, the contradiction between Indonesia's self-proclaimed "moderate" and "pluralist" Islamic status and its growing reputation for religious intolerance and violence grew sharper. For many years, and especially since the George W. Bush administration's "War on Terrorism" and concomitant programme to support democratization in the Muslim world, Indonesian leaders have cast their country as a model of religious harmony and democracy. Yudhoyono in particular has portrayed Indonesia as a leading moderate nation in the Islamic world. For example, in a speech at Harvard University in 2009 he stated that "Indonesia ... has a significant role to play [as a] bridge between the Islamic and the Western worlds. We can project the virtue of moderate Islam throughout the Muslim world. We can be the bastion of freedom, tolerance and harmony."[17]

But the reality of contemporary Indonesia is that this claim is grossly exaggerated. In the immediate post-Soeharto years, from 1999 to 2002, the country experienced savage sectarian violence in several regions, especially Ambon and Poso, which left a probable death toll in excess of 15,000 and many hundreds of places of worship destroyed. The level of violence dropped markedly from 2003 due largely to effective, if somewhat belated, responses from the state and civil society groups. But since 2010 religious attacks have been rising again, as also has the number of prosecutions of religious leaders on "deviancy" charges, particularly using the 1965 Blasphemy Law. According to the Setara Institute for Democracy and Peace, cases of religious intolerance have increased steadily over the past five years. In 2007, the Institute recorded 135 instances of intolerance, but in 2012 this number had risen to 264.[18] The Wahid Institute produced figures showing a similar trend. It recorded 363 breaches of religious freedom in 2012, which in the worst instances, led to the deaths of five people. This compares to 267 breaches of religious freedom in 2011, 184 in 2010, and 121 in 2009.[19]

State regulation of religious affairs, including restriction of religious freedoms, is also a growing problem. A recent study by Ismatu Ropi has argued that Indonesia has one of the most highly regulated religious spheres in the world, with an ever-expanding number of laws and regulations limiting religious practices.[20] Similarly, Tim Lindsey has shown that the Indonesian state is prosecuting larger numbers of people for perceived "deviancy" from officially defined orthodoxy. This often involves use of the 1965 Blasphemy Law, which allows heavy penalties for behaviour deemed insulting or denigrating to state-recognized faiths, most particularly Islam.[21]

In 2012, a number of developments confirmed the recent trend of intolerance. In past years, the main targets of intolerance were the allegedly "deviant" Ahmadiyah sect and Christian places of worship, and certainly both those groups continued to suffer execration and sometimes physical attack. There were new attacks on Ahmadiyah in various locations in West Java and Banten, as well as in West Nusa Tenggara. In Aceh, local governments shut down nine churches on the grounds that they lacked proper approval, even though some of the churches had been standing for many decades and had large congregations.[22] The highly publicized cases of the Filidelfia church in Bekasi and the Yasmin church in Bogor, both of which have been denied building approval by the respective local governments and whose congregations stage regular ceremonies outside their sites, continue to broil away with no immediate prospect of improvement.[23]

But by far the most significant religious development over the past year relates to the Shi'a minority, both in terms of the level of violence and also the polarizing effect of this issue within the government and mainstream Muslim community. The Shi'a have been present in Indonesia since at least colonial times but the size of the community has grown rapidly since the late 1970s and is currently estimated to be between one and three million people.[24]

Anti-Shi'a hostility came into sharp national and international focus on 26 August 2012 when a mob of several hundred local Sunni Muslims attacked a Shi'a community as they were sending their children to school in Sampang district on the East Java island of Madura. Two Shi'as were killed and thirty-five houses were destroyed.[25] Immediately after the bloodshed, officials evacuated some 220 Shi'as to a tennis stadium outside the village, where they have remained till early 2013. NGOs reported eyewitness accounts of police watching the attack but failing to intervene. Police only began arresting suspects after President Yudhoyono criticized them the following day for not preventing the attacks.[26]

The August Sampang attack was not the first in this district nor was this the only Shi'a community to experience violence and harassment in recent times. The Sampang case has a complex history. Its origins lie in the son of a prominent Sunni religious teacher, Tajul Muluk, becoming a Shi'a in the 1980s and establishing a Shi'ite boarding school in his village. This led to growing tensions within the family and attempts at mediation by the local MUI. One sticking point was Tajul's refusal to halt his preaching of Shi'a teachings. In December 2011, Tajul's school was set on fire by a group of Sunni protestors, though no lives were lost. In early 2012, the local MUI ruled that Tajul's views were "deviant" and he was subsequently arrested and charged with blasphemy by the police. In July, a local court found him guilty and sentenced him to two years' jail, a term which the East Java Supreme Court extended to four years in September.[27] A number of other Shi'a communities also suffered attacks and intimidation from disgruntled Sunni groups, though none were as serious as those in Sampang.[28]

The outbreak of violence against the Shi'a aroused sharply differing responses. Predictably, conservative Muslim groups and particularly *salafist* activists, who have long been antipathetic to the Shi'a, blamed the violence on Tajul and his followers and renewed calls for a ban on Shi'ism in Indonesia on the grounds that it was un-Islamic and also a source of social conflict. While many of these anti-Shi'a groups have deeply held doctrinal objections to Shi'ism, it is also true that many receive funding from Saudi and other Middle Eastern sources that encourage anti-Shi'a activism.

More surprising was the divisive effect of the Sampang attacks on mainstream Muslim groups and politicians. As noted above, the district MUI declared Shi'ism to be outside Islam, a ruling endorsed by the provincial MUI board. The National MUI, however, rejected this position and reasserted that it regarded Shi'a teachings to be within Islam. Nahdlatul Ulama (NU), Indonesia's largest Muslim organization and generally reckoned to be the most moderate of major Islamic groups was also split on the Shi'a issue. In East Java, the heartland of NU, the provincial board backed the local MUI fatwa against Shi'ism, despite the fact that NU's central board had long stated that Shi'as were not deviant.[29] Within cabinet, conflicting views were also evident. SBY's condemnation of the Sampang violence was unequivocal but his Minister for Religious Affairs, Suryadharma Ali, repeatedly told the media that Shi'as were not Muslims and that the easiest way for the Sampang Shi'as to return to their communities would be for them to "convert" to Sunni Islam.[30] SBY at no time reprimanded his minister for his inflammatory statements or for contradicting the position of the national MUI and most major Islamic organizations on the Shi'a issue. Din Syamsuddin, the chairman of Indonesia's second largest Muslim organization, Muhammadiyah, was more forthcoming, rebuking Suryadharma for being ignorant about Islamic civilization and doctrine. When a delegation of Sampang Shi'a visited Commission VIII, which deals with religious affairs in the national parliament, to tell of their plight their beliefs and ethnicity were ridiculed by MPs from both Islamic and secular parties.[31]

Meanwhile, the position of the 170-odd Shi'as still living in tents in the tennis stadium worsens. Despite their pleas to return home, the Shi'as are prevented from doing so by local government officials and police, supposedly because of the risk of more violence. NGOs working with the evacuees say that they are under constant pressure from officials to either relocate elsewhere or become Sunni in order to return to their home village. Tajul himself remains in detention due to a technicality, despite his sentence expiring in October 2012.[32] Other Shi'a groups have expressed their disillusionment with the government's handling of this and other Shi'a rights issues and have declared their lack of faith in Suryadharma Ali.[33]

The anti-Shi'a violence and prosecution of Tajul drew sharp criticism from both national and international human rights groups. Noted law academics condemned the conduct of Tajul's trial, claiming among other things that the judges showed prejudicial behaviour towards the defendant because of his religious beliefs.[34] Amnesty International made Tajul a "prisoner of conscience" and called on the Indonesian government to allow the Sampang Shi'as to return to their homes and to halt discrimination against religious minorities.[35] The United Nations Human Rights Commissioner, Navanethem Pillay, urged the government to rescind the Blasphemy Law and various regulations it deemed inimical to the freedom of religious minorities. She also asked that a UN Special Rapporteur on religious freedom be allowed to visit the country to investigate religious persecution, a request that the government rejected.[36] (Tajul Muluk's family later appealed to the UNHCR to take up their case.[37]) As with the anti-Ahmadiyah violence and discrimination, which attracted widespread international criticism and tarnished Indonesia's reputation for religious tolerance, the Yudhoyono government seems prepared to accept such disapproval rather than deal with the difficult socio-religious and political domestic issues that this case entails.

The Shi'a case is significant because it highlights the narrowing of religious discourses in Indonesia and the growing role of the state in defining what is orthodox Islamic behaviour and, by extension, who is to be regarded as part of the Muslim community. With Ahmadiyah, mainstream rejection of this sect is almost total and indeed, there is a long history of antipathy towards the Ahmadis. But the Shi'a provide a new test of religious, and particularly Islamic, inclusivity. Though major political and Muslim groups are still accepting of Shi'ism, pressure is building within conservative sections of the community for restrictions on Shi'a activities. Over the next decade, the treatment of the Shi'a will provide a measure of whether Indonesia's recent intolerance is a short-term aberration or part of a longer term sectarian trend.

Reflections

As Indonesians prepare themselves for the post-Yudhoyono period, they face important questions about the type of political and civic values, as well as the type of leadership, the nation should have over the next five to ten years. Yudhoyono may have been a hesitant, risk-averse president, but he has conducted himself in office with civility and integrity. Though sometimes over-reaching on diplomatic issues, he has nevertheless raised Indonesia's profile internationally and been widely applauded for his statesman-like qualities. The country's economic growth has exceeded, on average, 5 per cent per annum, one of the best growth rates in the region. He has also allowed anti-corruption cases to proceed without hindrance, even when party colleagues and even relatives are involved. He has respected the balance of powers between the executive, parliament, and judiciary and has been observant to a fault about due process. While talking much about pluralism, he has been equivocal in responding to sectarian tendencies in society. In all probability, history will judge him not so much a great reforming president but rather a steady, decent, stabilizing head of state. Under Yudhoyono, Indonesia has become a more prosperous, if less tolerant, nation.

While many scholars have written of the oligarchic and elite-driven political system in Indonesia as if ordinary electors were largely impotent, the events of the past year have shown that it is not always the establishment figure with the most money and biggest political alliances who wins. In the current environment, a charismatic candidate with new approaches and ideas, as well as people and media skills can attract enough support to best more fancied opponents. As the electorate becomes more critically minded and less beholden to large parties and institutions, it has considerable power to defeat seemingly entrenched forces. Thus, bottom-up processes are not always trumped by top-down ones. Voters can elect political leaders who are passive on or countenancing of religious intolerance or the winding back of democratic rights, or they can choose leaders who insist on substantive pluralism and the fostering of democratic values. Whoever becomes president in 2014, it will be perhaps less a case of who those at the pinnacle of politics, the economy, and society decide to foist upon the electorate, rather than who the electorate regards as most reflecting their own norms and predilections.

Notes

1. Edward Aspinall, "Indonesia: The Irony of Success", *Journal of Democracy* 21, no. 2 (2010): 20–34; Marcus Mietzner, "Indonesia"s democratic stagnation: Anti-reformist elites and resilient civil society", *Democratization*, iFirst (2011), available at <http://dx.doi.org/10.1080/13510347.2011.572620>; and Greg Fealy, "Indonesian

Politics in 2011: Democratic Regression and Yudhoyono"s Regal Incumbency", *Bulletin of Indonesian Economic Studies* 47 no. 3 (2011): 333–55.

2. "Dana Untuk Anas Dikesampingkan", *Kompas*, 21 April 2012; "Nazar tak dimiskinkan". *Suara Merdeka*, 21 April 2012; "Hukuman Nazaruddin Jadi 7 Tahun", *Kompas*, 23 January 2013; and "Supreme Court Sentences Nazaruddin to Seven Years", *Jakarta Post*, 25 January 2013.
3. "Angelina Tersangkut Proyek di 7 Universitas", *Kompas*, 29 April 2012; and "Angelina Jailed for 4.5 years, Fined Rp250 Million", *Jakarta Post*, 10 January 2013.
4. "Youth and Sports Minister resigns", *Jakarta Post*, 7 December 2012; "Andi Mallarangeng: Para Koruptor Bertobatlah", *Kompas*, 11 December 2012; "Andi: Saya Tak Bersalah", *Kompas*, 11 January 2013.
5. "Helikopter Dari Rumah Tuhan", *Tempo*, 17 February 2013, pp. 48–49.
6. "SBY takes over Dems Leadership", *Jakarta Globe*, 9 February 2013; and "SBY Minta Maaf Hasil Rapimnas PD tidak Bombastis", Detik.com, 17 February 2013.
7. Confidential interviews with political strategists and advisors in Jakarta, May and October 2012.
8. "Jokowi Named World's Third Best Mayor", *Jakarta Post*, 8 January 2013.
9. "Dangdut Star Doing his Duty in Warning against Ahok", *Jakarta Globe*, 4 August 2012; and "After Probe, Teary-Eyed Rhoma Reaffirms Stance", *Jakarta Post*, 6 August 2012.
10. "MUI Chief Gives Green Light to Vote for Non-Muslim Leaders", *Jakarta Globe*, 7 August 2013.
11. Komisi Pemilihan Umum, "Rekapitulasi Hasil Penghitungan Suara Pemilihan Umum Gubernor dan Wakil Gubernor Putaran Kedua di Tingkat Propinsi DKI Jakarta", 29 September 2013.
12. "Lawmaker, Anti-Graft Activist on PDI-P Ticket", *Jakarta Globe*, 8 November 2012.
13. Lembaga Survei Indonesia, "Pemilih Mengambang dan Prospek Perubahan Kekuatan Partai Politik", 15–25 May 2011.
14. John McBeth, "New Poll Shows Short-Tempered Prabowo's Rising President Stocks", *Straits Times*, 4 September 2012.
15. "LSI: Prabowo Pimpinan Kekuatan Poros Tengah", *Viva News*, 17 June 2012.
16. "Jokowi didoakan Gantikan SBY jadi Presiden", *Kompas*, 16 October 2012; "Young People Want Jokowi and Dahlan Iksan for President: Poll", *Jakarta Globe*, 3 December 2012; and "Jokowi Leads Top List of 2014 Presidential Candidates", *Indonesia Today*, 7 February 2013.
17. Susilo Bambang Yudhoyono, "Towards Harmony among Civilizations", delivered to the John F. Kennedy School of Government, Harvard University, 29 August 2009 <http://www.presidenri.go.id/index.php/eng/pidato/2009/09/30/1228.html>.

18. "Chistmas in Indonesia a Matter of Faith and Security", *Jakarta Globe*, 23 December 2012; and Ben Otto, "Indonesia Boosts Holiday Security", *Wall Street Journal*, 23 December 2012.
19. "Kebebasan Beragama: Butuh Pemimpin yang Melindungi", *Kompas*, 29 December 2012.
20. Ismatu Ropi, "The Politics of Religious Regulation in Indonesia", Ph.D. thesis, School of Culture, History and Languages, College of Asia and the Pacific, The Australian National University, Canberra, 2012.
21. Tim Lindsey, *Islam, Law and the State in Southeast Asia: Vol 1: Indonesia* (London: I.B. Taurus, 2012), pp. 401–44.
22. "Aceh's Christians Hope for a Christmas Miracle", *Jakarta Post*, 23 December 2012.
23. Sandra Hamid, "Indonesian Politics in 2012: Coalitions, Accountability and the Future of Democracy", *Bulletin of Indonesian Economic Studies* 48, no. 3 (2012): 325–45; "Indonesian Christians Protest over Intimidation", *Jakarta Globe*, 29 January 2012; and "GKI Yasmin Church Denied Christmas Services in Bogor Church Again", *Jakarta Globe*, 25 December 2012.
24. Bureau of Democracy, Human Rights and Labor, U.S. Department of State, *International Religious Freedom Report for 2011: Indonesia*. <http://www.state.gov/j/drl/rls/irf/religiousfreedom/index.htm#wrapper> (accessed 28 November 2012).
25. For a detailed account of the attack, see Solidaritas Anti-Kekerasan untuk Jamaah Syiah Sampang, "Press Release", 27 August 2012; and "Seven Suspects Arrested for Alleged Involvement in Sampang Attack", *Jakarta Globe*, 27 August 2012.
26. "SBY Orders Government Officials to Avert Future Shiite Attacks in Indonesia", *Jakarta Globe*, 27 August 2012; and "Seven Suspects Arrested for Alleged Involvement in Sampang Attack", *Jakarta Globe*, 27 August 2012.
27. "Penahanan Tajul Muluk Melanggar HAM", *Kompas*, 19 April 2012; Saif al Battar, "Ini dia ajaran sesat Tajul Muluk yang disebarkan di masyarakat Sampang", *ar-Rahmah*, 28 August 2012; and "Illegal Detention of Shia Leader is a Violation of Rights", *Jakarta Post*, 18 October 2012.
28. "Another mob attack breaks out as SBY calls for peace", *Jakarta Post*, 16 February 2012.
29. "PCNU Sampang Minta Syiah Dilarang", *ar-Rahmah*, 3 January 2012; and "MUI Jawa Timur Bantah Said Aqil yang Nyatakan Syiah Tidak Sesat", *Voice of Islam*, 31 August 2012.
30. "Minister says Shia Heretical", *Jakarta Post*, 27 January 2012; and "Shia Conversion is the Solution: Minister", *Jakarta Post*, 6 September 2012.
31. "Lawmakers Insult Shias at House", *Jakarta Post*, 23 November 2012.
32. "Illegal Dentention of Shia Cleric is a Violation of Rights", *Jakarta Post*, 18 October 2012.

33. "Shia Group wants Dialogue, not Sermon", *Jakarta Post*, 7 September 2012.
34. "Legal Scholars Back Shiite Cleric Jailed for Blasphemy", *Jakarta Globe*, 18 September 2012.
35. "Amnesty Calls for End to Discrimination Against Indonesian Shiites", *Jakarta Globe*, 16 January 2013.
36. "UN Urges Indonesia to Address "Lawful" Persecution", *Jakarta Post*, 14 November 2012; RI Refuses to Comply with UN on Human Rights", *Jakarta Post*, 13 September 2012.
37. "Sampang Shia ask the UN Commissioner for Help", *Jakarta Post*, 13 November 2012.

RESOURCE NATIONALISM AND CONSTITUTIONAL JIHAD

Ahmad D. Habir

Introduction

On 13 November 2012, the Constitutional Court or Mahkamah Konstitusi granted parts of a judicial review of the 2001 Oil and Gas Law No. 22. The petition for the judicial review was spearheaded by Muhammadiyah, the second largest Islamic organization in Indonesia. Joining Muhammadiyah were ten other Islamic-associated organizations and a number of prominent individuals who included Hasyim Muzadi, former chairman of Nahdlatul Ulama (NU), the largest Islamic organization in Indonesia, Salahuddin Wahid, also a leading NU figure and the younger brother of the late President Abdurrahman Wahid, Komaruddin Hidayat, Rector of Syarif Hidayatullah State Islamic University, and Fahmi Idris, former Minister for Labour and Minister for Industry in the first term administration of President Susilo Bambang Yudhoyono (SBY).

The ruling on the judicial review included the immediate disbanding of BP Migas, the upstream oil and gas regulator and implementing agency. While the action against Law No. 22 had been expected and, indeed, revisions to the Law had been under discussion in the House of Representatives (DPR) for several years, the dissolution of BP Migas took almost everybody, including the government, by complete surprise. The disbandment sent shock waves not only throughout the Indonesian oil and gas industry, but in much of the country as well. While the oil and gas sector continued its decline in production (Indonesia has for some time been a net importer of oil), the sector is still of major importance to the country, contributing approximately 20 per cent

AHMAD D. HABIR (DERRY) is a senior adviser at Bakrie University and a senior associate at Strategic Asia, an international policy advisory group.

of the country's national revenue. So it was not surprising that the Court's decision ignited media furore and public debate, not to mention the deep concern of foreign and national investors in the oil and gas industry regarding the status of their contractual agreements with BP Migas.

Public reactions that followed could be divided into two main categories. The first was that it was a dramatic manifestation of increasing resource nationalism that had already been evident, for example, in the mining sector. A regulation issued in 2010 relating to the mining sector required 20 per cent local ownership by the fifth year after the start of production. This was followed by another regulation in 2012 that required 51 per cent local ownership in the tenth year after production began. In the same year, a 20 per cent export tax was imposed on outgoing raw ores. In order to be able to continue to export raw ores, companies would have to build or obtain processing plants by January 2014.[1]

The second main reaction was that the petition for the judicial review was part of the expected political manoeuvring by political elites playing to populist sentiments in the lead-up to the 2014 legislative and presidential elections. Representative of such a view was a vitriolic attack on the ruling by Lin Che Wei that gained wide circulation, essentially accusing some of those involved of hypocrisy since they had been active in government at the time the law was promulgated.[2] However, the chairman of Muhammadiyah, Din Syamsuddin, claimed the petition was submitted to ensure that the country's natural resources were exploited for the benefit of the people. It was for that ostensible reason that he justified it as an act of "constitutional jihad".[3]

This chapter focuses on resource nationalism as exemplified by the petition and the Constitutional Court's ruling within the framework and dynamics of present-day democracy in Indonesia.

Global Resource Nationalism and Indonesia

The term "resource nationalism" is defined in different ways but can be summarized as "government efforts to maximize revenues from and exercise of greater state control over the exploitation of natural resources".[4] When sovereign states seek control over natural resources for strategic, political, and economic reasons, it is referred to as resource nationalism. A definition of resource nationalism that is specific to the oil and gas industry and to the Constitutional Court's ruling on the 2001 Oil and Gas Law No. 22 has "two components — limiting the operations of private international oil companies (IOCs) and asserting a greater national control over natural resource development".[5]

Engaged by developed and developing countries alike, resource nationalism and its causes are manifold and complex, encompassing as they do strategic, nationalistic and economic reasons. The drivers of resource nationalism can arise from either national circumstances (increasing domestic demand for a natural resource, for example) or international ones (for example, increasing commodity prices).

There can be a structural element to resource nationalism, often ignored by nationalists. This is related to the long lead times that are the norm in the extractive sectors, in particular the oil and gas sector, because of the large investments and advanced technology required. Long-term investment and production agreements tend not to be flexible enough to accommodate fluctuating prices or changing political and economic conditions. Governments then seek changes in what they consider outdated and unfair agreements.[6]

Because of the global resurgence of resource nationalism, Indonesian officials could look to other countries' resource nationalistic policies. The late Energy and Mineral Resources Deputy Minister Widjajono Partowidagdo, for example, could refer to Russia's policy towards foreign energy companies. "In the Sakhalin project by Shell in Russia, Shell got 60 per cent of the share, but after a new rule was applied, 55 per cent belonged to the government and the operator only got 45 per cent."[7] While stressing that the government was not seeking to copy Russia, he was adamant that Indonesia would like to have its fair share.

Resource nationalism has increased globally, due in part to a surge in global commodity demand particularly in the fast-growing economies of China and India. Consequently, foreign investors in natural resources face increasing risks worldwide. In at least one 2012 resource nationalism index, Indonesia ranked sixty-ninth in the "high risk" category.[8] Nine countries in the "extreme" resource nationalism risks by the index were Somalia (ranked highest at 1), DR Congo (2), South Sudan (3), Sudan (4), Myanmar (5), Turkmenistan (6), Yemen (7), Iran (8), and Guinea (9).

Eight of the twelve member nations of OPEC (Organization of the Petroleum Exporting Countries) were ranked in the index, including Iran (8), Venezuela (12), Iraq (13), Angola (18), Nigeria (21), Libya (22), Ecuador (29), and Algeria (52). These countries accounted for 21.3 per cent of global oil production.[9] Indonesia, an erstwhile member of OPEC, had for some time been a net importer of oil and had voluntarily withdrawn from the organization.

Domestic Conditions and Resource Nationalism

During the last few years, Indonesia has been portrayed by many outside observers as a rising power in Asia. As the narrative went, Indonesia was the fourth most populous country, the third largest democracy, *and* the largest Islamic country in the world. In a period of slow economic growth globally, Indonesia was one of the few countries showing continued strong economic growth of around 6 per cent annually. In November 2011, an international bank report mirrored other buoyant reports when it predicted Indonesia was on track to be the tenth largest economy in the world in 2020. By 2030, it would be a US$9 trillion economy, the sixth largest after China, the United States, India, Brazil, and Japan.[10]

However, on other important fronts, Indonesia ranked poorly. Transparency International ranked Indonesia 118 out of 176 polled in the annual Corruption Perceptions Index for 2012.[11] In the 2012–13 Global Competitiveness Report issued by the World Economic Forum, Indonesia was ranked 50 among 144 countries, behind Malaysia, China, and Thailand but ahead of the Philippines and Vietnam.[12] In a ranking of education in forty countries, the Global Index of Cognitive Skills and Educational Attainment published by Pearson and the Economist Intelligence Unit, Brazil and Indonesia came last.[13]

Nonetheless, the country's strong economic performance and the continued high demand for Indonesian natural resources stimulated resource nationalism sentiment as a growing number of government officials felt confident of being able to take advantage of the positive economic outlook, though others took a more moderate stance. As the former deputy minister for energy and mineral resources, Rudi Rubiandini stated, "Our officials should understand this bargaining position and should not just bow when it comes to representing Indonesia abroad. So should the analysts, some of whom have incorrect nationalist sentiments and are calling for a stop to exports [of minerals]. It's not about that kind of nationalism. We should explain about the real interests of Indonesia and seek collaboration to have fairness and a win-win solution."[14]

The 2001 Oil and Gas Law No. 22 and Constitutional Amendments

The 2001 Oil and Gas Law No. 22

The overall positive outlook was made more impressive in the light of Indonesia's recovery from the Asian crisis of the late 1990s that had devastated the Indonesian economy, bringing with it profound economic, social, and political changes. These included the referendum leading to the independence of Timor-Leste, freedom of the press, regional autonomy, and a series of economic reforms that included the submission in 1999 of a draft oil and gas law to be ratified by the House of Representatives.

After Soeharto's forced resignation in 1998, a successful 1999 legislative election was held. At the People's Consultative Assembly (MPR) General Session after the elections, Abdurrahman Wahid (Gus Dur) defeated Megawati Soekarnoputri for the presidency. Megawati became vice-president as a consolation prize. The same MPR General Session agreed by consensus to a review of the Constitution in order to introduce amendments that would prevent a return to an authoritarian regime.

A confrontation between President Abdurrahman Wahid and the MPR culminated in his removal from office by the July Special Session of the MPR in 2001, replacing him with Vice-President Megawati. It was later that same year that the 2001 Oil and Gas Law No. 22 passed as law under the presidency of Megawati. On 16 July 2002 as part of the implementation of the Law, BP Migas was established to take over the oil and gas sector regulatory role from the national oil company, Pertamina. In this way, a checks and balances system was introduced in the oil and gas sector in view of the history of corruption and patronage within Pertamina. The reorganization of the oil and gas industry was not left unchallenged for long as a number of organizations and individuals attempted to request a judicial review of the law from the Constitutional Court. One such request, submitted by the Pertamina labour union, was rejected by the Constitutional Court on 21 December 2004.

Pertamina was established in 1971 with powers to act as an operator to drill and produce oil, to select contractors to work oil and gas blocks, and to sign production sharing agreements. There had been a number of attempts to bring it under control. In 1996, the government had submitted a draft law to separate Pertamina's operating and regulatory roles but the House of Representatives rejected it. It was resubmitted in 1999 after the economic crisis as part of a series of economic reforms required to meet the conditions for receiving assistance from the International Monetary Fund (IMF).

However, despite the checks and balances introduced by the law, Indonesia became a net importer of oil as increased domestic fuel consumption outgrew stagnant oil production. In 2012, Indonesia ranked twenty-first in the world, producing about 1.2 per cent of world oil production. It ranked eighth in world gas production.[15] Crude oil production declined, with much of it coming from mature fields. Indonesia had been a net oil importer since 2004 and was now no longer an OPEC member. Declining oil production, festering opposition to the law and growth of democracy in the past decade led in 2012 to the submission of the petition to the Constitutional Court to review the 2001 Oil and Gas Law No. 22.

Constitutional Amendments

The wide-ranging amendments to the constitution by the People's Consultative Assembly after the fall of Soeharto included limiting the number of terms a president could serve to two five-year ones, constitutional affirmation of regional autonomy, bringing human rights for the large part in line with the Universal Declaration of Human Rights and empowering the House of Representatives which now does actually legislate, exercises oversight of the government, and approves the national budget.[16]

The third amendment of the Constitution included establishing the Constitutional Court as an independent guardian of the Constitution with the same standing as the Supreme Court. Indonesia became a state with constitutional checks and balances and separation of powers between the legislative, executive, and judiciary branches. The Court interprets the Constitution and has the authority to annul articles of a law or an entire law, making it a powerful and strategic institution.[17] Since its establishment in August 2003, the Court has ruled on a number of landmark decisions including the rehabilitation of the political rights of former members of the Indonesian Communist Party (PKI), the abolition of articles of the subversion law and of the defamation against the institution of the presidency. It is made up of nine justices and at the time of the petition on the Oil and Gas Law, it was led by Chief Justice Professor Dr Mohammad Mahfud, a senior politician of the National Awakening Party, a former member of the House of Representatives and a former cabinet minister.

"Constitutional Jihad"

The judicial review had been petitioned by a group of prominent Indonesian individuals and Islamic organizations wishing to challenge the Oil and Natural Gas Law No. 22 of 2001 arguing that it unduly favoured foreign interests and that it was in contradiction with Article 33(3) of the 1945 Constitution. That article states that "The earth and water and the natural wealth which they contain are under the power of the State and utilized for the maximum welfare of the people".

Why would a group of Islamic associations and prominent individuals associated with Islamic groups petition the Constitutional Court to review the 2001 Oil and Gas Law No. 22? This question was raised by Justice Harjono, who wrote the sole dissenting opinion among the nine justices. Justice Harjono argued that only those who are affected directly by the law should have the legal standing to be heard in court. In this case, he wrote, the Court had not sufficiently examined the damage the petitioners had suffered and therefore, the petition should have been dismissed.[18] On the substantive issue regarding BP Migas, he argued that the agency had a strong legal standing as a representative of the government, since it had been established by law through the presidency and the legislative branches of the government.

In an interview conducted not long after the ruling, Din Syamsuddin, the Chairman of Muhammadiyah, answered Justice Harjono's question at length. He said that the petition had been initiated by Muhammadiyah.[19] Muhammadiyah, the second largest Islamic association in Indonesia, boasted a proud heritage as an Islamic nationalist organization going back to Dutch colonial times. It prided itself on running a large number of schools, universities, and hospitals across Indonesia, among other activities besides its religious activities.

According to Din Syamsuddin, the organization was carrying out one of its mandates formulated at its 2010 National Congress or *Muktamar* which also celebrated the 100th anniversary of the organization. Prior to the Congress, the leadership board of Muhammadiyah had decided at the 2009 National Conference or *Tanwir* to investigate laws that were in contradiction to the Constitution, particularly in the field of energy. A team was formed made up of internal experts that worked for a year to do an inventory and study laws considered unconstitutional and that could be submitted for judicial review by the Constitutional Court. These laws included the 2001 Oil and Gas Law No. 22, the 2009 Law on Mining and Coal Law No. 4, the 1960 Agrarian Law No. 5, and the 2004 Law No. 7 on Water Resources.

The 2001 Oil and Gas Law No. 22 was the first law chosen for petition for judicial review by the Constitutional Court. According to the Muhammadiyah team, this law had brought the most loss to the country. It had also weakened the sovereignty of the nation over its natural resources and had unduly favoured foreign interests. Muhammadiyah implicated the IMF in the forced liberalization of the oil and gas sector through its conditionality of financial assistance to Indonesia during the Asian crisis. The team then invited other persons and organizations to join the petition.[20]

It may also be significant to note that in the larger national political context, the Muhammadiyah and its members were playing a far lesser role in formal politics than they had been used to, lamenting the distant relations between them and the second-term administration of President Susilo Bambang Yudhoyono and Vice-President Boediono. This was attributed to the support Muhammadiyah had given to former Vice-President Kalla in his 2009 bid for the presidency. As a result, after the re-election of SBY to his second term, Muhammadiyah was not represented in the cabinet of the SBY-Boediono administration.[21]

The petition, therefore, served not only to bolster the nationalist and populist standing of Muhammadiyah but also showed it could affect policies at a national level with the additional benefit of discomforting the government.

The Constitutional Court Ruling

At any rate, the Court accepted, for the most part, the petitioners' argument that the 2001 Oil and Natural Gas Law No. 22 of 2001, and BP Migas's standing in it, was in contradiction with Article 33 of the Constitution and needed to be changed. However, all production sharing contracts that had been entered into by BP Migas would remain valid until they expired.

The Court argued that BP Migas as a legal entity was not part of the government. However, its legal standing prevented the government from using its full authority over its oil and gas resources. Consequently it could not use its authority for the maximum welfare of the people.

According to the Court, the best option for exploiting the country's natural resources would be state-owned enterprises. This was in line with a major demand of the petitioners. The state enterprises could work with other parties, including private sector companies, to obtain the required capital, technology or management.[22] This implied the return of Pertamina to its previous role as both regulator and operator.

Post-Constitutional Court Ruling

The dissolution of BP MIGAS took effect immediately after the Constitutional Court ruling. Acting with alacrity to calm the industry and the investment market, and not least the suddenly stranded employees of BP Migas, President Susilo Bambang Yudhoyono issued Presidential Regulation No. 95 Year 2012 that transferred the responsibilities of BP Migas to the Minister for Energy and Mineral Resources on a temporary basis until the House of Representatives amended the 2001 Law on Oil and Gas No. 22 based on the Constitutional Court decision. In confirmation of the Court's ruling on contracts, the President's regulation also declared all contracts signed by BP Migas would be valid until their expiry.

The Minister for Energy and Mineral Resources, Jero Wacik, then established an Interim Working Unit for Upstream Oil and Gas Business Activities which was to report directly to the minister, taking over the duties and functions of BP Migas. The Unit was staffed by former BP MIGAS personnel. In the end only the head of BP Migas was not retained. In February, the President changed the status of the Working Unit from interim to permanent and appointed the deputy minister and a former senior official in BP MIGAS, Rudi Rubiandini, to head it.[23]

The petitioners were clearly unhappy with these developments as the status quo had been retained. Their aim had been to annul the 2001 Oil and Gas Law No. 22 and to return Pertamina to its former position as regulator and operator in the oil and gas sector. At first, they demanded the government to accelerate the revisions to the Oil and Gas Law so that the new Law could take effect within six months, presumably confident that it would be in line with the Constitutional Court ruling. However, the House of Representatives was already in the process of amending the Law and had been since 2010. The long legislative process made a six-month acceleration for completion highly unlikely.

House of Representatives Revision of the Oil and Gas Law

The revision of the law had been agreed by the executive and legislative branches since June 2010 at a joint meeting between Commissions IV, V, VI, and VII of the House of Representatives, and, from the government side, the Coordinating Minister for Economy, Minister for Energy and Mineral Resources, Minister for Industry, Minister for Trade, and Minister for State-owned Enterprises. The Commission VII was to have completed the background academic study on the revision in late 2011 to be sent to the plenary session of the House of Representatives for discussion. The scheduled completion for the revision would have been mid-2012 but it was postponed. However it was overtaken by the Constitutional Court's ruling and now had to take into account both the ruling and the government's post-BP Migas administrative reorganization.

The revision had been driven by dissatisfaction over the declining performance of the oil and gas sector. The Oil and Gas Law and the ensuing red tape it had engendered within BP Migas was blamed for much of the stagnation. Exploration of new oil and gas fields had encountered delays resulting in the continued reliance on mature oil wells.

At the same time, there has been an increased demand for more national control over the oil and gas sector. The demands came at a time when the government was in the process of deciding on upcoming extensions of contracts of oil and gas blocks managed by foreign production sharing contractors. Twenty-nine concessions were due to expire between 2013 and 2021. The revision of the draft was expected to favour the state oil company Pertamina and other private national oil companies.[24]

However, the outcome was still uncertain as the revision of the law was a tug-of-war between two groups. One group, in common with the petitioners to the Constitutional Court, wanted the Oil and Gas Law to be repealed and to move back to the Law No. 8 of 1971 and the dual role of Pertamina. Another group favoured the retention of the existing institutional framework in which Pertamina was to be operated as a purely commercial enterprise.[25]

Pertamina: Decline Amidst Rise of Other National Oil Companies

Another form of resource nationalism occurring globally has been the rise of national oil companies. In Asia, companies such as China National Offshore Oil Corporation (CNOOC), India's Oil and Natural Gas Corporation (ONGC), and the Korean National Oil Corporation have been expanding internationally in search of new fields and acquiring other companies.[26] As these companies expanded, Pertamina declined. The success of Petronas of Malaysia particularly gnawed at many Indonesians since, when first established, it looked to Pertamina as a model.

The decline of Pertamina came in part from its responsibility to distribute refined oil throughout the archipelago at a subsidized price. At the same time, it was notorious for being a cash cow for national projects and a source of patronage throughout its history. In one instance, a 1999 audit by

Price Waterhouse Coopers showed Pertamina had lost billions of dollars between 1996 to 1998 through corruption and inefficiency.[27]

Under its commercial status under the 2001 Oil and Gas Law No. 22, Pertamina was undergoing changes to become competitive internationally. Karen Agustiawan, appointed in 2009 as the company's president, was following a strategic blueprint that would make Pertamina a leading national oil company by 2023, even as it continued to struggle to erase its corruption-tainted image. After the Constitutional Court ruling on BP Migas, she emphatically rejected public demands that Pertamina should replace the agency in its regulatory role.[28]

Conclusion

The Constitutional Court ruling on the petition against the 2001 Law on Oil and Gas No. 22 left many loose ends. While the ruling had clearly surprised the government, it recovered quickly enough to keep the status quo more or less in place. The "traditional" resourcc nationalists, such as Din Syamsuddin and his "constitutional *jihad*", could take comfort that BP Migas, perceived as an unwanted child of liberalization of the Indonesian economy that had reduced the welfare of the people, had been dissolved.

Their misbegotten belief that state enterprises would do better than BP Migas, in the face of much evidence to the contrary, would have to wait for the passing of a new oil and gas law by the House of Representatives. Those with a patrimonial bent, the vested interests wishing a return to the patronage heyday of Pertamina, would also have to wait as the House of Representatives seemed more interested in politicking within electoral cycles (also constitutionally amended) than in passing laws expeditiously.

"Modernizer" resource nationalists such as Rudi Rubiandini and Karen Agustiawan could, for the time being, work at improving the competitiveness of their respective organizations as they too wait for the resolution to the new Oil and Gas Law issue and, indeed, for the upcoming elections in 2014, when they await with the rest of the nation, for a new president after SBY. President Susilo Bambang Yudhoyono would be the first president in the history of Indonesia to complete two terms and to step down in accordance with the Constitution.

Whether the new president will follow the inward-looking path of the "traditional" resource nationalists or the outward-looking path of the "modernizer" resource nationalists is an open question. Whatever path he or she chooses will be taken while leading a still messy democracy, albeit within a constitutional framework that offers a measure of stability. At the same time, there would be clear areas of national concern, that is, governance, competitiveness, and education, as underlined in Indonesia's rankings cited above.

In dealing with resource nationalism in the oil and gas sector, the new president could do well to listen to the advice of Ari H. Soemarno, a former head of Pertamina, who appealed that the lessons learnt from the dissolution of BP Migas be used to make changes beyond the issue of national sovereignty over natural resources. These should be, first, to formulate a national strategy of energy security; second, to understand that the era of cheap energy is over and that subsidies are no longer possible; third, to reformulate a comprehensive restructuring of the oil and gas sector; and finally, to assess correctly why Indonesia has failed to develop its oil and gas industry.

He noted the irony of trying to bring the management of the oil and gas sector in line with the Constitution while ignoring the increase in Indonesian oil and fuel imports that come from foreign sources.[29] This means the key to viable resource nationalism is an acceptance of the need for mutual interdependence with the outside world, rather than striving to win a zero-sum game.

Notes

1. Julian Hill, "The Case for Exploring the Unknown", *Strategic Review* 3, no. 1 (January–March 2013): 57–65.
2. Lin Che Wei, "BP Migas Dissolution: A Political Comedy", *Jakarta Post*, 17 November 2012.
3 "Ini Jihad Konstitusi", *Eksekutif*, December 2012, p. 22.
4. Halina Ward, "Resource Nationalism and Sustainable Development: A Primer and Key Issues", IIED Working Paper, March 2009.
5. Paul Stevens, "National Oil Companies and International Oil Companies in the Middle East: Under the Shadow of Government and the Resource Nationalism Cycle", *Journal of World Energy Law & Business* 1, no. 1 (2008), p. 5 <http://jwelb.oxfordjournals.org/>.
6. Philip Hill, David Lewis, James Pay, Audley Sheppard and Jo Delaney, "Resource Nationalism: A return to the bad old days?", *Practical Law Company*, 2012.
7. Concord Consulting, "Economic Nationalism: Here to Stay", p. 3 <http://www.ina.or.id/events/news/373-economic-nationalism-here-to-stay>.
8. "Indonesian Mineral Export Tax Highlights Resource Nationalism", 5 April 2012 <http://blog.maplecroft.com/2012/04/05/indonesian-mineral-export-tax-highlights-resource-nationalism-risks/>.

9. "44% of Global Oil Production Taking Place in Countries with a 'High Risk' of Resource Nationalism", 1 March 2012 <http://maplecroft.com/about/news/resource_nationalism_index_2012.html>.
10. "Indonesia's Economy to be in World's Top Six in 2030: Standard Chartered", *Jakarta Globe*, 27 November 2011 <http://www.thejakartaglobe.com/business/Indonesias-economy-to-be-in-worlds-top-six-in-2030-standard-chartered/481205>.
11. "Indonesia's global ranking drops in latest corruption index", *Jakarta Globe*, 5 December 2012 <http://www.thjakartaglobe.com/home/indonesias-global-ranking-drops-in-latest-corruption-index/560005>.
12. "Indonesia drops four places in WEF Global Competitiveness Ranking", *Policy and Business News*, 5 September 2012 <http://www.eurocham.or.id/joomla/index.php?option=com_content&view=article&id=562:indonesia-drops-four-places-in-wef-global-competitiveness-rankin&catid=39:policy-and-business-news&Itemid=124>.
13. "Two Opposite Education Systems Ranked on Top", *New York Times*, 1 December 2012 <http://www.nytimes.com/2012/12/03/world/europe/two-opposite-education-systems-ranked-on-top.html?_r=0>.
14. Yanto Soegiarto, "Talking about Energy Sovereignty (Interview with Rudi Rubiandini)", *GlobeAsia*, November 2012, p. 72.
15. "Oil and Gas in Indonesia, Investment and Taxation Guide 2012", *Price Waterhouse Coopers*, May 2012, 5th ed.
16. Andrew Ellis, "Constitutional Reform in Indonesia: A Retrospective", *IDEA*, March 2005.
17. Adnan Buyung Nasution, "Post-constitutional Amendments in Indonesia", *Jakarta Post*, 28 February 2009 <http://www.thejakartapost.com/news/2009/02/08/postconstitutional-amendments-indonesia.html>.
18. "Menyoal Keberadaan SK Migas", *GeoEnergi*, December 2012, p. 20.
19. "Ini Jihad Konstitusi", *Eksekutif*, December 2012, p. 22.
20. "Tiga Tahun Dalami Kelemahan BP Migas", *Tribunnews.com*, 16 November 2012 <http:www.tribunnews.com/2012/11/15/muhammadiyah-tiga-tahun-dalami-kelemahan-bp-migas>.
21. Benni Setiawan, "Pasang-Surut Hubungan Muhammadiyah dengan Pemerintah", *Koran Tempo*, 14 November 2012.
22. Michael S. Carl and Dewi Savitri Reni, "BP Migas Decision" <http://blog.ssek.com/index.php/2012/11/bp-migas-decision/>.
23. "Pertamina chief nixes regulatory role after dissolution of BP Migas", *Jakarta Post*, 22 November 2012 <http://www.thejakartapost.com/news/2012/11/22/pertamina-chief-nixes-regulatory-role-after-dissolution-bpmigas.html>.
24. Subkhan A.S., Saifudin and Abraham Logaligo, "Towards Oil and Gas Law Revision", *Tambang*, 10 January 2012 <http://m.majalahtambang.com/detail_berita-php?category=15&newsnr=5311>.

25. A. Rinto Pudyantoro, "Urgensi Pergantian UU Migas", *Bisnis Indonesia*, 10 July 2012.
26. Mikkal E. Herberg, "Asia's National Oil Companies and the Competitive Landscape of the International Oil Industry", National Bureau of Asian Research, NBR Special Report 31, September 2011, pp. 29–37.
27. Donald I. Hertzmark, "Pertamina, Indonesia's State-Owned Oil Company", The James A. Baker III Institute for Public Policy, Rice University, March 2007, p. 2.
28. "Pertamina Unwilling to Take Over BPMigas Functions, Says Chief", *Jakarta Post*, 21 November 2012 <http://www.thejakartapost.com/news/2012/11/21/pertamina-unwilling-take-over-bpmigas-functions-says-chief.html>.
29. Ari H. Soemarno, "Migas Setelah Pembubaran", *Kompas*, 25 January 2013.

Laos

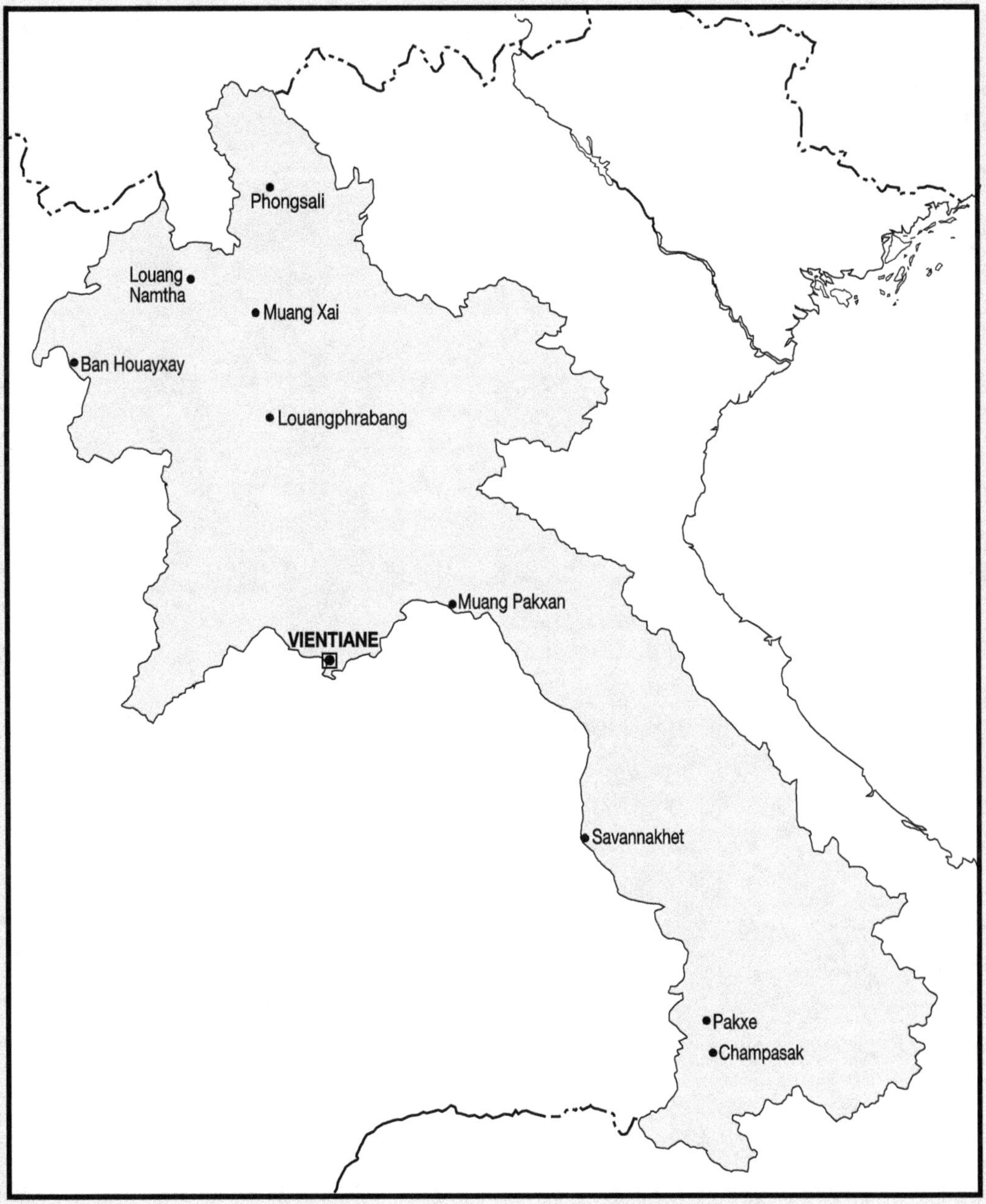
Phongsali
Louang Namtha
Muang Xai
Ban Houayxay
Louangphrabang
Muang Pakxan
VIENTIANE
Savannakhet
Pakxe
Champasak

LAOS IN 2012
In the Name of Democracy

Holly High

Introduction

"The Lao People's Democratic Republic: Peace, Independence, Democracy, Unity, Prosperity". Since the 1975 revolution, "democracy" has hung as an unfulfilled promise in both the official epithet and motto of the nation. Many previous chapters on Laos in *Southeast Asian Affairs* have speculated, mostly pessimistically, about when this repeated promise will be realized. Year after year we have read that Laos continues to be a one-party state ruled by a small, secretive elite resistant to international and internal pressures for reform. Just last year the contributor to this series wrote that "there is no credible challenge to its continued governance".[1] But the events of recent years have suggested that a different reading might be possible. It is notable, for instance, that the titles of the entries for Laos in *Southeast Asian Affairs* for 2009 and 2010 contained the words "contestation" and "debate"[2] respectively. Stavrakakis[3] defines democracy as a political system premised on recognition of imperfection, especially the inevitable failure to attain unity between different voices. Democracy by his definition is the never-ending and always-unresolved debate between differently held positions. This definition directs the analysis of so-called democratic polities to the question of the status differences of opinion in any given context: how is a space for argument facilitated or disabled? Cuing from this Stavrakakis definition, in this chapter I focus on forums for disagreement, debate, and complaint in Laos in 2012 as a means of taking the pulse of democracy there not as a name only, but as the systemic politics of disunity.

Holly High is Senior Lecturer in the Department of Anthropology, University of Sydney.

The definition of democracy has been debated and discussed critically within Laos, too. In one political theory handbook,[4] true democracy was defined as the reorganization of class relations away from the ruling class towards society in general: this is the goal of the current regime's political project. But the handbook also emphasized that "democracy" is a word that is used as an empty promise that stands in the place of this revolutionary prospect, and that in reality most so-called democracies do not grant political authority to the majority of people. In my discussions with Lao political leaders about the role of democracy and their hopes for the future of the nation, a similar ambivalence was evident. Although democracy is usually considered a core goal and an indisputable value, there is also a wariness that not everything done in the name of democracy is worth supporting. Some leaders suggested that a better educated population working from a base of secure development is needed first: until then the single party would lead on their behalf. One explained that without this, the field of democratic debate would just be senseless conflict and pointless argument, and the nation of Laos has already seen enough strife, war, and blood-shed in its recent history. Another criticism of multi-party democracy was that it is inherently unstable: invidious comparisons with the protests of Thailand are not uncommon. Some associate multi-party systems with tedious and drawn-out decision making, pandering to special interests and spending on immediate benefits rather than wise leadership for the long term. Another leader explained to me that steps towards democracy in Laos needed to be slow, incremental and balanced with other values, most notably equality (*khwam samoephap*) — especially between the various ethnicities and between genders — and unity (*ekaphap*). Other associated core political values that temper that of democracy include "harmony" (*pongdong*), "solidarity" (*samakhi*), and "consensus" (*hendi*).

There is a conflict here between the political value of democracy, which entails disunity, and the political values of unity, harmony, and solidarity.[5] The tension between these two currents of Lao political expression can be seen in the striking contortions political language sometimes takes in order to present dissent, contestation, or criticism as in fact a manifestation of unity. For instance, one particularly common style of dissent seen in 2012 was the technique of appealing to the letter of the law of the existing regime and the promises it has made it order to launch critiques against it. These are complaints against the state made in its own tongue, as it were. For instance, commenting on this widespread concern about land, Deputy Director General of the Land

Natural Resource Research Institute, Palikone Thalongsengchanh observed that "our law stipulates that compensation for affected villagers who have to give up their land for development projects needs to be sufficient to improve their livelihoods" but that the concerns raised by citizens showed that this law was not being upheld: "we have observed that many villagers end up poorer after losing their land to development projects, because of the inappropriate compensation provided," he explained.[6] In this style of critique, complaint is positioned as harmonious with the national project because it emerges from within the laws and goals set by the party-state. It complains about how the party-state's own stipulations and intent have not been faithfully carried out. The reproach to the party-state seems to be, "if only you were who you claim to be!".

Forms of dissent and criticism that do not adequately frame themselves within the overarching values of unity, solidarity, and harmony with the national project continued to struggle to find legitimacy in 2012. In early December, Helvetas Country Director Anne-Sophie Gindroz was expelled after she wrote a private letter circulated among "development partners" in Laos. In that letter, she described the current context as "democratically deficit" with little room for meaningful debate and repercussions for those who attempted to use it. She suggested that many NGOs remain silent about this because of fears that, should they speak up, their ability to operate in Laos would be reduced or removed altogether. But, she noted, there were elements in the Lao government and civil society pushing for greater openness, and that development partners ought to "show solidarity with those acting and calling for more inclusive dialogue". Towards the close of the letter, she argued strongly that open debate was fundamental to achieving the goals of development work, and called on other organizations to take a more critical stance. In the letter penned by the Ministry of Foreign Affairs instructing Helvetas on her expulsion, it was claimed that Gindroz had an "unconstructive attitude", "rejected" the Lao political system, and launched a "prejudicial anti-Lao Government campaign" by calling for development partners to turn against the Lao government. The letter went on to suggest that Gindroz was in violation of international and national law, although the only laws quoted in the letter did not persuade me of this. Both laws quoted did, however, mention the obligation of international non-governmental organization (INGO) staff to respect the "fine" traditions of the Lao people. Perhaps what the Ministry of Foreign Affairs found illegal about her letter, in these terms, was that it was styled as openly critical, agitating, and emphasized divisions, rather than subordinating her criticisms more firmly to the potent political values of unity, harmony, solidarity, and consensus.

In another case that drew far less English-media attention, in 2012 Dr Khamphouey Panmalaythong published an article in the Lao-langauge *Journal of Social Sciences*, published by the Lao Academy of Social Sciences.[7] In this piece, Khamphouey pointed out that in single-party systems that typically lack development, democracy, and freedom, opinions will always differ and even the best of ideas — including Marxist-Leninism — come from multiple sources and need to be adapted to local conditions. Laos should be wary of single-source ideology, he warned. This article followed his 2011 speech to the National Assembly (NA) where he questioned the appropriateness of Marxist-Leninist teachings for the particular case of Laos. His smooth delivery and cool demeanour were impressive and had some contributors to discussion boards rhapsodic: perhaps Laos had found her Aung Sang Suu Kyi, one speculated. Others warned that his impeccable party affiliations suggested to the contrary that his public statements were a trap laid to lure the opposition out of hiding. Trained in Vietnam and the USSR, by 2010 he was a member of the Central Committee of the Party and of the National Assembly, Secretary of the Party Secretariat, and President of the National Institute of Social Sciences. In May 2012 he was replaced as President of the National Institute of Social Sciences. Some have suggested that this reshuffling might be a reprimand for his critical and public remarks, but that it is too soon to draw any conclusions.[8]

Previously in analysis of politics in Laos, the classic observation was that — off-the-record — everyone knows that laws are not fairly enforced, that elites hold the power in reality, and that economic growth and increasing foreign investment have only tended to confirm their position and privilege above their countrymen. "Everyone knows" that to criticize elites is to invite punishment and perhaps even imprisonment. "Everyone knows" that corruption is the norm, that policy on paper means nothing on the ground, and about the power of provincial and district chiefs and their cronies who are often said to hold the last word on anything of import within their localities. And "everyone knows" better than to risk pointing this out. By 2012, it was not quite so clear that everyone knew this. Instead, 2012 saw such supposedly unspeakable topics thrust repeatedly into expression. Gindroz and Khamphouey spoke openly about their concerns with the party-state, and there were many other lower profile examples in 2012 as well. Many of these took the form of the first style

I identified above, presented through the language of the law itself in very conciliatory terms.

In a sense, complaint and criticism of a certain style has been a common, and even an encouraged, form of political engagement in Laos since the revolution: for instance, self-criticism is often found in official documents and speeches, where "weaknesses" of existing policies and problems encountered to date are often pointed out and targeted for improvement. Attention to previous failings and rallying calls for ever-strengthened efforts going forward is a standard part of party-state meetings. One of the striking aspects of political debates in Laos more recently is that they have taken this pre-existing form of constructive criticism and expanded it into a meta-level debate about the role and form of debate itself. One recurring theme of political expression in 2012 was criticism about how criticism itself was being delivered and dealt with. Khamphouey's article was a key example of this, but there were also complaints about the complaints procedures at the NA and laws drafted about how to protect those who alert us of breaches of the law. There were raging debates on discussion boards about the lack of space for debate. That is to say, the role of debate, dissent and complaint was itself one of the subjects of debate in 2012.

If one follows Stavrakakis in defining democracy as a political system of disunity, one can understand this debate about debate as a debate about democratic possibilities. While it might be tempting to dismiss these small examples as cosmetic niceties that paper over the underlying fact of ongoing suppression of dissent in Laos, I argue that they are important not only for their content, but also for their form, the way they phrase and imagine the potential for democracy in Laos. Below, I will provide three examples that were significant in 2012. The first is the NA; the second is in the regional and international context; and the third is cyberspace and media forums.

The National Assembly Steps Up

In many ways it is no surprise that Dr Khamphouey's controversial 2011 speech took place in the NA. In recent years, the NA has elbowed its way into recognition as one of the primary forums for political debate and criticism in Laos. The NA consists of elected representatives (either members of the Lao People's Revolutionary Party or independents) charged with representing their constituent's concerns and instructing the government. The NA regularly undertakes routine tasks such as ratifying international agreements, electing the President of Laos (this year, Choummaly Sayasone was re-elected) and the Vice-

President (Bounnhang Vorachit) and appointing the Prime Minister (Thongsing Thammavong) and endorsing the government cabinet. Ordinary sessions are held twice a year, each hemmed in before and after with consultative meetings and extraordinary sessions for particular issues. The NA is tasked with monitoring the performance of the government, and part of this is representing complaints of constituents about the government. For instance, The NA receives petitions from citizens to its central office to which parliamentarians then respond.

While in the past the role of the NA was often dismissed as a mere symbolic nod towards representational politics and a rubber stamp for party directives, perceptions have changed in recent years with the NA now thought of as a key avenue for popular recourse. This may be related to the NA's new leadership. NA President Pany Yathortou rose to the leadership of the NA after the controversial removal of Bouasone Bouphavanh as Prime Minister in 2010, when the then President of NA Thongsing Thammavong was promoted to Prime Minister. Madame Pany and other NA members have been vocal in discussing ways to improve the Assembly's activities. For instance, the member for Vientiane and member of the NA Standing Committee, Souvanpheng Bouphanouvong, raised the suggestion that the cumbersome and time-consuming meetings organized before or after each ordinary NA session between representatives and their constituents be changed to more focused, issue-based meetings between interested community members and their representatives. The newspaper article that reported this noted that "she didn't criticise the way NA members met with their constituents in the past, but confirmed that the NA is working to avoid what some feel are mostly symbolic meetings".[9] This quotation is interesting for two reasons: first it demonstrates that Souvanpheng was operating within the style that I outlined above, where she assures us that her suggestion for improvement is not to be taken as a harsh critique of the past, but as constructive criticism within an overarching unifying and harmonious orientation. Secondly, it expresses the goal to move away from merely "symbolic" engagement between representatives and their constituents towards a more robust engagement. This small example shows the delicacy of the terrain in which Pany, Souvanpheng, and some other NA members are operating: they are pushing for reform but in a context where criticism is offered cautiously in the guise of unity and non-conflict.

In media reports, the NA is often presented as speaking as a single voice on behalf of "the people". Souvanpheng was quoted in a newspaper report about the need for better auditing of government spending as saying:

> This is why the NA is in a very serious battle to prevent the leakage of money, and is trying hard to build regulations to control the situation, for the budget was allocated correctly and clearly. If there is any pressure or violation of regulations by officials, the NA is ready to stand by the side of the disadvantaged people. What we're doing is for transparency and the benefit of the entire nation.[10]

On the one hand, this looks like an example of open political critique because the NA is ostensibly taking a critical view of the spending activities of the government and committing to take a stand against corruption. But on the other hand, this is phrased as if the NA speaks with one, unified voice. If the NA was truly representative of the diversity of its constituents, then surely there would be a multitude of views that could not be contained in such a single standpoint. A commitment to the political value of unity can be seen in another characteristic of NA media releases: tempering criticism with praise. For instance, another report noted that Souvanpheng stated: "The National Assembly (NA) yesterday pointed out several areas where the government could do more, while applauding the government for its strong performance overall".[11] This presents her criticism as friendly and constructive, rather than truly oppositional. My point is that even in moments where "criticism" is deliberately aired in the NA, it often remains subordinated to a more subtle but all the more pervasive political value of unity.

One of the most fascinating aspects of the NA's attempt to be the voice of the people is its hotline. When the Assembly is in session, comments and concerns can be submitted by any citizen of Laos via a free-call number, letter, or e-mail. These complaints are then submitted to the Government Office, and from there to relevant ministries and departments with the request that a report be returned directly to the NA about the response taken. Some of these cases are taken up for debate and discussion within the NA session periods. In the mid-year session of 2012 there were 280 calls over seventeen days.

In a summary of the complaints raised in that session, Deputy Head of the NA's Administrative Office, Viseth Savengseuksa, explained that "most" of the calls were about land issues.[12] Over the past few years, economic growth has gathered pace in Laos as large resource exploitation undertakings have started to bring in revenue, most notably mining, hydropower, and agribusiness.[13] These are part of a much broader "land as capital" strategy that has seen many Lao people effected by resettlement. Compensation claims for reallocated land have often been tense, and rural livelihoods have been squeezed. Mr Viseth noted that while these land concessions were aimed at national development, there was widespread popular dissatisfaction. The immediate effect for ordinary people was often impoverishment as the loss of land directly impacted on subsistence livelihoods. The other major complaints raised were, in order of frequency: the rule of law; environmental degradation and logging; and the corruption or extravagant living of civil servants. True to the general formula of NA announcements, press reports about the hotline also included ruminations on the weaknesses of the hotline itself and plans for its improvement.[14]

The recent endeavours of the NA can be interpreted as a move to bolster it as a forum for political expression and recourse in Laos. On the one hand, the NA has been active and vocal in airing and addressing concerns, including controversial issues like land concessions and corruption, and Khamphouey's speech. The NA of recent years has challenged many old taboos and clichés about political criticism in Laos: one can hardly continue to claim that all public political criticism in Laos is strictly censured. On the other hand, the space for critique and debate that the NA is carving out remains limited. The critical statements aired there are typically carefully phrased as constructive criticism from within the law, in terms that are supportive and praising of the party-state rather than divisive. The Assembly's criticisms of the party-state uphold the political values of unity and harmony to such an extent that, counter-intuitively, the Assembly is often presented as speaking with a single voice, rather than in the disharmonious cacophony of democratic debate.

Debate in International Forums

Laos hosted a visit from Hillary Clinton in July, the first from a U.S. Secretary of State since 1955. Before her arrival, Clinton spoke from Mongolia pointing to that nation as a role model for post-socialist transitions to democracy. She commented, "This is the right time to talk about democracy in Asia, as many countries in this region grapple with the question of which model of governance best suits their society and circumstances. The path they choose will shape the lives of billions of people and the future of this region."[15] That said, there was little media discussion of democracy during her visit to Laos, with the focus instead on trade, unexploded ordnance and missing U.S. servicemen. She did, however, weigh in on the controversial Sayaburi dam issue, calling for its suspension.

That dam dogged Laos' international relations in 2012. It will be the second constructed on the Mekong (the first is located in China). Opponents have raised concerns about environmental impacts and viability, especially for downstream nations Thailand, Cambodia, and Vietnam. In response, the Lao government proposed to hold off construction while further studies and revisions were completed. However, in November the ground-breaking ceremony took place and other preparatory works continued. One of the striking aspects of this long-running dispute is the divide that it exposed between the public stances of the Lao and Vietnamese governments. These two typically present a unified front, referring to one another as "younger and older brother". In 2012, fifty years of diplomatic relations between the two was marked with a series of high-level commemorative events strung together as the Laos-Vietnam Year of Solidarity and Friendship. In such a context, Vietnam's call for a ten-year moratorium on all dams on the Mekong was unusual. As it happened, it was also fleeting: by year's end Vietnam had withdrawn her opposition to the Sayaburi dam.

In another major event for Lao international relations, it was announced that the country had finally completed all the requirements to accede to the World Trade Organization (WTO). It has been a long path for Laos to reach this point. Legal frameworks were modified extensively or written completely from scratch in order to satisfy the eligibility requirements. Laos' Industry and Commerce Minister, Nam Viyaketh, spoke with disarming frankness about the difficulties he had encountered not only in the international negotiations, but domestically:

> We, however, underestimated the difficult negotiations we would have to undergo at the internal front. Quite frankly, trying to convince our trading partners of the position of Lao PDR only to go home, and to convince our internal partners of the justification of the reforms requested, was one of our most difficult and hard tasks.[16]

Some of the future effects of such internationally influenced changes to the Lao legal framework may have been presaged by a story that captured the attention of international journalists in 2012: Lao Holdings N.V. and its wholly-owned subsidiary, Sanum Investments Limited, both filed suits against the Government of the Lao People's Democratic Republic for its attempts to seize assets, impose fines, and revoke licences to operate, acts which Sanum argues were baseless, corrupt and in violation of numerous international treaties. The suits will be handled by the World Bank's International Center for the Settlement of Investment

Disputes under treaties signed by Laos designed to protect foreign investment. The details of the case are complex and have been well reported elsewhere, partly because of the talkativeness of Sanum's president, Jody Jordahl, who has given a series of interviews to international media outlets. For the purposes of this chapter, the pertinent aspect to note is the appeals made to the law, laws which are increasingly framed within an international context. For instance, Jordal stated: "We invested in good faith in the Lao PDR. We believed the former Prime Minister when he told us the Lao Government would uphold the rule of law".[17] This is a contestation of the party-state spoken in the language of the current legal framework, a framework that has been importantly modified by international agreements and their attendant domestic reforms.

Perhaps the most significant event in Lao international relations in 2012 was the hosting of the Asia-Europe Meetings (ASEM). As one commentary put it, it is almost as if the aim of hosting these meetings, and a bevy of other international events in recent years, is to secure an international image of Laos as "charming"[18] and of the ruling party-state as internationally well connected:[19] viewers of Lao national television were subjected each evening to news reports of the meetings a repeated announcement requesting one and all to be hospitable to the visiting delegates. The Asia Europe People's Forum (AEPF) was held in the lead up to the ASEM meetings. Intended as a forum for non-government voices, much of the discussion and critique emerging from it at the time was about the format itself (did the forum truly support free speech? Or was the format rigged to favour governmental voices?). While this style — debate about the role of debate — was not unexpected given the form of the other debates of 2012, the events that followed AEPF made this a meeting that would not quickly be forgotten. On 15 December 2012, Sombath Somphone, a key member of the forum's National Organizing Committee (Laos), was abducted directly after a routine police check of his car in Vientiane. The Lao government denied any responsibility and announced that a careful investigation would be undertaken. However, the year closed with no news of any advances made in identifying the whereabouts of this respected civil society leader and winner of the Ramon Malagasy Award. A panel hosted by the Thai Foreign Correspondent's Club discussed his disappearance as test case for the new ASEAN Human Rights Framework. Some observers tentatively linked Sombath's disappearance to the expulsion of Ms Gindroz: both were key supporters of the AEPF,[20] although again it is too soon to tell whether or not this disappearance was linked to Sombath's civil society work.

Debate in Cyberspace and the Media

The CCTV clip of Sombath's disappearance was released on YouTube. Dr Khamphouey's academic article was scanned and circulated on Flickr and Facebook. His NA speech has been watched by thousands of people on YouTube (over 35,000 views at time of writing). Gindroz's "private" letter was circulated widely via e-mail. Jordahl's complaints against the Lao state were flashed across numerous websites. While access to the Internet in Laos remains small overall (only 7 per cent of the population in 2010) it is growing fast, doubling each couple of years by some accounts and set to accelerate as the Internet becomes standard on mobile phones. While the state-run media remains restricted, there are no similar restrictions on Internet access in Laos and no sites are blocked.[21] Lao44, established in 2009, is a Lao-language online discussion board that facilitates debate and provides access to documents that might otherwise be difficult to locate, particularly legal provisions, some of which are essential for launching critiques of the style I have identified where criticism is made more conciliatory through its framing as within the law. Lao44 is named after the constitutional Article 44 that stipulates Lao citizen's rights for "freedom of speech, press and assembly".

Lao44 and the many other online forums pertinent to Laos remain intimately linked to, and even dependent on, more traditional forms of media. Many of the exchanges on them are sparked by the circulation of news breaking in more traditional forms of media, such as newspaper articles, which are then discussed, often critically and acrimoniously online. Importantly, these forums have the potential to bring into discussion members both from within and outside Laos, and people of various nationalities. The Internet, then, is fast becoming one of the most important forums for political debate in and about Laos, and it is changing the nature of the debate in the process.

One of the most talked about media events of 2012 was undoubtedly the Lao National Radio show *Talk of the News*. The show rose to even greater prominence when it was abruptly cancelled without notice or explanation in late January. The popular call-in programme had run for four years, providing a forum where Vientiane listeners could call in and offer their opinions, anonymously, on current events. Hosted by Ounkeo Souksavanh, the programme heard complaints that were similar to those noted as raised in the NA: land issues, rule of law, and corruption were high on the agenda. The show was cancelled by the Minister for Information, Culture and Tourism, Bosengkham

Vongdara. This was interpreted by some as a blow to the hopes for democracy in Laos, as it ended a thriving forum of debate. However, the closure of the show did not quell debate: to the contrary it became a kind of *cause célèbre* as the show's disappearance itself drew criticism in cyber forums. Lao44, for instance, ran a poll allowing people to vote on whether they wanted *Talk of the News* to be returned to air: 87 per cent of 1,601 respondents replied "yes". Newsgroups such as LaoFAB, soc.culture.laos, and LaoLink also saw popular disgruntlement with the show's halt aired and linked to perceptions of the Lao government as secretive, unfair and oppressive. International media reports were also highly critical of the closure and sympathetic to Ounkeo's plight, pointing to Article 44 of the national Constitution and Laos' ratification of the International Covenant on Civil and Political Rights (ICCPR) in 2009, which also provides for the protection of political speech.

Ounkeo is one of a small but significant number of Lao journalists and activists who are testing the limits and possibilities for a more critical political expression under the new legal protections which have often been drafted to international standards of human rights and freedom of speech. Critical articles and editorials in the Lao papers do remain rare but they are by no means absent. Characteristically they take up the same issues that are found in the other forums for popular complaint discussed so far: complaints about the gap between the provisions and securities guaranteed by the law and the reality on the ground; about the stark disparity between poor people, who are often asked to make sacrifices in the name of national development, especially as far as land is concerned, and the officials and elites who appear to be benefiting disproportionately from the nation's new wealth. Typically, the arguments are not phrased as revolutionary but rather as conservatively requesting merely that laws ought actually be enforced and that development in reality should be more like the promises made about it. Speaking on a listserv, one Lao journalist explained that: "In our circumstances, we need to ensure that our criticism is constructive. We are supposed to push gradually — if not we won [sic] be allowed to at all". Prime Minister Thomsing Thammavong released a scathing critical attack of the standard of media reporting in 2012, claiming that the media's avoidance of critique was hampering the development of informed national debate. In his criticism he called for more criticism, not only of internal events but also a domestic critique of international representations of Laos.

Conclusion

So, what do all these debates about debate, criticisms calling for more criticisms, and complaints not *with* the law but *within* the law amount to? One thing is for certain: these prove decisively that there is popular dissatisfaction in Laos with corruption and inequality. The complaints raised so repeatedly in these forums put to rest any lingering idea that there might be a "cultural" reason for, or even acceptance of, corruption and elitism in Laos.

But there is a bigger picture than this small (but important) point. These forums indicate a significant pattern in the Lao political terrain. This pattern has been building for several years now, and despite continual setbacks and repercussions it is nevertheless ongoing. This is a pattern where, rather than debate being censured and impossible in public, it is not only "tolerated" but called for, publicized and responded to. There are still unspoken parameters to what counts as acceptable criticism, but significantly these parameters are themselves being subjected to debate.

I will conclude with an observation from Zizek, a man who knows a thing or two about totalitarianism and its demise from first-hand experience. He noted that totalitarian situations are characterized by an obscene (that is, off-scene, unutterable) rule: "The obscene rule is here that any form of political opposition is unconditionally prohibited; however, this rule itself is strictly unutterable — anyone who dares to state this prohibition publicly is immediately condemned for the slander of socialist democracy".[22] The pre-revolutionary moment, by contrast, is marked by a different orientation towards such utterances: "the more a regime ... is uncertain of itself, of its legitimacy, the more it hesitates and makes concessions to the opposition, the more it is attacked by the opposition as an illegitimate tyranny. ... the true reproach of the opposition is that the regime *is not strong enough*, that it doesn't live up to is mandate of power...".[23] That is, the pre-revolutionary moment is characterized not by the total suppression of debate, nor by the total rejection of the existing regime, but by a loud and repetitive insistence that the law ought to be correctly and thoroughly adhered to and that the regime ought to deliver on its own promises: "if only you were who you claim to be!" This resembles some aspects of political expression in Laos today.

This raises the question, then: is Laos in a pre-revolutionary moment? Considering the events of Laos in 2012, one gets the sense that a tense, internal battle is taking place off-scene among leaders and elites, with only the surface ripples visible to interested outsiders. There are clearly elements of the Lao leadership who support more open forums for debate. But it is just as clear that there are powerful opponents to these moves, and that those who venture to utilize the growing spaces for political expression may meet with severe and unpredictable repercussions. This is not a smooth trajectory: while the new limits to free speech are tested by some, others launch new reprisals aimed at curbing it. It is important to note, for instance, that only weeks prior to the expulsion of Ms Gindroz, Helvetas staff spoke optimistically on a newsgroup about their engagements with the government: even on "hot topics" such as mining, a staffer wrote, a door was opening for dialogue. That this door was slammed shut only weeks later indicates that as long as this internal battle takes place, mixed signals are likely to be sent about the place of open political debate in Laos and its limits.

It is easy to be cynical about the possibilities for real change in Laos. It is also possible to be carried away with optimism sparked by very small gains. It is true that 2012 was a year brimming with examples of political expression in Laos, and it is also true that these were dogged by injustices, disciplining actions and yet more complaints about how complaints are currently dealt with. One of the greatest challenges, and the one I have drawn attention to in this short chapter, is that these tentative moves towards increased debate and criticism have been so far subordinated to those other powerful and persistent political values: unity, solidarity and harmony. Part of having a non-utopian vision of democracy is to accept the presence of disagreement. The test will be whether debate and criticism will continue to be merely "allowed" on certain occasions and in certain forms, tolerated only in order to be "resolved" (or even expelled altogether, as with Ms Gindroz) within a space that is in reality dominated by the norms of unity, solidarity and harmony, or whether openly held and expressed differences will come to be appreciated as permanent and valued aspects of a genuinely Lao democracy.

Notes

1. Christopher B. Roberts, "Laos: A More Mature and Robust State?", *Southeast Asian Affairs 2012*, edited by Daljit Singh and Pushpa Thambipillai (Singapore: Institute of Southeast Asian Studies, 2012), p. 153.
2. H. High, "Laos: Crisis and Resource Contestation", *Southeast Asian Affairs 2010*, edited by Daljit Singh (Singapore: Institute of Southeast Asian Studies. 2010), p. 153; and S. Creak, "Laos: Celebrations and Development Debates", *Southeast Asian Affairs 2011*, edited by Daljit Singh (Singapore: Institute of Southeast Asian Studies. 2011), pp. 107–28.

3. Y. Stavrakakis, *Lacan and the Political* (London and New York: Routledge, 1999).
4. Ministry of Information and Culture, "Pasatipatay (What is Democracy?)", in *Undertakings of Great Merit in Politics, Thought and Culture* (Vientiane: Ministry of Information and Culture 2010), pp. 129–33.
5. This holds true for the debates that I observed personally in my fieldwork in the rural south of Laos and also my knowledge of Vientiane politics through interviews and reading media reports. It does not preclude the possibility that other, more violent and extra-legal forms of dissent aimed at revolutionary overthrow of the regime took place in 2012, but I have no first-hand knowledge nor reliable source that could confirm such events. Rumours of rebellion do continue to circulate especially in Laos but media reporting on violence and arrests remains slim. In this chapter, I will confine myself to those arenas of debate and contestation that I was able to witness first-hand or confirm through secondary sources.
6. Vientiane Times Reporters, "Govt needs to examine land compensation, experts say", *Vientiane Times*, 17 July 2012.
7. Khamphouey Panmalaythong, "Some Thoughts on the Problems of the Ruling Party", *Walasan Withnyasansangkhom (Journal of Social Sciences)* 6, no. 11 (2012): pp. 1–6.
8. S. Creak and K. Barney, "Distressing Developments in Laos", 23 December 2012 <http://asiapacific.anu.edu.au/newmandala/2012/12/23/distressing-developments-in-laos/>.
9. Vientiane Times Reporters, "NA plans relevant meetings with constituents", *Vientiane Times*, 3 September 2012.
10. S. Sengdara, "National Assembly gets tough", *Vientiane Times*, 1 September 2012.
11. Vientiane Times Reporters, "NA spotlights areas where govt could do better", *Vientiane Times*, 21 June 2012.
12. S. Vaenkeo, "Laos National Assembly to quicken response to public concerns", *Vientiane Times*, 5 July 2012.
13. Ibid.
14. One major modification under consideration is to make the hotline available all year round in order to enable speedier resolution of citizen concerns. There were also concerns raised about the confidentiality of calls: originally the full details of the complaint were disclosed to the local authorities, but now Viseth suggested that the identity of callers be protected, known only to the NA and not passed on to government officials.
15. B. Klapper, "Clinton urges free markets with democracy in Asia", *Huffington Post*, 9 July 2012.
16. WTO Press Release, "Laos' WTO membership terms agreed — next stop: General Council" <http://www.wto.org/english/news_e/news12_e/acc_lao_28sep12_e.htm>, 28 September 2012.

17. BusinessWire, "Lao People's Democratic Republic: Alleged to Be Unsafe For Foreign Investment" <http://www.businesswire.com/news/home/20120814006693/en/Lao-People's-Democratic-Republic-Alleged-Unsafe-Foreign>, 15 August 2012.
18. Creak and Barney, "Distressing Developments".
19. Creak, "Laos: Celebrations and Development Debates".
20. Creak and Barney, "Distressing developments".
21. G. Kunze, "Laos and the Internet" <http://thediplomat.com/sport-culture/2012/04/17/laos-and-the-internet/>, 17 April 2012.
22. S. Zizek, "Invisible Ideology: Political Violence between Fiction and Fantasy", *Journal of Political Ideologies* 1, no. 1 (2007): 21.
23. Ibid., p. 26.

Malaysia

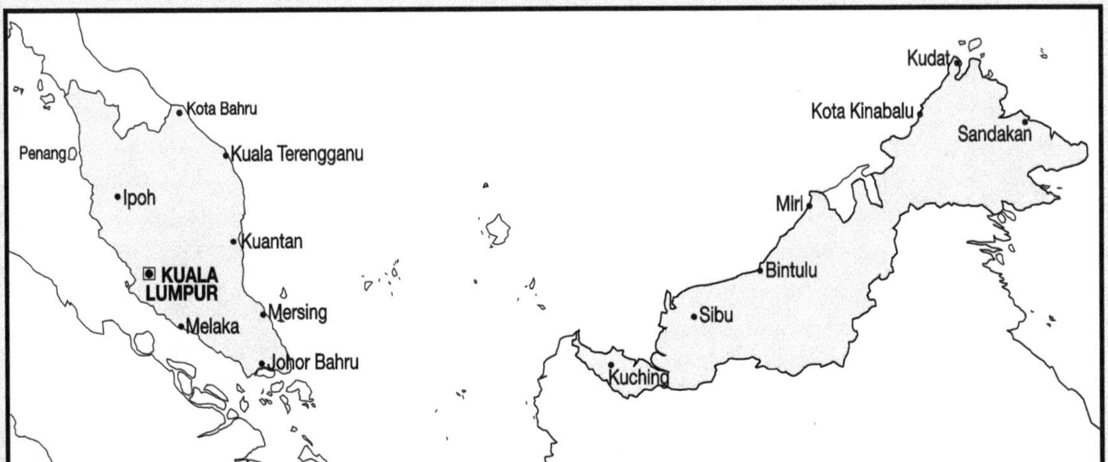

Kota Bahru
Penang
Kuala Terengganu
Ipoh
Kuantan
KUALA LUMPUR
Mersing
Melaka
Johor Bahru
Kudat
Kota Kinabalu
Sandakan
Miri
Bintulu
Sibu
Kuching

MALAYSIA IN 2012
Promises of Reform; Promises Met?

Graham K. Brown

The year 2012 in Malaysia was one of expectations: expectations of reform, set in place by Prime Minister Najib Tun Razak's National Day speech in 2011 when he had committed his government to a swathe of legal reform; and expectations of an election, which many had expected to be called in late 2011 and which, when that failed to arrive, few doubted would be called during the course of 2012. As it turned out, no election was called in 2012, although political parties across the divide remained in virtual campaigning mode throughout the year. By mid-2012, however, the Barisan Nasional (BN) government was sufficiently confident that it had met the expectations of reform — and, no doubt, with an eye to the elections which must be called in the first half of 2013 — that it launched a campaign slogan of *Janji Ditepati*: Promises Met.

Throughout his tenure as prime minister, Najib has been caught in a reformist dilemma. In early 2012, the *Economist* carried an appraisal of Najib that concluded he was "a well-intentioned man [who] has reformed just enough to alienate his own party and too little to convince the centre ground".[1] While it is beyond the scope of this article to evaluate just how far Najib's reformist drive is "well-intentioned" against how far it is driven by the necessity of reform in the face of an increasingly articulate and demanding electorate, it is clear that in many ways political and economic developments in 2012 embodied this dilemma. The view that the BN must reform or die has been growing even among government supporters, but this imperative is arguably particularly strong for Najib, who is unpopular among large sections of his party and who continues to be tainted by allegations of corruption, from the labyrinthine web of allegations surrounding the purchase of Scorpene submarines during his tenure as Defence

GRAHAM K. BROWN is Reader in Social and Policy Sciences, Institute of Policy Research, University of Bath, United Kingdom.

Minister and the murder of the Mongolian translator Shaariibuu Altantuuya in relation to the deal to the behaviour and habits of his wife, Rosmah Mansor. The latter's purported profligacy is deeply unpopular with sections of the public who increasingly see her as a Malaysian Imelda Marcos. For the BN as a whole, 2012 was arguably one long campaign year. For Najib, the necessity of winning popular support was not just a matter of party survival but personal political survival.

Legal Reform

In a speech on the eve of the annual Independence Day celebrations in August 2011, Najib had promised a swathe of reforms that appeared to address the perennial concerns of liberal opposition parties and civil society organizations. Most noteworthy was his promise to replace the notorious Internal Security Act (ISA), which allowed for effectively limitless detention without trial on the order of the Home Minister, and to lift three declarations of Emergency that date back decades but had never been lifted. But he also expressed a broader commitment to re-examine legislation that impinged upon the desire for a "more open and dynamic democracy". By the time of the 2012 Independence Day, the emergency declarations had indeed been lifted, the ISA repealed and replaced, and a number of other reforms enacted. Promises Met (*Janji Ditepati*) was the theme of the 2012 celebrations, and these reforms, on face value, gave the claim credence.

While few commentators dispute that the legal reforms of 2012 remove a number of impediments to fundamental liberties in the country, many opposition politicians, civil society activists, and commentators have cried foul over the reforms, arguing that what was conceded in terms of extra liberties has been more than made up for by new restrictions.

The replacement for the ISA, the Security Offences (Special Measures) Act (SOSMA), has met with a mixed reception from civil society. The new act contains an explicit commitment that "no person shall be arrested and detained … solely for his political belief or political activity",[2] a clause that was welcomed by many civil society organizations. Moreover, the Home Minister's powers to order extended detention without trial in the ISA were not renewed in SOSMA and the period under which the police are able to detain individuals for security reasons has been shortened from the sixty days of ISA to twenty-eight days, equivalent, as government spokesmen observed, to the powers of the British police under anti-terrorism legislation. In a rather more unusual legal requirement, however, the Act insists that anyone tried but acquitted under the Act must be held in custody if the prosecution appeals, and that they should remain in custody throughout the entire appeal process. With a full appeal process potentially taking years, critics claimed that the new law revoked formal detention-without-trial powers but created a new informal system in its place. In addition, the Act perpetuates the BN tradition of wording security legislation in vague ways that allow for a wide and broad range of interpretations. SOSMA defines security offences as "an act prejudicial to national security and public safety", while associated amendments to the Penal Code define additional security offences very broadly as "activity detrimental to parliamentary democracy".[3]

As has arguably always been the case, while the ISA (and SOSMA as its successor) was the *bête noire* of the human rights movement, the arsenal of coercive legislation in Malaysia is embodied in a range of other acts, many of which have far greater impact on the day-to-day lives of ordinary Malaysians than the ISA and SOSMA. Along with SOSMA, the year 2012 saw the passage of a number of acts and amendments that tightened these more quotidian restrictions on individual liberties. The Peaceful Assembly Act, passed by parliament at the end of 2011 but gazetted in early February 2012, in many ways replicated the approach of SOSMA by removing some of the "headline" restrictions that had been the target of sustained criticisms but introducing new, potentially more restrictive mechanisms in their place. The Peaceful Assembly Act abolishes the previous requirement for police permits for any form of public assembly, although the organizers are obliged to notify the police at least ten days before the planned assembly and comply with any restrictions imposed. But the act also explicitly prohibits any form of street protest and prohibits non-citizens and children from taking part in any public assembly.[4] Fines for breaking any of these restrictions are set at up to RM10,000 (around US$3,000). Critics claim that the law actually gives the police greater power because although permits are no longer required, the police have absolute discretion in the restrictions they impose without judicial oversight.

Other major legislative changes of the year were less widely publicized but no less important amendments to the Evidence Act, the Election Offences Act, and the University and University Colleges Act. The amendments to the Evidence Act dealt with standards of evidence relating to online activity. Since the days of the Mahathir administration, the Malaysian government has been more cautious than its neighbour Singapore in regulating the Internet, largely due a commercially driven commitment not to censor the Internet. The main substance of the amendment was the insertion of a section (114A) that dealt with the "presumption of fact" in online publications and contained two controversial clauses: that anybody depicted online as being the publisher of online material is indeed presumed to be the publisher "unless the contrary is proved" (section 114A[1]); and, that the owner or possessor of a computer which is identified as the origin of an online publication is presumed to be the publisher, again unless the contrary is proved (section 114A[3]).[5] While the act was passed through parliament rapidly and without fanfare, opposition to the act quickly escalated, with critics accusing it of undermining the principle of innocence until proven guilty. The Malaysian Bar Council, which had expressed general but vague concerns about the provisions of SOSMA and the Peaceful Assembly Act, was much more explicit in calling for the repeal of this Act.[6]

The amendments to the Election Offences were passed through parliament equally quickly, and provoked subsequent condemnation. In particular, the deletion of a provision that election advertisements must carry the name and address of its publisher and printer was interpreted by the Bersih movement for electoral reform as giving impunity to "defamatory, racist, or sexist poster" and constituted a negative step in the drive to reform the electoral system (see below).[7] The amendment also restricted considerably the ability for party representatives to observe the polling process and to challenge the identity of intended voters.

Almost parenthetically, the Universities and University College Act was also revised to remove a prohibition on students joining political parties, although this was a moot point as the Court of Appeal had already ruled this provision unconstitutional in late 2011.[8]

Beyond the substance of the acts themselves, the legal reforms of 2012 raise two broader questions. Firstly, as mentioned above, civil society in Malaysia is questioning whether the legal reforms taken as a whole constitute progressive change in fundamental freedoms or whether they are simply old wine in new bottles. In some respects, however, asking the question this way obverts attention from a more subtle question: *how* have these reforms changed fundamental liberties in Malaysia? The answer to this seems to lie in the apparent "downstreaming" of coercive powers. Headline powers that allowed detention without trial of opposition leaders are gone, but the new measures are much more readily applicable to the everyday Malaysian discontented with BN rule. The infamous 1987 *Operation Lalang* when over a hundred opposition politicians and activists were detained without trial under the ISA is unlikely to be repeated, but the legal reforms make it much more risky for individual Malaysians to become actively involved in contentious politics, whether on the street or in the cybercafé.

The second question that the legal reforms raise is how far they are reflective of a broader political shift towards, in Najib's own words, a more "open and dynamic democracy", or whether they are rather an attempt to stave off such political reform through symbolic concessions. To begin to answer such questions, we need to look at the broader political dynamics of 2012.

Political Reform

As argued above, for the BN as a whole, reform is now largely accepted as a necessity to ensure its long-term survival. But for many within the coalition, and particularly in the dominant United Malays National Organization (UMNO), their short-term interests are endangered by reform. For Najib, however, his short-term political survival is dependent upon reform. Arguably only through winning the *rakyat* over to his reform agenda and delivering a resounding election victory, could he win his own party over to his continued leadership. Hence, Najib is in many ways setting himself alongside the *rakyat* against his own party. The tightrope act this entails was played out in full in 2012.

The year 2011 had been a year of high-street drama, with the second mass Bersih (Clean) rally prompting a pre-emptive lockdown of Kuala Lumpur by federal police and, in no small way, contributing to the formulation of the Peaceful Assemblies Act. The protest and its associated movement for electoral reform enjoy high levels of popular support among a wide swathe of the Malaysian public, irrespective of ethnicity, and the heavy-handed response to the 2011 rally had been widely criticized. After the rally, Najib had announced a Parliamentary Select Committee would look at electoral reform, and the committee, constituted by five BN MPs, three opposition MPs, and an independent, presented its report to parliament in March 2012. The report contained twenty-two recommendations, eighteen of which were agreed by all committee members irrespective of party, that covered areas from the automatic registration of new voters, greater flexibility in voting location, and mechanisms for easier voting for overseas Malaysia to a broader commitment to study the possibility of alternative electoral systems, including proportional representation. While these areas were uncontested, however, the opposition MPs on the committee sought to append a "minority report" that dealt with a further set of issues primarily relating to acquisition of voting rights by non-citizens and further measures to clean up the electoral role. When the Committee Report was tabled in parliament, the Speaker's refusal to accept this minority report led to a stand-off with opposition MPs; the Speaker ruled that the opposition clearly did not wish to debate the report and sent it straight to a vote without the minority report. Moreover, while the recommendations of the main report were consensual, critics within the opposition parties and civil society decried it for being, in the words of the Bar Council, "incomplete and inadequate".[9] The Bersih committee complained that while many of the proposals were positive, implementation was to be left to the Election Commission which, they charged, "has shown itself to be incapable or unwilling to initiate reforms".[10]

By early April, then, the confluence of the select committee report with the passage of the Election Offences Amendment Act had refocused public attention on electoral reform. The revelation that chairman and deputy chairman of the nominally apolitical Election Commission were both registered UMNO members hardly placated fears that electoral reform was heading backwards, not forwards. In this context, the preparation for the planned third Bersih rally later that month, dubbed Bersih 3.0, presented the government a challenge that embodied its reforming dilemma: whether to allow it to go ahead unfettered and accept the prospect of mass opposition activism in the national capital; or, to oppose it and risk further alienating the electorate. More specifically, the rally was, in Najib's own words, "the first test" for the new Peaceful Assembly Act. Public statements by both the Home Minister Hishamuddin Hussein and "Law Minister" Nazri Aziz[11] confirmed that the government would not oppose the rally as long as it complied with the Peaceful Assembly Act.

It may be that Najib and his supporters hoped that the new Act would take the sting out of the protest by corralling it into a specified venue, and to some extent the Bersih organizers appeared willing to play ball with this. On the one hand, the organizers complied with the Act's requirement to provide the police with notification of their intended venue, but the venue they chose — Dataran Merdeka (Independence Square) — was clearly chosen at least in part to test the limits of the new law. While the square is not a public road *per se* — and hence did not appear to fall under the explicit prohibition on street protests — the number of people expected at the venue would have necessarily spilled out onto the surrounding streets. The selection of the site did indeed test the limits of the law. On the one hand, the protestor organizers and their supporters noted that none of the provisions of the new Act allowed the police to *ban* an assembly from a particular venue, only to impose conditions. On the other hand, however, the act does oblige organizers to gain permission from the venue owner — in this case, the Kuala Lumpur City Hall (DBKL) — although no penalties are stipulated for failure to do so. Unsurprisingly, the mayor of Kuala Lumpur — a federal government appointee — refused permission for

Dataran Merdeka to be used. Subsequently, the police responded to the official notification with an official refusal to allow the protest to go ahead despite, as protestor organizers noted, no clear legal provisions for such a ruling to be made. With the Bersih committee and the DBKL deadlocked, the day of the protest arrived. Estimates of the size of the crowds that converged on central Kuala Lumpur vary significantly but unsurprisingly. Protest organizers claim 300,000 protestors;[12] a police spokesman estimates the figure at 25,000.[13] Barricades had been set up around Dataran Merdeka, Federal Reserve Units and water-cannon deployed, but some of the protestors broke through. While the police arrested around 500 people, this was far less than the number of arrests in the previous year's rally and all were released relatively quickly. Subsequently, however, opposition leader Anwar Ibrahim and two other opposition politicians were arrested and charged under the Peaceful Assembly Act; their trial is set for July 2013.[14]

While parliament refused to accept the "minority report" of the Parliamentary Select Committee, in June Najib bowed to increasing pressure over one particular issue and announced the creation of a Royal Commission of Inquiry on illegal immigrants in the East Malaysian state of Sabah. Sabah has long been recipient of high levels of international migration from Indonesia and the southern Philippines. The year 2010 recorded more than a quarter of the population of the state as non-citizens, most of whom are Muslim in a state where the largest indigenous groups have historically been Christian. Local politicians and activists have long alleged that many illegal immigrants gain citizenship under dubious circumstances in return for government support, under a scheme dubbed "Project IC".[15] The commission was formally constituted in November 2012, but its hearings are scheduled for 2013.

Beyond the high-election (and high-street) politics of the Bersih movement, the political reform agenda promoted by Najib struggled through 2012. High-profile corruption cases continued to beleaguer the BN. The "cowgate" scandal broke in late 2011 when it was claimed that a private company run by family members of Shahrizat Abdul Jalil, the Minister for Women, Family and Community Development had used government loans meant for the development of the domestic beef industry to buy luxury condominiums. Despite long protestations of denial of any wrongdoing, Shahrizat finally resigned her ministry in April 2012, although retained her position at the head of the Women's wing of UMNO. Her husband was charged with corruption shortly afterwards. Around the same time, the opposition Parti Keadilan Rakyat (PKR, or People's Justice Party) claimed to have evidence that the lavish engagement reception of

Najib's daughter in a luxury Kuala Lumpur hotel, costing around RM400,000, had been charged to the Prime Minister's Office. In December 2012, the release of the annual Transparency International corruption perceptions data carried mixed news for Malaysia; its ranking had improved six places on the overall Corruption Perception Index from 60th to 54th (although still far worse than its ranking a decade previously), but the country reportedly topped the Bribe Payers Survey that estimates the prevalence of bribery in thirty countries.[16]

Social Reform

Throughout 2012, the BN government continued its campaign of broad social reform under the rubric of the 1Malaysia slogan, a broad but fuzzy vision of ethnic and religious harmony. 1Malaysia initiatives, rolled out since 2010, had included cash hand-outs to poor families (BR1M, or Bantuan Rakyat 1Malaysia), health clinics in poor areas, and the creation of a chain of government-subsidized general stores dubbed Kedai Rakyat 1Malaysia (KR1M, or 1Malaysia People's Store). In July 2012, the government announced new initiatives for 1Malaysia bookstores and fabric stores. The purported link between initiatives such as these and the social reform goals of the 1Malaysia project remain ambiguous and ill-defined.

Despite the apparent good intentions of the 1Malaysia concept, ethnic and religious tensions in Malaysia remained high in 2012. Over recent years, a discourse has emerged among some conservative sections of Malay society purporting an underhand Christian plot to undermine Islam in Malaysia, politically and socially. In March, official agencies in the southern state of Johor appeared to lend their support to these claims when the state Education Department along with the state Mufti's office organized a seminar on "Strengthening the faith, the dangers of liberalism and pluralism and the threat of Christianization towards Muslims".[17] Protests from Christian groups saw the phrase over the "threat of Christianization" dropped from the seminar title, but state and federal officials refused to comment on the issue.[18]

Other perennial religious issues continued to simmer throughout 2012, including the controversy over the use of the word "Allah" to refer to God in Malay-language Christian bibles; and the debate over the implementation of *hudud* laws in the country. A long-standing goal of the opposition Pan-Malaysian Islamic Party (PAS), *hudud* is vehemently opposed by PAS' somewhat reluctant partner in the Paktan Rakyat opposition coalition, the Chinese-based Democratic Action Party (DAP). In 2011 Najib reaffirmed the BN's equally long-standing position that while *syariah* law applies to Muslims in Malaysia, *hudud* is not appropriate because of the country's multi-ethnic make-up,[19] but the BN lost few opportunities to raise the issue and to point out the inconsistencies between PAS' stand and the DAP's. Moreover, occasional mixed messages from within the BN emerged. In September 2012, the Minister for Islamic Affairs Jamil Khir Baharom appeared to contradict Najib by asserting in parliament that the implementation of *hudud* would not affect non-Muslims but that a "comprehensive study" must be done "before any form of *hudud* could be implemented".[20] Earlier in the year, an UMNO state assembly representative in the state of Johor had advocated the implementation of *hudud* in that state. Many commentators see the BN as quite deliberately sending out such mixed messages — in part to sow seeds of discord among the fragile opposition coalition, in part to strengthen the government's appeal among conservative Malay Muslims. Certainly, it achieved the latter; during the *hudud* spat, Nasharudin Mat Isa, a senior PAS member and former deputy president from the conservative wing of the party, explicitly called for PAS to leave the opposition coalition in the face of the DAP's opposition to *hudud*. Yet, whatever the political mileage in the debate, the net social impact of this controversy is decidedly negative.

Economic Reform

Despite global uncertainty, Malaysian economy grew well in 2012, early estimates suggesting a growth of around 5 per cent in GDP over the year. With Najib's attempt to roll back affirmative action under the rubric of the New Economic Model effectively stalled by vehement opposition from within his own party, continued economic reform focused instead on the parallel but less politicized Economic Transformation Programme (ETP) that is designed to help Malaysia escape the "middle income trap". While the country's economy has continued to grow throughout the global crisis, the government deficit escalated likewise, reaching RM484.6 billion (around US$150 billion) in the third quarter of 2012, up 10 per cent on the equivalent figure for 2011,[21] and equivalent to 51.8 per cent of GDP. At the end of the first quarter, when the figure stood closer to 54 per cent of GDP, both Standard & Poor's and Moody's threatened to downgrade the country's credit rating.[22]

In no small part, this increasing deficit was due to extensive subsidies, particularly on fuel and, to a lesser extent, basic food stuffs; subsidies accounted for around 18 per cent of government operating expenditure over the year. While the government is committed to reducing these subsidies and implementing new consumption taxes to broaden its revenue base under the ETP's Strategic Reform Initiatives, in the extended election fever of 2012, it was never likely to introduce unpopular economic measures. Indeed, in his budget speech in September 2012, Najib (who also holds the Finance Ministry) acknowledged that reductions in subsidies are politically sensitive; cuts in the fuel subsidy in 2008 had met with furious protests in Kuala Lumpur and other cities. Instead, the 2012 budget was an unabashedly electioneering budget, with a raft of populist measures, including a second round of RM500 (US$160) cash transfers to low-income families under the BR1M scheme and RM250 (US$80) to unmarried people on low incomes, a cut in income taxes and a bonus payment equivalent to 1.5 month's salary for public sector workers.

Stumbling Government; Stumbling Opposition

While the package of BN-led reforms in the political, social, and economic realms all stuttered in 2012, the opposition movement built around the post-1998 slogan of *Reformasi* (reform) was unable to capitalize on these failures to strengthen its own position considerably in the country. The opposition began the year on a high, with the acquittal of its totemic leader Anwar Ibrahim from a charge of sodomy, bringing back memories of his imprisonment in 1999 on similar charges. Political motivations had been widely read into the charges. While the verdict allowed Anwar to claim a victory for justice and, perhaps more importantly, to free him from the time-consuming activities of the trial, the government was also quick to make political mileage out of the verdict, claiming that it gainsaid the constant opposition charges that the police and the judiciary were politically biased.

In large part, the failure of the opposition to build upon the stumbling performance of the BN in 2012 was due to the increasingly evident tensions within the opposition coalition, both between and within its component parties. As discussed above in relation to the *hudud* issue, PAS and DAP have never sat particularly comfortably in the PR coalition, and are only really held together by Anwar's PKR occupying the centre ground. While PKR is the mainstay of the coalition, however, the party was over the course of the year increasingly beset by a distancing of its leadership from its grassroots support. Bringing together a broad alliance of civil society activists and political reformers from across the spectrum, PKR was always something of a coalition in itself, but Anwar Ibrahim was an effective glue that bound the party together. Increasingly, however, Anwar is losing his sheen even within the party. The BN has long made much of the concentration of Anwar's family members among the high echelons of the party to claim that PKR is not free of the nepotism of which it accuses the government. The sense that Anwar and his close confidantes are out of touch with the rest of the party has, however, started to penetrate the ranks. In the East Malaysian state of Sabah, for instance, the party scored an apparent victory with the defection of two high-profile BN MPs, Wilfred Bumburing and Lajim Ukin. Both MPs became "Pakatan-friendly" independents rather than officially join PKR. While Anwar was able to trump this as a political victory at the national level, the realization at the local level that the two MPs would most likely be parachuted in as PKR candidates for the upcoming election generated considerable disillusionment among grassroots activists who had long been campaigning against Bumburing and Lajim themselves. More broadly, factional divides within the party became increasingly evident, highlighted by a very public feud between party deputy president and Anwar loyalist Azmin Ali and Khalid Ibrahim, the party Treasurer-General and current chief minister of the Pakatan-controlled state of Selangor.

Conclusions

For Malaysia, the year 2012 was one of held breath, with the country expectantly awaiting an election that never arrived. Across the board, longer term government reforms stalled or were displaced by measures that appeared primarily designed to shore up the short-term survival of the BN, whether through legal measures like the non-too-subtle amendments to the Election Offences Act or through the financial inducements in the budget give-away. For some within the government ranks, the short-term political gains from stirring up the *hudud* issue and stoking tensions within the opposition coalition outweighed the longer term negative impacts the controversy has on religious and ethnic tolerance in the country. In a country where democracy activists often bemoan the exceptionally short official campaign periods for elections, the year 2012 was if nothing else a salutary warning of the dangers of overly long campaign periods as well.

Notes

1. "Najib at bay", *The Economist*, 4 February 2012; available online at <http://www.economist.com/node/21546026>.
2. Security Offences (Special Measures) Act 2012, Part II, 4(3). For the full text, see <http://www.parlimen.gov.my/files/billindex/pdf/2012/DR152012E.pdf>.

3. For more discussion of the new act, see Mickey Spiegel, "Smoke and mirrors: Malaysia's 'new' internal security act", *Asia-Pacific Bulletin* no. 167, Washington, D.C., EastWest Center <http://www.hrw.org/sites/default/files/related_material/2012_Malaysia_EastWest.pdf>.
4. Peaceful Assemblies Act 2012, Part II, Section 4. The Act lists certain types of assembly, such as funeral processions and wedding assemblies, to which these measures variously do not apply. For full text, see <http://www.parlimen.gov.my/files/billindex/pdf/2011/DR422011E.pdf>.
5. For the full text of the Act, see <http://www.parlimen.gov.my/files/billindex/pdf/2012/DR162012E.pdf>.
6. See press statement at <http://www.malaysianbar.org.my/press_statements/press_release_repeal_section_114a_of_the_evidence_act_1950.html>.
7. "Amendment to the Election Offences Act 1954", Press statement by Bersih 2.0, 20 April 2012 <http://www.globalbersih.org/2012/04/20/20-april-2012-bersih-2-0-press-statement/>. For the full text of the amendment, see <http://www.parlimen.gov.my/files/billindex/pdf/2012/DR042012E.pdf>.
8. "Court rules UUCA section 15(5)A violates freedom of expression", *The Star*, 31 October 2011 <http://thestar.com.my/news/story.asp?file=/2011/10/31/nation/20111031122643&sec=nation>.
9. "Final report of PSC incomplete, and inadequate to achieve free and fair elections", press statement by the Malaysian Bar Council, 4 April 2012; available online at <http://www.malaysianbar.org.my/press_statements/press_release_final_report_of_psc_incomplete_and_inadequate_to_achieve_free_and_fair_elections.html>.
10. "Highly likely that electoral fraud will continue", *Bersih* press statement, reproduced in *Aliran Monthly* 2012 (4) <http://aliran.com/9491.html>.
11. Technically, Nazri is minister without portfolio, but he is universally referred to as "de facto law minister".
12. "300,000 at Bersih 3.0, Ambiga claims success", *Malaysiakini*, 28 April 2012 <http://www.malaysiakini.com/news/196344> [subscription required].
13. "Police violence marks Malaysia reform rally", *Aljazeera*, 28 April 2012 <http://www.aljazeera.com/news/asia-pacific/2012/04/20124286221449574.html>.
14. "Anwar and Azmin charged in court over April 28 Bersih rally", *The Star*, 22 May 2012 <http://thestar.com.my/news/story.asp?file=/2012/5/22/nation/20120522094202&sec=nation>.
15. IC is the common acronym for the identity cards that bestow Malaysians with citizenship and voting rights.
16. "Malaysia tops bribery table", *Wall Street Journal*, 11 December 2012 <http://blogs.wsj.com/corruption-currents/2012/12/11/malaysia-tops-bribery-table/>. For TI data on Malaysia, see <http://www.transparency.org/country#MYS>.
17. Pemantapan Aqidah, Bahaya Liberalisme dan Pluralisme serta Ancaman Kristianisasi terhadap Umat Islam.

18. "Do we have faith in the politics of fear?", *Aliran* media statement, 30 March 2012 <http://aliran.com/8681.html>.
19. "Najib: No to hudud in Malaysia", *The Star*, 25 September 2011 <http://thestar.com.my/news/story.asp?file=/2011/9/25/nation/9571868&sec=nation>.
20. "Hudud will not impact non-Muslim, minister says", *The Malaysian Insider*, 24 October 2012 <http://www.themalaysianinsider.com/malaysia/article/hudud-will-not-impact-non-muslims-minister-says/>.
21. Bank Negara, *Monthly Statistical Bulletin*, December 2012.
22. "Malaysia faces credit ratings cut", Channel News Asia, 27 April 2012 <http://www.channelnewsasia.com/stories/economicnews/view/1197885/1/.html>.

SHADES OF CITIZENSHIP
Betwixt the Civic and the Ethnic[1]

Lee Hock Guan

In 1991, Mahathir Mohamad, then Prime Minister of Malaysia, declared his aim to transform Malaysia into a fully developed nation by the year 2020.[2] To achieve this goal, he identified nine strategic challenges that must be overcome, a key challenge being the creation of a united Malaysian nation, or a "bangsa Malaysia", that would cultivate an inclusive national citizenship. Subsequently, several non-Malay individuals interpreted the concept to mean a future community of equal citizens where Malays would no longer possess special rights. The Malay reaction was initially low-keyed,[3] but gradually ballooned to strident criticisms of non-Malays who equated "bangsa Malaysia" with equal rights for all citizens, regardless of ethnicity. On the contrary, they insisted that their special position and special rights, enshrined in the Constitution, cannot be questioned.

The "bangsa Malaysia" controversies highlighted once more the long-standing contest between the ethnic groups over the rights to citizenship status and the status of citizenship rights in Malaysia. To better understand the notion of "bangsa Malaysia" and the heated debates over it, this chapter will consider the colonial constructions of membership and disputes over acquisition of and terms of membership status in the peninsula. British indirect rule identified the Malay states with a particular ethnicity, defined by indigeneity, and established ethnic hierarchies between natives and non-natives in the colony. Consequently, colonial authorities used a mixture of *jus sanguinis* (right of blood) and *jus soli* (right of the soil) principles to classify the Malays and non-Malays into different classes of membership that have access to differential rights and privileges. Based on the principle of *jus sanguinis*, the Malays as the indigenous group were conferred special rights and preferential treatment, which were denied to the Chinese who were regarded as an immigrant group. Arguably then, British colonial policies

---

LEE HOCK GUAN is Senior Fellow at the Institute of Southeast Asian Studies, Singapore.

and compromises contributed extensively to the development of a Malaysian citizenship that is wedged betwixt a civic element that regards citizenship as an effect of membership of a nation and an ethnic element that regards citizenship as an effect of membership of a native or non-native group.

Subjects, Protected Persons, and Resident Aliens in Pre-war Malaya

Prior to the Japanese invasion of Malaya, the peninsula was administered in the form of two distinct colonial entities: the Crown Colony of the Straits Settlements[4] and the British Protectorates of the Federated and Unfederated Malay States.[5] By and large, the British colonial state classified an individual's membership status in the Malay States and Straits Settlements according to *jus sanguinis*, *jus soli*, and place of origins. Those who qualified were classified into three classes of membership: subjects of Malay Rulers, British subjects, and Protected Persons. The three classes of membership were accorded differential access to residence and rights. Most importantly, the overwhelming majority of Chinese in the colony did not qualify for membership in British Malaya and remained as resident aliens.

In a Malay State, a Malay[6] born in that State or born of a father who was a subject of the State would automatically qualify to be a subject of the Ruler of the State. Another category of persons who qualified to be subjects of the Ruler of a State was any person who belonged to an aboriginal tribe resident in that State. While the Malays in the Federated and Unfederated States were subjects of the Malay Rulers, Straits Settlements-born Malays were granted British subjecthood and thus, in principle, owed their allegiance to the British Crown.

In the Malay States, the principles of *jus sanguinis* and *jus soli* were not extended to the Chinese as the British and Malay authorities regarded them as belonging to an immigrant community (or *kaum pendatang*) that did not "belong" to the peninsula. That the place of origin of a person mattered was confirmed by the fact that it was generally much easier for local-born Malays, or even Indonesians, to become naturalized subjects of a Malay State than for Chinese born in that State. In addition, subjects of a Ruler were divided into Native and non-Native subjects, and only Malays were eligible for the status of Native subjects with access to varying privileges of that status.

In the prevailing British concept of nationality, the primary determinant of allegiance was *jus soli* such that all persons born in a Crown territory owed allegiance to the British Crown. Accordingly, since the Straits Settlements were a Crown Colony, then Straits-born Chinese (Straits Chinese, for short) would qualify to become British subjects.[7] While in principle a person could also attain British subjecthood through naturalization, it was rarely employed in the Straits Settlements and thus few foreign-born Chinese became naturalized British subjects. In the Straits Settlements, similar to the Malay States, British policy designated their Malay subjects as Native subjects and the Straits Chinese as non-Native subjects.

Through the various treaty agreements with the Malay Rulers, the British assumed indirect control over the Malay States, which were converted into protectorates where the Rulers retained their sovereignty. Because the Malay States were not under the sovereignty of the British Crown, the *jus soli* principle to attain British subjecthood was not extended to persons born in the Malay States. This meant that Malay States-born Chinese could not become subjects of the Rulers or qualify to become British subjects.

In theory, under the then British Nationality Law, a person born in a British Protectorate would be classified as a Protected Person. In the Malay States context this aspect of the British Nationality Law, while debated and considered, was in actual fact sparingly enforced. In part, this was because the Malaya situation was complicated by the Nationalist Chinese Government support of the 1929 Chinese Nationality Law, which asserted, "that persons of the Chinese race, wherever born, were considered technically as subjects of China".[8] Consequently, while the British authorities could offer to a Malay State-born Chinese a Protected Person status, the latter could choose to acquire a China nationality instead.[9] This was further compounded by the British's lukewarm enthusiasm to push the Protected Person issue, and thus until the late 1930s only a minority of Malay States-born Chinese acquired Protected Person status.

Before the Second World War, the Straits Chinese and Chinese Protected Persons together constituted a small minority of the total Chinese population in British Malaya. Membership status was denied to the Chinese who were China-born and as well as to the majority of those born in the Malay States. The British colonial state thus classified most Chinese as resident aliens and classified them as nationals of China who were in Malaya on a temporary basis with no intention of settling down permanently. Chinese resident aliens possessed no right of abode in Malaya and could be deported back to China for various criminal or political offences. The Straits Chinese, as British subjects, enjoyed certain rights such as the right of abode in the Straits Settlements, but not in the Malay States, and the colonial state's protection. Since the British did not regard Chinese Protected Persons as a nationality, in fact a Protected Person was eligible only for a certificate of nationality in lieu of a British passport; they did not enjoy the same rights or protection as the Straits Chinese.[10]

Varying British policy towards the Malays and Chinese was also influenced by the terms of the various treaty agreements with the Malay Rulers and by the prevailing British conception of Malay as the indigenous community and Chinese as a foreign community. Up to the Second World War, the British treated the Chinese as foreigners who did not "belong" to Malaya and thus did not feel they owed them any obligations or treated them the equals of Malays. The Chinese community had to essentially fend for and look after themselves, and their inferior status was clearly exemplified by certain British policies and practices towards the Straits Chinese who were British subjects. That was most apparent in the exclusion of the Chinese from the administrative ranks of the colonial service — even in the Straits Settlements, which was a Crown Colony. When the British began to admit non-Europeans into the lower ranks of the administrative service, only Malays as Native subjects were recruited while the Straits Chinese regarded as non-Native subjects were excluded.

The Malay Rulers were recognized as the heads of sovereign governments with whom the British authorities negotiated and signed treaty agreements. Designating themselves as the Malays' temporary trustees, or "protectors", British officials repeatedly claimed that they were administering the Malay States on behalf and for the benefits of the Malays. The notion of trusteeship[11] influenced the ways the British conducted themselves in their relationships with the Malay Rulers, and the Malays in general. Hugh Clifford, one of the earliest Malayan pioneers, insisted that "the public servants to whom is entrusted the task of administering and developing" the Malay States should be aware "that the welfare and well-being of the indigenous inhabitants [i.e. Malays] must always be the first care of the Federal and State Governments".[12]

Thus, in part to fulfill their trustee obligations, the colonial government pursued what could generally be regarded as a "pro-Malay" policy. In the Straits Settlements, Malays as Native subjects were granted Malay Customary Land Rights, although these were annulled eventually. In the educational sector, British authorities established Malay educational institutions to provide free education for the Malays, albeit only on a modest scale. The colonial state also provided scholarships for qualified Malays to pursue higher education both locally and overseas. The "pro-Malay" preferential policy was most apparent in the employment of Malays into the colonial bureaucracy. Preserving the "Malay" character of the Malay States led the British to assume the tutelage role to teach and groom the ruling elites and their male progenitors in the business of governing: the Malay College Kuala Kangsar[13] was established in 1905 for this purpose. In the aftermath of the First World War, several factors led the British to expand their recruitment of Malays such that by "the early 1930s there had appeared among the Malays a group, still extremely small but growing, of English-educated government servants".[14]

The view that Malays were the definitive people of Malaya were reinforced by various policies demanded and practices implemented by the Malay ruling elites. A prevalent practice in the Malay States, especially in the Unfederated Malay States, was to make it mandatory that only Malays were eligible to become officers in the local administrative bureaucracy.[15] Moreover, in the Unfederated Malay States, since very few Europeans were employed in the local governments, their Malay character was largely preserved. Hence, various state policies and practices in the Malay States entrenched the status of the Malays as Native subjects of the Rulers who were entitled to special rights and preferential treatment.

Nevertheless, other than the employment opportunities in the administrative service, the British largely failed to fulfil their obligations to protect and look after the welfare of the Malays while rapidly developing the Malay States. The vast majority of Malays remained poor peasants eking a subsistence living off their land in the rural areas, which, due to British policies of reducing the impact of and rate of socio-economic change at the village level, were largely underdeveloped.[16] In terms of the non-European populations, the Chinese became the foremost beneficiaries of the rapid economic development of the Malay States. Thus when the British decided to increase their recruitment of non-Malay British subjects, specifically the Straits Chinese, into the lower echelon of the colonial service, sections of the Malay community felt threatened and appealed to the British to safeguard their interests. Indeed, the Malays acutely felt threatened by the Chinese when the Straits Chinese demanded equal rights in the early 1930s.[17] Before the Second World War then, emerging Malay nationalists were already growing wary of Chinese economic dominance and were especially suspicious of the Straits Chinese demands for equal rights. Malay nationalists felt that developments in the first three decades of the twentieth century showed that the British had not lived up to their trustee role, with the economy largely under the control of Europeans and Chinese while the majority of Malays were left behind, stuck in the impoverished peasant economy.

Malayan Union, *Tanah Melayu*

During the Japanese Occupation interlude, British colonial officials began to explore and debate the idea of reconstituting Malaya into a unitary nation-state with a common national citizenship for all those who qualified.[18] While British post-war policy intended to amalgamate the Straits Settlements and Malay States into a unitary nation-state, there was no consensus in terms of how to reconstitute Malaya. Many proposals and opinions were presented, and they "can be grouped under one of two headings: those in favour of making the old system work better, and those advocating a break with the past".[19] The former insisted that the British must live up to their trusteeship role of protecting and preserving the Malay special position and that Malaya was and must remain the Land of the Malays (Tanah Melayu).[20] Those who advocated a break with the past proposed the creation of a common national citizenship where every fully recognized citizen would have equality of rights, regardless of ethnicity or place of birth.[21]

The Malayan Union Plan proposed to construct a citizenship that "would not be confined to the Malays, but would also be open to persons of whatever race, who may have been born in the country or who have genuinely adopted Malaya as their home".[22] Several existing factors convinced the British that a future Malaya was best served by granting the majority of Chinese Malayan citizenship. The Malayan Union Plan projected a generous set of criteria for the acquisition of a Malayan citizenship.[23] It was clear that these liberal citizenship provisions would enable nearly all Straits Chinese and Chinese Protected Persons, and the majority of Chinese resident aliens to acquire Malayan citizenship. The Malayan Union Plan also proposed that every fully recognized Malayan citizen be conferred "with all the rights and obligations which that term implies" and contended that "no one must rely upon past privilege, or regard Malaya simply as a source of material wealth".[24] The rationale was that political equality would only achieve universality in Malaya if Malayan Chinese citizens were granted the same bundle of rights as their Malay counterparts.

The extension of Malayan citizenship status to the Chinese would carry with it complete equality of rights including admission to the administrative civil service, which the Straits Chinese had demanded and the Malays resisted. Proposals were made by the British to recruit non-Malay Malayan citizens into the higher echelons of the administrative service, which previously was the exclusive domain of the Malays, especially in the Federated and Unfederated Malay States. The rationale was that if in the Malayan democratic polity all the ethnic groups equally shared in the tasks of administering and governing, then there would be racial harmony as no ethnic group would feel discriminated against.

While planning to create a common Malayan citizenship, the British policy-makers were also cognizant of the post-war Malay anxieties regarding their special position and the Chinese economic dominance. Malays indeed feared that the Chinese might just overwhelm them; already economically and, if the Chinese were granted equal rights, politically as well. They also viewed the opening up of the civil service to the non-Malays as violating the symbol and substance of the Malay-based polity. The British evidently did not entirely ignore and abandon their obligations to the Malays as the Malayan Union White Paper reiterated the need to introduce policy measures to alleviate the Malay economic standing as well as protect their political dominance. What was not included in the White Paper were proposals that could be construed as supporting and entrenching the idea of Malay special position or that their special position would entitle them to a different category of rights, namely special rights.

The proposed Malayan citizenship was at its core based on a civic form of citizenship where all those who acquired Malayan citizen would be conferred with equality of rights, regardless of ethnicity and place of origin. The Malayan Union Plan was designed to universalize civic citizenship in Malaya that could act as a unifying factor in its effect on the many diverse peoples. Besides being inclusive, the Malayan civic citizenship was also ethnically sensitive in that the White Paper recognized the need to address the increasing ethnic inequalities in the society.

The Malays, led by the United Malays National Organization (UMNO), mounted a successful campaign against the Malayan Union Plan. They raised two critical objections. First, they were against the plan to establish a new centralized government in which the Malay Rulers would forfeit their sovereignties to the British Crown; that is, the Malay States would be converted from protectorates into a crown colony. Their second objection was against the idea and the liberal terms for acquiring a common civic citizenship. They argued that the Malayan Union Plan would breach the various treaty obligations that bounded the British, legally and morally, to preserve the Malay special position and Malay character and identity of the Malay States.

Reacting to the Malayan Union proposals to create a civic citizenship, Onn Ja'afar, the founder-president of UMNO, declared:

> We know very well that there is not only one race staying in Malaya, there are also other Asiatic races inhabiting this land. We have kindly allowed them to stay here but now they have even started to clamour for our land. But notwithstanding all their attempts we shall always maintain that this land belongs to us. I speak so because I notice that the other

> races in the peninsula affirm that they have the right to demand equality of treatment. Whatever comes we will never consent to this. We wish to make them understand that they are only tenants of the house but not the owners.[25]

UMNO regarded the Malay States to be the domain of the Malays and that since Malays have no alternative allegiance or other country, which they could regard as their homeland, they occupied a special position and possessed rights, which must be safeguarded. In contrast, they insisted that the Chinese were immigrants, or *pendatang*, from another country and thus were "lodgers" who could not and should not be treated as the equal of their Malay "landlords". UMNO thus strongly rejected a Malayan citizenship that would endow every citizen with equality of rights, regardless of ethnicity and place of origins.

The Federation of Malaya Agreement

Several factors contributed to the defeat of the Malayan Union Plan and the subsequent establishmcnt of the Federation of Malaya (Persekutuan Tanah Melayu) Agreement. Although the Federation Agreement retained the British objectives to create a central government and a common citizenship for all who accepted Malaya as their homeland, it also made several key concessions to UMNO and the Malay Rulers. Indeed, "the special position of Malays must be safeguarded" was one of the key concessions made and which dictated the Federation Agreement Working Committee proceedings.[26] The Federation Agreement restored many aspects and features of the pre-war Malay States: the individuality of each of the Malay States, the sovereignty of the Malay Rulers, and measures to safeguard Malay special position. Most importantly, the Federation Agreement abandoned the notion of a civic Malayan citizenship for all and radically altered the terms for the Chinese to acquire citizenship status, making it very difficult for them to acquire Federation citizenship. The Malays essentially were only willing to accept as Federation citizens Chinese who were British subjects, even then with stringent conditions added.[27] For Chinese Protected Persons and resident aliens to become naturalized Federation citizens, the terms were such that few could qualify. In addition, Chinese applicants would have to show that they were "truly Malaya minded" and of good conduct, and intend to settle permanently in Malaya and speak either Malay or English.

Malays would automatically acquire Federation citizenship through the provision that citizenship would be granted to any person who is a subject of the Malay Rulers. Given the existing definition of Malay, Indian Muslims and

Arabs who had intermarried with Malays and Indonesians would also qualify for Federation citizenship status. While the majority of Malays, around 2 million, automatically became Federation citizens, only a small fraction of the Chinese acquire Federation citizenship; an estimate was that only 320,000 out of nearly 2 million (about 16 per cent) Chinese attained Federation citizens.[28] In the Federation of Malaya polity then, Malay political dominance was ensured by the fact that Malay citizens would make up more than 80 per cent of the total citizenry in the future Federation.

The Malay citizens' numerical majority over the Chinese was further strengthened by the establishment of a Federation polity that restored selected features of the pre-war Malay Protected States. The sovereignty and independence of the Rulers of the Malay States were to a certain extent reinstated. Regaining their position as legal sovereigns also meant that the British Crown would have to work together with the nine Rulers to create the future Federation polity. A British High Commissioner would exercise the executive powers of the federal government, but he would be assisted by an executive council where Malay members predominated. Malay political dominance was obvious in the former Federated and Unfederated states' local governments. The executive authority of each Malay State would be exercised by the Ruler of that State where a State Executive Council would assist him; the State Executive Council should consist of at least of five members and again with a Malay majority. Hence the structure and composition of the Federation polity would ensure that in the Malay States were restored their Malay character and dominance.

Significantly, the Federation Agreement did not contain any provisions to ensure the fundamental rights and liberties of citizenship, but, instead, included provisions to safeguard the special position and privileges of the Malay community. The responsibility to look after the special position of the Malays was delegated to the British High Commissioner who was required to safeguard "the special position of the Malays and of the legitimate interests of the other communities".[29]

British officials, however, were aware that two Federation provisions could be viewed as overt discrimination between races. One, the differential treatment in the automatic qualification for Federation citizenship between Malays, Straits Chinese, and Chinese who were not British subjects, and two, the principle of common citizenship and of its relationship to assurances that the special position of Malays would be safeguarded. While the Malays would automatically qualify for Federal citizenship by birth alone, the majority of Chinese could not become Federation citizens because of the stringent criteria imposed on them: even for

Chinese who were British subjects, to acquire citizenship the *jus soli* principle was not sufficient as additional conditions were imposed. In their defence, British officials claimed that the usage of some distinctions between racial categories in the automatic qualification for Federation citizenship was consistent with the "fundamental principle that political rights in Malaya should be extended to all those who regard Malaya as their real home and as the object of their loyalty".[30] In other words, British officials skirted around the racial discrimination accusation by claiming that the majority of Chinese would be denied citizenship because they did not regard Malaya as their homeland and country of allegiance and not because of their place of origin.

With regard to the measures introduced to safeguard Malay special position, the argument was that the special measures "designed to safeguard the Malay race have always been envisaged as operating in relation to specific matters, amongst which citizenship has not (repeat not) been included".[31] The specific matters referred to Malay reserved land, free education, and employment in the public sector. This would suggest that, for the British, the measures to safeguard Malay special position and interests in the Federation Agreement were designed to address specific Malay needs and would in no way create a special category of rights for the Malays as a consequence of their special position. British officials indeed asserted that since the common citizenship created would confer all who qualified with equality of rights, it would rule out discrimination based on ethnicity.

In contrast, UMNO held different views. For UMNO, the Malays were the definite people of the peninsula such that the country belonged to them; in other words, Malaya is Tanah Melayu. It thus would suffice for Malays to automatically qualify for citizenship by birth alone. Also, since Malays are the "landlords" it would be for them to decide who among the Chinese they would accept into the Federation. UMNO also did not see a conflict between the principle of civic citizenship and measures to safeguard Malay special rights since they were of the view that the Chinese being *pendatang* and tenants should not be expected to be treated as the equal of the Malays, their "landlords". Hence many in UMNO viewed that Malays should have "special rights" because of their native status.

The defeat of the Malayan Union Plan marked a major turning point in the development of the concept and practice of citizenship in the peninsula. In the Federation Agreement, the UMNO leadership did make a concession to the British colonial state — the extension of a limited citizenship to a limited number of Chinese. The recognition of Malay special position and safeguards to protect it, however, were included in the Federation Agreement. Hence, while the Malayan Union Plan would have created only one class of citizen, the Federation Agreement created a citizenship that included the notion of special rights for Malays as a consequence of their native status.

Construction and Consolidation of the "Historic Bargain"

On March 1956 the Alliance Party[32] established the Alliance Ad Hoc Political Working Committee to draw up a common memorandum for the Merdeka constitutional negotiations. The English-educated leaders of the UMNO, Malayan Chinese Association (MCA), and Malayan Indian Congress (MIC) dominated the working committee.[33] While there were obvious points of disagreement between UMNO, its coalition partners, and among members of each party, the Alliance English-educated leaders were given the "mandate" to bargain for their respective parties. The constitutional compromises were accordingly the result of a "gentlemen's agreement" among the English-educated elites of UMNO, MCA, and MIC. It was also apparent that in the constitutional negotiations the British authorities gave the Alliance constitutional proposals the most legitimacy and consideration.[34] Consequently, the 1957 Merdeka Constitution could be construed as a product of negotiations and compromises between UMNO, MCA, and MIC, and between the Alliance Party, Malay Rulers, and British authorities.

As with the Malayan Union Plan and Federation Agreement, two intensely contested issues in the Merdeka constitutional negotiations were with regard to equal citizenship and Malay special position. The majority opinion in UMNO wanted to stick to the 1948 Federation Agreement terms: for the Chinese, limited application of the principle of *jus soli* and stringent naturalization criteria, and for the Malays, principle of *jus sanguinis* as the sole criterion and measures to safeguard Malay special position. A vocal group in UMNO, in fact, held fast to the view not to grant citizenship status to the Chinese.[35] The party's manifesto, The Basis of UMNO's Struggle (Dasar Perjuangan UMNO),[36] avowed that UMNO would strive "for the privileges, sovereignty, and priority (*hak, kedaulatan, keistimewaan*) of Malays as the owners of this country", but also acknowledged that non-Malay citizens would receive "specified" rights. The MCA, on the other hand, insisted on a liberal application of the principle of *jus soli* and the adoption of a common civic citizenship where every fully recognized citizen would be endowed with equal political, economic, and cultural rights.[37]

The oft-repeated "historic bargain" made between UMNO and MCA was this: UMNO would agree to a liberal application of the principle of *jus soli* and in exchange the MCA would support measures to safeguard the Malay special position. The liberal application of the principle of *jus soli* proposed by the Alliance included: automatic citizenship qualification of all those born in Malaya on and after the date of independence, while those Chinese born in Malaya before independence would qualify if they have resided in the country for five out of seven years preceding the date of application for citizenship. For foreign-born Chinese they would "before, on or after the appointed date qualify after a period of eight out of twelve years".[38] Thus, the majority of Chinese would gradually acquire citizenship status in Malay(si)a.[39] The Alliance constitutional memorandum also proposed that all citizens be accorded equal rights, privileges, and opportunities and that there must not be discrimination on grounds of race or creed.

In return for enabling the majority of Chinese to acquire citizenship status, the Alliance memorandum upheld that Malays have a special position as a consequence of their being the original sons of the land and because of the terms of the various treaty agreements. The Malay(si)an Sultan would be assigned the constitutional responsibility to safeguard the special position of the Malays and reserve for the "Malays a reasonable proportion of lands, posts in public service, permits to engage in business or trade, where such permits are restricted and controlled by law, grant scholarships and such similar privileges accorded by the Government, [and] ... in pursuance of this special responsibility, the Government would not infringe on the legitimate interests of the other communities or adversely affect or diminish the rights and privileges at present enjoyed by them".[40]

The Alliance's proposal on the Malay special position was, after much heated debates, included in the Merdeka Constitution as Article 153:

(1) It shall be in the responsibility of the Yang Di-Pertuan Agung (YPA)[41] to safeguard the special position of the Malays and other natives and the legitimate interests of other communities in accordance with the provisions of this Article.

(2) Notwithstanding anything in this Constitution, but subject to the provisions of this Article, the YPA shall exercise his functions under the Constitution and federal law in such manner as may be necessary to safeguard the special position of the Malays and other natives and to ensure the reservations for Malays and other natives of such proportion as he may deem reasonable of

positions in the public service ... and of scholarships, exhibitions and other educational or training privileges or special facilities.

However, unlike the Federation Agreement, provisions to protect the equality of rights of citizenship were also enshrined in the Merdeka Constitution in the Fundamental Liberties Section (Articles 5 to 10). Article 8, for example, addresses the issue of equality of opportunities and privileges:

(1) All persons are equal before the law and entitled to the equal protection of the law

(2) Except as expressly authorized by this Constitution, there shall be no discrimination against citizens on the ground only of religion, race, descent or place of birth in any law or in appointment to any office or employment under a public authority or in the administration of any law relating to the acquisition, holding or disposition of property or establishing or carrying on any trade, business, profession, vocation or employment.

(3) There shall be no discrimination in favour of any person on the ground that he is a subject of the Ruler of any State.

The juxtaposition of the provisions that ensure the equality of rights, opportunities and privileges of every citizen with measures to safeguard Malay special position invariably created a conflict. When it was first formulated in the Alliance memorandum, the MCA, while agreeing "in principle on the need to assist the Malays economically", was apprehensive "on the nature of the provisions on the Malay special position in the new constitution".[42] Consequently, the earlier drafts of the Alliance memorandum, with the MCA strong prodding, declared that there would be a review of the measures to protect Malay special position fifteen years after the independence. But this provision for a time frame was omitted in the final version of the Alliance memorandum to avoid criticisms from both within UMNO and from other Malay political groups.

The Reid Commission,[43] established to draft the Constitution of the Federation of Malaya, was aware of the potential for conflict. On the one hand, the Reid Commission went along with the preservation of Malay special position for two reasons: one, it was recognized and safeguarded by various past policies[44] and, two, given the existing economic standing of the community "the Malays would be at a serious and unfair disadvantage compared with other communities if they were suddenly withdrawn".[45] On the other hand, the Commission argued that "if the protection of the special position of the Malays signified the granting of special privileges, permanently, to one community only and not to the others",[46] it would be difficult to reconcile this with the provisions stipulating that all citizens have equal rights, privileges and opportunities and there must be no discrimination on grounds of race and creed.

The Reid Commission thus recommended that "transitional and temporary clauses" be added which would entail reviewing the possible removal of the Malay special rights after a period of fifteen years after independence:

> The Malays should be assured that the present position will continue for a substantial period, but that in due course the present preferences should be reduced and should ultimately cease so that there should be no discrimination between races or communities ... [and] that after 15 years there should be a review ... and the legislature should then determine either to retain or to reduce any quota or to discontinue it entirely.[47]

In short, while the Reid Commission supported the inclusion of special rights as a means to improve the socio-economic standing of the Malay community, they also saw the necessity — in the long run — to ensure that the fundamental principle of equal rights is upheld.

The Reid Commission recommendations on measures to safeguard Malay special position received contradictory responses from the UMNO, MCA, and MIC. Strident reactions from the Malay community and from within the rank and file of the party led UMNO to reject the Reid Commission recommendation to review the Malay special rights fifteen years after independence. The UMNO leaders, particularly the second echelon and grassroots, appeared to interpret the Malay special position as a consequence of their being the natives of the country, and thus the constitutional provision as permanent guarantee of their status. Thus, a resolution passed in the UMNO General Assembly that met on 28 March 1957 insisted "there should be no time limit for Malay special privileges".[48]

The MCA reacted disapprovingly to UMNO's resolution to remove any time limit for Malay special privileges, but reiterated that they support the measures to safeguard the Malay special position as a temporary means to improve the Malays' socio-economic position. Tan Siew Sin expressed his worry that if the wording of the article in the Constitution was not drawn up properly, it could be interpreted to the disadvantage of the Chinese *ad infinitum*.[49] Similarly, the MIC, in its General Assembly on 19 April 1957, "proposed that the Malay special position be continued for 15 years, after which any safeguard or protection be given to backward sections of the population irrespective of race, creed or community".[50] In the end, despite their reservations, the MCA and MIC agreed with UMNO to remove the Reid Commission recommendation to review the Malay special position fifteen years after independence. In its place, the Working Party Report outlining the constitutional proposals, instead of stating a fixed period, inserted the phrase "from time to time" for a review of the provision safeguarding Malay special position.

In summary, as the principle of *jus soli* was to be liberally applied and the naturalization terms relaxed, the majority of Chinese would gradually acquire Malay(si)an citizenship status. The British and non-Malay support for the creation of a common equal citizenship for all qualified persons, irrespective of ethnic background, was incorporated in the Merdeka Constitution under the fundamental liberties provisions. However, the provisions enshrining the equality of rights of citizenship were precariously juxtaposed with provisions to safeguard Malay special position and preferential treatment. As a result, ever since independence, the different ethnic groups have interpreted differently the meanings of the provisions regarding the equality of rights of citizenship and Malay special position and privileges, and their relationship.

Conclusion: Betwixt Civic and Ethnic Citizenship

What has emerged from this overview of the development of citizenship in the peninsula is how the principles of *jus sanguinis* and *jus soli* were used to classify and differentiate membership status before the Japanese Occupation, in the Malayan Union Plan, and in the Merdeka constitutional negotiations. In the last, compromises between the British officials and Alliance leaders led to the making of a citizenship that included a civic element that regarded citizenship as consequence of membership of a nation-state and an ethnic element that linked citizenship to membership in a native or non-native group. Non-Malays naturally supported the civic citizenship, or a "Malaysian Malaysia", that would endow every citizen, regardless of ethnicity, equality of rights. The UMNO-led Malays, however, insisted on an ethnic citizenship where Malays are granted special rights by virtue of their indigenous position. The inclusion of the civic and ethnic elements in the terms of citizenship in the Merdeka Constitution invariably generated different interpretations by the different ethnic groups.

In his 1971 book, *The Malay Dilemma*, Mahathir wrote,

> I contend that the Malays are the original or indigenous people of Malaya and the only people who can claim Malaya as their one and only country [as definitive people]. In accordance with practice all over the world, this confers on the Malays certain inalienable rights over the forms and obligations of citizenship which can be imposed on citizens of non-indigenous origin." (p. 133).

Politically, of course, since a two-third majority is needed to amend the constitution, Malays obviously would have the final say on Malay special position and special rights, and the rights of the non-Malays. The future "bangsa Malaysia" would depend on whether the Malays view the special rights provision as a temporary measure or a permanent status quo.

In 1971, in his parliamentary speech Tun Razak, then Deputy Prime Minister, expressed his hope that "one day the special rights of the Malays as enshrined in the Constitution will become merely a historical event for the country and will not become a political issue. This could only happen when the economy of the Malays is put at par with the non-Malays".[51] The argument here suggests that the special rights arc just temporary measures to assist the Malays to realize an equal distribution of some resource and opportunity.

In recent years, there has emerged a tendency to view the Malay special rights provisions not as temporary measures, but, rather, as a permanent status quo. Frequently, reference is made to the informal "historic bargain" between the Alliance leaders, now interpreted to be a "social contract" between Malays and non-Malays, to justify the status quo.[52] That is, Malays agreed to grant citizenship status and rights to the non-Malays who, in return, endorsed Malay special position and rights. However, historically the MCA and MIC leaders, the Reid Commission, and probably the majority of non-Malays had viewed the special rights provisions as temporary measures to redress the Malay economic handicaps.

Ronald Dworkin (1977)[53] made a distinction between the right to equal treatment and the right to treatment as an equal. If right to equal treatment is concerned with the right to an equal distribution of some resource or opportunity, the right to treatment as an equal, in contrast, is the right to be treated with the same respect and concern as anyone else. In this sense, the second is fundamental whereas the first is derivative. Thus, if Malay special rights provisions are just temporary measures to help equalize the ethnic economic inequalities, then the concept of equality here is the right to equal treatment. As soon as the equal distribution of resources and opportunities objective is achieved, then the ethnically discriminating special rights should be discarded, and the civic form of citizenship where every citizen have equality of rights and opportunities be the cornerstone of the Malaysian nation. On the other hand, if Malays believe that membership in an indigenous group confers them special rights, then Malaysian citizens' right to treatment as equals will continue to be thwarted by discriminatory practices based on their native versus non-native origins.

Notes

1. Civic citizenship refers to membership in a nation where every citizen has equality of rights and receives equal treatment by the state (see Ronald Dworkin, *Taking Rights Seriously* (Cambridge, MA: Harvard University Press 1977)). In the Malaysian Constitution, the fundamental liberties provisions protect citizens' equality of rights. Ethnic citizenship implies that membership status in a nation is determined by ethnicity; in the case of Malaysia the ethnicity is linked to native or non-native dichotomy.
2. Mahathir Mohamad, "Malaysia: The Way Forward (Vision 2020)", Speech to Malaysian Business Council, Kuala Lumpur, 1991.
3. Cheah Boon Kheng, *Malaysia: The Making of a Nation* (Singapore: Institute of Southeast Asian Studies, 2002).
4. Composed of Penang, Malacca, and Singapore, the Straits Settlements became a Crown Colony in 1867.
5. Federated Malay States were made up of Perak, Selangor, Negeri Sembilan, and Pahang, and the Unfederated Malay States of Johore, Trengganu, Kelantan, Perlis, and Kedah. The system of indirect rule used to administer the Malay States preserved the Rulers' sovereignty and symbolic importance as the Head of State except that the latter's sovereignty was reduced to jurisdiction over issues that concerned Malay customs and Islam. In other matters, the terms of the various treaty agreements and the realities and demands of colonial administration ensured that the British officers, known as Resident in the Federated Malay States and Advisers in the Unfederated Malay States, appointed to "advise" the Rulers, became the real power behind the throne.
6. By the 1930s, it was generally accepted that a person was considered a Malay if the person (a) habitually speaks the Malay language, (b) professes the Muslim religion, and (c) conforms to Malay custom. The official census in the 1930s had began to include "Indonesians" under the Malay category, and Malay nationalism had expanded to include the descendants of the Arab and Indian-Muslim communities who had intermarried with Malays. See Charles Hirschman, "The Meaning and Measurement of Ethnicity in Malaysia: An Analysis of Census Classifications", in *Journal of Southeast Asian Studies* 46 (August 1987): 555–82, and William Roff, *The Origins of Malay Nationalism* (Kuala Lumpur: University of Malaya Press, 1967).

7. Important to note here is that the Kuomintang government in China maintained the view that treated any Chinese living abroad as a national of China. In the 1930s the Chinese government refused to accept the British position that the Straits Settlements Chinese could become British subjects by birth.
8. Albert Lau, "Malayan Union Citizenship: Constitutional Change and Controversy in Malaya, 1942–48", *Journal of Southeast Asian Studies* 20, no. 2 (1989): 218.
9. Given the Chinese emotional attachment to and identification with China then, most likely a majority of Malaya-born Chinese would have opted for a China nationality. The British could have circumvented the international law if they get the Malaya-born Chinese to be subjects of the Rulers, but this was not feasible, as the Rulers would not accept the Chinese as their subjects.
10. For example, Chinese Protected Persons' right of abode in the Malay States was not fully recognized, especially by the Malay Rulers. In the deteriorating political crisis after the Japanese occupation, the British amended the Banishment Act to facilitate the legal deportation of Chinese Protected Persons to China. The status of the Chinese Protected Person was obviously one inferior to that of the Straits Chinese.
11. In the latter part of British colonialism, Edmund Burke's writings on trusteeship became particularly influential.
12. Hugh Clifford's sentiment was widely shared and often throughout the duration of colonial rule reiterated by members of the British administrative elite. Quoted in Rex Stevenson, *Cultivators and Administrators: British Educational Policy towards the Malays 1875–1906* (Kuala Lumpur: Oxford University Press, 1975).
13. While initially students were selected from sons of the ruling elites, gradually it was opened up to Malays of ordinary background as well.
14. Roff, *Origins of Malay Nationalism*, p. 111.
15. In Johore, the 1895 State Constitution stipulated, "Ministers must be of the Malay nationality and Johore subjects" (1895 Johore State Constitution). In Kedah, it was stipulated that "the administration of this State shall so far is possible, be carried out by Malay Officers, preference being given generally to Malays domiciled in Kedah and more specifically to natives of the Country" (1923 Kedah Treaty).
16. This was largely because British introduced policies and practices to "keep the Malay on the land and, as far as possible, employed in cultivating his traditional staple" (Roff, *Origins of Malay Nationalism*).
17. Lim Ching Yan, a member of the Penang Legislative Council, first triggered the controversy in 1931 when he asserted that the Chinese could equally claim that Malaya is their country. In general, the Straits Chinese were growing critical of the British pro-Malay policy that continued to exclude non-Malays from the administrative ranks of the colonial government (see Roff, *Origins of Malay Nationalism*, p. 111).

18. "Our policy will ... give equal citizenship rights to those who claim Malaya to be their homeland" (George Hall, Secretary of State for the Colonies, Parliament 10/10/45 in *Malaya, Part I: The Malayan Union Experiment, 1942–1948*, edited by A.J. Stockwell (London: HMSO Publications, 1995)).
19. A.J. Stockwell, *British Policy and Malay Politics During the Malayan Union Experiment 1942–1948* (Kuala Lumpur: MBRAS Monograph no. 8, 1979), p. 164.
20. This position was supported by a prominent group of ex-Malayan officials who publicly voiced their rejection of the Malayan Union proposals. Among the Malays, the opposition to the Malayan Union cut across class and parochialism.
21. The Malayan Union proposal was supported by very few ex-Malayan officials; in fact only one publicly spoke out in its defence — Victor Purcell. For various reasons, among the Chinese community, it received support only from the Straits Chinese.
22. G.D. Hall, "Policy in regard to Malaya and Borneo: Cabinet Memorandum 29 August, 1945", in *Malaya, Part I*, edited by A.J. Stockwell (1995), p. 117.
23. Categories of persons who would be conferred citizenship included: (1) any person born in the peninsula before the date when the Order comes into force, (2) any person aged 18 or above who has resided in the peninsula for a period of 10 years during the 15 years preceding 15 February 1942, and who swears allegiance, (3) any person born in the peninsula after the date when the order comes into force, and (4) any person whose father is a Malayan citizen. Through the naturalization process of acquiring Malayan citizenship, applicants must satisfy: (1) residence in the peninsula for a period of one year immediately preceding the date of application and for a further period of four years during the last eight years before application, (2) good character and have an adequate knowledge of the Malay or English language, and (3) the intention, if the application is granted, to reside in the Malayan Union or Singapore. *Malayan Union and Singapore: Statement of policy on future constitution* (Malayan Union White Paper) (Kuala Lumpur: Government Printers, 1946).
24. G.D. Hall, in *Malaya, Part I*, edited by Stockwell (1995), p. 139.
25. Cited in John Funston, *Malay politics in Malaysia: A study of the United Malays National Organization and Party Islam* (Kuala Lumpur: Heinemann Educational Books (Asia), 1980), p. 137.
26. The Working Committee was composed of British officers, UMNO leaders, and representatives of the Malay Rulers.
27. Thus Chinese who were British subjects would qualify for Federation citizenship if they were: (1) Straits-born (excluding Singapore) British subjects who had settled permanently anywhere in the Federation, and (2) Federation-born British subjects whose father had been born in the Federation or had lived there continuously for fifteen years. Federation-born Chinese, both of whose parents were born in and had resided there continuously for not less than fifteen years, would also qualify for Federation citizenship.

28. Cited by Joseph M. Fernando, *The Making of the Malayan Constitution* (Kuala Lumpur: MBRAS, Monograph no. 31, 2002), p. 73.
29. Federation Agreement, Article 19.
30 H.T. Bourdillon, "Malayan Citizenship: Note, November 1946", in *Malaya, Part I*, edited by Stockwell, p. 277.
31. G.D. Hall in *Malaya, Part I*, edited by Stockwell (1995), p. 269.
32. The Alliance Party was a multi-ethnic coalition party established by UMNO, MCA, and MIC.
33. See Alliance Party, *Memorandum to Reid Commission* (Kuala Lumpur: Alliance, 1956). Among those representing UMNO were Tunku Abdul Rahman, Tunku Abdul Razak, Dr Ismail Abdul Rahman, Khir Johari, Senu Abdul Rahman, Rahman Talib, Aziz Ishak, and Abdul Kadir Mohammed. Among those representing the MCA were Tan Siew Sin, Ong Yoke Lin, T.H. Tan, H.S. Lee, Leong Yew Koh, Too Joon Hing, and Yong Pung How.
34. The reason was simply due to the fact that the Alliance won 51 of the 52 seats in the 1955 federal election — a problematic outcome because of the limited franchise, based on the Federation Agreement citizenship proposals, excluded the majority of the Chinese population. It was estimated that Malays made up 84 per cent, Chinese 11 per cent, and Indians 5 per cent of the voting public. Clearly, the MCA was the weaker partner as they would have to depend on the UMNO to win the Malay votes.
35. In addition to this, the UMNO was unanimous in demanding for the constitutional protection of Islam as the official religion and Malay as the sole official and national language.
36. United Malay National Organization, *Constitution of the UMNO of Malaya* (Kuala Lumpur: UMNO, 1949).
37. The Chinese-educated second-echelon leaders and the majority of the rank and file members wanted *Kuo Yu* to be an official language and its usage be allowed in the elected legislative assemblies, and Chinese education be given equal consideration.
38. Alliance Memorandum 1956.
39. Until today there is still a significant number of Indians who have not received citizenship status.
40. Alliance Memorandum 1956.
41. The Yang Di Pertuan Agung has to act on the advice of the elected government. If the monarch is amenable, the constitution says he must act on the advice of the government.
42. Fernando, *Making of the Malayan Constitution*, pp. 85–86.
43. Named after Lord William Reid who was appointed by the British to head the commission to draft the constitutional proposals.
44. (1) In the Malay States there were extensive Malay reservations of land, and the system of reserving land for Malays has been in operation for many years, (2) there

are now quotas for admission to public services, (3) quotas in respect of issuing of permits or licences for the operation of certain businesses, and (4) many classes of scholarships, bursaries and other forms of aid for educational purposes preference given to Malays.

45. Reid Commission Report 1957, pp. 71–72.
46. Ibid, p. 71.
47. Ibid, pp. 72–73.
48. Fernando, *Making of the Malayan Constitution*, p. 154.
49. To assure the MCA and MIC, Razak said "At any rate, there is recourse to the Court for redress in the event of the provisions of the Constitution being unreasonably interpreted" (cited in Fernando, *Making of the Malayan Constitution*, p. 156).
50. Ibid., p. 157.
51. Abdul Razak Hussein, *Speech in Parliamentary Debates* (Kuala Lumpur: Government Printers 1971), p. 136.
52. A Merdeka Centre survey conducted in 2010 found that nearly 60 per cent of Malay/*bumiputera* accepted the idea that as the "original inhabitants" they should be accorded special privileges and rights.
53. Dworkin, *Taking Rights Seriously.*

Myanmar

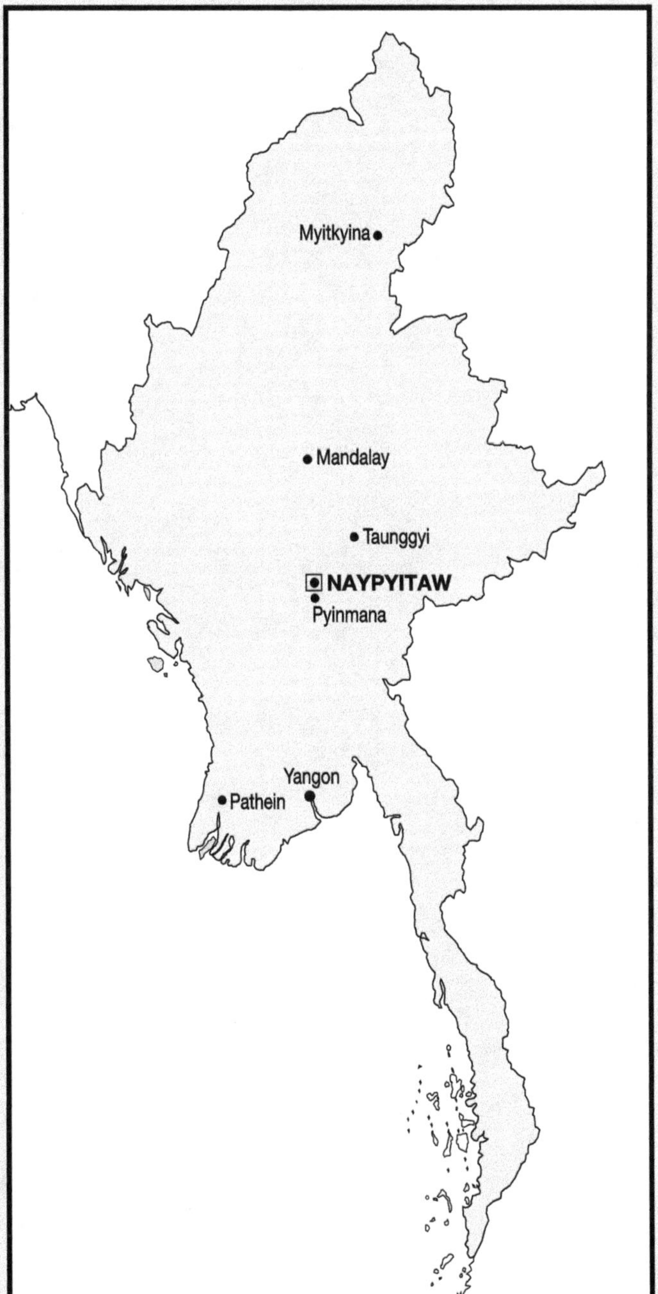

Myitkyina
Mandalay
Taunggyi
NAYPYITAW
Pyinmana
Yangon
Pathein

MYANMAR IN 2012
mhyaw ta lin lin or Great Expectations

Robert H. Taylor

After years of being held up as one of the outposts of tyranny and the only pariah government in Southeast Asia, by the end of 2012 Myanmar was being toasted as a newly reformed champion of political opening and democratic transition, a model for persisting "tyrannies" to emulate. What a difference a year makes. The 2008 Constitution of the country is now seen as a worthy document, but in need of amending,[1] and the government of President Thein Sein, formed after the 2010 general elections, which were roundly condemned as a fraud and sham by Western nations, is now heralded as the friend of everyone and the enemy of none. Western political leaders, from British Secretary of State for Foreign Affairs, William Hague, at the start of the year, to U.S. President Barack Obama near the end, queued to have their pictures taken with President Thein Sein, with a side trip for another photo opportunity with Nobel Prize winner, Daw Aung San Suu Kyi, the leader of the National League for Democracy (NLD). She, along with more than forty other NLD members, was elected to the lower house of parliament, the *Pyithu Hluttaw*, following a by-election held on April Fools' Day of the year under review.[2]

And yet, for all of the unexpected goodwill and *bonhomie*, including the first visit by a head of state of Myanmar to the United Nations and the United States since 1966, much still seemed the same in Myanmar as before. While the media attention has gone from negative to largely positive, and the United States, Australia, and the European Union have suspended almost

---

ROBERT H. TAYLOR is Visiting Professorial Fellow at the Institute of Southeast Asian Studies, Singapore.

all of the economic sanctions which had been applied, in some cases for more than two decades, little Western trade and investment has yet to result. There is much talk, and some would say too much talk, as Western non-governmental organizations (NGOs) and would-be fund managers and foreign investment consultants, held seminars and forums on the new Myanmar in the new world, and lessons to be learnt from studying the experience of others or fanciful academic theories. Myanmar civil servants were thus experts on the rhetoric of decentralization, open governance, federalism, women's role in development, banking sector reform, international human rights law and reconciliation processes, political party development, and ethical investment. But as occurred during the last period of party government, rhetoric does not change reality and old practices are deeply imbedded in institutional practices going back decades.

Many of the seminar organizers were well intended but little aware of the historical and political context of the issues they were discussing. The desire to treat Myanmar as a *tabula rasa* seemed overwhelming. It got to the point that civil servants complained of having no time to do their job as they are attending seminars of little value to them in their day-to-day responsibilities. If the minister wanted to keep the foreigners happy and concede their requests for seminars, they had to pay the price in time and patience. While the continual flow through of foreign dignitaries boosted the morale and legitimacy of the government and Naypyitaw hoteliers enjoyed a mini-boom, little action, and less money, has actually materialized to change the lives of the average Myanmar citizen. People in Naypyitaw and Yangon began to complain of the appearance of many foreign "carpetbaggers", but as they were rarely seen outside of airport lounges and hotels, most of the population remained immune to their intentions. Still, it made a difference in as much as fewer seminars are now held abroad to propose solutions to Myanmar's many ills.

Political Liberalization Continues

One of the reforms introduced during the year was the near abolition of pre-censorship of the press and Internet. Freedom of speech is now acknowledged as a human right in practice as well as in principle. While the Press Scrutiny Board had since the latter part of the last decade begun relaxing its rules which, since the 1960s, had limited what Myanmar newspapers and other media could print and broadcast, it was abolished on 20 August. While there are laws that publications can still fall foul of if they publish secret, defamatory, or inflammatory articles, and a degree of self-censorship no doubt prevails, press freedom is the most extensive since before 1962. Existing state-owned media, feeling competition from the thriving private sector press, vowed to attempt to turn themselves into public service distributors of news and information, and sought advice from the British Broadcasting Corporation (BBC) on how to do so. Meanwhile, President Thein Sein, having repeatedly met with members of the fourth estate during his trip to the United States, held his first, two-hour-long, press conference on 22 October 2012 within Myanmar. He encouraged his ministers to also be more open and free with the press, saying he was himself no longer intimidated by the process of questioning. The President's Office now regularly issues press releases on his activities and legislative and policy proposals.

The opening of the press brought many mixed signals to the public. While there was much freer discussion of political parties and their avowed policies and leaders, and much more news on everyday occurrences such as road accidents and fires, some censorship had to be reimposed to reign in potentially destabilizing issues. Particularly of concern was how Internet bloggers and others reported their views on the so-called "Rohingya", or Bengali Muslim, issue in western Myanmar. This long-festering problem, which has lain largely fallow since the early 1990s, once more caused the fear of anti-Muslim and anti-Buddhist riots across the country. However, by and large, the press remains mainly unfettered and many newspapers are soon intending to begin printing on a daily, rather than weekly, basis and the government is planning two more new papers to meet public demand in Mandalay and Naypyitaw.

Another reform, called for by Western nations, was the further release of so-called political prisoners. While the government has always denied that it holds persons in prison for other than violation of the law, this is contested by a number of groups, including the NLD. However, the issue became increasing muted in discussions between Western governments and President Thein Sein's administration as clear definitions of what is a political prisoner, and agreed lists of those persons so classified, were not produced. Like the allegations previously heard that Myanmar had established a plan, supported by North Korea, to develop a nuclear capability, such rumours are now replaced with goodwill. Even the Myanmar armed forces will be invited to observe the next annual Cobra Gold joint military operations undertaken by the United States and Thailand with other regional countries. Cobra Gold was seen by previous Myanmar governments as provocative and an annual reminder that Thailand is the most important mainland Southeast Asian ally of the United States, and Myanmar's historical enemy.

The Economy and Public Finances

The economy has continued its modest growth, with few sectors seeing any significant change, other than perhaps tourism, but even that on a comparative scale, has been reasonably modest set against the tourist numbers of other destinations in the region. About a third of more than 330,000 who arrived by air were travelling on business or for family reunions, while more than half of the total tourist numbers of more than 800,000 were cross-border tourists, mainly from China and Thailand, in 2011. Numbers through Yangon international airport were up by more than a third for the first four months of 2012 with about the same proportion of non-tourist arrivals. However, increasing flights to Yangon have been put in place by a number of airlines and others planned as global interest has grown but these facilitate the export of labour as much as the growth of trade or investment. The rise in tourist numbers have allowed hoteliers to increase prices for even modest accommodation to uncompetitive levels, forcing the government to intervene to set maximum rates. The limited capacity of Yangon International Airport places a constraint on international tourist growth through the country's primary port of entry, leading both to the upgrading of facilities at other airports, primarily Mandalay and Naypyitaw, and commencement of construction of a new airport sixty miles from Yangon, near Bago, Hanthawaddy International, during 2012.

Where some modest investment occurred was largely in the sectors that previously received attention from Asian investors: energy, mainly natural gas and hydropower, and mining. Manufacturing has seen little new. Approximately US$133 million worth of foreign direct investment (FDI) was pledged in the current fiscal year by July, for nine projects, and almost all from Asian investors. Foreign investors, of course, were put off by the late production of a new foreign investment law as it was being passed back and forth between the President and the Hluttaw, having been repeatedly promised to be issued "soon". The final version emerged from the Hluttaw in mid-November. The President had sent back an earlier draft which placed significant conditions and restrictions on foreign investors in order to protect domestic industrialists from foreign competition. Even after it was promulgated, the high value of the kyat, and continuing problems in the provision of electricity and poor transport infrastructure, will put off investors who are looking to export other than in labour-intensive industries such as garment production. The persistent strength of the kyat, trading at 852.5 to the U.S. dollar in late November, makes Myanmar exports expensive in comparison with other developing countries. However, a boost to manufacturing exports was provided when the European Union decided to bring Myanmar back into the Generalized System of Preferences (GSP), designed to give developing nations' goods preferential tariff rates. Meanwhile, the strong currency has encouraged the import of large numbers of motor vehicles and spares, for the first time in five decades. The abolition of the monopoly on auto imports previously held by the army's two giant holding companies will have an impact on the resources they can provide their owners, including the Myanmar War Veterans Organization.

The government's finances, long a problem as a result of the previous government's liberal printing of money to finance the public deficit, and the absence of foreign economic assistance for more than two decades, still remain perilous. It was announced in the Pyithu Hluttaw in October that total foreign debt stood at over US$15 billion, up by a factor of nearly three from two decades previously. Most of this debt is bilateral, as multinational lenders stopped loaning to Myanmar after 1989 and the government then fell into arrears in making repayments. While the World Bank and other lenders have begun to make modest loans for specific rural development projects, a condition for significant funding is a requirement to make up the arrears. However, Japan, Myanmar's largest aid source before 1988, has agreed to give up much of the bilateral debt-owing. Like so much, Myanmar is still in the stage of great expectations. Domestic debt is also a burden for the government, amounting to 9,900,000 million kyat, according to the government, a huge increase over earlier estimates as a result of the exchange rate rectification that replaced the old official rate of about 6 kyat to the U.S. dollar to prevailing regulated market rate.

Myanmar's foreign trade continued to grow during the year, reaching US$6.6 billion in the first five months of the fiscal years to August. Imports slightly exceeded exports as car spares and petroleum products consumption outpaced the growth of exports of natural gas and beans and pulses, the two largest trade items. Jade sales declined, thanks to additional taxation on the commodity as well as political unrest in the production areas in the Kachin state. Final trade figures for the 2011–12 fiscal year to April showed a slight surplus for Myanmar's balance of payments position, with a total of trade of US$18.15 billion. Fiscal year 2012–13 is expected to surpass that record and overall, the country looks to grow at about 6 per cent of GDP, with an inflation rate of 5 to 6 per cent.

Constitutional Learning Curve

The delay in passing the foreign investment law and the openness of the government in revealing previously highly confidential information are both signs that the new constitutional order is working, at least in the sense that the legislative branch is exercising its powers to "check and balance" the executive. In one conflict involving the judiciary, the presidency, and the legislative branch, a crisis arose over a ruling by the nine-person Constitutional Court, which has the power of interpreting the new and, in some places, self-contradictory document. The Court ruled that the committees of the legislature were not "union-level" (i. e., state) agencies, but just what they are, legislative committees. While that would seem obvious to a lay reader, the lower house took umbrage at the decision and rather, as suggested by President Thein Sein, than amend the Constitution to fit their wishes; they voted to impeach the members of the Court. The Court resigned before that could occur, causing the appointment of nine new judges. However, the previous decision stands unaltered.

One of the newest members of the Pyithu Hluttaw became chairperson of a newly created committee entitled the Committee for the Rule of Law and Peace and Stability in August, Daw Aung San Suu Kyi. Its fifteen members had hardly had time to take their seats when the committee began to receive requests from citizens to intervene on their behalf over land disputes. Such disputes also became the main complaints to reach the independent but government-appointed Human Rights Commission. Local land records are clearly in disarray following sixty years of land reform and bureaucratic ineptitude and until and unless a system of land registration is introduced, capitalizing on rural land will be a moot proposition, holding back the growth of the agricultural sector.

During the year, Daw Aung San Suu Kyi, often misleadingly described as "the leader of the opposition", made visits to Bangkok, northwestern Europe, including the United Kingdom, the United States, and India. She was lionized at all points, and made speeches acknowledging her receipt of the Nobel Peace Prize in 1991 in Stockholm and a joint meeting of the British Parliament in the Palace of Westminster, and received the United States Congressional Gold Medal in Washington, D.C. Even President Thein Sein lauded her celebrity status in his speech to the UN General Assembly in late September. However, unlike in previous years, her hesitancy in condemning communal conflict between Myanmar Buddhists and Bengali Muslims in northern Rakhaing State led some to criticize her carefully crafted, non-inflammatory words, on what is a very emotive subject among the majority of the Myanmar population.[3]

The legislative branch had some of its decisions questioned, as well. In early July, U Tin Aung Myint Oo, one of two vice-presidents and regarded by the tea shops as a "hardliner" on advancing political reforms, resigned on health grounds. It was then up to the military members of the two houses of the legislature to nominate a replacement. Their initial choice was former General Myint Swe, the Chief Minister of Yangon Region. However, the parliamentary scrutiny committee established to confirm his eligibility, refused to do so, finding he was disqualified as his son is married to an Australian, in violation of the constitutional provision requiring that the president and vice-presidents have no entangling relationships with foreigners. The military members then chose the head of the Myanmar Navy, Admiral, now U, Nyan Tun, as their nominee. He was found fit and duly sworn into office in mid-August. The entire affair was of little consequence as the vice-president's powers are very limited, but it did lay down a marker for those who insisted that Daw Aung San Suu Kyi might be elected president following the 2015 election. Given that she was married to a United Kingdom citizen and her two sons have foreign citizenship, as the Constitution now reads, she is ineligible for the office.

President Thein Sein undertook his first cabinet reshuffle finally in August. In one of the most prolonged and publicly discussed changes of any government, four existing ministers, all known to be in favour of the president's reform agenda, were moved into his office as super-ministers to coordinate policy formulation and implement in a bureaucracy historically inept at internal communications. U Aung Min, who had sported the title of Railways Minister while doing many other things for the president, was elevated to coordinate the peace process with ethnically designated insurgent groups, political exiles, and newly elected members of the legislature from outside the majority Union Solidarity and Development Party (USDP). U Soe Thane, Chairman of the Investment Commission, was similarly elevated from his previous post as Industry Minister, to coordinate economic development and industrialization tasks. Two others were moved upwards to coordinate economic planning, state finances, and revenue generation.

The President's speech to the UN General Assembly, the first such address ever by a Myanmar head of state, reiterated the foreign policy position of every Myanmar government since 1948, the country's pursuit of "independent and active" foreign policy. In addition to drawing attention to the ongoing reform processes, he articulated the government's desires for peace and stability in all of the country, including the Kachin State and Rahkaing State, in order to achieve the country's economic and social plans, in line with the UN Millennium Development Goals. In conclusion, he drew the Assembly's attention to the personage of U Thant of Myanmar, the first Asian Secretary-General of the UN, another unprecedented remark in an international forum.

Looking forward to the elections in 2015 for all of the seats in the union and state/regional level legislatures, political parties were in the mood to consider how to capitalize on their assets. In the case of the USDP, they wish to maintain their dominant majority in the government. In the case of the NLD, their goal is to gain a majority in order to be in a position to begin to bargain on amending the Constitution in line with their demands that the power of the military be reduced and persons such as Daw Aung San Suu Kyi might be eligible to be chosen as president or vice-president. At the USDP annual conference, rather than revitalizing the party as many expected, given its poor performance in the April by-elections, the old leadership was once more reconfirmed. Contrary to expectations, U Thein Sein was re-elected as party leader, despite the constitutional prohibition on the president participating in a political party. Similarly, the NLD remains essentially a one-person party, as no fundamental decisions are taken until Daw Aung San Suu Kyi indicates her preferences, and the day-to-day management of party affairs remains under the control of octogenarian former general Tin Oo. Meanwhile, new parties spring up regularly but they probably will wilt just as rapidly. The party scene, thus, like many sectors of the government, looks little changed, but suffused with great expectations.

Waning, but Not Ending, Armed Conflicts

Among the political issues for which the year only found some partial solution was the perennial problem of insurgency and conflict caused by armed conflict between ethnically designated armies in the more remote and mountainous regions of the country in the northern and eastern border areas. As part of the reform programme introduced by President Thein Sein were a number of initiatives to end the armed conflict and reach negotiated settlements with the insurgent leaders. However, only partial success was achieved. U Aung Min, leading the Union Peace Implementation Working Committee, held peace talks with the Karen National Union (KNU) and the New Mon State Party, as well as several other small groups both within Myanmar, and unprecedentedly publicly acknowledged, in neighbouring Thailand several times during the year.

Peace agreements were reached, leading to the provision of foreign economic assistance to resettle displaced persons in eastern Myanmar. Also, the government agreed with General Mutu of the Karen National Liberation Army that the KNU could open an office in Hpa-an, the capital of the Kayin State, though this and other agreements were brought into question by the civilian leadership of the organization. By year end, the rivalry within the KNU remained in check, the organization's ninety-three-year-old leader, Tamla Baw, indicated he would stand down, and peace largely prevailed in the area.

The main area of armed conflict remained isolated in the Kachin State and small part of the neighbouring Shan State. Shan, Bama, Kachin and other ethnically self-designated individuals and groups live throughout both states, though Kachin tend to reside in the higher and more remote elevations. While Kachin groups, which had previously been aligned with the now defunct Burma Communist Party, have reached agreements to turn their troops into border guard units under the command of the central army, the Kachin Independence Army (KIA), which once had a near monopoly of the lucrative jade smuggling operations, refused to accept the terms laid down by the government. Their supporters in various human rights and "independent news" outlets accuse the army of violating the order of President Thein Sein to install a ceasefire in the area, leading others to argue that the army is outside the control of the president. Of course, the army maintains the right of self-defence and in the close quarters in which they operate with their avowed enemy, they state that the shots are necessarily returned when they are attacked.

Who controls the natural resources of the Kachin State has been under contention for many years. Last year, and earlier when a ceasefire was entered into between the previous military government and the KIA, no peace terms were ever agreed. The suspension of the construction of the Chinese financed and constructed Myitsone Dam was cited by many as proof that President Thein Sein was listening to the people, and therefore the new constitutional order was working. This, however, did not convince the KIA and conflict resumed last year and into this, with bridges blown up, towns attacked, land mines laid and general disorder. Though the Union Peace Implementation Working Committee and Kachin State government and local military officers met for talks with the KIA leadership, both in Myanmar and in neighbouring countries several times, almost to the point of agreement, still there was no resolution. Consequently, villagers continue to face coercion from both sides as they try to push each other out of the contested territory. In the meantime, the demands made upon the government by the leaders of ethnically designated armed and unarmed groups remain the same as they have been for the past forty years, and no one has found a creative way out of what is an interminable conflict.[4]

Other than with regard to the ongoing insurgency of the KIA, the country faced little armed conflict in 2012, one of the most peaceful and optimistic years in Myanmar's turbulent history. Talks continued with Shan, Kayin, Mon, Kayinni, Chin and other groups at both central and state/regional level, with the provision of modest inputs of supporting resources from foreign donors and international agencies. However, poverty remains widespread in large areas of the country and this has in part led to a growth again in opium production in the northernmost sectors. Farmers, mainly in the Shan State, accounted for 23 per cent of world production of opium the previous year, second only to the much larger producer, Afghanistan, and production in 2012 was up again for the sixth consecutive year, according to the United Nations. Ending production of opium, and also chemically based amphetamines, in the area requires a degree of government control and investment not now available. The legacy of earlier years, in the case of illicit drugs going back to the KMT intervention in the late 1940s, continues to plague the country. The government indicated during the year that a peace settlement must still be reached with the Wa and Mongla autonomous zones, a difficult task given those areas close integration with Yunnan on the other side of the border.

An even older issue is that of northern Rakhaing State, particularly the districts of Buthidaung, Maungdaw and Rathedaung, but spreading further south to reach the capital of the state, Sittwe, as well. This area, into which many immigrants from what was then the Bengal Province of British India settled in the colonial period, and especially when the area was largely unadministered by any government during the Japanese occupation, became heavily armed during the Second World War. This provided the weaponry for the so-called Mujahedein which fought both the British and Myanmar armies before and after independence, in a failed bid to merge with then East Pakistan. While the insurgents were largely disarmed, immigration continued into the area and, by 1975, according to the Bangladesh ambassador to Myanmar, approximately half a million illegal immigrants were living in northern Rakhaing State.[5] Three years later, responding to public pressure over land competition in Rahkaing, the government conducted a campaign, Operation Naga Min, of checking on the nationality of persons living in the area. As a consequence, several hundred thousand crossed into Bangladesh, creating an international incident. Eventually, many returned under UN auspices, but when another immigration check, Operation Pyi Thaya, was made in 1991–92, a similar response occurred.

Relations between the Muslim minority, especially those of relatively recent arrival in the country, and the Buddhist majority have long been tense. There have been communal clashes in every decade since the 1930s. The current wave began following the rape and murder of a Buddhist woman by three Muslim men in late May. The three were subsequently arrested and one died in prison while two were tried and found guilty. In the meantime, however, Buddhists killed ten Muslims unconnected with the affair and then the communal clashes spread to other areas. According to the government, whose figures have been accepted as accurate, unlike prior to the coming to power of President Thein Sein, 50 persons were killed, 54 wounded, and 2,230 homes and 14 places of worship were destroyed before the army and police could restore calm in mid-June. Thousands of Muslims were relocated to refugee camps and UN agencies and NGOs began to provide assistance. The government has been very open about the problem and many foreign delegations have visited the area. In addition, the government appointed a twenty-seven-person commission to investigate the cause of the clashes and to make recommendations. Leading members of the Myanmar Muslim community are involved as well as other notable figures from political parties and the broader civil society.

The issue of Buddhist-Muslim relations in Rakhaing is further complicated by the claim, at least outside Myanmar, that the Muslims in question belong to an unrecognized ethnic group known as the "Rohingya". This is a term never heard of prior to the late 1950s, and its origins are in great dispute. It appears in no known colonial or post-colonial records, including the 1931 census of India from which stems the claim that there are 135 ethnic groups, or "national races", in Myanmar. Many of the persons in the area are stateless and neither Myanmar nor Bangladesh recognizes them as having citizenship rights.

The clashes resumed in late October, leading to the death of another 60 to 100 persons, adding another 22,000 displaced persons to the already 75,000 living in refugee camps. In the October unrest, it was claimed that government troops fired at Buddhists who were threatening to attack Muslims. This follows accusations, from international human rights and Islamic organizations, that the army and police had been biased and had previously been targeting Muslims. As these continuing clashes are seen to be potentially destabilizing to the ongoing political reforms in the country, as deep and ultimately probably irreconcilable claims are being made, the government attempted to suppress the conflict, imposing a state of emergency in six townships in Rakhaing, including the tourist destination of Thandwe, and attempting to ensure that the communal tensions do not spread, as they have in the past, to other parts of Myanmar.

International Relations

In a year which in which the Myanmar situation was frequently discussed in the international media, and the government was courted by many in the West who for the previous two decades were highly critical, there was no reorientation of Myanmar's foreign policy. As the President made clear in his United Nations speech, Myanmar clings to the principles of non-alignment articulated in the 1950s at the Bandung conference. Furthermore, by agreeing to send for ratification by the Hluttaw of the additional protocol of the International Atomic Energy Small Quantities Protocol, which permits onsite inspection of nuclear facilities, the President reconfirmed Myanmar's commitment to Southeast Asia as a nuclear-free zone, and undermined arguments that Myanmar was possibly cooperating with North Korea in the development of nuclear weapons.

The visit by President Obama probably ended any speculation that Myanmar was not a suitable nation to assume the chairmanship ASEAN in 2014. When President Obama called the country, for the first time in public and with a phrase in Burmese, "Myanmar", rather than the British name "Burma", he put a seal of approval on the new government. Therefore, some saw the visit as evidence of a reorientation of Myanmar's foreign policy away from China and towards the West. That rather overstates the case. China made no comment on the Obama visit, but would have been content with it. Underscoring Myanmar's close ties with China, the commander of the Myanmar army, General Soe Win, met with the Chinese national defence councillor and other senior Chinese military figures just three days before the Obama visit. The lifting of American sanctions in time may help stimulate the Myanmar economy which will be positive for the economic development of Yunnan Province in China's southwest. Moreover, the emphasis on the consistency of Myanmar's foreign policy for the past sixty years underscores that it is a fundamental tenet of the government that it will not enter into a relationship which implies a military alliance with a potential opponent of China. Proximity, in Naypyitaw, trumps prospects and there is no dissent on this by any political leader.

Year end found Myanmar facing many of the same problems which it had faced at the beginning of the year and perhaps a few more. However, the international climate in which the government operates, and the support the Thein Sein administration has received from foreign government and international agencies, as well as its nominal domestic political opponents, bodes well for 2013. Expectations may have to be reigned in and a more realistic set of expectations put in place of 2012's *mhyaw ta lin lin*. As Pip, the orphan who is lifted out of penury by the benefaction of Abel Magwitch discovered in Charles Dicken's novel, money and opportunity, even when they come easily, do not necessarily lead to love and fulfilment. Life has too many unknown variables to predict whether one's great expectations will be fulfilled. The past cannot be changed and it holds a legacy that wishful thinking cannot alter.

Notes

1. The main targets of those who wish to reform the Constitution are eight articles which in various ways provide the army with ultimate powers to preserve state security, obviating the need for *coup d'etat* in the future. See Larry Diamond, "The Opening in Burma: The Need for a Political Pact", *Journal of Democracy* 23, no. 4 (October 2012): 138–49, p. 142. The former ruling military State Peace and Development Council (SPDC) indicated that in the fullness of time, these might be removed or amended as the new constitutional order became more firmly established. However, there is little chance of amendment, despite the desire to do so by the National League for Democracy and some ethnically designated political parties, prior to the next general elections in 2015.
2. For the details of the by-election and the aftermath, see the article by Tin Maung Maung Than in this volume.
3. See, for example, Mark MacKinnon, "Suu Kyi Must Balance Politics and Principles", *Toronto Globe and Mail*, 22 June 2012; or Andrew R.C. Marshall, "Special Report: Suu Kyi's Perilous Pivot from Icon to Party Boss", Reuters, 4 October 2912, in which the head of the Burma Campaign (UK), long an advocate of sanctions in support the Daw Aung San Suu Kyi's previous position, states that the lack of criticism of the Myanmar government of the issue of communal discord in Rakhaing State is attributable to her remaining non-committal on the subject. Also, Akbar Ahmed and Harrison Akins, "Aung San Suu Kyi, the Rohingya of Burma and the Challenge of Faith", *Washington Post*, 24 October 2012.
4. See, for example, the Statement of the Ethnic Nationalities 2012 Conference at <http://euro-burma.eu/doc/Ethnic_Natioalities_Conference_Statement_-_EN_-_16.09.2012.pdf> (in Burmese) and accompanying six point "political programme".
5. "Talk with Mr K.M. Kaiser, Bangladesh Ambassador in Rangoon", by T.J. O'Brien [United Kingdom Ambassador to Burma], 23 December 1975, British National Archives (PRO), FCO 15/2041.

MYANMAR'S 2012 BY-ELECTIONS The Return of NLD

Tin Maung Maung Than

Introduction: The Constitutional Roots of Myanmar's By-Elections

If not for the unique features of Myanmar's 2008 Constitution there would not have been any by-election of the sort that engrossed Myanmar's polity and much of the West as well as Asia in April 2012.

Myanmar's third constitution in six decades is controversial as it has been seen by the military's detractors and the advocates of liberal democracy as codifying military control over the political process and extending its dominance over state and society.[1] Nevertheless, it was overwhelmingly endorsed at the national referendum in May 2008 despite a "vote no" campaign by its opponents.[2] Having secured 92.5 per cent of the votes (98.1 per cent turnout), the Constitution of the Republic of the Union of Myanmar popularly known as the 2008 Constitution was promulgated by the ruling State Peace and Development Council (SPDC) on 29 May 2008, paving the way for the multi-party general elections under the supervision of the SPDC-appointed Union Election Commission (UEC).

However, in this Constitution, it is stipulated in article 232(i), that "if the Union Minister is a representative of a Hluttaw (i.e. MP or member of parliament), it shall be deemed that he has resigned from the day he is appointed as a Union Minister".[3] The same stipulation applies to the person appointed as deputy minister and as attorney-general according to article 234(f) and 237(f) respectively.[4] In the case of the chairman and the member of the Election Commission the Constitution's article 398(b)(8) states that the appointee "shall not be a Hluttaw representative".[5]

TIN MAUNG MAUNG THAN is Senior Research Fellow at the Institute of Southeast Asian Studies, Singapore.

The general elections held on 7 November 2010 brought into power a civilian government formed by President U Thein Sein who was the chairman of the Union Solidarity and Development Party (USDP) which captured nearly 79 per cent of the Lower House (Pyithu Hluttaw) constituencies and some 77 per cent of the Upper House (Amyotha Hluttaw) seats. It also won around 75 per cent of the contested seats in the fourteen provincial assemblies (Region and State Hluttaw).[6] On the other hand, the National League for Democracy (NLD), which refused to recognize the Constitution and which had convincingly won the May 1990 general election was absent as it refused to re-register as a political party under the revised election laws and by-laws that were seen as too restrictive and discriminatory to be acceptable.[7] As such, the party became defunct and lost its status as a legal entity under the prevailing election rules. Nevertheless, the NLD continued to operate in a business-as-usual manner albeit under a constant threat of being declared an unlawful organization. Meanwhile, the party leader Nobel Peace Laureate Daw Aung San Suu Kyi who was released from seven years of house arrest on 13 November expressed her intention to continue her struggle for democracy by saying that "there are always some who participate in politics inside Parliament, and others who are involved in politics outside Parliament. We will be in the latter category. Since we have some experience with how they [the USDP] engage in political activities, we will use various means to carry out our political activities outside the Parliament."[8]

Subsequently, President U Thein Sein, who was the former Secretary-1 of the SPDC and the incumbent prime minister prior to the elections, formed the Union executive with personnel drawn mainly from the USDP members of parliament (MP). As such, the seats of those MPs who were appointed, on 30 March 2011, to the Union Government (the President, two Vice-Presidents, Ministers, and the Attorney-General) and as deputy ministers as well as members of the reconstituted election commission became vacant in conformity with the provisions of the Constitution.

The Return of NLD to Mainstream Politics

President U Thein Sein's government, whose legitimacy was questioned by the exiled opposition groups and many Western politicians, quickly initiated political and economic reforms that surprised its detractors and supporters alike. In a significant move towards political reconciliation the new reformist government released 14,578 convicted prisoners in an amnesty that reportedly included fifty-eight "political prisoners".[9] Moreover, in an apparent overture,

Labour Minister U Aung Kyi (who had been previously liaising with Daw Aung San Suu Kyi during her house arrest) met with Daw Aung San Suu Kyi (who became the chairperson of NLD) on 25 July at a state guesthouse in Yangon to discuss "possibilities for co-operating in the interests of the people".[10] It was followed by a second meeting on 12 August that resulted in a rare press conference.[11] Then, just a week later, virtually everybody was surprised when U Thein Sein met Daw Aung San Suu Kyi at his official residence in Nay Pyi Taw (Myanmar's capital) on 19 August 2011 and announced that both sides were willing to set aside differences and work together to establish "common grounds" for cooperation "in the interests of the nation".[12] Furthermore, she stayed on to attend, on 20 August, the morning session of the second day's proceedings of the first-ever "National Workshop on Reforms for National Economic Development" and was given VVIP treatment.[13] This rapprochement set the stage for implementing further measures to facilitate the return of the NLD to the political arena under relaxed rules of the game.[14] In particular, the law for political party registration was amended by the Second Regular Session of the Union Parliament (Pyidaungsu Hluttaw) and promulgated by the President on 4 November 2011. The amended law, by replacing the phrase that required political parties to preserve and safeguard the 2008 Constitution with the phrase "respect and observe" and also removing "the clause that prohibited anyone serving a prison sentence from joining a political party", could be seen as significant concessions to accommodate the NLD.[15] These changes apparently prompted the NLD to justify a reconsideration of its decision to stay out of the electoral process due to its rejection of the Constitutional framework that underpins it. On 18 November the NLD central committee members unanimously agreed in an "oral" vote "to support reactivating the NLD as a legal political party" under prevailing laws and regulations.[16] Finally, on 23 December, Daw Aung San Suu Kyi led a group of NLD members to Nay Pyi Taw and re-registered the party with the UEC.[17] This paved the way for the NLD to enter the forthcoming by-elections and Daw Aung San Suu Kyi to contest the polls.

Towards By-Elections

The UEC announcement on 30 December that the by-election date was fixed for 1 April 2012 set the stage for an unprecedented contest in Myanmar's electoral history in terms of publicity and expectations. The UEC's deadline for the submission of candidature list for the forty-eight vacant constituencies was 31 January and the newly registered party that could not field a minimum of three candidates stood to lose its registration.[18] The distribution of vacant seats among the three parliaments was as follows: forty in the Lower House, six in the Upper House, and two in the provincial parliaments (one in Bago and another in Ayeyarwady). As the UEC suspended (on 23 March 2012) three Lower House seats in the Kachin State for lack of security, only forty-five seats were left for the contest.[19]

Altogether 17 political parties were successful in registering (see Table 1), and there were 158 candidates including 7 independents for the original 48 constituencies. However, one NLD candidate for the Upper House and a National Unity Party candidate for the Lower House were disqualified by the UEC for failing to satisfy the nationality requirement and the field was further reduced by eleven candidates (one independent) after three constituencies in the Lower House were suspended, leaving only 37 constituencies in the Lower House for the polls.[20]

TABLE 1
Political Parties in Contest for the By-Elections

No.	*Party Name*	
1	AMRDP	All Mon Region Democracy Party
2	DP (M)	Democratic Party (Myanmar)*
3	KDUP	Kokang Democracy and Unity Party*
4	LNDP	Lahu National Development Party*
5	MNC	Myanmar National Congress
6	MNSDP	Myanmar New Society Democratic Party*
7	MPP	Modern People's Party
8	NDF	National Democratic Force*
9	NLD	National League for Democracy
10	NNDP	New National Democracy Party
11	NUP	National Unity Party*
12	PDP	People's Democracy Party
13	PNO	Pa-O National Organization*
14	SNDP	Shan Nationalities Democratic Party*
15	UMFNP	Union of Myanmar Federation of National Politics*
16	UPP	Unity and Peace Party
17	USDP	Union Solidarity and Development Party*

Note: * denotes parties that contested the May 1990 elections.
Source: Michael F. Martin, "Burma's April Parliamentary By-Elections", CRS Report for Congress (28 March 2012), p. 4; and "Will the Winner Take All", EBO Analysis Paper No. 1/2012 (March 2012), p. 2.

The President and the UEC Chair repeatedly reaffirmed their promise to hold a free and fair election.[21] To facilitate campaigning, the UEC issued an announcement on 13 February 2012 inviting all eligible political parties to apply for permission for participating in the state-sponsored media programme. Each party was required to submit the manuscript of the presentation to be scrutinized by the UEC in coordination with the Ministry of Information. The content of the presentation was subject to nine prohibitions that included statements: detrimental to the three Main National Causes; detrimental to security, law and order, peace and tranquility; undermining the Constitution; tarnishing or harming the State's image; leading to the military's disintegration or tarnishing its image; leading to religious, ethnic, communal or individual conflict and undermining morale and dignity; using religion as a tool; detrimental to peaceful pursuit of education; inciting service personnel to take anti-government actions and to perform duties perfunctorily.[22] Permitted statements were allowed 15 minutes of airtime for radio and television with another 15 minutes each for party songs.[23] On 17 February the UEC announced the daily broadcasting schedule from 7 March to 12 March allowing two broadcast each for the seventeen parties in pairs of two.[24] However, a critical media veteran who returned to Myanmar after running an exile media organization in India commented that there was virtually nothing else by way of information on the by-elections in the state-owned media while the coverage by the newly liberated private media's was more than expected despite some weakness in the area of in-depth reports.[25]

The government also decided to let in international observers and media personnel albeit quite late in the run-up to the polling day. The Association of Southeast Asian Nations (ASEAN) acknowledged on 20 March that Myanmar (a member since 1997) had invited five observers from the grouping and eighteen parliamentarians from its other nine member states. The European Union (EU), the United Nations, and the United States were also invited, on 22 March, "to send a limited number of election observers".[26] Tours were organized for groups of representatives from diplomatic missions to visit polling stations on elections day.

The campaigning started in February once the approved candidature list was announced, well before the formal presentation of party positions through the state media in March. It soon became apparent that due to a lopsided imbalance in financial and human resources that favoured the USDP and NLD the other smaller parties found themselves struggling to get the attention and support of the voters. Moreover, (private) media attention (both local and foreign) was overwhelmingly focused on Daw Aung San Suu Kyi and the NLD campaign.[27] In fact the NLD apparently banked on the charisma and appeal of the NLD leader, and its branding centred on her sheer personality probably attracted voters much more than its platform premised upon rule of law, internal peace, and Constitutional change (to become more democratic).[28] The democratic opposition movement's dream of a "grand coalition" against the dominant USDP never materialized and the NLD reportedly refused to cooperate with the smaller parties to prevent fielding candidates against one another in their fight with the USDP.[29] In fact, both the NLD and the USDP fielded candidates for all available seats whereas the National Unity Party (NUP) and NDF (the two largest parties among the rest) could manage only twenty-three and thirteen contestants respectively.[30]

No major untoward incidents occurred during the hustings, and most observers agreed that there were far fewer irregularities that hampered campaigning by opposition parties than in the 2010 election. However, there were also allegations of inaccurate voters registration lists in favour of the USDP, bribing, coercion and intimidation of voters, and official impediments to the holding of NLD rallies.[31] There were also lack of voter education and failure to address complaints.[32] There was some controversy over the disqualification of two opposition candidates as the NUP candidate was previously allowed to contest the 2010 election while the NLD candidate had won a seat in the 1990 election.[33] However, it was also observed that the "media coverage" was "significantly freer than the last election" and "the international community had full freedom to cover the election events".[34] The generally optimistic mood that the election would be free and fair as promised by both President U Thein Sein and UEC Chair U Tin Aye (a former junta member) was reflected by the remark of Mr Chheang Vun, a Cambodian observer, who said "We're happy with what we've seen".[35]

On the eve of elections, anecdotal information suggested an NLD victory but, except for the NLD spokesperson who predicted a win of some 85 per cent of contested seats, many did not anticipate a landslide win.[36] On the other hand, the USDP leader U Htay Oo appeared to be quite confident that the incumbents' proven track record would be appreciated by the public. He warned that "if the product is not as good as its advertisement" there would be "adverse effects".[37] Meanwhile, it was reported that "[m]any MPs agreed that the NLD's presence would improve the credibility of the hluttaws — both at home and abroad."[38]

The Polls

The polling was peaceful, secure, and orderly. Though there were some discrepancies in the interpretation of relevant rules and regulations leading to unhappiness on the part of affected media persons and party representatives, it was on the whole relatively free and fair. There were some shortcomings like the poor quality of pen and paper, missing entries in the voting list, inability for workers to vote due to the opening of some workplaces on this public holiday, and improper procedures resulting in spoilt votes.[39] Moreover, under real time reporting and live coverage by the private media, the counting process appeared to be relatively transparent and non-controversial with no serious complaints over "advance" voting which was the major issue during the 2010 elections.[40]

NLD's Landslide Victory

Though there was widespread expectation that the NLD would win a sizeable portion of available seats, even the party itself was surprised by its virtually clean sweep of the field, securing forty-three out of forty-four constituencies in which it competed. The NLD's young candidates triumphed even in the USDP's "safe" constituencies in Nay Pyi Taw's four townships that formerly belonged to President U Thein Sein, Vice-President-1 U Tin Aung Myint Oo, Agriculture and Irrigation Minister U Myint Hlaing, and President's Office Minister U Kyaw Swar Khine.[41] Not only did Daw Aung San Suu Kyi (NLD chairperson) win a Lower House seat[42] but three other Central Executive Committee (CEC) members and several young activists who were former political prisoners also won on the NLD ticket. The party's sole loss was in the Upper House slot for the Shan State, won by a native candidate from the regionally based Shan Nationalities Democratic Party (SNDP), popularly known as the White Tiger Party by virtue of its symbol. Another Upper House seat in the Sagaing Region where the NLD candidate was disqualified earlier went to the USDP candidate. In terms of overall votes the NLD garnered a 66 per cent share while the USDP managed only 27 per cent. While the total number of valid votes cast was 4,091,840, only 146,265 votes (or 3.6 per cent) were advance votes. The voter turnout was 68.19 per cent, which was significantly lower than the approximately 77 per cent in 2010 despite the relatively high interest and awareness of the campaign.[43]

Reactions

Though the UEC's official announcement of results only appeared in state-owned newspapers on 3 and 4 April, the NLD's victory was celebrated by jubilant supporters in Yangon soon after the polls closed as unofficial results rolled in.[44]

Even though the NLD complained that they had received reports of waxed ballot papers[45] that prevented voters from properly marking their preference for the NLD candidate, most observers agreed that the polls were free and fair. In fact, the Yangon-based managing editor of *Mizzima* (former opposition media agency-in-exile) commented on the day of the elections that it could be considered a free and fair election.[46] Also, on 2 April a statement issued by the ASEAN observers said "the by-elections had been conducted in a 'free, fair, and transparent manner'".[47]

On the other hand, the USDP representatives filed complaints on 10 May against four NLD MPs on charges of committing illegal actions during the by-elections. However, the UEC tribunals that investigated the allegations ruled that such allegations were false and dismissed the plaintiff's cases.[48]

Daw Aung San Suu Kyi, on 2 April, told her supporters that "We hope that this is the beginning of the new era where there will be more emphasis on the role of the people in the everyday politics of the country".[49] She added that "What is important is not how many seats we have won …, but the fact that the people are so enthusiastic about participating in the democratic process". Furthermore, she expressed her "hope that all other parties that took part in the elections will be in a position to cooperate with us to create a genuine democratic atmosphere in our nation".[50]

In the interview with Radio Free Asia Myanmar service on 4 April, the USDP party General Secretary U Htay Oo rationalized the NLD's big win as due to "the popularity of the party leader Daw Aung San Suu Kyi. This is the main factor." He also contended that "voting was based on what people think they know, rather than [on whether they] … love or hate the USDP party".[51] Dr Nay Zin Latt, political advisor to the President, told Britain's *Daily Telegraph* that "the president believes Aung San Suu Kyi's NLD group of MPs will liven the relatively new parliament's proceedings and improve the quality of its debates". U Ko Ko Hlaing, the chief presidential political advisor, told the *Washington Post* that "I could guess that the NLD would take the lion's share in these elections, but I didn't expect this much of a landslide victory".[52]

Endorsements from the international community came quickly as the usual critics were pleasantly surprised by NLD's resounding victory in what they acknowledged as a free and fair election. ASEAN Leaders attending the annual summit of the regional grouping in Phnom Penh "called for the lifting of international sanctions" on Myanmar.[53] United States President Obama's press secretary stated, on 2 April, that "We hope it is an indication that the government of Burma intends to continue along the path of greater openness, transparency and reform". Meanwhile, "the U.S. business community … welcomed the election results as an important milestone and said that Washington should continue and expand its diplomatic outreach to the country".[54] On the other hand, Secretary of State Hilary Clinton, in Istanbul, cautioned "it is too early to know what recent progress means and whether it will be sustained".[55]

After the by-elections, the tempo of visits by Western leaders and politicians who made it a point to call upon Daw Aung San Suu Kyi seemed to have increased with U.K. Premier David Cameron arriving on 13 April and E.U. High Representative for Foreign Affairs and Security Catherine Ashton flying in on 28 April for a three-day visit. On the domestic front there was a second meeting between President Thein Sein and Daw Aung San Suu Kyi on 11 April in Nay Pyi Taw where issues relating to democratization and peace-making were reportedly discussed. This was preceded, on 8 April, by a 2-hour meeting with the Karen National Union (KNU) peace-talk delegation (led by KNU General Secretary and it military chief) which called upon her home in Yangon after meeting President U Thein Sein on 7 April.[56]

The easing of Western sanctions quickly followed on the heels of the by-elections with Secretary Clinton announcing the partial lifting of U.S. financial and investment sanctions on 4 April and Norway lifting its economic sanctions, except the arms embargo, on 15 April. Australia also announced on 16 April that it "would lift financial and travel restrictions for more than 260 persons in Burma, including President Thein Sein". On 23 April the EU "decided to suspend [its] sanctions against Burma for a year" though maintaining the arms embargo. Similarly, on 24 April, Canada's foreign minister "announced that "Ottawa would suspend sanctions on imports, exports, and financial transactions … but would maintain the arms embargo".[57] Moreover, on 5 April the Inter Parliamentary Union admitted Myanmar's parliament as a member on 5 April. Germany's Development Minster revealed on 23 April that "Germany will resume full-scale development aid" while U.K. Foreign Secretary Hague said, on 26 April, that "U.K. will no longer discourage trade" with Myanmar.[58] On 17 May President Obama "suspended" the U.S. "ban on investments and financial services" though Secretary Clinton stated that "sanctions would remain on the book" in the form of an "insurance policy" against a reversal of reforms.[59]

At the same time, calls for further easing or lifting of sanctions were made by prominent persons and friendly states. China's "foreign ministry spokesman Hong Lei called on the international community to lift sanctions ... as soon as possible". U.K. premier Cameron said, after meeting Daw Aung San Suu Kyi, that "he would support the suspending of EU's sanctions". U.N. Secretary General Ban Ki-moon who arrived in Myanmar on 29 April "urged Western nations to lift all sanctions."[60]

The Way Forward: A Dynamic Parliament?

Though the NLD's win in the by-elections elevated the party to the forefront of the opposition bench as the third largest grouping after the USDP and military representatives group, it constituted a mere 6 per cent of the total parliamentary seats and some 11 per cent of the Lower House MPs. It would take extraordinary effort and superb negotiating skills on the part of Daw Aung San Suu Kyi and her colleagues to fulfill the party's campaign promise of establishing rule of law, fostering internal peace, and changing the Constitution to be more "democratic".

Just the day before the Third Session of the Hluttaw convened on 23 April, the UEC announced an unprecedented substitution of fifty-nine military representatives in the Upper and Lower House (twenty and thirty-nine respectively) whereby majors were replaced by eight brigadiers, fourteen colonels, and thirty-seven lieutenant colonels. This was seen by some observers as the military's attempt to enhance coherence and bolster its strength in anticipation of NLD's imminent presence in parliament.[61]

However, an apparent technicality in the swearing in process threatened to derail NLD's entry into parliament when the party's elected representatives failed to show up at the Third Session of the First Hluttaw on 23 April. It was revealed that the NLD objection to the wording of the oath of office that required MPs to "safeguard" the Constitution which the NLD had refused to recognize. This impasse, with the potential of having all the NLD MPs disqualified if they exceeded the grace period for oath-taking, was finally resolved when, under adverse public reaction and criticism from some stakeholders, the NLD relented on 30 April "as a gesture of respect to the desires of the people".[62] The NLD MPs were officially sworn in on 2 May 2012, and afterwards Daw Aung San Suu Kyi reiterated her aim to make the legislative bodies "more democratic" (read changing the Constitution). Perhaps, alluding to unelected military representatives, she explained that "[w]e would like our parliament to be in line with genuine democratic values. It's not because we want to remove anybody, as such".[63]

Since then Daw Aung San Suu Kyi and NLD as well as other parties in the respective Hluttaws have come a long way in terms of debate and discussion as well as on reviewing, amending and formulating laws. Daw Aung San Suu Kyi had travelled abroad many times since May 2012 and was treated like a state leader while she and her colleagues were assigned responsibilities in various parliamentary committees and commissions. In particular, Daw Aung San Suu Kyi was appointed chairman of the newly formed Committee for Rule of Law and Peace and Stability, at the Fourth Session of Pyithu Hluttaw (Lower House) on 7 August 2012 and she was also appointed by the President on 1 December 2012 to chair the investigative commission for the controversial Letpadaungtaung Copper Mining Project.[64]

But for the by-elections all the aforementioned developments might not have unfolded and Myanmar would be poorer on the democratic front. Of course, one cannot attribute every subsequent change for the better in the domestic and international arenas to this singular event. Thus far Daw Aung San Suu Kyi and NLD have been unable to progress substantially towards fulfilling the party's three main election promises and the NLD has yet to form a "grand alliance" of democratic parties in the parliaments and to embrace the ethnic parties as well. However, it is fair to say that both the government and the NLD have enjoyed the dividends from the "historic compromise" and the parliaments have also gained more credibility and stature on account of the pluralism brought about by the by-elections.[65] It remains to be seen whether this by-election is a harbinger of things to be expected in the 2015 general election as three years is a painstakingly long time in politics.

Notes

1. See, for example, *Impunity Prolonged: Burma and Its 2008 Constitution* (New York: International Center for Transitional Justice, September 2009).

2. For details, see Tin Maung Maung Than, "Myanmar in 2008: Weathering the Storm", in *Southeast Asian Affairs 2009*, edited by Daljit Singh (Singapore: Institute of Southeast Asian Studies, 2009), pp. 200–04.
3. Constitution of the Republic of the Union of Myanmar (2008), n.p., May 2009, p. 86.
4. Ibid. pp. 89, 92.
5. Ibid. p. 160.
6. For election details, see Tin Maung Maung Than, "Myanmar's 2010 Elections: Continuity and Change", in *Southeast Asian Affairs 2011*, edited by Daljit Singh (Singapore: Institute of Southeast Asian Studies, 2011), pp. 190–207.
7. The NLD issued a statement on 30 March announcing its refusal to re-register as a political party on account of "absolutely unjust" electoral laws, citing a unanimous decision by the Central Committee on 29 March.
8. Interview with the editor of *Irrawaddy* (an exile publication based in Chiang Mai), published online at <www.irrawaddy.org>, 22 November 2010.
9. The government did not recognize the existence of "political prisoners"; regarding all prisoners as convicted criminals. See "Not all that glitters is gold", ALTSEAN "Issues & Concerns", vol. 8 (October 2012), p. 5.
10. See "Aung San Suu Kyi meets government minister Aung Kyi", BBC online, 25 July 2011 <http://www.bbc.co.uk/news/world-asia-pacific-14271464?print=true>.
11. See *New Light of Myanmar* (NLM), 13 August 2011. There were two more meetings 30 September and 30 October which might have some bearing on the NLD's decision to consider re-registering in the November conclave of central committee members.
12. See, *NLM*, 20 August 2011.
13. Personal observations at the workshop.
14 Three more amnesties followed (on 12 October 2011, 4 and 13 January 2012) in which 13,666 prisoners, including 578 political prisoners, were released ("Not all that glitters", ALTSEAN "Issues & Concerns", p. 5).
15. See ALTSEAN, "Burma Bulletin", Issue No. 58 (October 2011), p. 6.
16. See Euro-Burma Office, "Political Monitor", No. 34 (12–18 November 2011), p. 3.
17. See ALTSEAN, "Burma Bulletin", Issue No. 60 (December 2011), p. 4.
18. This rule applies only if there are three or more seats available for contestation. See, for example, Michael F. Martin, "Burma's April Parliamentary By-Elections", CRS Report for Congress (28 March 2012), p. 3.
19. All forty-eight seats belonged to USDP MPs of which forty-five had taken up executive positions, two were "removed" and one died (ibid. p. 1).

20. The three constituencies Phakant, Mogaung and Bamaw NLD and USDP fielded three candidates each, and NDF two and NUP one. The SNDF and independent had one each. See "Will the Winner Take All", EBO Analysis Paper No. 1/2012 (March 2012).
21. See, for example, Martin, "Burma's April Parliamentary By-Elections", p. 5.
22. See UEC Announcement No. 12/2012 dated 16 February 2012, in *NLM*, 17 February 2012.
23. Ibid.
24. The political party must seek permission from the UEC at least seven days before its allotted date. See "Timetable for radio and TV talk programmes for political parties", *NLM*, 17 February 2012.
25. See Ko Pauk, "It could be said that it was a free and fair election" (in Myanmar), Interview with U Sein Win, *Mizzima online*, 1 April 2012 <www.mizzimaburmese.com/2012-03-09-12-19-18.html>.
26. See Martin, "Burma's April Parliamentary By-Elections", p. 6. The last minute scramble for entry visas created some anxiety and inconvenience but the authorities concerned managed to secure timely clearance for all legitimate observers and accredited media personnel. Anecdotal evidence suggested that quite a number of academics, journalists and interested foreigners also managed to enter individually and conduct informal observations. However, the executive director of ANFREL (Asian Networks for Free Elections) was expelled, on 20 March, for contravening the terms of her tourist visa. Two of her assistants were also asked to leave the next day (Zin Linn, "Is Burma's election monitoring a window dressing?", *Asian Tribune*, 23 March 2012 <http://www.asiantribune.com/news/2012/03/22/burma%E2%80%99s-election-monitoring-window-dressing>).
27. See, for example, Kyaw Hsu Mon, "Small Parties Struggle Amid NLD Media Storm", *Myanmar Times*, 12–18 March 2012 <http://www.mmtimes.com/2012/news/618/news61801.html>; and Esmer Golluoglo, "Aung San Suu Kyi's celebrity eclipses splintered Burmese opposition", *The Guardian*, 30 March 2012 <http://www.guardian.co.uk/world/2012/mar/30/aung-san-suu-kyi-burmese-opposition>.
28. See "The NLD 2012 By-Election Manifesto" (in Myanmar), 31 January 2012.
29. See Kyaw Hsu Mon, "Small Parties".
30. The NUP is the former Burma Socialist Programme Party that controlled Myanmar from 1974 to 1988. The NDF was formed by two senior members of the NLD who disagreed with the party's decision to boycott the 2010 elections. It managed to garner twelve seats in the two houses of parliament and was the second largest national-level party, after the NUP (seventeen seats) in the opposition camp. However, of the NDF's total of sixteen representatives (including four in the

region/sate assemblies) five left to form a new party in 2011 and three more defected to join the NLD in April 2012 (Peter Aung, "After losing members, party looks to restructure", DVB online <http://www.dvb.no/news/after-loosing-members-party-looks-to-restructure/22116>).

31. Nevertheless Daw Aung San Suu Kyi drew large crowds in her rallies as she tried to visit as many constituencies as possible in a whirlwind tour throughout the campaign period (Martin, "Burma's April Parliamentary By-Elections", p. 5).
32. See, for example, ibid., pp. 4–6; and "Election Monitoring Report #1", 7 April 2012, unpublished report by the independent Election Monitoring Network (Myanmar), pp. 2–3.
33. Ibid., p. 3.
34. Ibid., p. 4.
35. Daniel Ten Kate, "Suu Kyi's Party Declares Landslide as Myanmar Opens Up", Bloomberg online, 2 April 2012 <www.bloomberg.com/news/print/2012-04-01/aung-san-suu-kyi-wins-myanmar-by-election-seat-party-says.html>.
36. See Shwe Yinn Mar Oo, "MPs will follow our lead: NLD", *Myanmar Times (Elections Special)*, 30 March–8 April 2012. See also Win Ko Ko Latt, "Nay Pyi Taw by-elections: too close to call", *Myanmar Times (Elections Special)*, 30 March–8 April 2012; and "Election predictions", *Myanmar Times (Elections Special)*, 30 March–8 April 2012.
37. Shwe Yinn Mar Oo, "USDP actions speak louder than words: U Htay Oo", *Myanmar Times (Elections Special)*, 30 March–8 April 2012.
38. Soe Than Lynn, "Hluttaw reps ready for arrival of NLD", *Myanmar Times (Elections Special)*, 30 March–8 April 2012.
39. "Election Monitoring Report", pp. 4, 5.
40. Ibid., p. 6.
41. The four NLD candidates in Nay Pyi Taw scored between 51 and 55 per cent of the casted votes (*Myanma Alin*, 9 April 2012, Special Supplement, in Myanmar).
42. She won by a large majority of some 82 per cent in the Kawhmu constituency in Yangon Region (ibid.)
43. See "Network Myanmar" blog <http://www.networkmyanmar.org/component/content/article/88/By-Elections>. For detailed results of all constituencies, see *Myanma Alin*, op. cit.
44. See, for example, "The lady of all landslides?", *Economist* blog, 2 April 2012 <www.economist.com/blogs/banyan/2012/04/myanmars-elections>.
45. Ibid. U Nyan Win, secretary of the central campaign team of NLD, lodged a formal complaint on 1 April regarding the waxing of ballot papers to the UEC but the latter's investigation found no evidence to support the allegation (*NLM*, 9 May 2012) and dismissed the case. The NLD then backed down from its claims referring to second-hand reports and admitted that there was "not enough time to

find the evidence" (Sandar Lwin, "NLD backs away from 'waxed' ballot claim", *Myanmar Times* online, 14–20 May 2012 <www.mmtimes.com/2012/news/626/news62617.html>). Subsequently, the UEC filed a lawsuit against U Nyan Win for making false accusations ("Court rejects NLD spokesperson's motion over libel suit", Democratic Voice of Burma online, 30 January 2013, in *BurmaNet News*, 30 January 2013).

46. See Ko Pauk, "It could be said".
47. ALTSEAN, "Burma Bulletin", Issue No. 64 (April 2012), p. 2.
48. See "All NLD people's representatives won cases of illegal votes filed by USDP" (in Myanmar), *Weekly Eleven* online news, 23 September 2012 <www.weeklyeleven.com/index.php?option=com_content&view=article&id=15645:---nld--&catid=42:2009-11-10-07-36-59&Itemid=112>.
49. "Burma's Opposition Party Wins By-Election in Landslide", VOA online news, 1 April 2012 <www.voanews.com/content/burmas-opposition-party-wins-by-election-in-landslide-145727485/181259.html>.
50. Kate, "Suu Kyi's Party Declares Landslide".
51. "'Suu Kyi won because of father'", *Mizzima* online, 6 April 2012 <www.mizzima.com/news/inside-burma/6911-suu-kyi-won-because-of-father.html>.
52. Dean Nelson, "Burma Elections: President Thein Sein Happy with Result", *Daily Telegraph* online, 3 April 2012 <www.telegraph.co.uk/news/worldnews/asia/burmamyanmar/9183220/Burma-elections…>.
53. Ibid.
54. "U.S. hails Myanmar election as step for democratic change", Reuters, 2 April 2012 <www.reuters.com/article/2012/04/02/us-myanamr-idUSBRE83109120120402>.
55. Kate, "Suu Kyi's Party Declares Landslide".
56. See Euro-Burma Office, "Political Monitor", No. 10 (8 to 14 April 2012), p. 4.
57. "Burma Bulletin", Issue No. 64, pp. 8, 9.
58. Ibid., pp. 10, 11.
59. ALTSEAN, "Burma Bulletin", Issue No. 65 (May 2012), p. 9.
60. "Burma Bulletin", Issue No. 64, pp. 7, 8, 10.
61. Ibid., p. 2. For details, see Euro-Burma Office, "Political Monitor", No. 11 (15 to 21 April 2012), pp. 6, 7.
62. "Burma Bulletin", Issue No. 64, pp. 2, 3.
63. "Burma's Aung San Su Kyi Makes History with Parliamentary Oath", VOA online news <http://blogs.voanews.com/breaking-news/2012/05/02/burmas-aung-san-suu-kyi-makes-history-with-parliamentary-oath/>.
64. See President's Office Notification No. 92/2012, dated 1 December 2012 <http://www.president-office.gov.mm/en/print/1155>. This was after a public and international outcry over a violent crackdown, on 29 November, of protestors at the Letpadaungtaung copper mining site after they refused to disperse despite a

curfew imposed by local authorities. See, for example, Euro-Burma Office, "Political Monitor", No. 37 (1–7 December 2012), pp. 3, 4, 6–9.

65. See, for example, "Top Ten Events of 2012- No. 2, Aung San Suu Kyi's NLD sweeps April by-elections", *Mizzima* online, 30 December 2012 <www.mizzima.com/news/inside-burma/8660-top-10-events-of-2012no-2.html?tmpl=components&print=1&layout=default&page=>.

Philippines

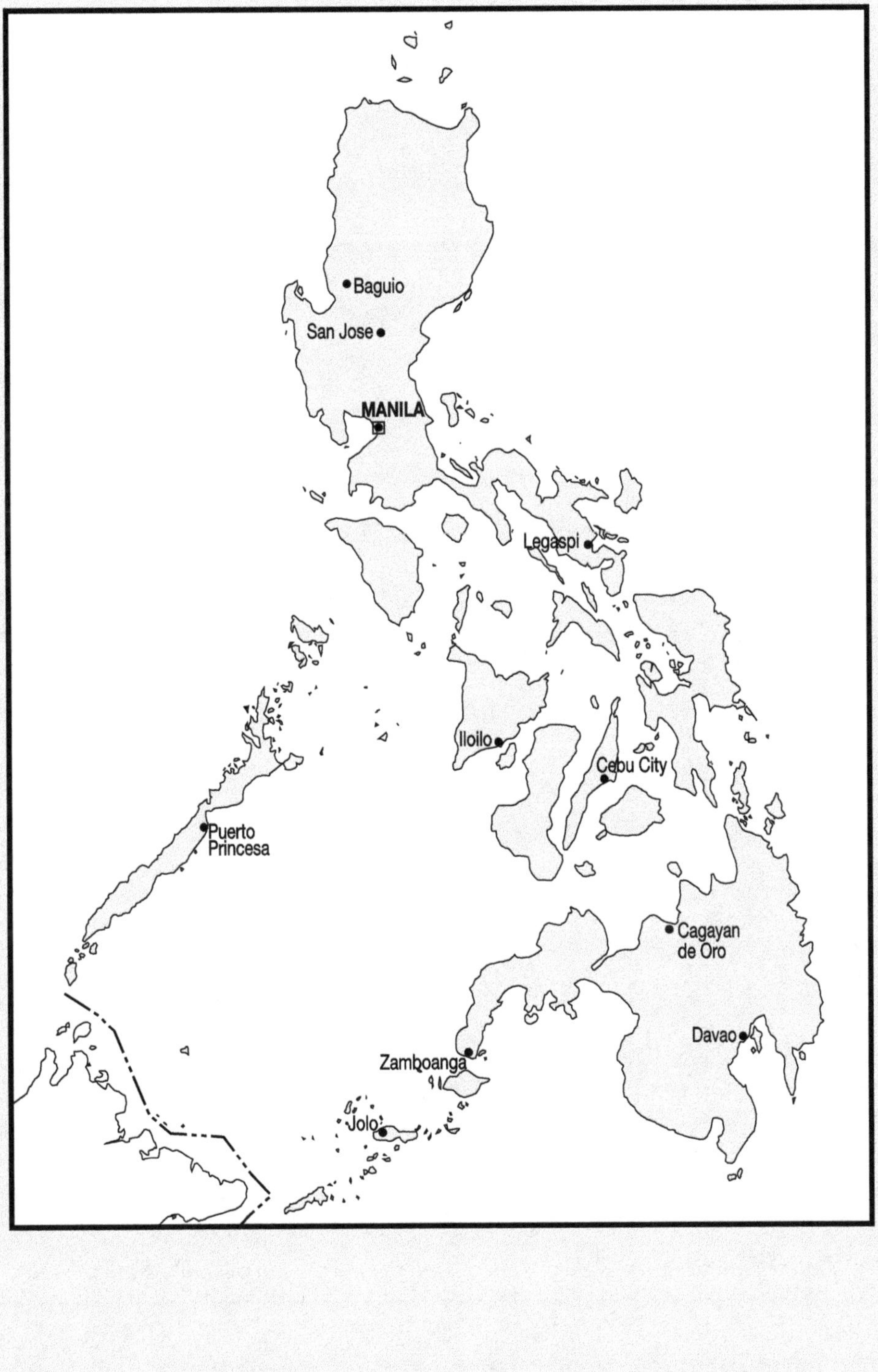

THE PHILIPPINES UNDER AQUINO III, YEAR 2
A Ponderous Slog Continues

Patricio N. Abinales

President Benigno Aquino III's Third State of the Nation address on 23 July 2012, to the joint houses of the legislature, is probably the best starting point for this chapter. For what was notable about the speech was that it was not simply a listing of his accomplishments after a year in office. It also set out to show how long a way he had come in changing the manner of conducting politics and governance that his predecessor, Gloria M. Arroyo, had purportedly tarnished.[1] Despite understating the obvious, the comparison to the Arroyo administration permeated most of the speech.

Where Arroyo exacerbated the practice of looting the state, Aquino declared success in implementing a variety of administrative and political reforms that cut wasteful spending and "held offenders accountable for their actions".[2] Where the increase in rice importation under Arroyo exemplified a deterioration of the rural economy, under Aquino extreme import dependence on this primary staple had gone down, and the country was back in pursuit of food self-sufficiency. And where Arroyo showed only perfunctory concern for the poor, her successor boasted that by giving more serious attention to past programmes like the Conditional Cash Transfer (CCT), the government had successfully assisted 3.1 million poor Filipinos in gaining access to primary health and getting their children to school.[3]

Aquino closed his speech by declaring that his presidency had "showed … the world that the Philippines is now open for business under new management".[4] This confidence is anchored on the president's continuing popularity, reinforced

Patricio N. Abinales is Professor at the School of Pacific and Asian Studies, University of Hawai'i at Manoa, United States.

by the country's remarkable general economic performance. Past overviews of the country have grudgingly acknowledged how these two distinctive features of the Aquino presidency have persisted despite an unwieldy, spoils-infected, elite-controlled, factionalized, and administratively fragile state structure, and a president who has been described as "lacklustre and reactive".[5] An earlier evaluation focused on his doggedness in pursuing his administrative agenda, while others point more to a consistently positive economic growth that had, in turn, fostered a strong sense of hope that the country will finally overcome its underdevelopment.[6]

Aquino Remains Personally Popular

In his speech, Aquino III referred to the Filipino public as his "bosses", a term which, together with such mundane action as to ban the use of sirens by government officials when on the road, further endeared this son of one of the country's most powerful oligarchic families to the people. "PNoy", as he is now simply called by everyone including critics, has tapped on this political capital to maintain a substantial majority approval/satisfaction rating.[7] Pulse Asia, one of the country's two top poll survey groups, reported that his Pulse Asia's September 2012 *Ulat ng Bayan* (Report to the People) survey showed the president's approval rating at 78 per cent, improving 11 percentage points from an earlier May survey. This consistently high mark earned for Aquino as president the longest approval rating among his peers (including his late mother Corazon) since 1986.[8]

Aquino III scored highly on only three of the eleven issues listed for a sample group to comment on: his efforts to fight corruption in government (52 per cent), criminality (56 per cent) and "enforce the law equally on all citizens" (52 per cent). What clearly influenced this positive view was Aquino III's determined pursuit of the corruption cases against his predecessor, Arroyo, in the courts, and her perceived judicial defender, former Supreme Court Chief Justice Renato Corona, in the Senate impeachment hearing.

Prosecuting Arroyo was almost a no-brainer; when she finished her term, the country's fourteenth president was tagged the most unpopular of all post-war presidents. Aquino was less sure as to whether he had enough votes in the Senate to impeach the Chief Justice. In the end, however, it was Corona who did himself in, and the contempt he displayed towards the senator-judges led to an overwhelming 20–3 vote in favour of his removal from office — the first government official ever convicted by an impeachment court in Philippine history.[9]

Aquino, however, continues to be outstaged by his vice-president, Jejomar Binay, whose performance rating of 85 per cent was 7 percentage points ahead of Aquino's.[10] This was a repeat of 2011 when Binay also topped Aquino as the most trusted top government official.[11] The vice-president has been modest about this feat, suggesting that he was simply riding on Aquino III's coat-tails.[12] More acute observers, however, point to Binay's astute use of "pork barrel" funds (US$4.8 million annually) to maintain patronage ties with local officials in cities and provinces that, coincidentally, are also the top vote-rich localities of the country.[13] Binay is expected to run for president after Aquino III's term ends in 2016.

Coming in third was Senate President Juan Ponce Enrile, with a 62 per cent "trust rating" that was the result of his adept handling of the impeachment proceedings against former Supreme Court Chief Justice Renato Corona (more on this later).[14] Enrile, a remarkable political survivor, has outlasted and personally outlived two of his former bosses — the authoritarian Ferdinand Marcos and the constitutionalist Corazon Aquino.

At the tail-end of the list is Speaker of the House of Representatives Feliciano Belmonte, who only had a trust rating of 36 per cent, and the new Supreme Court Chief Justice Ma. Lourdes Sereno, who received the lowest rating at 23 per cent.[15] Pulse Asia does not explain these low percentages, but this is most likely the result of these two senior officials being seen less as leaders of their respective autonomous branches of government than as close allies and even subalterns of the president.[16]

These surveys have boosted Aquino's confidence, and he has parlayed this to brush off criticisms of flaws in his anti-poverty programme and his alleged lethargic approach to leadership.[17] This political cachet had also been very useful in pushing through the signing of a framework agreement with the Moro Islamic Liberation Front (MILF), formally ending the latter's armed quest to separate the island of Mindanao, the Sulu Archipelago, and Palawan Island from the Philippines (more on this below). Aquino's confidence has even reached a point where he could — indeed with some relish — poke fun at Arroyo and Corona and still deflect critics' charges of his acting "unpresidential".[18]

Enrile has recast himself as a Grand Statesman of the Republic, emerging from an autobiography that included a series of revisionist views on the declaration of martial law by Marcos in 1972 and his role in the latter's overthrow in 1986. One of the most surreal scenes of the year was a portrait from the grandiose launch of *Juan Ponce Enrile: A Memoir*, which had the Senate

President seated at the centre beside his estranged wife, with President Aquino to his left, and the infamous Imelda Marcos seated to his right. The irony was not lost even on a straightforward news item, which noted how "Mrs Marcos gamely traded niceties with President Aquino whose mother, the late President Cory Aquino, ousted her husband."[19] Enrile, of course, had tried to overthrow both Marcos and Mrs Aquino, although all the coup attempts he and his military officers launched had failed miserably.

... but Institutions Are Not

If the surveys suggest public confidence in these leaders, this positive public reception is markedly different with regard to offices and their programmes. The disapproval rates are particularly high on attempts by "the national administration" to deal with inflation (54 per cent). Pulse Asia adds: "The plurality of opinion concerning the Aquino administration's environmental efforts is one of appreciation (46 per cent) but towards its initiative to control the increasing prices of basic goods, it is one of disapproval (40 per cent). Inflation is an issue deemed urgent by a sizeable majority of Filipinos (68 per cent)."[20]

This level of cynicism if not mistrust towards the government's ability to solve poverty suggests that state/institutional legitimacy persists as an issue. The public will put its faith in the president-as-person, but remains uncertain as to the state agencies' capacity to deal with fundamental problems like the economy. For despite a seemingly robust economic growth in 2012, pervasive poverty is still what meets many a Filipino's eye, despite assurances by government economists that poverty levels will be going down by the end of Aquino III's term. In fact, the poverty rate's rise from 24.9 per cent in 2003 to 26.4 per cent in 2006, and finally to 26.5 per cent in 2009 is what accounts for the public's ambivalence about the government's anti-poverty initiatives.[21]

To be fair, the government did make the appropriate moves to strengthen state capacities by institutionalizing reforms that make the delivery of goods and services more efficient, expanding health care particularly to the poor, and making transparency the norm in local and national governance.[22] It has intervened actively in gradually eliminating spoils through a zero-based budgeting programme, curbing red tape, and adopting a full-disclosure policy using new technologies.[23] The result was a budget surplus of 2.5 billion peso (US$61 million).[24]

Implementing these programmes, however, experienced some drawbacks, notably the death of Jesus M. Robredo, the hugely popular and widely regarded incorruptible secretary of the Department of Interior and Local Government. Robredo died in a plane crash while allegedly investigating a suspicious purchase of high-powered rifles by his own deputy.[25] His replacement, former Trade Secretary Manuel "Mar" Roxas II, has yet to make a mark that could equal if not surpass that left by his predecessor.

The private sector has responded well to these moves, but such positive news is often mitigated by recurring institutional problems, the most notorious of which is the government's failure to achieve revenue targets. Aquino III's term is no exception.[26] There had been some euphoria in mid-year when the Bureau of Internal Revenue announced that its collection of 81.34 billion peso (US$2.03 billion) by the end of the month was higher by 13.8 per cent compared to June 2011.[27] Alas, this turned out to be a brief exceptional moment. Come July, it was back to the old problem of missing targets: the 83.5 billion peso (US$2.02 billion) collected was 4.4 per cent short of the amount collected a year ago. In fact the total January–July 2012 collection of 604.7 billion peso (US$14 billion) was way below the target of 622.7 billion peso (US$15.1 billion).[28]

The regressive impact of another chronic problem, namely, government waste due to inefficiency and corruption, continued to be evident. The government's Commission on Audit admitted being unable to track around 101.8 billion peso (US$2.47 billion) at the end of 2011. And in the case of the CCT, the auditing office noted that only 10.71 billion peso (US$244 million) out of the total allotment of 14.5 billion peso (US$351 million) was accounted for.[29]

Revenue collection has likewise suffered considerably because of the power of the illicit sector.[30] One Arroyo critic pointed out that smuggling had dramatically flourished under Aquino III. Citing the International Monetary Fund's "Direction of Statistics", Rigoberto Tiglao wrote that smuggling had reached an amazing US$19.6 billion since Aquino III became president, dwarfing the figures during the administrations of President Joseph Estrada (US$3.1 billion) and President Arroyo (US$3.8 billion).

Accordingly, the spillage into the informal economy is evident in the trade with China, with the huge discrepancy between what the latter has reported as the value of exports to the Philippines (US$33.3 billion between July 2010 and June 2012) and the Philippine government's report on imports from China during the same period (US$14.7 billion). As a result, argues this critic, the Bureau of Customs lost potential revenue amounting to about 327 billion peso (US$9.1 billion).[31]

The Limits to Growth

It is in this context of a severely limited state capacity that one can understand the contradictions in the economy. Economic observers have lauded the government for presiding over a remarkable 7.1 per cent economic growth by end November, surpassing an initial growth target of between 5 to 6 per cent.[32] Government officials attributed this to "robust domestic consumption" and "higher government spending", but, as the past years, it is the remittances by overseas Filipino workers (OFWs) (totalling 1.319 million peso in 2011) that are the main fuel for this growth. In September 2012 alone, the flow of money had already reached a record US$1.8 billion, up 5–9 per cent from the US$1.7 billion in 2011.[33] The government estimates that by the end of 2012, OFW remittances will reach US$21 billion.[34] The news had enhanced Philippines' economic competitiveness on a list of 144 countries from 75th in 2011 to 65th in 2012, and the country's credit ratings had been upgraded by agencies like Moody's and Standard and Poor's to one level below investment grade.[35]

There was, however, one major element that was absent in this "surprising" growth: foreign investments. The inflow of foreign capital into the country had "fallen steeply" in the first two years of Aquino III, argued Rigoberto Tiglao, in yet another column that showed the downside of the economy. Using statistics produced by the World Bank and the United Nations Conference on Trade and Development (UNCTAD), Tiglao showed that foreign investment "under Aquino amounted to only $1,367 million, compared to the $2,171 million under Gloria Macapagal-Arroyo's watch from 2005 until 2010, and the $1,746 million under Joseph Estrada's years". Arroyo's former chief of staff added: "[The] Philippines even during the global financial crisis from 2008 to 2009 — considered worse than the 1920s Great Depression — still attracted substantial foreign capital under [Arroyo's] watch. During the politically volatile 2006–2007 years when the opposition threw everything … to overthrow [Arroyo], FDI [foreign direct investments] inflows were even the highest in our history, nearly reaching $3 billion annually."[36]

But perhaps the more potent counter-narrative to this official story of "surprising" growth is that it had not brought about any significant changes in income levels or a reduction of the poor. In fact, the country's elites continue to be the main beneficiary of the robust economy. *Forbes Asia* included forty Filipinos on its list of Asian billionaires and multimillionaires, resulting from a rise in their wealth from US$13 billion in 2011 to US$47.4 billion in 2012, or a 37.8 per cent jump! To further underscore this outstanding feature of the vaunted 6.4 per cent growth, economist Cielito Habito compared the Filipino rich to:

> the wealth of the 40 richest people in Japan, [which] rose by $10.7 billion, a mere 2.8 per cent of the economy-wide increase in income (GDP) of $381 billion. Closer to home, Thailand's 40 richest increased their fortunes by US$9 billion to US$45 billion [a 25-per cent increase], with the rise equivalent to 33.7 per cent or one-third of their overall income growth. Malaysia's top 40 got richer by US$2.3 billion (to US$64.4 billion), a 3.7-per cent rise... This is equivalent to a mere 5.6 per cent of the total increase in the Malaysians' (sic) incomes in 2011.

Meanwhile, at the other end of the spectrum, the poorest of the poor continue to rise in number, from 9.1 million to 11.1 million, "or 10 percentage points from 45 last December (2011) to 55 per cent".[37]

The sluggish domestic economy was able to offer only 1.5 million new jobs, half of what Aquino III had promised in his Third State of the Nation Address. In fact, unemployment and underemployment had risen from mid-2010 to early 2012 (see Table 1). The Asian Development Bank's Country Director cautioned that "job generation remains inadequate" and "poverty remains high at 26.5 per cent in 2009, compared to 26.4 per cent in 2006, and 24.9 per cent in 2003".[38] Moreover, while consumer confidence among recipients of OFW remittances stayed high, growing fears of hard times have also mitigated the desire to spend.[39] Around 67 per cent of those surveyed said "they would rather put [their monies] into savings" while 28 per cent would use the funds to pay off debts and credit card loans.[40] Government officials were predicting though

TABLE 1
Employment under Aquino
(in millions of Filipinos)[38]

Status	*July 2010*	*April 2012*	*Change*
Employed	36.3	37.8	1.5
Unemployed	2.7	2.8	0.1
Underemployed	7.0	7.8	0.8
Unemployed + underemployed	9.7	10.6	0.9

Source: National Census Statistics, as cited in Rigoberto Tiglao, "11M bosses now without work, not enough work", *Philippine Daily Inquirer*, 26 July 2012 <http://opinion.inquirer.net/33363/11m-bosses-now-without-work-not-enough-work> (accessed 15 November 2012).

that the 7.1 per cent third-quarter growth will "translate to more jobs and better incomes for Filipinos".[41] The media, however, did not sense any signs of general enthusiasm; in fact the general response was muted. Guarded optimism remained the norm by the end of 2012.

The Politics of Accommodation and Opposition

Economic glitches, however, almost always end up in the inside pages of national dailies that favour the excitement and hoopla of political combat. Here, as pointed above, Aquino III clearly has had the edge over his enemies. Arroyo has been kept in hospital detention, and Corona has been impeached and replaced by someone seen as more sympathetic to the president. Aquino III's Liberal Party has geared itself for the 2013 mid-term elections, forming a coalition of "strange bedfellows" that included the wife of a former presidential opponent, a representative from the Left, a family member, the daughter of a late movie star, a former coup plotter, and the scions of known traditional politicians.[42] The Liberal Party also "concluded" a "partnership agreement" with the rival National Union Party (NUP) and "shares" candidates with another rival, the United Nationalist Alliance (UNA).[43]

Critics have been quick to accuse Aquino III of political opportunism, but most Filipinos seem hardly surprised by such moves. Temporary and shifting coalitions have always been the norm in Philippine electoral politics, and even the communist party's front organizations have become adept at the practice, for example, by "adopting" several "traditional politicians" in its Senate slate.[44]

Aquino III's biggest political triumph to date, however, was in the Philippine south. On 7 October 2012, the government and the MILF signed a "framework of agreement" to create "a new political entity", the Bangsamoro (Moro nation), which "symbolizes and honors the struggles of our forebears in Mindanao, and celebrates the history and character of our nation".[45] Both sides appear to have learned the lessons of the past failed agreements well: the panels had taken pains to consult every other "stakeholder" (foremost local Muslim and Christian political leaders); sought the assistance of a range of influential outside players, from the Malaysian government to the American non-profit organization Asia Foundation; and endeavoured to make the negotiations as transparent as possible. The formal signing was followed by the creation of a transition commission that would take charge of working out the details of this new entity. Intense discussions are expected on issues such as what constitutes "fair and equitable share of taxation, revenues and the fruits of national patrimony", the role of non-Muslim communities in this new autonomous body, and the relationship between republican and *sharia* law.[46]

With the MILF agreement signed and sealed, the only remaining threat to the government is the Communist Party of the Philippines (CPP). Its New People's Army (NPA) continues to be an irritant in the countryside, with its occasional small-arms skirmishes with government troops even as it carries on extorting enterprises operating in the guerrilla zones.[47] As always, businesses that refused to pay "revolutionary taxes" had their equipment burned down or their employees harassed.[48] With the considerable reduction in the number of extrajudicial killings — the summary execution of communist activists and cadres carried out supposedly by the military under Aquino III compared to the Arroyo years, these organizations have ratcheted communist propaganda war against both the government and rival Left-wing groups. Still, the Left and human rights groups have not ceased their criticism of government, assailing Aquino III for not moving decisively on the prosecution of perpetrators.[49]

The government has responded to these small assaults and extortion activities on the part of the NPA by putting a bounty of 466.8 million peso (US$11.3 million) for the capture of top communist leaders. Whether this will work remains to be seen.[50] With its "war of the flea" still decades from becoming a full-blown conventional war, the CPP must continue to rely on its front organizations to pick up the slack, particularly in promoting its political line. In October 2012, the CPP's front organizations actively sought to disqualify a smaller Left-wing coalition from the party-list organizations allowed by the Commission on Elections (Comelec) to participate in elections, on the grounds that the appointment of its senior leaders to government positions had effectively ended its status as a voice of the marginalized.[51]

The fierce intra-Left-wing cat fight that followed made national news but hardly made any dent on the public's attention. A month later, Comelec officials resolved the conflict by upholding the party-list organizations of both groups and their right to field candidates in the 2013 mid-term elections.[52]

The enduring irony of leftist politics in the Philippines has continued in 2012. The larger, more coordinated, and Stalinist CPP network failed to go beyond making feeble attempts at nationalizing its "people's war" in the countryside while remaining unable to muster "warm bodies" in the cities to back up its rural war. In legal open politics, its front organizations had been bested by a smaller rival, Akbayan — a coalition of academics, ex-CPP cadres, social democrats, populists, trade unionists and peasant leaders, and NGO/civil society activists — which had done well in influencing government policy-making. In the coming year the CPP is expected to intensify its attacks on Akbayan in an attempt to claim sole possession of the extreme Left in the country's political spectrum. Its chances for success are slim, short of physically eliminating Akbayan.

Foreign Affairs

The stand-off between the Philippines and China as to who has sovereignty over a shoal in the South China Sea was not resolved in 2012, with diplomatic discussions stalled following the forced retirement of the new Philippine ambassador to China after suffering a stroke.[53] In this confrontation, the Chinese government had the edge in terms of actual presence in the area; at best, that of the Philippine navy was symbolic, for all it could pit against the Chinese navy was its newest ship, a Coast Guard cutter first commissioned in 1967 and retired in early 2012, and transferred to the Philippines under the United States Department of Defense's Excess Defense Article Program.[54]

With the United States unwilling to make any categorical statement favouring the Philippine position, the latter has sought support among fellow members of the Association of Southeast Asian Nations (ASEAN). When ASEAN failed to reach a consensus over the territorial dispute with China, the Philippines went ahead with a year-end plan to discuss the issue with Brunei, Malaysia, and Vietnam — the three other claimants of the isles around the South China Sea.[55] Territorial disputes, however, appear to have very little bearing on economics. In the first half of 2012, Chinese investments in the Philippines totalled US$3.4 billion, and Philippine import revenues from trade with China amounted to US$3.2 billion (China is the Philippines' third-largest export market). And as a sign that these ties would bind, the Philippines sent fifty of its top exporters to the China-ASEAN Expo in September 2012.[56]

There was very little change in Philippine-American relations in 2012, with military cooperation, particularly joint exercises between American and Filipino troops, becoming more frequent. Politicians and the Left continue to protest against the viability of the Visiting Forces Agreement, but no one seems interested in pursuing its termination whether in the legislature or out on the streets.

The only notable shift in American policy towards the Philippines is the ending of the more than fifteen years of substantial American economic assistance to the island of Mindanao. There will be no fourth phase for the Growth with Equity in Mindanao (GEM), the largest and most successful economic programme of the U.S. Agency for International Development (USAID). GEM, which counts among its major projects the reintegration of more than 40,000 former fighters of the Moro National Liberation Front, had fallen victim to its success (which did not interest the American policy and media world that seem to favour broadcasting failures and military adventures), its smallness (compared to larger projects in places like Afghanistan and Iraq), intra-office rivalries, and an American strategic thinking that values military options more than civilian and economic ones. Success stories like GEM are expected to fall into the wayside as the American foreign policy machine moves on to the next "threat" interest (China?).[57]

What's Next?

As the year ended, Aquino III and his allies scored one more victory. A "Reproductive Health Bill", that includes provisions allowing women to access birth control pills and promotes condom use, was passed by Congress, despite fierce opposition from the Catholic Church.[58] President Benigno Aquino III thus closed the year with less and less reason to worry that his term would be subjected to the same stresses his predecessor underwent. His political victories and other small, if charming, gestures will sustain his popularity among Filipinos. Thus, despite the corruption, personality- and clan-driven politics, inefficiencies, factionalism, and pettiness on the one hand and a wobbly economy with weak domestic foundations and the persistence of cacique democracy on the other, the Philippines has found a way to stabilize itself somewhat. The political economy moves ponderously, with Filipinos not expecting any dramatic change for the better. The prevailing general sentiment is that they can live with what they have — provided that the outlet to go abroad and find jobs with better pay remains open.[59]

Notes

1. For a full transcript and video of Aquino's speech, see "Benigno S. Aquino III, Third State of the Nation Address, 23 July 2012", Office of the President of the Philippines Official Gazette <http://www.gov.ph/2012/07/23/benigno-s-aquino-iii-third-state-of-the-nation-address-july-23-2012/> (accessed 3 November 2012).
2. Christine O. Avendaño and Norman Bordadora, "SONA is President's narration of changes", *Philippine Daily Inquirer*, 24 July 2012 <http://newsinfo.inquirer.net/234841/aquino-nothing-is-impossible> (accessed 12 November 2012).

3. And thus receiving praise from funders like the World Bank. See "Philippines: Good Governance contributes to growth that is beneficial to the poor – World Bank", *World Bank News and Views* <http://www.worldbank.org/en/news/2012/05/09/philippines-good-governance-contributes-to-growth-that-is-beneficial-to-the-poor-world-bank> (accessed 8 November 2012).
4. Christine O. Avendaño and Norman Bordadora, "SONA is President's narration of changes", *Philippine Daily Inquirer*, 24 July 2012 <http://newsinfo.inquirer.net/234841/aquino-nothing-is-impossible> (accessed 12 November 2012).
5. Renato Cruz de Castro, "The Philippines in 2011: Muddling through a year of learning and adjustment", *Asian Survey* 52, no. 1 (January/February 2012): 210–19; and Bjorn Dressel, "The Philippines: How much real democracy?", *International Political Science Review* 32, no. 5 (November 2011); 529–45.
6. Aileen S.P. Baviera, "Aquino: Pushing the envelope, single-mindedly", in *Southeast Asian Affairs 2012*, edited by Daljit Singh and Pushpa Thambipillai (Singapore: Institute of Southeast Asian Studies, 2012), pp. 241–56.
7. Aquino's nickname is wordplay on "Pinoy", the popular informal slang that Filipinos, especially those abroad, use to call each other.
8. Ronald D. Holmes, "Moving forward but for how long? 26 months into the Benigno S. Aquino (sic) Administration", paper delivered at the Philippine Update 2012: Prospects for Peace in Mindanao conference, School of International, Political and Strategic Studies, College of Asia and the Pacific, Australian National University, 11 October 2012.
9. Sheilo Mendoza, "Chief Justice Renato Corona: Guilty as charged", Yahoo Southeast Asia Newsroom, 29 May 2012 <http://ph.news.yahoo.com/verdict-is-out.html> (accessed 15 October 2012). Arroyo, in the meantime, remains under "hospital arrest", after being rearrested on a charge of "plunder" of government resources. Max Sangil, "Arroyo arrested for plunder", *Sunstar*, 4 October 2012 <http://www.sunstar.com.ph/breaking-news/2012/10/04/arroyo-arrested-plunder-246350> (accessed 7 November 2012).
10. Pulse Asia, "September 2012 nationwide survey on the performance and trust ratings of the top national government officials and performance ratings of Congress and the Supreme Court", Media Release, 4 October 2012, p. 3.
11. "Binay still most trusted top gov't official, says Pulse Asia", *Philippine Daily Inquirer*, 21 September 2011 <http://newsinfo.inquirer.net/62327/binay-still-most-trusted-top-gov't-official-says-pulse-asia> (accessed 2 November 2012).
12. See, for example, the contrast between these two accounts: "Binay: I owe high survey ratings to PNoy", *ABS-CBN news.com*, 15 September 2012 <http://rp3.abs-cbnnews.com/video/anc/09/14/12/binay-i-owe-high-survey-ratings-pnoy> (accessed 8 November 2012); and "Who's afraid of Jojo Binay?", Editorial, *Daily Tribune*, 20 August 2012.

13. Malou Mangahas, "Binay bags P200-M PDAF: Pork training to Malacanang?", *Philippine Center for Investigative Journalism,* 22 July 2012 <http://pcij.org/stories/binay-bags-p200-m-pdaf-pork-train-to-malacanang/> (accessed 3 November, 2012). "PDAF" stands for Priority Development Assistance Fund, which is part of the annual budget approved by Congress. In local parlance, political leaders call it "pork barrel", an allusion to the use of these public funds as spoils.
14. Maila Ager, "Pulse Asia: Majority approve of, trust Aquino, Binay, Enrile", *Philippine Daily Inquirer*, 7 June 2012 <http://newsinfo.inquirer.net/207737/survey-aquino-binay-enrile-score-high-approval-ratings> (accessed 5 November 2012).
15. Pulse Asia, "September 2012 nationwide survey on the performance and trust ratings of the top national government officials and performance ratings of Congress and the Supreme Court", Media Release, 4 October 2012, p. 6.
16. Nestor Mata, "Not Noynoy's 'puppet'?", *Malaya*, 30 August 2012 <http://www.malaya.com.ph/index.php/column-of-the-day/11906-not-noynoys-puppet> (accessed 12 October 2012).
17. James Hookway, "'Noynoying' poses challenge to Philippine leader", *Wall Street Journal – Southeast Asia*, 20 March 2012 <http://blogs.wsj.com/searealtime/2012/03/20/noynoying-poses-challenge-to-philippine-leader/> (accessed 18 September 2012). Leftists have especially been acerbic in their attacks on Aquino III's conditional cash transfer programme. See Gil C. Cabacungan and Jerry E. Esplanada, "Change CCT scheme, lawmakers urge gov't", *Philippine Daily Inquirer*, 29 October 2012 <http://newsinfo.inquirer.net/297306/lawmakers-call-for-review-of-cash-dole-out-program> (accessed 7 November 2012).
18. Maricel Cruz, "Aquino's un-presidential quip bashed", *Manila Standard Today*, 26 October 2012 <http://manilastandardtoday.com/2012/10/26/aquinos-un-presidential-quip-bashed/> (accessed 4 November 2012).
19. Cathy C. Yamsuan and T.J. Burgonio, "Unthinkable: Guess who came to Enrile book launch", *Philippine Daily Inquirer*, 29 September 2012 <http://newsinfo.inquirer.net/279262/unthinkable-guess-who-came-to-enrile-book-launch> (accessed 9 November 2012). Apart from Marcos and Aquino, two other presidents — Fidel V. Ramos and Joseph Estrada — were at the launch, including senior government officials led by Vice-President Jejomar Binay, House Speaker Feliciano Belmonte, members of the Senate and House Representatives, and even former student activists that Enrile had jailed during the martial law. As a finishing touch to this series of ironies, ABS-CBN Publishing, an outfit owned by the Lopez family, one of the oligarchic families whose businesses suffered when Marcos declared the martial law, published the memoir. See Carmela Fonbuena, "JPW writes his memoir, 'corrects' history", *Rappler Beta*, 28 September 2012 <http://www.rappler.com/nation/13219-jpe-writes-his-memoir,-seeks-to-correct-history> (accessed 2 October 2012).

20. Pulse Asia's March 2012 *Ulat ng Bayan* Survey: Media Release on the National Administration's Performance Ratings on Selected issues and Filipinos' Urgent National Concerns, 17 April 2012, p. 4.
21. Pulse Asia's September 2012 *Ulat ng Bayan* Survey: Media Release on the Performance and Trust Ratings of President Benigno S. Aquino III and the performance ratings of the National Administration on Selected Issues, 11 June 2012, p. 8.
22. "PH govt working to bring down 2012 poverty levels", *Asian Journal: The Filipino-American Community Newspaper*, 19 July 2012 <http://www.asianjournal.com/dateline-philippines/headlines/16712-ph-govt-working-to-bring-down-2012-poverty-levels.html> (accessed 5 October 2012); and Mayvelin Caraballo, "Government transformation, transparency attracting PPP investors", *Manila Times*, 12 November 2012, as reprinted in the Philippine government's Public-Private Partnership Center <http://ppp.gov.ph/?p=11980> (accessed 15 November 2012).
23. Holmes, "Moving forward", pp. 4–5.
24. Ronnel W. Domingo, "Gov't posts budget surplus of P2.5B", *Philippine Daily Inquirer*, 7 September 2012 <http://business.inquirer.net/84130/govt-posts-budget-surplus-of-p2-5b> (accessed 23 November 2012).
25. Anthony Taberna, ABS-CBN News, 7 September 2012, as cited in <http://www.ellentordesillas.com/2012/09/07/robredo-probing-puno-on-arms-deal-before-crash/> (accessed 8 November 2012).
26. Bernie Cahiles-Magkilat, "PCCI says transparency inspires investors", *Manila Bulletin*, 30 August 2012 <http://www.mb.com.ph/articles/371591/pcci-says-transparency-inspires-investors#.UKnp-o6ZqIk> (accessed 22 October 2012).
27. "BIR exceeds June target tax collections", *Rappler*, 12 July 2012 <http://www.rappler.com/business/8476-bir-exceeds-june-target-tax-collections> (accessed 20 September 2012).
28. Ronnel W. Domingo, "BIR misses tax collection target anew", *Philippine Daily Inquirer*, 17 August 2012 <http://business.inquirer.net/82086/bir-misses-august-collection-target> (accessed 5 November 2012).
29. Charlie V. Manalo, "Corruption pervasive under Noy gov't", *Daily Tribune*, 11 October 2012.
30. Just how integrated the illicit sector is in the country's political history? See the path-breaking study of historian Alfred W. McCoy, *Policing America's Empire: The United States and the rise of the surveillance state* (Madison: University of Wisconsin Press, 2009).
31. Rigoberto Tiglao, "Smuggling at its worst under Aquino", *Philippine Daily Inquirer*, 14 November 2012 <http://opinion.inquirer.net/40814/smuggling-at-its-worst-under-aquino> (accessed 14 November 2012).
32. Riza T. Olchondra, "Suprising 7.1% growth", *Philippine Daily Inquirer*, 29 November 2012 <http://business.inquirer.net/95447/philippine-economy-grows-7-1-in-third-quarter> (accessed 29 November 2012).

33. Michelle V. Remo, "Remittances hit new record high in Sept", *Philippine Daily Inquirer*, 16 November 2012.
34. Michelle V. Remo, "Stop illegal remittance agents, BSP urged", *Philippine Daily Inquirer*, 14 November 2012 <http://business.inquirer.net/93066/stop-illegal-remittance-agents-bsp-urged> (accessed 15 November 2012).
35. Klaus Scwhan, "Philippines", *The Global Competitiveness Report: 2012–2013* <http://reports.weforum.org/global-competitiveness-report-2012-2013/> as cited by Holmes, "Moving forward", p. 7.
36. Rigoberto Tiglao, "Foreign investments steeply fall under Aquino", *Philippine Daily Inquirer*, 29 November 2012 <http://opinion.inquirer.net/41695/foreign-investments-steeply-fall-under-aquino> (accessed 29 November 2012).
37. Cielito Habito, "Economic Growth for All", *Philippine Daily Inquirer*, 25 June 2012 <http://opinion.inquirer.net/31439/economic-growth-for-all> (accessed 14 November 2012).
38. Asian Development Bank, "Philippine economy strong but more jobs needed — ADB report", 3 October 2012 <http://www.adb.org/news/philippine-economy-strong-more-jobs-needed-adb-report> (accessed 18 November 2012).
39. An indicator of this confidence was the surge in credit card debts to 137 billion peso (US$3.3 billion), up nearly 13 per cent since a year ago. Michael Remo, "Credit card debts surge 13% to P137B in 1st semester", *Philippine Daily Inquirer*, 29 October 2012 <http://business.inquirer.net/89812/credit-card-debts-surge-13-to-p137b-in-1st-semester> (accessed 18 November 2012).
40. Daxim L. Lucas, "PH consumers among the world's most bullish", *Philippine Daily Inquirer*, 31 October 2012 <http://business.inquirer.net/90440/ph-consumers-among-worlds-most-bullish> (accessed 6 November 2012).
41. Riza T. Olchondra, "Suprising 7.1% growth".
42. "Liberal Party to field full senatorial slate", *Sunstar-Manila*, 25 September 2012 <http://www.sunstar.com.ph/manila/local-news/2012/09/25/liberal-party-field-full-senatorial-slate-244748> (accessed 22 October 2012).
43. Christian Esguerra, "Strangest bedfellows on Aquino senate slate", *Philippine Daily Inquirer*, 27 September 2012 <http://newsinfo.inquirer.net/278094/strangest-bedfellows-on-aquino-senate-slate> (accessed 5 November 2012).
44. Christian Esguerra, "Makabayan adopts 5 senatorial bets from 2 major slates", *Philippine Daily Inquirer*, 9 November 2012 <http://newsinfo.inquirer.net/304178/makabayan-adopts-5-senatorial-bets-from-2-major-slates> (accessed 12 November 2012).
45. President Benigno Aquino III, "Speech delivered on 7 October 2012, on the preliminary peace agreement between the Government of the Philippines (GPH) and the Moro Islamic Liberation Front (MILF)", as reproduced in *Rappler Beta*, 16 October 2012 <http://www.rappler.com/thought-leaders/13752-agreement-paves-way-for-enduring-peace-in-mindanao> (accessed 5 November 2012).

46. KD Suarez, "PH govt, MILF reach peace deal", *Rappler Beta*, 16 October 2012 <http://www.rappler.com/nation/13750-ph-govt,-milf-reach-agreement-bangsamoro-soon-on-map> (accessed 5 November 2012).
47. See, for example, "7 soldiers, 5 rebels killed in Isabela clash", *Philippine Daily Inquirer*, 17 November 2012 <http://newsinfo.inquirer.net/308548/7-soldiers-5-rebels-killed-in-isabela-clash> (accessed 20 November 2012).
48. Frances Mangosin, "Suspected rebels burn equipment worth P20M", *Philippine Daily Inquirer*, 5 September 2012 <http://newsinfo.inquirer.net/264654/suspected-rebels-burn-equipment-worth-p20m> (accessed 12 November 2012).
49. "Philippines: Two years under Aquino, abuses go unpunished", *Human Rights Watch*, 27 June 2012 <http://www.hrw.org/news/2012/06/27/philippines-two-years-under-aquino-abuses-go-unpunished> (accessed 18 November 2012).
50. Delfin T. Mallari, "CPP hits P467-M cash bounties for rebel leaders", *Philippine Daily Inquirer*, 15 November 2012 <http://newsinfo.inquirer.net/307604/cpp-hits-p467-m-cash-bounties-for-rebel-leaders> (accessed 15 November 2012).
51. Angela Casaua, "It's war: Akbayan vs. Anakbayan", *Rappler Beta*, 16 October 2012 <http://www.rappler.com/move-ph/conversations/14302-akbayan-vs-anakbayan> (accessed 18 November 2012).
52. Dennis Carcamo, "Comelec Oks Akbayan, Bayan Muna party-list bids", *Philippine Star*, 20 November 2012 <http://www.philstar.com/headlines/2012/11/20/869341/comelec-oks-akbayan-bayan-muna-party-list-bids> (accessed 20 November 2012).
53. Fat Reyes, "Philippine ambassador to China suffers stroke", *Philippine Daily Inquirer*, 24 August 2012 <http://globalnation.inquirer.net/47982/ph-ambassador-to-china-brought-to-hospital-in-beijing> (accessed 18 November 2012).
54. Michael Valliant, "Coast Guard Cutter Dallas is transferred to the Philippines", *United States Coast Guard Service Lines*, 15 June 2012 <http://www.uscg.mil/servicelines/archive/20120615-DallasTransferred.asp> (accessed 15 November 2012).
55. Veronica Uy, "Philippines to host 3 other South China Sea claimants in discussion of dispute", *Interaksyon*, 21 November 2012 <http://www.interaksyon.com/article/48584/philippines-to-host-3-other-south-china-sea-claimants-in-discussion-of-dispute> (accessed 22 November 2012).
56. Lovelyn M. Quintos, "It's business as usual with China – DTI officials", *The Manila Times*, 14 September 2012, <http://www.manilatimes.net/index.php/business/top-business-news/31022-it-s-business-as-usual-with-china-dti-official> (accessed 10 November 2012). Chinese officials did warn that an escalation of the South China issue will affect Chinese investments. Li Jiabao, "Trade warning to the Philippines," *China Daily*, 14 May 2012 <http://www.chinadaily.com.cn/bizchina/2012-05/14/content_15283502.htm> (accessed 4 November 2012).
57. My current research includes a comprehensive study of GEM in Mindanao. Its initial findings can be accessed at Patricio Abinales, "The Other Americans in the 'Second Front in the War on Terror': The Politics of USAID in the Southern Philippines",

presentation at the Woodrow Wilson International Center for Scholars, Washington, D.C., 5 September 2011 <http://www.youtube.com/watch?v=l7yvS4pUqlI>.

58. Cathy C. Yamsuan, Christian V. Esguerra, and Leila B. Salavierra, "Congress passes RH bill", *Philippine Daily Inquirer* <http://newsinfo.inquirer.net/326013/congress-passes-rh-bill> (accessed 18 December 2012). For a good summary of the opposing positions, see Sam Yap, "The RH Bill: Pros and Cons", 10 August 2012 <http://xvdph.multiply.com/journal/item/3355/The-RH-Bill-Pros-and-Cons-by-Sam-Yap> (accessed 23 November 2012).
59. The Overseas Workers Welfare Administration reported 3,700 Filipinos leaving the country daily to various parts of the world for employment. Elias O. Baquero, "Workers' exodus continues", *Sunstar Cebu*, 8 June 2012 <http://www.sunstar.com.ph/cebu/local-news/2012/06/08/workers-exodus-continues-225779> (accessed 23 November 2012).

THE PHILIPPINES IN THE SOUTH CHINA SEA
Out of Time, Out of Options?

Maria Ortuoste

Background

The Philippines began claiming parts of the Spratly Islands — the Kalayaan Island Group or KIG — in the 1950s when Tomas Cloma discovered them unoccupied. Since then, the Philippines has promulgated laws on archipelagic baselines and the geographic scope of its exclusive economic zone (EEZ), and placed the KIG under the administrative jurisdiction of Palawan province. In 2009, the Philippines submitted the geographical coordinates for its archipelagic baselines to the United Nations. Using the "regime of islands" principle under the UN Convention on the Law of the Sea (UNCLOS), the coordinates show Scarborough Shoal (Bajo de Masinloc) to be within the country's EEZ. The government routinely protests the actions of other claimants, and its coast guard arrests fishermen and poachers in the KIG and in the EEZ. The Philippines currently occupies eight islands in the KIG.

These actions are not unique to the Philippines. All South China Sea (SCS) claimants have followed a pattern of (re-)naming, claiming, mapping, occupying islets, protesting each other's statements or actions, and arresting fishermen and other would-be encroachers. The Philippines has held bilateral consultations with China on SCS-related issues since 1995 but progress has been slow and insignificant.

The Philippines, however, differs from other SCS claimants in two ways. It is the only claimant who has a formal alliance with a major power, the United States. Attacks on Philippine or American vessels could potentially lead

MARIA ORTUOSTE is Assistant Professor in Political Science at the California State University East Bay, United States.

to confrontation with China. Second, the Philippines uses multilateral forums to obtain recognition for its claims as well as to call attention to China's destabilizing actions. Since 2002, the Philippines and ASEAN have been trying to draft a Code of Conduct (COC) in the South China Sea in order to prevent the dispute from escalating, as well as to guarantee freedom of navigation.

Several events in 2012, however, have shown the limits of using the alliance and multilateralism. While supportive of the Philippines, the United States has yet to specify the geographic scope of their treaty. The impasse during the ASEAN foreign ministers' and leaders' meetings showed the divide among ASEAN members, some of whom were more easily influenced by China.

Developing a Minimum Credible Defence Posture

The Scarborough Shoal stand-off demonstrated the power asymmetry between China and the Philippines. While the Philippines sent one cutter-turned-"warship", the Chinese deployed thirty-three ships from civilian agencies such as fishery administration and maritime surveillance. This incident galvanized the Philippine Congress into passing the Armed Forces of the Philippines (AFP) Modernization Act of 2012. Divided into three stages, the fifteen-year plan hopes to develop a *minimum credible defence posture* by upgrading aircrafts, coast guard vessels, and monitoring capabilities. But will the Philippines be able to sustain this programme?

The Philippines still faces internal security challenges from the communist insurgency, the Muslim secessionist movement, and intermittent terrorist attacks. The government hopes that its framework agreement with the Moro Islamic Liberation Front (MILF) will lead to lasting peace and free up money and manpower for external defence. Philippine President Benigno Aquino III wants a new autonomous political entity to be established by the end of his term in 2016. Both groups seem to be open to compromise but the process could be scuttled if certain issues (such as power and revenue sharing) are inadequately addressed, if the newly elected Philippine Congress does not adopt the necessary legislation, or if the agreement's constitutionality is challenged. There are also two possible spoilers to the peace process — the MILF breakaway group known as the Bangsamoro Islamic Freedom Fighters and the former politicians of the first autonomous government formed in 1989. The Aquino administration is confident that these groups do not pose a credible threat, but it would be unwise for the government to not maintain the flexibility to respond to both internal and external security threats.

Another challenge is limited financial resources. The military budget will depend on the country's economic health. The World Bank and the Asian Development Bank project a 5 per cent economic growth for the Philippines in 2012. Its economy, however, remains susceptible to external shocks as it relies on exports and remittances from overseas Filipino workers (OFWs). A previous defence modernization plan was barely implemented because the 1997–98 financial crisis led to a currency devaluation which added US$2 billion to the estimated costs of the plan. To address this problem, the 2012 Modernization Act identifies other sources of revenue, such as proceeds from the sale of military reservations, the lease or joint development of military reservations, the sale of products of the government arsenal, donations from local and foreign sources, and the Malampaya gas-to-power project in Palawan.

The government also has to counter endemic corruption in order to make full use of its limited resources. In 2011, there were numerous reports about "official" corruption in the highest echelons of the military including hefty "retirement" gifts. President Aquino promised to get rid of corruption, but whether he will be successful in changing bureaucratic culture or whether that campaign will continue after 2016 is doubtful.

Even with these remedies, Philippine defence expenditures will be a modest US$1.2 billion per year for the first five years.[1] In comparison, China's 2011 defence expenditures (US$129.3 billion) make up 8.2 per cent of world military spending, second only to the United States. Rapid economic growth has spurred this spending: "China has increased its military spending by 170 per cent in real terms since 2002, and by more than 500 per cent since 1995."[2] Its East and South Sea Fleets have 203 naval craft, and it commissioned its first aircraft carrier in 2012. If the Philippines' modernization programme does survive, its minimum credible defence posture could increase patrolling and monitoring, interdiction and arrests, and even search and rescue. But this could also lead to more minor skirmishes which could easily escalate. If so, the Philippines would be out-gunned and out-manned by China, leaving the country to rely on its formal ally.

U.S. Assistance and Commitment

On the sixtieth anniversary of the 1951 Mutual Defence Treaty (MDT), the United States pledged a US$30-million foreign military finance package to help the AFP develop "a robust, balanced, and responsive security partnership including cooperating to enhance ... defence, interdiction, and apprehension capabilities".[3] And in early 2012, Secretaries Hillary Clinton and Leon Panetta reaffirmed U.S. treaty obligations during their 2+2 meeting with Secretaries Alberto del Rosario and Voltaire Gazmin.[4] Despite these pledges, there are serious problems with these arrangements.

First, the final decision on the amount of financial assistance and the type of equipment transferred lies solely with the United States. Realizing the US$30-million pledge depends on the United States averting the "fiscal cliff" by 2013. However, even if agreement is reached, the 2012 Budget Control Act means that the Department of Defence will have a flat budget up till 2021.

In terms of equipment, the United States cannot share its modern systems because of their classified nature. Thus, the Philippines has had to accept equipment that has seen better days. The vessel deployed during the Scaborough Shoal incident, the *BRP Gregorio del Pilar*, is a "modernized" Hamilton-class cutter introduced in 1967 and recently decommissioned. This obsolescence is a problem because 94.2 per cent of the total arms transfers to the Philippines (in 2011) came from the United States.[5]

The Philippines is, therefore, diversifying its equipment sources. Philippine Defence Secretary Gazmin announced 138 modernization projects slated for 2012–17. They hope to obtain patrol boats from Japan, search-and-rescue vehicles from Australia, jet fighters from South Korea, patrol vessels from France, and fighter jets and attack helicopters from Italy, Russia, or South Africa. How well these ships will be integrated with the AFP's current equipment and how they will be maintained are unclear.

The second issue is the U.S. guarantee of external defence. Up until 1992 when the Military Bases Agreement (MBA) was abrogated by the Philippine Senate, the United States patrolled the waters around the country inadvertently contributing to the AFP's lack of external defence capability. Realizing their vulnerability after Chinese structures were found on Mischief (Panganiban) Reef in 1995, the Philippines negotiated the Visiting Forces Agreement (VFA) with the United States to allow the deployment of American soldiers for military exercises.

Since the American government announced its U.S. "pivot" to Asia in 2010, it has been increasing its maritime presence and upgrading bilateral military arrangements. The Philippines already hosts 500–600 American soldiers of the Joint Special Operations Task Force, a component of Operation Enduring Freedom. American presence will become more substantial: in fact, more U.S. warships are now passing through Subic Bay, a former U.S. base in the Philippines, located near the SCS. The United States also has significant "signals intelligence and satellite communications facilities" on the western and northern coasts of Australia, and hopes to gain access to Vietnam's Cam Ranh Bay to safeguard freedom of navigation and commerce in the SCS.[6]

For the Philippines and other Southeast Asian countries, U.S. presence is reassuring. The Philippines possibly sees this presence as some sort of tripwire to trigger U.S. action against an aggressor. Article V of the MDT states: an armed attack will "include an armed attack on the metropolitan territory of either of the Parties, or the island territories under its jurisdiction in the Pacific ocean, its armed forces, public vessels or aircraft in the Pacific". However, Article IV implies that U.S. response will not be automatic and subject to Congressional approval. It states: "Each party recognizes that an armed attack in the Pacific area on either of the Parties would be dangerous to its own peace and safety and declares that it would act to meet the common dangers in accordance with its constitutional processes."

The MDT does not delineate the Philippines' "metropolitan territory". The Philippines considers its EEZ and the KIG as part of that metropolitan territory, and argues that letters from previous American officials support this interpretation. The 1979 Vance-Romulo letters, reaffirmed by Ambassador Thomas C. Hubbard in 1999, states that an attack on Philippine or American vessels "would not have to occur within the metropolitan territory of the Philippines or island territories under its jurisdiction in the Pacific in order to come within the definition of Pacific area in Article V". Moreover, Hubbard noted that then Defence Secretary William Cohen stated that "the U.S. considers the South China Sea to be part of the Pacific Area".[7] Despite reaffirming its treaty obligations, there are no other official statements confirming these interpretations. If the United States wanted to signal a firmer commitment, it could have negotiated defence guidelines as it did with Japan in 1997. Those guidelines detail "actions in response to an armed attack against Japan" which includes Japan's "surrounding waters and ... sea lines of communication".

But the Philippines will probably not be able to secure similar affirmations for two reasons. Current U.S. policy not to take sides in territorial disputes will be compromised if it protected Philippine ships in the KIG. The United States' strategic ambiguity is also necessary in its relations with China. While recalibrating bilateral ties in the Asia-Pacific, U.S. officials are quick to say that they are not creating bases. Secretary Panetta visited Beijing in 2012 to deepen bilateral military ties which were broken in 2010 over U.S. arms sales to Taiwan.

Panetta assured Beijing that the United States was not trying to contain China, but rather trying to initiate a "new model" relationship.[8] China is still more important to the United States than the Philippines: not only does China hold US$3.2 trillion in foreign exchange reserves, but China's cooperation in the UN Security Council is necessary to respond to other issues such as Iran's nuclear weapons programme.

This ambiguity is probably acceptable to other Southeast Asian countries who also want to improve economic ties with China. In fact, some ASEAN members were uncomfortable with the Philippines' vociferous calls for U.S. involvement during the Scarborough Shoal incident. China protested American "meddling" when it called on all parties to resolve the dispute peacefully. Any American statement stronger than that might push China to be more hostile. Thus, the revitalization of American ties in the Asia-Pacific is a way for the United States to signal its commitment to its regional allies and partners without upsetting the Chinese even more.

The sad and inevitable conclusion is that Philippine external defence capability depends on America's "resolve and capability to assert itself as a Pacific nation and to remain the primary Pacific power".[9] American commitment will be constrained by limited finances, Congressional bickering, or more urgent security concerns. The Philippines' diversification of military equipment suppliers may not sufficiently replace U.S. weapons transfers. The Philippines has approached other countries for military cooperation: Russia said that it was open to joint exercises on anti-piracy and search-and-rescue operations, while the Philippine Senate ratified the Philippines-Australia Status of Visiting Forces Agreement in July 2012 following the Scarborough Shoal incident. The bill, which languished in the Senate for more than four years, was overwhelmingly approved by 17–1, much to the satisfaction of the Defence Department which hopes to conduct exercises on humanitarian assistance, disaster relief, and border and maritime security. It remains to be seen whether, without defence treaties, the Philippines can rely on middle powers to come to its aid.

Bananas and Nationalism

Military preparations notwithstanding, the Philippines still needs to maintain positive relations with China to pave the way for a political settlement as well as to benefit from its economic growth. After the 1995 Mischief Reef incident, the two governments agreed on the principle that territorial disputes "should not affect the normal development of their relations".[10] In 2000, they even decided to elevate bilateral relations through defence cooperation, scientific collaboration, and increased trade, tourism and people-to-people exchanges. With regard to the SCS, they agreed to consult with each other, cooperate in their working group on confidence-building measures (CBMs), and possibly hold negotiations in accordance with international law (including the UNCLOS). They also agreed to "contribute positively toward the formulation and adoption of the regional code of conduct" in the SCS.[11]

For the Philippines and its neighbours these were signs that China would be a responsible international player. Tangible progress in bilateral relations was made. China is now the Philippines' third largest trading partner with two-way trade valued at US$12.1 billion in 2011.[12] Philippines-China economic relations have actually surpassed U.S.-Philippines trade: 28 per cent of all Philippine exports in 2011 went to China and Hong Kong compared to only 13.8 per cent to the United States which is the Philippines' traditional market. Philippine investments in China totalled US$2.8 billion in 2011, while Chinese investments in the Philippines stood at US$500 million. Chinese investors have expressed interest in investing in infrastructure, agriculture, energy and tourism.[13] Tourism from China grew by 20.9 per cent from 2009 to 2010 and during the first seven months of 2012, the Chinese were the fourth in tourist arrivals in the Philippines. There are also plans to increase bilateral trade to US$60 billion by 2016, and the Philippines is the first country to host a resident Chinese investment advisor.[14]

Progress on SCS issues, however, was underwhelming. In 1995, they agreed on principles for a code of conduct which included CBMs, a gradual process leading up to negotiation, the use of UNCLOS, maritime cooperation, and protecting freedom of navigation. In 2000, they exchanged draft codes of conduct but they disagreed on geographic scope, freezing further constructions, maritime military activities, and the detention of fishermen.[15] Talking did not prevent either country from bolstering their claims legally or militarily. In the last few years, China has become very aggressive in the SCS.

However, China does not rely solely on naval superiority. During the Scarborough Shoal incident, China exerted economic pressure on the Philippines. The government impounded Philippine bananas due to alleged pest problems. Later, it issued a travel advisory warning Chinese tourists that they may be harmed in the Philippines due to the ongoing disputes. These are all sensitive points for the Philippines: bananas are the country's fifth largest export with sales to China reaching US$360 million in 2011.[16] Tourism accounts for around 5 per cent of the country's total receipts: this travel advisory led to the cancellation of scheduled airline seats by approximately 15–20 per cent according to the Centre for Aviation. Many Filipinos were also concerned that China's government would retaliate against the OFWs in the mainland and in Hong Kong. While not the top destination for OFWs, remittances from China have been increasing since 2003: they now account for 15 per cent of remittances from Asia according to the Philippine Central Bank.

Partly because of this pressure, the Philippines declared that it will bring the SCS dispute to international courts. But this move is problematic for both parties. First, since they are dismissing each other's claim outright, they would probably never agree on a legal venue. Besides, China entered a declaration to the UNCLOS and, therefore, does not recognize the authority of the International Tribunal on the Law of the Sea (ITLOS). Second, both claimants need to refine their legal cases. China's nine-dash line is beyond any of the boundaries set in UNCLOS, while the Philippines still has to resolve important issues such as distinguishing which features are islands and which are rocks, and dealing with the overlap of its EEZ with Palau, Taiwan, and Japan.[17] Thus, it might be premature even for the Philippines to seek advisory opinions from ITLOS. Finally, any compromises will be difficult as both sides issued statements effectively putting their leaders on the line: China by claiming indisputable sovereignty and the Philippines by stating that "[i]t would be an impeachable offense if the President would cede any part of our territory".[18]

Any settlement in the SCS will be political. The UNCLOS, according to Sam Bateman, "only comes into play when sovereignty over land features has been agreed" and the convention is therefore not intended to address sovereignty disputes.[19] But the political atmosphere in 2012 has been toxic in both countries due to domestic power plays and nationalist rhetoric.

China's aggressiveness is either an attempt to divert attention from domestic problems or to demonstrate the country's power to its citizens. In 2012, China's leadership transition was occurring amidst scandals, and growing public dissatisfaction with corruption and socio-economic inequality. The International Crisis Group also raised the possibility that Chinese actions are the result of bureaucratic politics involving civilian agencies, military establishments, national and local governments, energy companies, and other government ministries without effective control by the central government.[20] Regardless of the accuracy of these claims, the fact is that these machinations prevent

of the United States. China is also deeply involved in projects on mainland Southeast Asia involving Cambodia, Laos, and Myanmar such as in the Mekong River.

China had generated such goodwill that sometimes Vietnam and the Philippines are asked by other members to temper their statements against China. Nevertheless, frustration was developing as COC negotiations dragged on, and China remained unflinching. It continued to reject multilateral venues to discuss the topic, griped about ASEAN's ganging up on China, insisted that China will agree to a COC when the time is "ripe", and asked for a seat in ASEAN discussions when the Philippines circulated an informal working draft on the COC.[24]

Matters came to a head during the 2012 ASEAN meetings in Cambodia. In July, for the first time in its forty-five-year history, the ASEAN foreign ministers did not issue a communiqué because of their disagreement on mentioning China's actions in the SCS. Numerous alternatives were drafted but most were rejected by the Cambodian host who, in the end, declared that there was no consensus despite the apparent consensus reached by other members. Subsequently, Indonesian foreign minister Marty Natalegawa's shuttle diplomacy managed to patch up some differences allowing ASEAN to issue its "Six Point Principles", which called for the "early conclusion" of a regional COC on the SCS. The self-congratulation was short-lived. At the November ASEAN Summit, a Cambodian foreign ministry official said that Southeast Asian leaders "had decided that they will not internationalize the South China Sea from now on" when Japanese Prime Minister Noda raised the issue. President Aquino disputed the Cambodian statement and his spokesman later said: "The ASEAN route is not the only route for us. As a sovereign state, it is our right to defend our national interests."[25] Hopes that a legally binding COC or at least a Declaration would be issued during the ASEAN-China Leaders' meeting were unrealized.

These developments are problematic in many ways for the Philippines. First, it means the loss of trust in a key diplomatic partner over the years. ASEAN is important to the Philippines not because the organization will support the legal bases of its claims, but because the organization supports dialogue. A regional COC addresses not only the Philippines' concern of possible conflict, but also the interests of other ASEAN members who are concerned about freedom of commerce and navigation.

Second, it calls into question ASEAN's "centrality" in regional security arrangements when its own members are not united and even mired in their territorial disputes and diplomatic spats. The goal of building an ASEAN Community was a chance to reassert the organization's legitimacy but absent a new convergence of interests among its members, the Community will exist only in name.

Third, it also highlights the dependence and vulnerability of ASEAN to external powers. China exerts strong influence over Cambodia, Myanmar and Laos — a fact that was on display during the Phnom Penh meetings, and a cause of concern when the latter two countries assume chairmanship of ASEAN in 2014 and in 2016. Will there be more setbacks? The United States, for its part, is adopting China's "charm diplomacy" of the late 1990s in order to build better ties with Southeast Asian countries. During the July meetings, Secretary Clinton brought a large contingent of businesspersons to explore possible investments in Cambodia, and in November, President Obama became the first sitting American president to visit Myanmar. The United States now has a seat in the East Asia Summit and has formed a Trans-Pacific Partnership, which includes Brunei, Malaysia, Singapore, and Vietnam, to enhance trade and investments. Finally, the United States voices strong support for a regional COC, a "rules-based" approach to disputes, and encourages a unified ASEAN position towards the SCS. While such support is good, the question is, how long will it last?

This situation has now spurred the Philippines to call for a "minilateral" meeting with Vietnam, Malaysia, and Brunei to discuss viable options to move the peaceful resolution of the SCS dispute forward. Such a meeting is long overdue — throughout the past decade of discussions, the ASEAN claimants had not talked among themselves either because they did not want any disagreement to compromise ASEAN unity or because they were trying to develop cordial relations with China. Does this signal the beginning of the end for ASEAN? Most probably not — there is still too much at stake for ASEAN to not remain as one entity. Actually, by removing this contentious issue off the ASEAN table, it might actually help other ASEAN projects to proceed at a faster pace. But there are troubling signs: the proposed 12 December 2012 meeting was postponed due to "scheduling problems", while some diplomatic sources said that Malaysia and Brunei did not want to offend China.[26] Nevertheless, would this potential meeting lead to a defence alliance against China? Certainly not — at the most it would lay out principles and identify not only areas of cooperation but also legally binding rules to prevent the outbreak of hostilities. One can hope that enforcement mechanisms or at least an impartial tribunal is formed, but that would be extremely difficult. Will China be shut out from the process or any agreement? ASEAN asked China during the November meetings to discuss the COC but the latter was non-committal. It is possible that the four claimants would agree to China's constructive participation, especially its accession to any agreement the four countries might develop. Ironically, it is China's own actions in the SCS and its efforts to divide ASEAN that led to this proposed four-nation meeting which is, perhaps, the last best hope for the Philippines.

Notes

1. Benigno Aquino III, "Third State of the Nation Address", 23 July 2012 <http://www.gov.ph/2012/07/23/english-translation-benigno-s-aquino-iii-third-state-of-the-nation-address-july-23–2012/>.
2. SIPRI, "Background paper on SIPRI Military Expenditure, 2011" <http://www.sipri.org/research/armaments/milex/sipri-factsheet-on-military-expenditure-2011.pdf>.
3. "Manila Declaration on US-Philippine Alliance", 16 November 2011 <http://www.state.gov.r.pa.prs.ps.2011.11.177226.htm>.
4. "Hillary Clinton's remarks with Secretary of Defense Leon Panetta, Philippines Foreign Secretary Albert del Rosario, and Philippines Defense Secretary Voltaire Gazmin after their [2+2] Meeting", Washington, D.C., 30 April 2012 <http://www.state.gov/secretary/rm/2012/04/188982.htm>.
5. SIPRI Arms Trade Database <http://armstrade.sipri.org>.
6. John O'Callaghan and Manuel Mogato, "The U.S. Military Pivot to Asia: When Bases are not Bases", Reuters, 14 November 2012 <http://www.abs-cbnnews.com/-depth/11/14/12/us-military-pivot-asia-when-bases-are-not-bases>.
7. "Statement of Foreign Affairs Secretary Albert F. del Rosario regarding the Philippines-US Mutual Defense Treaty", Public Information Services Unit, 9 May 2012.
8. Thom Shanker and Ian Johnson, "In China, Panetta says American focus on Asia is no threat", *New York Times*, 18 September 2012 <http://www.nytimes.com/2012/09/20/world/asia/panetta-meets-with-xi-easing-doubts-on-chinese-leader.html?_r=0>.
9. Renato Cruz de Castro, "Future Challenges in the US-Philippines Alliance", *Asia-Pacific Bulletin*, no. 168, 26 June 2012 <http://www.eastwestcenter.org/sites/default/files/private/apb168.pdf>.
10. "Joint Statement, Republic of the Philippines-People's Republic of China Consultations on the South China Sea and on Other Areas of Cooperation", 10 August 1995 <http://www.scribd.com/doc/61125477/Joint-Statement-PRC-and-RP>.
11. "Joint Statement between China and the Philippines on the Framework of Bilateral Cooperation in the Twenty-First Century", Beijing, 16 May 2000 <http://www.fmprc.gov.cn/eng/wjdt/2649/t15785.htm#>.
12. Thomas Lum, "The Republic of the Philippines and U.S. Interests", *CRS Report for Congress*, 5 April 2012, p. 10 <http://www.fas.org/sgp/crs/row/RL33233.pdf>.

13. "PNoy brings home $11-billion investment deals from China", GMA News Online, 4 September 2011 <http://www.gmanetwork.com/news/story/231398/news/nation/pnoy-brings-home-11-billion-investment-deals-from-china>.
14. Roy C. Mabasa, "Philippines welcomes China investment advisor", *Manila Bulletin*, 27 March 2012 <http://mb.com.ph/node/355580/philippine>.
15. Carlyle A. Thayer, "ASEAN's Code of Conduct in the South China Sea: A litmus test for community building", *Asia Pacific Journal: Japan Focus*, vol. 10, issue 34, no. 4 (20 August 2012).
16. Joseph Santolan, "Philippine protests further escalate tensions with China", 11 May 2012 <http://www.wsws.org/articles/2012/may2012/phch-m11.shtml>.
17. Rodolfo C. Severino, "The Philippines' National Territory", in *Southeast Asian Affairs 2012*, edited by Daljit Singh and Pushpa Thambipillai (Singapore: Institute of Southeast Asian Studies, 2012), pp. 257–62.
18. Matikas Santos, "Lacierda: Aquino won't give up Scarborough Shoal", *Inquirer Global Nation*, 23 July 2012 <http://globalnation.inquirer.net/45205/lacierda-aquino-wont-give-up-scarborough-shoal>.
19. Sam Bateman, "Managing the South China Sea: Sovereignty is not the issue", *RSIS Commentaries* no. 136/2011, 29 September 2011 <http://www.rsis.edu.sg/publications/Perspective/RSIS1362011.pdf>.
20. ICG, "Stirring up the South China Sea (I)", 23 April 2012 <http://www.crisisgroup.org/~/media/Files/asia/north-east-asia/223-stirring-up-the-south-china-sea-i>.
21. Gil C. Cabacungan, "Aquino's back channel to China is Trillanes", *Philippine Daily Inquirer*, 19 September 2012 <http://globalnation.inquirer.net/50558/aquinos-back-channel-to-china-is-trillanes>.
22. ICG, "Stirring up the South China Sea".
23. Thayer, "ASEAN's Code of Conduct".
24. Ibid.
25. Jason Szep and James Pomfret, "Tensions flare over South China Sea at Asian summit", Reuters, 19 November 2012 <http://www.reuters.com/article/2012/11/19/us-asia-summit-idUSBRE8AI0BC20122119>.
26. Kyodo News Agency, "PH scraps meet of 4 ASEAN claimants in S. China Sea disputes", *ABS-CBN News.com*, 7 December 2012 <http://www.abs-cbnnews.com/nation/12/07/12/ph-scraps-meet-4-asean-claimants-s-china-sea-disputes>.

Singapore

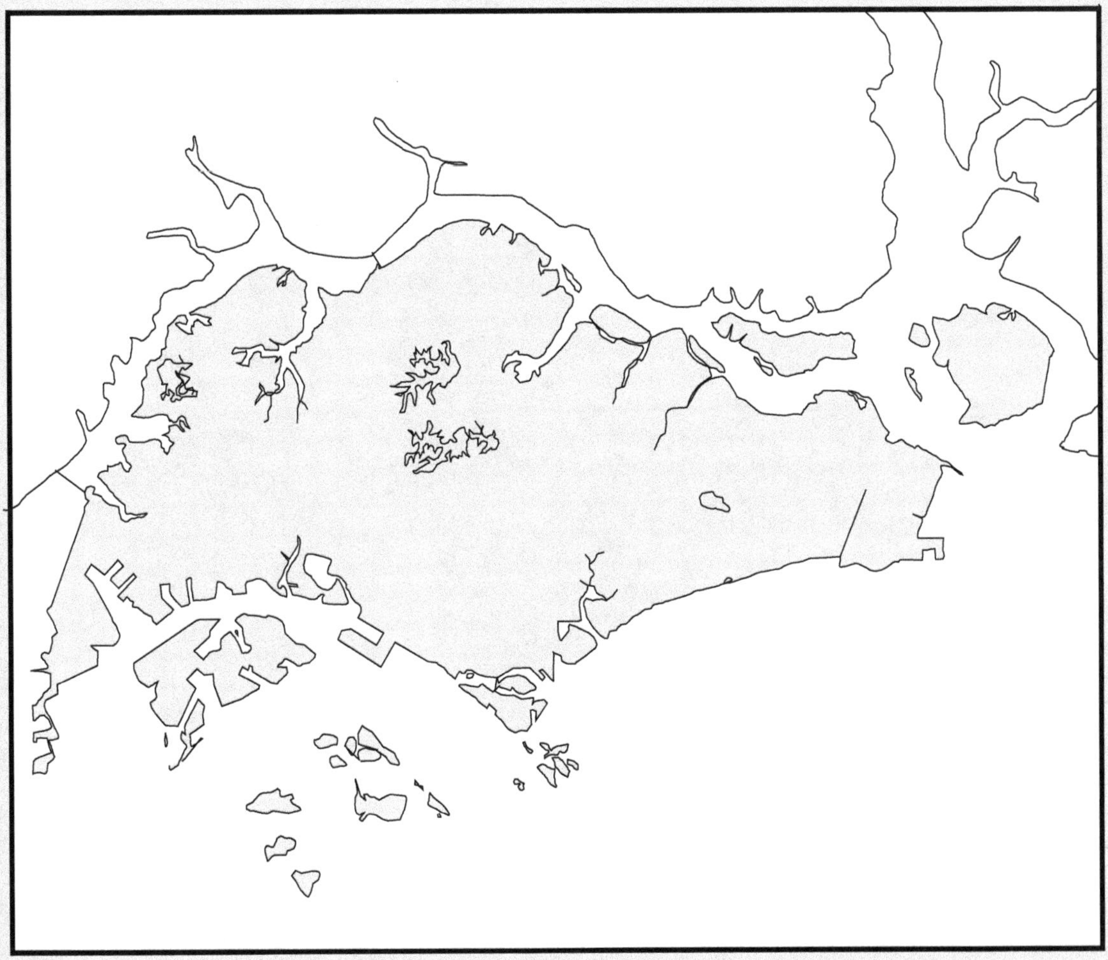

SINGAPORE IN 2012
A Year of Scandals, Attempted Political Engagement, and Socio-economic Anxieties

Narayanan Ganesan

Introduction

The year 2012 began with a scandal that involved two senior civil servants who were arrested and charged with corruption for granting government contracts in exchange for sexual favours. Later in the year, another fifty-one individuals including some rather prominent personalities were charged for procuring commercial sex from an underaged girl. In the political arena, the single member ward of Hougang was the scene of a by-election when the Member of Parliament (MP) for the constituency, Yaw Shin Leong, was sacked from the Workers' Party (WP) that he had previously represented. The sacking came in the wake of allegations of extramarital affairs and the party's inability to get him to account for his behaviour that was deemed to be in the public interest. The by-election was subsequently won by the Workers' Party again though with a marginally narrower lead of 62.1 per cent over the People's Action Party (PAP). Towards the end of the year in December, PAP MP and Speaker of Parliament, Michael Palmer, resigned his seat in the single-member ward of Punggol East over an extramarital affair. It is likely that a by-election will be called in order that the constituents have representation in Parliament. Apart from these highlights, Prime Minister Lee Hsien Loong announced a National Dialogue to uncover domestic preferences on important issues and values going forward. And in the socio-economic realm there was a concerted effort to raise the base wages of the lowest income earners while anxieties persisted regarding property

NARAYANAN GANESAN is Professor at the Hiroshima Peace Institute, Japan.

prices and availability, the high cost of living, and the overload on the country's infrastructure. Legal action against the City Harvest Church for misuse of funds also attracted some attention. The issue of the large number of foreign workers in the country continued to draw attention, notwithstanding government pronouncements to raise the salary bar for special individual work permit holders and slow the intake of foreigners to assuage local anxieties. Furthermore, in late November, foreign bus drivers from China staged a strike that rattled the government's management of industrial relations.

Domestic Political Issues: Hougang By-election and National Dialogue

The most important political event in 2012 was the by-election for Hougang constituency's single-member ward. The seat fell vacant when incumbent Yaw Shin Leong was sacked by the WP. Yaw who was rumoured to be involved in extramarital affairs did not respond to the WP's call to explain his behaviour. The incident naturally put the WP in a negative light, and it went to great lengths to explain to the public that it was unaware of Yaw's trysts and chose to sack him to retain the party's integrity and support. The WP, which had risen to significant political popularity in the general election of 2011 by winning a total of six seats, was clearly put on the defensive and had its work cut out for it in terms of convincing the over 23,000 voters that the indiscretions of its previous member had no bearing on the party. In a clever and orchestrated strategy, the party immediately fired Yaw and went public with its pronouncements that such lapses in conduct were irresponsible and unacceptable, hoping to claim the high moral ground and emerge from the situation unscathed in terms of voter support and public perception regarding the party.[1] There was some discussion at the local constituency level on whether the by-election would disadvantage the WP or whether the generally negative mood against the PAP government at the national level would prevail.[2] Whatever the public perceptions at the ground level were, the WP's Png Eng Huat eventually recaptured the seat with 62.1 per cent of the votes on an approximately 94 per cent turnout of eligible voters in the constituency.[3] In the previous election, Yaw had polled 64.8 per cent of the votes to win the seat. Consequently, there was a marginal erosion of support for the WP but it came out of the situation relatively unscathed. The by-election indicates that support in the ward nurtured by WP leader Low Thia Khiang, the ward's MP from 1991 to 2011, continues to be strong for the WP. This support is likely to pose a problem for the PAP in its future attempts to dislodge the WP there.

The by-election attracted a number of other side plots that are worth mentioning briefly. The first of these were the apparent attempts by two other candidates to contest in the by-election that eventually came to naught. The first candidate hopeful, Dr Poh Lee Guan who is also from the WP, caused some confusion among observers since the WP denied knowledge of his professed intention to stand as a reserve candidate. However, although he did not file his nomination papers, he was sacked by the WP for his unacceptable behaviour. The other independent candidate, Zeng Guoyan, who has a history of showing up at such events, had his application rejected. A more interesting sub-plot was the suit filed by a resident of Hougang constituency, Vellama Marie Muthu, that the Prime Minister did not have "unfettered discretion" in calling for a by-election and for the courts to order him to do so within three months or a reasonable time. The applicant had also offered to withdraw the bid if the Prime Minister made a declaration in Parliament to that effect.[4] The High Court allowed for the case to be heard in open court against the appeal of the Attorney General's Chambers (AGC). Eventually the case was indeed heard as a public issue of general importance, and the AGC again attempted to seek costs against the applicant, a cleaner. The High Court waived costs against the applicant for the case and eventually dismissed an appeal by the AGC against that decision as well.[5] The petitioner, however, failed in her attempt to get the Prime Minister to set a deadline in calling for a by-election. This suit is interesting to the extent that it may well set a norm at least for single-member wards on when and how soon by-elections may be called in the future if the seat falls vacant. The WP in this instance clearly felt a need for the by-election so that its representation in Parliament would not be eroded. In the past, the PAP government had argued that by-elections in Group Representation Constituencies (GRCs) were not necessary since the remaining MPs in the GRC can represent the interests of an MP who is unable to discharge his/her duties.

The lawyer representing the applicant in the Hougang by-election case, M. Ravi, has in the past taken on a number of high-profile cases. He himself was seemingly subjected to some harassment in court when a Law Society official, Wong Siew Hong, approached the bench twice during the by-election trial and submitted a medical report stating that M. Ravi had bipolar disorder and was unfit to practise law.[6] This rather odd development led, in turn, to M. Ravi suing the Law Society and Wong Siew Hong, who had made the representation in court in the first place. An extraordinary general meeting called by the society's members in September for the executive to explain the situation came to naught. Subsequently, however, both Wong Siew Hong and the society's President, Wong Meng Meng, stood down from office and lawyer M. Ravi withdrew his defamation suits. The manner in which the developments unfolded left many unanswered questions but the resolution appears to indicate a settlement behind the scenes that was acceptable to all parties. It was also disclosed that M. Ravi had produced a more detailed psychiatric report in court in his defence, and he was allowed to continue practising law if he subjected himself to a more robust medical regime.[7]

Michael Palmer's resignation from the PAP and as his constituency's MP in Punggol East is likely to lead to a by-election some time in 2013. The simple reason for this assertion is that a single-member ward, unlike a GRC, cannot be dealt with in the long run by a different MP. Since the national election was held only in 2011 and the current government still has a lengthy mandate to serve the country, it will be difficult for the PAP-led government not to call for a by-election. The PAP will also have to match the performance and position of the WP when its MP fell afoul of political norms or risk accruing negative political capital which will be deleterious to its standing. The by-election will pose a significant challenge for the PAP to retain the seat if it is a straight fight with the WP since Palmer won the seat with 54.5 per cent of the votes in 2011 in a three-cornered fight.

In other political developments, Prime Minister Lee Hsien Loong announced the inauguration of a National Dialogue meant to engage a broad spectrum of society and identify their preferences and concerns regarding the national development process. The committee that will lead the discussion comprising some twenty-six members drawn from many different backgrounds is headed by Education Minister Heng Swee Keat. Lee himself went on to hold a television forum in September with fifty guests called "A Conversation With PM Lee".[8] These activities were described as being conducted in order to determine the next chapter of the Singapore Story — a reference to how the country has morphed since political independence in 1965. This dialogue is still in the early stages and it remains to be seen how representative it will be and the direction that it will take.

The bills introduced to amend the Parliamentary Pensions Act and Civil List and Pension Act in August have gone some way to placate public disquiet at the high salaries that were previously paid out to political appointment holders and their ability to draw a pension after serving eight years or more in office after attaining the age of fifty. This pension provision was removed, and the removal was part of the recommendations of the committee that had been tasked to review the salaries of political appointment holders in the country. There had previously been widespread disquiet regarding the high salaries drawn by such appointees and their entitlement to a scheme that was not available to the average citizen. These changes bring the post-retirement arrangements of political office holders more in line with those of others and are meant to pacify public anger at what was perceived to be the disproportionate and self-rewarding practices of previous governments.

The final development of some significance for the year was the government's announcement of the detention of two persons under the Internal Security Act (ISA) in March and June. The two were described as senior members of the Jemaah Islamiyah (JI) terrorist organization who had undergone training in Afghanistan and fled Singapore in 2001. One of them was arrested by Malaysian authorities and the other by Indonesian authorities and then deported to Singapore where they were detained under the ISA. The Ministry of Home Affairs added that three JI members were released between March and September 2012 and restriction orders against seventeen others were allowed to lapse on account of their cooperative behaviour and responsiveness to rehabilitation efforts.[9]

Dominant Economic Issues: Wages, Inflation, and the Foreign Workforce

The government's budget allocation for the fiscal year emphasized a number of important issues that will have a direct impact on local savings and spending. The first of these initiatives is an increase in the employers' and employees' contribution to the Central Provident Fund (CPF) rates for older workers above the age of fifty. With effect from September 2012, the total contribution rates to the fund for those aged between fifty to fifty-five will increase by 2.5 per cent, for those from fifty-five to sixty by 2 per cent and those from sixty to sixty-five by 0.5 per cent.[10] Interestingly, the bulk of the increase is drawn from the employers' contribution that will not lessen the take-home salaries of workers substantially. Similar but lesser increases were also mandated for self-employed workers. The earned income tax relief of older workers was also effectively doubled from S$3,000 to S$6,000 for workers from fifty-five to fifty-nine years of age and from S$4,000 to S$8,000 for those above sixty years of age. Other interesting schemes to benefit older citizens included cash bonuses of up to $20,000 for home owners who downgraded from larger to smaller public housing flats. This and a reverse mortgage scheme that has already been introduced may well free up some larger public housing units and provide senior citizens with sufficient cash to maintain a reasonable quality of life. The previous government mantra of upgrading and asset enhancement meant little since cashing out would have meant the loss of house and home. Other initiatives included greater support for health care and those with disabilities, and cash offsets for the Goods and Services Tax (GST) and rising medical costs to be paid into the Medisave funds of citizens. As with previous years, given the redistributive nature of these policies, the greatest gains accrued to those regarded as the most needy, based on their housing type or annual rental value of the premises.

Cost of living is another major domestic concern especially for those in the low-income categories. The cost of living in Singapore in the last two decades has far outpaced the rise in wages of many workers especially those in the middle and lower income groups. Booming prices of housing and transportation and persistently high inflation that averaged around 4.5 to 5 per cent has led to a decline in real wages for many in these categories. The seriousness of the situation was highlighted by former National Wages Council (NWC) chief Dr Lim Chong Yah's call for shock therapy to increase the wages of those who earn S$1,500 a month or less by 50 per cent over a three-year period. Concurrently, he advocated freezing the salaries of high-income earners with salaries in excess of S$15,000 during the same period.[11] This in his view would help stabilize the rising income inequality in Singapore and ensure that living became more affordable for the less well-off. He had also suggested a minimum monthly wage of S$1,000 for those earning below that amount. Whereas the government initially dismissed his suggestions as simplistic, there is evidence to suggest that some concerted effort is being made to increase the wages of those in such situations.

The first sign of the government's seriousness in addressing the issue was its acceptance of the NWC's recommendation to increase the salaries of those earning below S$1,000 by S$50 monthly and also include a percentage salary increment beyond the S$50 in 2012.[12] It was also reported that an agreement has been reached between the government, unions, and cleaning companies for cleaners to draw a minimum monthly wage of S$1,000 as the starting salary in the sector. This was said to be a 23 per cent increase in wages over the current median wage of S$815 according to figures from the Ministry of Manpower (MOM).[13] The government has in the past introduced fixed quanta in addition to percentages only for the payment of bonuses. Consequently this move that was put forward by the National Trades Union Congress (NTUC) represents an attempt to structure a wage system that better attends to the necessity to pay a base wage that takes into account the actual cost of living. Separately, it was also reported that some 10,000 cleaners from the office and commercial buildings, food and beverage establishments and conservancy sectors will get a wage increase that raises the basic wage to between S$1,000 and S$1,200.[14] Another sector that reported significant wage increases is the health care sector where 16,000 public health care administrative, ancillary and support staff are expected to benefit from a wage increase of 4 per cent to 10 per cent from September 2012.[15] Finally, it was also announced that some 26,000 teachers will benefit from a salary increase from 5 per cent to 15 per cent effective from September 2012.[16]

The government appears to be slowly putting in place a progressive wage model that gradually increases the salaries of low-wage earners in the country. The importation of low-cost foreign labour whose wages were also depressed by unscrupulous labour agents have truly had a deleterious impact on local low-wage earners. Consequently, initiatives that raise the basic salaries of these workers should have been forthcoming much earlier, given the rise in the country's cost of living and persistently high inflation that lowers the value of real wages. Pronouncements by NTUC leaders and MPs from the PAP make it clear that the situation needs to be remedied. A big differential between the wages of top earners and those at the bottom is well known to lead to frustration and social disquiet. This, added to the fact that Singapore spends little on social welfare compared to other countries at a similar level of development in East Asia like Taiwan and Hong Kong, leaves low-wage earners especially vulnerable to cost of living issues.[17] Additionally, it spends little on domestic social reproduction by accepting a large number of migrants into the country for residence.

The price and availability of housing and the increasing number of foreign workers in the country continued to be two other major economic considerations in 2012. Housing prices, including those of new and resale public housing, have seen remarkable increases in the last decade. In the third quarter of the year alone, resale Housing and Development Board (HDB) prices climbed 2 per cent higher. An increase of 0.5 per cent was recorded for private property prices.[18] These prices come on the back of annual rises that have seen prime resale units fetch up to a million dollars, feeding the already existent anxieties at the ground level and in particular among young couples keen to start a family. Stung by widespread criticisms of an overload on infrastructural facilities to service the large intake of foreigners into the country, the HDB has ramped up supply in order to play catch up to the situation. It announced that a total of 11,300 HDB flats and 12,500 non-landed private housing units were being completed in 2012, much more than in previous years.[19] The government also announced that the number of new private properties coming up for sale has reached 100,000 units at the end of the third quarter.[20] Finally, in order to cater to the housing needs of lower income families, the HDB has announced the building of 2,000 additional rental flats with the aim of raising the total number of such units to 57,000 by 2015.[21]

The government does indeed appear to have been caught off guard with regard to the robust demand for housing in Singapore. This is in large part because the population has grown significantly in recent years through liberal immigration policies for foreign workers without careful coordination to ensure that the city-state is able to sustain the enlarged population now reported at 5.31 million according to the government's statistics.[22] This total comprises a citizen population of 3.29 million, a permanent resident population of 0.53 million that was reported as stable; the biggest increase came from the non-resident population at 1.49 million, up from 1.39 million a year ago. These robust increases in population size since 2005 when the population was only 4.265 million have clearly stretched Singapore's current infrastructure including housing. The government on its part has responded by building more units and lately also curbing the tenure of home mortgages to a maximum of thirty-five years. And it has introduced a 10 per cent premium on the purchase of properties by foreigners that lulled sentiments for a short while. In fact Hong Kong has introduced a similar but higher 15 per cent levy as well as a 5 per cent levy at the time when the property is sold.

Public housing and being able to meet the housing needs of citizens at an affordable price is an important social and political issue in Singapore. Good quality and reasonably priced public housing and good infrastructure facilities were a selling point for the PAP government from the 1970s and enormously raised the party's popularity and support at the polls. The same issues as well as the cost of living are now clearly bearing down on the popularity of the government. Although public housing now accounts for only 82 per cent of the total housing needs compared to 86 per cent in the past, the vast majority of citizens look to the government to provide affordable housing. In the Singapore case, the skyrocketing prices of these properties have serious negative consequences for the population as well as the PAP government, and much more can clearly be done to arrest the upward momentum on the basis of public policies.[23] Whereas the situation is partly the outcome of an excess of capital in international markets and historically low interest rates for mortgages, the government cannot escape a good measure of responsibility for it.

To begin with, the government is the largest landowner in the country, having purchased large tracts of land at very low prices in the 1970s. It therefore owns land that can be sold for development, which means it controls the demand and supply of housing. Secondly, it needs to exercise more stringent oversight in the resale public housing market that tends to have a knock-on effect on the entire housing market. For example, whereas private property owners are unable to buy public housing, those who already own public housing are allowed to buy private properties without relinquishing the public housing. Extending the mandatory residential requirement from the current five years to a much longer period will also dampen prices, and the levy for foreign buyers can be significantly raised especially if it is meant to curb speculation. In other words, those who buy and sell public housing properties for capital gains can be penalized through the introduction of a tax regime. Similarly, in order to cater to low-wage earners, it can introduce units that cannot be sold for much longer periods at significant discounts in order to encourage home ownership — a key PAP policy platform in the past. Other ideas include the sale of foreign-owned properties only to citizens at the time of relocation like in Australia. In short, there are many ways to overcome this housing problem and the government should seriously consider introducing more legislation to curb the seemingly runaway situation.[24]

The other major economic anxiety among locals appears to be the rising number of foreign workers in the country. In order to assuage such anxiety, the government announced that it was significantly tightening the income criteria for holders of Personalised Employment Passes (PEPs).[25] Whereas the previous requirement was an annual income of S$34,000, it was raised to S$144,000 with effect from December. Additionally it was announced that the duration of the passes that cannot be renewed has been shortened from five years to three years. For existing pass holders, the income limit comes into effect from December 2014. Internet postings clearly indicated bewilderment at the liberal nature of previous policies amid fears that such pass holders may accept a lower salary just to stay on in the country and further worsen the plight of low-wage earners.[26] The Ministry of Trade and Industry (MTI) also announced that there was a strong case to be made for calibrating Singapore's immigration policy to cope with an ageing workforce in order to retain economic productivity. It was also revealed that some 41 per cent of the more than 400,000 foreign workers are in the services sector like food and beverage, retail, finance, landscaping, and security.[27] This revelation confirmed the suspicions of many that low-wage earners in Singapore faced pressures from low-paid foreign workers who can afford to live without a family in the country at a much lower cost and then repatriate their wages back to their home country. Against this backdrop, it was also revealed that 70 per cent of the 122,600 jobs created in the country in 2012 went to foreigners.[28] Additionally, it was revealed that despite attempts to prune the foreign workforce in the country, their total number stood at 1,234,100, reportedly the highest since 2007.[29]

In the face of such statistics, it is not surprising if there has been the perception that the government is placing economic productivity above the clearly expressed plight of citizens and that policy-makers do not realize that low- and middle-income wage earners bear a disproportionate burden of escalating costs of living and putting up with the inconveniences of an overloaded infrastructure, pressures to which policy-makers are immune. It is only very recently that some of those in charge of policy seem to have gone down to the ground level in order to get a better feel of ground sentiments. It is not clear if this initiative has been replicated elsewhere in policy-making circles. The grievances of the local population with regard to their current situation have the potential to unravel the post-independence social contract between the PAP government and its citizenry.

Dominant Social Issues: Corruption Scandals, Underaged Sex, Disease Outbreaks, and Ethnic Misgivings

The year 2012 witnessed an unusual number of high-profile cases in the courts. The year began with an announcement in late January from the government that two senior civil servants had been arrested for corruption by the Corrupt Practices Investigation Bureau (CPIB). The two were identified as Peter Lim Sin Pang, the head of the Singapore Civil Defence Force (SCDF) and Ng Boon Gay, the Director of the Central Narcotics Bureau (CNB). They were charged under the Prevention of Corruption Act (PCA) for "serious personal misconduct". It was subsequently revealed that both men were accused of obtaining sexual gratification while holding office in return for favourable treatment in the award of government contracts in information technology. Whereas Peter Lim who had ten charges brought against him opted to plead guilty and his trial is scheduled for early 2013, Ng hired a lawyer, Senior Counsel Tan Chee Meng, who mounted a robust and animated defence of his client. Tan's contention was that Ng had been involved in an intimate relationship with the woman, Cecilia Sue, who he was accused of corruptly giving preferential treatment to, and that he had not sought any sexual gratification in the course of the relationship. If no gratification was sought, there was no corruption charge to answer. Despite the clever line of reasoning, the prosecution argued that the line of reasoning was mischievous and that regardless of whether Ng felt the sexual acts to be satisfactory or adequate, it still constitutes a corrupt act of gratification during Ng's term of office as a civil servant.[30] Eventually the prosecution prevailed and Ng was deemed to have a case for him to answer. These two cases appear to indicate, in an age of greater scrutiny via social media, an enhanced concern in the government in ensuring that the elite ranks of the Singapore civil service stay clean, despite the country's generally good reputation in such matters.

The second sensational trial for financial irregularities involved the City Harvest Church and five of its senior members. The probe launched by the police came after complaints from the Commissioner of Charities. The five charged are the founder of the church Kong Hee, his deputy Tan Yee Peng, former board member John Lam Leng Hung, church investment manager Chew Eng Han, and church finance manager Sharon Tan Shao Yuen. They were accused of financial irregularities for a sum of S$24 million to finance the secular music career of Kong Hee's wife, Ho Yeow Sun, from the church's building fund.[31] It was also revealed that the group had conspired to appropriate another S$26.6 million to avoid scrutiny of the earlier misappropriation. The money misappropriated was apparently used to fund a grand plan called the Crossover Project, an "ambitious endeavour to expand the reach of Christianity through Ms Ho's secular music".[32] At early pre-trial hearings three of the accused were granted permission to travel abroad since their passports had been impounded. Indications thus far are that the accused will enter "not guilty" pleas and contest the charges which will make for a highly watched trial. The government's position in the case is that monies from charitable and non-profit organizations cannot be utilized to further non-charitable causes. It also maintains a regulatory regime to monitor the activities of such organizations.

The final case involved charges brought against fifty-one men for procuring commercial sex from an underaged girl. The case was sensational for the sheer number of men involved and the social standing of some of them. They included

Howard Shaw from the Shaw Organization family whose name is synonymous with movie theatres in Singapore, a former school principal, and a senior banker with the Union Bank of Switzerland (UBS). Most of those charged were given jail terms ranging from nine to thirteen weeks with a possible third of the sentence commuted for good behaviour.[33]

Among other major social developments worth noting are the large and sustained outbreaks of hand, foot and mouth disease (HFMD) that affected young kindergarten and school-going children and a racist Facebook rant by an NTUC official against Malays. Singapore has had problems coping with HFMD as a public health issue for some years now, but 2012 saw the number of cases spike up well beyond epidemic levels. The large increases began from March and the reported number of cases for the week ending 28 April was 1,590, and it spiked even higher to 1,610 cases by the week ending 12 May.[34] The Ministry of Health's (MOH) threshold for an epidemic is when cases go above a count of 780 and, at its peak, the count was more than double the benchmark for declaring an epidemic. Preventive measures undertaken by the MOH included spot checks and the forced closure of eight childcare centres and kindergartens. Fortunately only a mild variant of the virus that did not lead to any fatalities was involved. Nonetheless, HFMD and dengue haemorrhagic fever have become public health concerns lately.

As for the case involving the NTUC official, one of the labour organization's senior employees, Amy Cheong, had posted racist remarks against Malays on her Facebook page that went viral. These remarks were quickly condemned by the political elite as being misplaced, wrong, and totally unacceptable. There was a groundswell of anger against the posting, and she was subsequently sacked by the NTUC shortly afterwards in what the organization's secretary-general and senior PAP politician Lim Swee Say described as a "painful decision".[35] Amy Cheong then packed up and returned to Australia where she had come from to work in Singapore. The groundswell of disquiet in Singapore against the large number of foreign workers in the country often morphs into generalized attacks against foreigners whenever one of them runs afoul of local norms.

Foreign Affairs: Relative Calm and Strengthening of Bilateral Relations

It was a rather lacklustre year in foreign affairs that mostly saw the strengthening of important relationships. There was a small hiccup in June when online posts in Malaysia reported the active participation of three Singapore diplomats at the Bersih 3.0 Rally that campaigned for transparent elections in the country. Although Singapore's Ministry of Foreign Affairs (MFA) clarified that its officers did not don the yellow colours of the campaign, its ambassador to Malaysia, Ong Keng Yong, was summoned by Malaysia's Foreign Minister Anifah Aman to convey the Malaysian government's displeasure.[36] Ong is the previous Secretary-General of the Association of Southeast Asian Nations (ASEAN). Singapore's MFA simply maintained that its officers were at the Rally as "impartial observers" monitoring political developments rather than being involved in domestic politics. Nonetheless, the Malay rights group Perkasa staged a protest involving some 300 persons outside the Singapore High Commission and sought an official apology and the recall of the three diplomats involved.[37] Perkasa has recently acquired a measure of prominence and notoriety as an NGO because of the extreme position it takes and owing to the United Malays National Organization's (UMNO) quiet support for it, especially on matters pertaining to Malay-Muslim interests. In an unrelated development, Singapore announced a tightening of rules on male foreign workers from Sabah and Sarawak after a number of brutal murder incidents on the island were traced to these nationals. Rather than admit them for employment from a minimum age of eighteen, the government revised the age requirement upward to thirty-five.[38] Notwithstanding these hiccups, Singapore's bilateral relations with Malaysia has been good recently and especially since leadership transition in Malaysia after Mahathir Mohamad in 2003. Important outstanding issues like the overlapping territorial claims over the Horsburgh Lighthouse and the ownership and development of Malayan Railway land have been resolved. Singapore has also indicated interest in investments in the proximate Iskandar project in Johor state, and Malaysia continues to be Singapore's most important trading partner.

Similarly, ties with the United States were reaffirmed with the visit of U.S. Secretary of State Hillary Clinton to Singapore in November 2012. Additionally, earlier in the year it was announced that the United States would deploy up to four of a new class of coastal warships — Littoral Combat Ships (LCS) — on a rotational basis to Singapore from 2013.[39] This arrangement strengthens Singapore's already deep security ties with the United States since the two countries signed a Memorandum of Understanding in 1990. Singapore's relations with China were also good, and Prime Minister Lee Hsien Loong visited China in September 2012 and held talks with President Hu Jintao. Strategic and environmental cooperation agreements were signed with Jiangsu province and Nanjing during the visit. Bilateral relations with China have steadily strengthened since the two countries normalized diplomatic ties in 1990 and the value of bilateral trade rose 6.4 per cent in 2011 to $80.5 billion in 2012. Singapore has also taken the position that the territorial disputes in the South China Sea that involve China should be peacefully negotiated even though such a process may take a long time to bear tangible results.

In other developments, Singapore's bilateral relations with Australia, Brunei, and New Zealand were enhanced with official visits by Prime Minister Lee Hsien Loong. Other developments included the signing of a strategic partnership agreement between France and Singapore in October when French Prime Minister Jean-Marc Ayrault visited Singapore.[40] Finally, Singapore signed a tax evasion treaty with Germany, mostly aimed at preventing German nationals from stashing money in the city-state to avoid paying taxes on them.[41]

Conclusion

The year 2012 saw the WP retain its seat in the Hougang by-election. There was the resignation of the Speaker of Parliament Michael Palmer from his Punggol East seat and this is likely to lead to a by-election in 2013. The government also announced the start of a National Dialogue to engage a broad spectrum of the country's citizens to try and determine the course of the country's future development. In economic matters, there were worries over the price and availability of housing and persistently high inflation. In the social realm, a number of high-profile sex and corruption cases stole the limelight. In foreign affairs it was mostly a case of staying the course and strengthening important bilateral relations. As the year drew to a close the local economy had slowed and the government predicted a lowered annual growth of 1.5 per cent to 2.5 per cent for the entire year.[42] There was also a much-publicized mass strike action by bus drivers from China at the Singapore Mass Rapid Transit (SMRT) system. A total of 171 workers stopped work on 26 November and 88 continued the action into the following day. After investigations by the government over the workers' unhappiness regarding wages and living conditions, four workers were charged in court for instigating the strike action and another twenty-nine were eventually deported from the country back to China. This strike action that the government called an "illegal strike" poses challenges for how Singapore manages industrial relations with foreign workers.

Notes

The author would like to thank Benjamin Wong, Lam Peng Er, Michael Montesano, and Daljit Singh for their comments on an earlier draft of this article.

1. "Yaw broke trust of WP and the people", *Straits Times*, 16 February 2012.
2. Goh Chin Lian, "By-election: Local focus or barometer of national issues?", *Straits Times*, 10 May 2012.
3. Phua Mei Pin, "Workers' Party wins 62 per cent of Hougang by-election votes", *Straits Times*, 26 May 2012.
4. "Hougang resident's offer to Prime Minister", *Straits Times*, 20 June 2012.
5. Andrea Ong, "Hougang by-election case: Judge dismisses AGC's ruling against 'no costs' appeal", *Straits Times*, 14 November 2012.
6. "M Ravi seeks court order to expel Law Society council members", AsiaOne News, 2 September 2012.
7. "Lawyer M. Ravi allowed to continue practising law", *New Paper*, 25 November 2012.
8. "PM Lee to hold TV forum with 50 guests from all walks of life", Channel News Asia, 13 September 2012.
9. "Two persons detained in S'pore for terrorism activities", Yahoo News, 11 October 2012.
10. See "Singapore Budget 2012 – Key Budget Initiatives" <http://www.mof.sg/budget_2012/key_initiatives/families1.html>.
11. "Ex-NWC chief proposes changes to help narrow income gap", Channel News Asia, 25 October 2012.
12. "Gov't accepts NWC proposal for wage increase", Yahoo News, 23 May 2012.
13. Toh Yong Chuan, "New proposed cleaners' basic pay to start from $1,000", *Straits Times*, 19 October 2012.
14. "10,000 cleaners set to get pay increases", Channel News Asia, 18 October, 2012.
15. "16,000 healthcare staff to get salary increases from September", Channel News Asia, 14 September 2012.
16. "Over 26,000 teachers to benefit from up to 15 per cent pay rise", Yahoo News, 31 August 2012.
17. "Social welfare per capita: Hong Kong spends 76 per cent more than Singapore", The Online Citizen, 11 November 2012. Comparative data for countries in Asia across sectors can be accessed at the website of the Asian Development Bank.
18. Daryl Chin, "HDB resale prices hit record highs, even with supply ramped up", and Esther Teo, "Singapore's Q3 private home prices rise 0.5 per cent", *Straits Times*, 1 October 2012.
19. "Significantly more housing units to be completed in 2014", Channel News Asia, 15 October 2012.

20. Rachel Chang, "Coming up: Over 100,000 housing units", *Straits Times*, 30 October 2012.
21. Daryl Chin, "2,000 flats to be built for lower-income families", *Straits Times*, 24 October 2012.
22. Janice Heng, "S'pore population up to 5.31 million due to 'strong manpower demand'", *Straits Times*, 28 September 2012.
23. See the interesting article by Dr Wong Wee Nam, "The deleterious effects of high property prices", The Online Citizen, 6 November 2012. A Yahoo poll of 21,470 persons identified housing as the most pressing concern among Singaporeans (28 per cent), management of flow and integration of foreigners (21 per cent), and narrowing the income gap (17 per cent) as the second and third most important worries of locals. See "Cost of housing No. 1 concern: Yahoo poll", Yahoo News, 25 September 2012.
24. See, for example, Yeoh Lam Keong, Donald Low and Manu Bhaskaran, *Rethinking Singapore's Social Compact* (Singapore: National University of Singapore, 2012).
25. Janice Heng, "Stricter criteria for personalized work passes for foreign professionals", *Straits Times*, 7 November 2012.
26. See Leong Sze Hian, "Premium Employment Pass: Was only $34,000?", The Online Citizen, 8 November 2012.
27. "Strong case for Singapore to continue with calibrated immigration policy", Channel News Asia, 25 September 2012.
28. Sharon Chen, "Singapore Will Take in Foreigners at Comfortable Pace, Lee Says", Bloomberg News, 26 September 2012.
29. Daryl Chin, "Singapore on right track to cut foreign labour dependency", *Straits Times*, 1 October 2012.
30. Claire Huang, "Ng Boon Gay trial adjourned till after lunch", *Straits Times*, 19 November 2012.
31. "Prosecutors shed light on alleged misuse of church funds", and Tan Dawn Wei, "Ho Yeow Sun: '$23 million bid for stardom'", *Straits Times*, 27 June 2012.
32. Ibid.
33. Elena Chong, "Howard Shaw begins jail term for sex with underaged prostitute", *Straits Times*, 5 October 2012.
34. Melissa Pang, "HFMD cases at record high", *Straits Times*, 19 May 2012.
35. Jennani Durai, "Sacking of Amy Cheong a 'painful decision' for NTUC chief", *Straits Times*, 9 October 2012.
36. Phua Mei Yin, "MFA rebuts allegations diplomats participated in Bersih Rally", *Straits Times*, 22 June 2012; and "Diplomatic flurry over Singapore envoys at Bersih rally", *Straits Times*, 23 June 2012.
37. "Protests outside Singapore High Commission in KL", *Straits Times*, 26 June 2012.

38. Nelson Benjamin, "Singapore tightens labour rules on Sarawakian males", *The Star*, 10 September 2012.
39 "U.S. plans 10-month warship deployment to Singapore", Reuters News, 10 May 2012.
40. "Singapore, France sign strategic partnership agreement", Channel News Asia, 18 October 2012.
41. "Singapore and Germany agree deal to tackle tax evasion", BBC News, 15 October 2012.
42. "Singapore will grow between 1.5 per cent and 2.5 per cent this year: MAS", Channel News Asia, 30 October 2012.

SINGAPORE'S POPULATION CONUNDRUM
The Great Balancing Act 2

Yap Mui Teng

In January 2013, the Singapore government is expected to issue a White Paper on Population which will be debated in Parliament. This is the culmination of a year's work and consultations involving various stakeholders. At issue are the ultra-low Total Fertility Rate (TFR), imminent rapid population and workforce ageing and decline, and the population's aversion to more in-migration, a policy lever which could ameliorate the above mentioned impacts. The White Paper represents another attempt by the government to come to grips with Singapore's population conundrum.

What Is at Stake?

Singapore's population has been experiencing below replacement level TFR since 1977. Since 2003, the TFR has in fact fallen below the "ultra-low"[1] level of 1.3 births per woman. According to the eminent demographer, Peter McDonald, no country whose TFR has fallen below 1.5 births per woman has successfully returned to the replacement level of about 2.1.[2] The National Population and Talent Division (NPTD), which is a part of the Prime Minister's Office, projected that with a constant TFR of 1.2 births and average life expectancy of eighty-two years, the number of deaths among its citizens will outstrip births by 2025 and the citizen population will begin to decline, if there is no net in-migration.[3] The NPTD goes on to show that raising the TFR to the replacement level will only delay and slow the rate of decline and that an

YAP MUI TENG is Senior Research Fellow at the Institute of Policy Studies, Lee Kuan Yew School of Public Policy, National University of Singapore.

annual inflow of between 20,000 and 25,000 immigrants "will keep the citizen population size stable".[4]

Another factor that will begin to change the demographic scene dramatically in Singapore is the ageing of the post-World War II baby boomers. According to the NPTD:

> (b)etween now and 2030, Singapore will experience an unprecedented age shift, as over 900,000 Baby Boomers will retire from the workforce and enter their silver years ... As more citizens retire and fewer enter the working-age band of 20–64 years, the number of citizens of working ages will start to shrink. At current TFR and without immigration, the size of our working-age citizen population will shrink drastically ... Immigration will slow down the decline of citizens in the working-age band. An inflow of 25 (thousand) new citizens per year would keep the size of our working-age citizen population relatively stable.[5]

In another paper put out as part of its public consultation exercise, the NPTD spells out the implications of population ageing and decline for Singapore, as follows:

> An ageing population coupled with increased longevity will lead to higher national healthcare and long-term care expenditure for the elderly. Even at current rates of subsidy, the national expenditure on healthcare will rise, given that there will be (three) times the number of citizens aged 65 and above by 2030. With fewer children to support parents and grandparents, and increasing numbers of elderly living alone, more paid help such as domestic workers, home-based caregivers and nurses will also be needed.
>
> Government revenue comes mostly from income taxes, consumption taxes and asset taxes, all of which are dependent on economic growth. A shrinking and ageing population and workforce will make it more difficult to sustain public finances, especially when this is coupled with increasing needs for higher expenditure to support a much larger elderly population. We may need to cut expenditure in some areas, or find new sources of revenue to balance our budget.[6]

Why Now?

As mentioned in the NPTD paper, 2012 marks the year when the first of the baby boomers, identified in Singapore as those born over the years 1947 to 1964, reach age sixty-five, marking their entry into retirement and senior citizen status.[7]

Although baby boomers, particularly the later-born ones, are better educated and likely to be better prepared for old age than the current elderly, the ratio between economically active and inactive population will change unless measures are taken to change existing attitudes and institutions to adapt to the new reality. These include changes in attitudes and policies towards the employment of older workers. It may be noted that a survey on baby boomers conducted in 2007 found that a sizeable proportion of them expect to remain in the workforce beyond the retirement age, either because they felt they needed a job for financial reasons or because they wanted to remain active.[8]

The ageing of the baby boomers and its impact on the population and society have been anticipated for years, indeed since the 1980s. The factor that has probably contributed to the heightened urgency to review and discuss the future of the Singapore population at this point in time is immigration. This is in turn related to the further decline of the TFR and annual births to unprecedented low levels in the decade of the 2000s in spite of the strengthening of policy measures to promote marriage and childbearing. Raising the TFR and immigration, as mentioned in my contribution in the 2001 edition of this publication, are the main demographic levers that the government can use to address the demographic challenges.[9] Recent developments in these areas will be discussed in greater detail below.

Ultra-low TFR

The decade of the 2000s saw Singapore's TFR plunge below 1.3 births per woman, the level which demographers consider "ultra-low". Singapore's current TFR ranks well below that of France, the United States, and the Nordic countries; even among East Asian countries which are well known for their low fertility levels, only Hong Kong and Taiwan have TFRs that are at or lower than Singapore's.[10]

As Figure 1 shows, the TFR has hovered around 1.2 births per woman since 2003. This is unprecedented in Singapore's demographic history. Prior to the 2000s decade, the only times when the TFR had fallen below 1.5 births per woman was in 1986 (when the TFR was 1.43) after Singapore experienced its first recession since independence in 1965 and in 1998/99 in the aftermath of the Asian financial crisis (when the TFR was 1.48 and 1.47 respectively).[11] The ultra-low fertility levels in the 2000s follow periods of economic uncertainty in Singapore and elsewhere following the 2001 dot-com bust, the September 11 attacks on the United States in 2001, and the Severe Acute Respiratory Syndrome

FIGURE 1
Resident Live-births and Total Fertility Rate, 2000–11

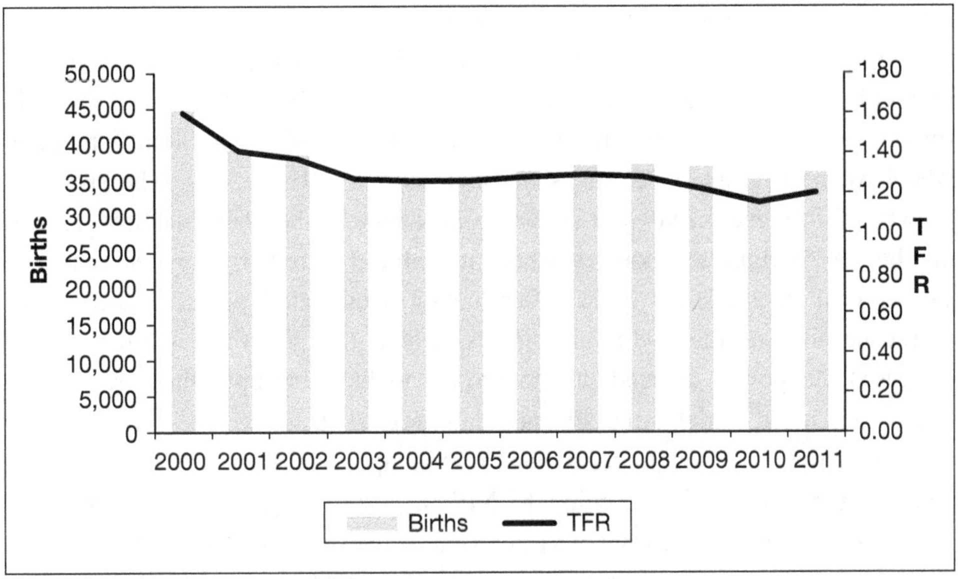

Source: Department of Statistics, *Population Trends 2012*, Table A4.1 <http://www.singstat.gov.sg/pubn/popn/population2012b.pdf>.

(SARS) epidemic in the Asian region in 2003. The TFR dipped further to 1.16 births per woman in 2010, following the 2008/09 U.S.-led recession. Singapore, being a very open economy, is strongly affected by developments elsewhere, and its TFR tends to track changes in its economic performance quite closely. The number of babies born annually over this period hovered around 35,000, which is well below the more than 60,000 born during the baby boom and also below the average numbers of 42,000–46,000 born in the 1980s and 1990s (only in 1983 and 1986 did the number of births fall below 40,000). The decline in annual births means that there will be fewer young men and women entering the workforce, and this is not helped by the increasing tendency for the young to pursue higher education and remain in school longer. Over the course of the 2000s (in 2001, 2004, and 2008), the government had enhanced its suite pro-family policy measures that were first introduced in 1987 when it switched from the previous anti-natalist policy to a pro-natalist one (albeit selectively at first). In 2012, the government has again embarked on a review of its package of measures to boost marriage and childbearing and an announcement is also expected in January 2013.

Immigration

To make up for the "shortfall" in births, the Singapore government has been liberalizing its immigration policy to allow more foreigners to work in the country and to become permanent residents (PRs) and citizens where appropriate. The growth in the foreign population has been such that in 2012, non-citizen, non-PR foreigners made up 28 per cent of the total population of 5.3 million. Foreigners who have been granted PR status made up another 10 per cent. The speed of growth of foreigners over the past two decades can be seen in Table 1. The number of foreigners ("non-residents" in Table 1) grew by 15 per cent and 19 per cent in 2007 and 2008 (after having averaged 9 per cent and higher in the decades of the 1980s and 1990s) which the government attributed to increased manpower demand due to growth in business opportunities.[12] While fluctuating more widely, the PR population grew by 11.5 per cent in 2009 as more foreigners sought to remain in Singapore in view of the economic conditions elsewhere.[13] According to NPTD, "(w)e ... took in an average of 58,000 Permanent Residents (PRs) per year between 2004 and 2008, but have tightened our immigration framework since late-2009 and reduced the intake to an average of 28,500 per year from 2010 onwards".[14] Former Deputy Prime Minister Wong Kan Seng, the then minister in charge of population matters, explained the reason for the increase thus: "(w)e wanted to take advantage of the strong economy in the mid 2000s to attract and retain suitable foreigners to sink roots here, and to make up for our low TFR".[15] It may be noted that only 62 per cent of the Singapore population in 2012 are citizens. This figure includes new citizens whose intake increased "from an average of 8,200 per year between 1987 and 2006, to about 18,500 per year in the last 5 years".[16]

The influx of foreigners triggered unprecedented unhappiness among Singaporeans, and the immigration issue is said to have affected the results of the 2011 General Elections in which the ruling People's Action Party (PAP) had a relatively poorer showing compared to past elections, winning only 60 per cent of the popular votes.[17] The increase in foreigners is blamed for a host of woes faced by the local population, including competition for jobs, rising housing prices, and overcrowding in public transport and other amenities. Differences in socio-cultural behaviour are highlighted, even between those who are supposedly of the same ethnic origin (for example, Chinese Singaporeans and newcomers from mainland China).[18] Negative sentiments are especially strongly expressed on social media — and such feelings are not always one-sided. While the government has taken steps to ramp up the supply of housing

TABLE 1
Singapore Population Size and Growth by Residential Status

Year	Total Population	Number ('000)			Non-Residents	Average Annual Growth[a] (%)				
		Singapore Residents				Total Population	Singapore Residents			Non-Residents
		Total	Citizens	PRs			Total	Citizens	PRs	
1990	3,047.1	2,735.9	2,623.7	112.1	311.3	2.3[b]	1.7[b]	1.7[b]	2.3[b]	9.0
2000	4,027.9	3,273.4	2,985.9	287.5	754.5	2.8	1.8	1.3	9.9	9.3
2006	4,401.4	3,525.9	3,107.9	418.0	875.5	3.2	1.7	0.9	8.1	9.7
2007	4,588.6	3,583.1	3,133.8	449.2	1,005.5	4.3	1.6	0.8	7.5	14.9
2008	4,839.4	3,642.7	3,164.4	478.2	1,196.7	5.5	1.7	1.0	6.5	19.0
2009	4,987.6	3,733.9	3,200.7	533.2	1,253.7	3.1	2.5	1.1	11.5	4.8
2010	5,076.7	3,771.7	3,230.7	541.0	1,305.0	1.8	1.0	0.9	1.5	4.1
2011	5,183.7	3,789.3	3,257.2	532.0	1,394.4	2.1	0.5	0.8	–1.7	6.9
2012	5,312.4	3,818.2	3,285.1	533.1	1,494.2	2.5	0.8	0.9	0.2	7.2

Note: Data from 2003 onwards exclude residents who have been away from Singapore for a continuous period of 12 months or longer as at the reference period.

a. For 1990 and 2000, growth rate refers to the annualized change over the last ten years. For 2006 onwards, growth rate refers to the change over the previous year.

b. Growth rate is computed using population estimates based on de facto concept (i.e. the person is present in the country when enumerated at the reference period).

Source: Department of Statistics, Population Trends 2012, Table 1.1, p. 1 <http://www.singstat.gov.sg/pubn/demo.html#popntrend>.

and infrastructure, this will take time to complete. It has also accepted a recommendation by the 2008 Economic Strategies Committee to keep the share of foreign workers at no more than one-third of the workforce and taken steps to tighten immigration. However, it would seem that for some Singaporeans, any further intake is one too many. The term "xenophobia" or "xenophobic" has crept into the public discourse and media and used to characterize Singaporeans, although writer and naturalized Singaporean, Asad Latif, would argue, "Singaporeans are not a xenophobic people — because there is no single ethnic identity for xenophobia to coalesce around — but they are a people who are immensely proud of what they have achieved collectively in less than 50 years of independence. They place value on being Singaporean. Singaporeans believe that foreigners who wish to make Singapore home cannot change those terms of existence unilaterally".[19] He also expressed the belief, and hope, that anti-foreigner sentiments are only a passing phase "but it is perhaps a necessary phase to be undergone for Singapore's social value system to evolve".

Going forward, can Singapore afford to close its doors to immigration, both temporary and permanent, and if not, what is the level of intake and of what type? It is apparent from both the NPTD projections on citizens, and projections on the resident population made by the Institute of Policy Studies (IPS), that the population of working ages will decline while there will be more older people in the population. Regardless of the projection used, the domestic workforce is likely to grow more slowly in the future than has been the case in the past. Will a slower workforce growth affect economic growth in the future, or can the slower workforce growth be offset by increases in productivity? Is slower growth desirable for the country, or can the country accept a more rapid workforce growth (and ultimately a larger population and a larger foreign population) without lowering the quality of life and social relations?

Prime Minister Lee Hsien Loong, in a speech to PAP members at a party conference in December 2012, argued that economic growth is needed to provide Singaporeans with quality living and quality jobs, revealing also that the government is "aiming for a sustainable 2 to 3 per cent per year" as workforce growth slows, not the "7–8 per cent, some years 10 per cent or even more" of the past.[20] He elaborated that slower growth would mean

> (s)maller increments, smaller bonuses, fewer jobs created. Harder to do business... The lower pay workers (will be affected first), because they are already in a tough spot, and there is (sic) really going to be very difficult for them to move up. Young people will be affected, because they are looking for

> opportunities, they are looking for adventure, they are looking for challenge. No growth, nothing happening, many will be off. Off to Australia, off to America, off to China, India, where the big cities are, where the bright lights are, where the opportunities are. And then we will become an old folks home in Singapore, and we will not achieve our hopes, and we will not achieve our hopes for our children.

The other ways that foreigners can contribute to Singapore's growth has been argued by the Ministry of Trade and Industry (MTI) in an Occasional Paper "Population and Economy" published in October 2012. First, foreign manpower complement the resident workforce doing the lower skilled jobs that Singaporeans reject, including those in health care and elder care. Indeed, a subsequent paper by the NPTD projected the additional foreign worker requirements in health care, domestic services and construction in 2030, as follows: an additional 28,000 foreign health care professionals and support care workers on top of the 13,000 in 2011; an increase in foreign domestic workers from 198,000 in 2011 to 300,000 by 2030; and 250,000 to 300,000 foreign construction workers, up from 250,000 in 2011.[21] The MTI also argues that foreigners contribute to Singapore's tax base — "while foreigners currently account for 20 per cent of all income taxpayers, they contribute more than 25 per cent of our total personal income taxes. Foreigners ... also add to our GST tax base".[22]

The Acting Minister for Manpower, Tan Chuan Jin, warned, however, that "Singapore cannot continue to rely on low-cost foreign labour to grow our economy" and that the government "will manage the pace of foreign manpower tightening carefully ... at a sustainable rate that enables businesses to grow…".[23] In any case, Singapore may not have much choice as more foreigners, including foreign domestic workers, are reportedly either choosing to remain in their home countries due to a narrowing of wage differentials or headed for other destinations that pay them more or provide better working conditions.[24] The impact of a reduction of foreign inflow, effective since late 2009, is already being felt. According to Singapore economist, Chua Hak Bin, "Singapore's economy could have grown nearly twice as fast (in 2012) if not for the stricter rules placed on the hiring of foreign workers".[25] The reduced access to foreign workers has affected small and medium enterprises more, with eight in ten reporting in a survey that "manpower shortages were hampering expansion plans, with some suggesting they may have to relocate operations or close if they did not get relief".[26] Productivity growth may be an alternative to labour; however, the Singapore Business Federation has appealed to the government to review its productivity goal of 2–3 per cent growth, saying it is "a stretched target".[27] Companies are also asking the government for help to raise worker productivity.[28]

Concluding Remarks

Singaporeans are eagerly awaiting the release of the White Paper on Population, given the rapid changes in Singapore's population size and composition in recent years and the impact of these developments on everyday lives. When it is released, there is no doubt that the debates will extend well beyond Parliament. It will probably be one of the most major balancing acts that the government will have to juggle given the breadth and depth of its potential impact. It will also be a major political test for the government, whether or not it will be able to persuade Singaporeans to accept and adapt to its vision of the "new reality" on the demographic front. However, "replacement migration" is not a panacea to all of Singapore's population woes; it is still desirable to raise the TFR to as close to the replacement as possible, perhaps topped up by a small number of immigrants, for population stability in the longer term future. In this regard, it is appropriate to continue to put in place all the social institutions that will help Singaporeans to replace themselves.

Notes

1. See Gavin Jones, Paulin Tay Straughan, and Angelique Chan, eds., *Ultra-low Fertility in Pacific Asia: Trends, Causes and Policy Issues* (New York: Routledge, 2009).
2. Peter McDonald, "Very Low Fertility Consequences, Causes and Policy Approaches", *Japanese Journal of Population* 6, no. 1 (March 2008) <http://www.ipss.go.jp/webj-ad/webjournal.files/population/2008_4/02mcdonald.pdf>.
3. National Population and Talent Division, Prime Minister's Office, "Citizen Population Scenarios", Occasional Paper, April 2010 <https://www.nptd.gov.sg/content/NPTD/home/_jcr_content/par_content/download_1/file.res/Occasional%20Paper%20-%20Citizen%20Population%20Scenarios.pdf>, p. 6.
4. Ibid, p. 7.
5. Ibid.
6. National Population and Talent Division, Prime Minister's Office, "Our Population Our Future", Issues Paper, July 2012 <https://www.nptd.gov.sg/content/NPTD/home/_jcr_content/par_content/download/file.res/Issues%20Paper%20-%20Our%20Population%20Our%20Future.pdf>, p. 16.
7. Although the official retirement age remains at sixty-two, the government has enacted the Retirement and Re-employment Act which, beginning in 2012, requires employers to offer their employees that are nearing retirement age, the opportunity

to be re-employed until age sixty-five, though not necessarily on the same terms (see <http://www.mom.gov.sg/employment-practices/employment-rights-conditions/retirement/Pages/retirement.aspx>).

8. Angelique Chan and Yap Mui Teng, "Baby Boomers Survey", 2009 <http://app.msf.gov.sg/Portals/0/Summary/pressroom/02-2009.pdf>.
9. Yap Mui Teng, "On Babies, Foreign Talent, and Older People: The Great Balancing Act", in *Southeast Asian Affairs 2001* (Singapore: Institute of Southeast Asian Studies, 2001), pp. 310–22.
10. See Occasional Paper on Marriage and Parenthood Trends in Singapore, published by the National Population and Talent Division, Prime Minister's Office, June 2012 <https://www.nptd.gov.sg/content/NPTD/home/_jcr_content/par_content/download_0/file.res/Occasional%20Paper%20on%20MP%20Trends%20_For%20Media%20Briefing%2028%20Jun%202012_w%20annex.pdf>.
11. Department of Statistics, Population Trends 2012, Table A4.1, p. 81 <http://www.singstat.gov.sg/pubn/popn/population2012b.pdf>.
12. Tharman Shanmugaratnam, Budget Debate Round-up Speech 2010 <http://www.mof.gov.sg/budget_2010/download/FY2010_Budget_Debate_Round_Up_Speech.pdf>.
13. Cassandra Chew, "PR hopefuls qucueing overnight", *Straits Times*, 1 February 2009, accessed 3 February 2009.
14. National Population and Talent Division, "Our Population Our Future", Issues Paper, July 2012, p. 6.
15. Wong Kan Seng, "DPM's Speech on Population at the Committee of Supply 2010", 4 March 2010 <https://www.nptd.gov.sg/content/NPTD/news/_jcr_content/par_content/download_34/file.res/DPM's%20speech%20on%20population%20at%20COS%2020100304%20-%20final.pdf>.
16. National Population and Talent Division, "Our Population Our Future", Issues Paper, July 2012, p. 6.
17. See, for example, Zakir Husain, "Rising home prices hit PAP's vote share: Mr Lee", *Straits Times*, 14 August 2011.
18. Andrew Jacobs, "In Singapore, Vitriol Against Chinese Newcomers", *New York Times*, 26 July 2012 <www.nytimes.com>, (accessed 6 December 2012).
19. Asad Latif, "The year of values", *Straits Times*, 27 December 2012.
20. Ng Jing Yng, "Finding the right balance to meet Singapore's goals", *Today*, 3 December 2012; Rachel Chang, "PM defends three core principles of Singapore", *Straits Times*, 3 December 2012; "Secretary-General Lee Hsien Loong's Speech at 2012 Party Conference, 2 December 2012" <http://maintmp.pap.org.sg/uploads/ap/8435/documents/secgen_party_conference_speech_2012.pdf>.
21. National Population and Talent Division, Prime Minister's Office, "Projection of Foreign Manpower Demand for Healthcare Sector, Construction Workers and Foreign Domestic Workers", Occasional Paper, November 2012 <https://www.nptd.gov.sg/content/NPTD/home/_jcr_content/par_content/download_16/file.res/OP-Projection%

20of%20foreign%20manpower%20demand%20for%20healthcare%20sector%20construction%20workers%20and%20foreign%20domestic%20workers.pdf>.

22. Ministry of Trade and Industry, Occasional Paper on Population and Economy, September 2012 <http://www.mti.gov.sg/MTIInsights/Documents/MTI%20Occasional%20Paper%20on%20Population%20and%20Economy.pdf>.
23. Saifulbahri Ismail, "Govt may further tighten inflow of foreign workers", *Today*, 26 October 2012.
24. Amelia Tan, "New sourcing ideas for maids, workers", *Straits Times*, 2 January 2013; and "Low pay may deter foreign workers", *Straits Times*, 3 January 2013; Channel News Asia, "China's job agencies say Singapore no longer the preferred work destination", 5 December 2012 <http://www.channelnewsasia.com/stories/eastasia/view/1241278/1/.html>.
25. Yasmine Yahya, "Tighter foreign worker rules cut growth by half: economist", *Straits Times*, 26 October 2012.
26. "Addressing manpower needs of SMEs", *Straits Times*, 16 October 2012; Phua Mei Pin, "SMEs facing labour crunch: DPM Teo", *Straits Times*, 10 October 2012.
27. Jonathan Kwok, "Productivity goal tough: Federation", *Strait Times*, 29 December 2012.
28. Ng Jing Yng, "Companies want more help to raise productivity", *Today*, 8 January 2013.

Thailand

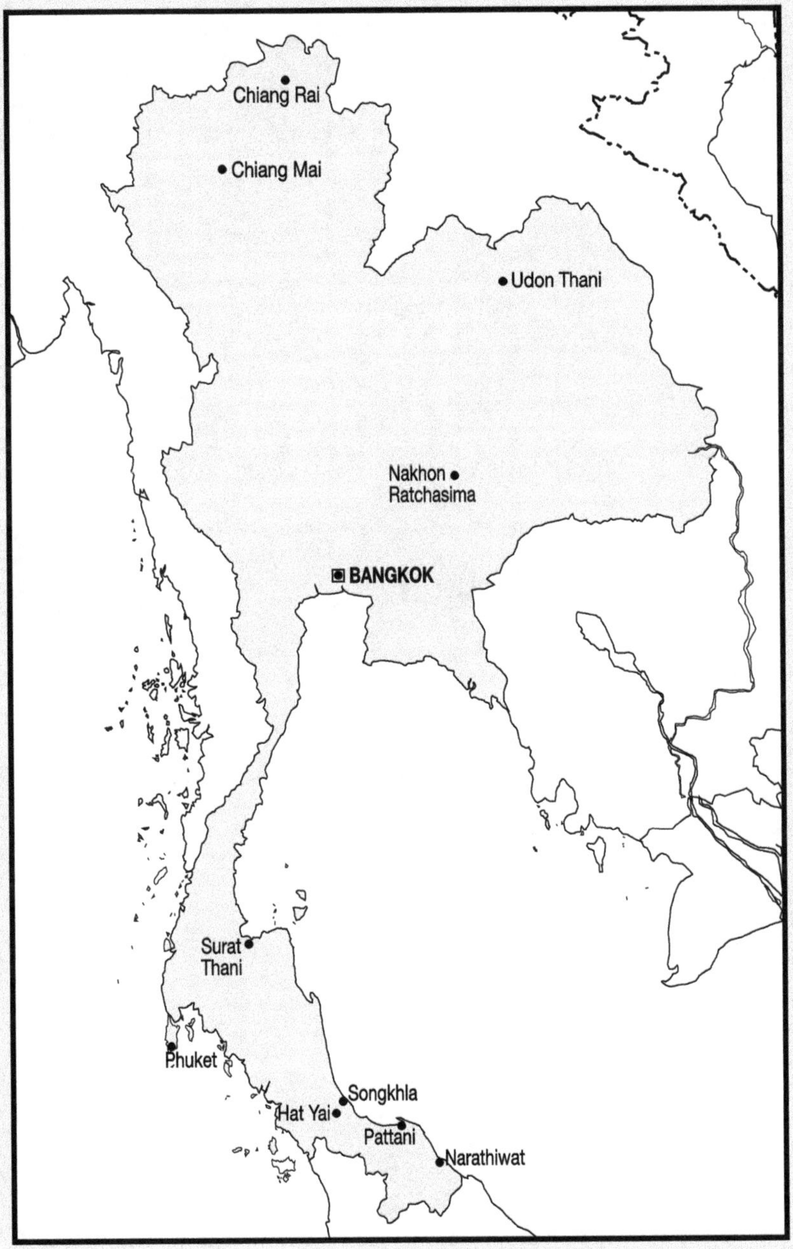
Chiang Rai
Chiang Mai
Udon Thani
Nakhon Ratchasima
BANGKOK
Surat Thani
Phuket
Songkhla
Hat Yai
Pattani
Narathiwat

THAILAND IN 2012
A Year of Truth, Reconciliation, and Continued Divide

Chairat Charoensin-o-larn

Eternal Recurrence of Political Dramatization[1]

On 26 May 2012, the *Bangkok Post* ran this line on its front page: "King makes historic return". The previous day, King Bhumibol, accompanied by Queen Sirikit and Princess Sirindhorn, had made an official visit to Thung Makham Yong in Ayutthaya Province. Some four hundred years ago the area had been a battleground between Thai and Burmese troops. In recent times it has been used as a paddy field, promoted by the royal household as a showcase of the royally initiated *kaem ling* (monkey cheek) project to hold and conserve water for use in the dry season and to manage flood water during the rainy season. On this occasion, the king wore his green army uniform, signifying his cordial relationship with the Thai military institution.[2] It was "historic" because this was the first official trip outside Bangkok by King Bhumibol after having been hospitalized in September 2009 for lung inflammation. As usual, he was greeted by a huge crowd of well-wishers wearing all sorts of coloured shirts.

The day after the royal trip, the Yellow Shirt People's Alliance for Democracy (PAD) started its rallies, first at Lumpini Park, then at the Royal Plaza, and finally in front of parliament to protest against the proposed reconciliation bills.[3] The bills offered a blanket amnesty for politicians, state officials, and people involved in the political rallies that had taken place between 15 September 2005 and 10 May 2010. This means that former Prime Minister Abhisit Vejjajiva, his

---

CHAIRAT CHAROENSIN-O-LARN is an associate professor of political science at Thammasat University in Bangkok, Thailand.

Deputy Prime Minister Suthep Thaugsuban, and the army chief and personnel who were responsible for the violent crackdown on the Red Shirt United Front for Democracy against Dictatorship (UDD) as well as leaders and ordinary Yellow and Red Shirt protesters would be set free. The bills further sought to annul orders and legal requirements initiated by the coup-appointed Assets Scrutiny Committee (ASC) to pave the way for a new judicial review and to return political rights to political party executives who were not involved in the poll fraud that led to the dissolution of their parties.

The ASC investigation led to the ruling in 2010 by the Supreme Court Criminal Division for Political Office Holders to seize assets worth 46 billion baht from Thaksin's family after finding that he had abused his power to benefit his family's telecom business. The attempt to annul the work of the ASC was interpreted as an avenue to return the seized assets to Thaksin. In the eyes of the PAD, the opposition Democrat Party, and anti-Thaksin groups of all kinds, the bill was nothing but a blatant attempt to whitewash Thaksin. In the process, a heavy blow would have been dealt to the justice system.

In parliament, the opposition Democrat Party derailed the House sessions in order to stop the consideration of the reconciliation bills. On 30 May, the Democrat MPs tried to physically pull House Speaker and ex-officio Parliament President Somsak Kiatsuranont from his bench and removed his chair after he called for votes to move the bills up for urgent consideration. On 31 May, Democrat MPs hurled objects and shouted tirades at Somsak, who was guarded by scores of parliament police after the Pheu Thai Party successfully voted to move the bills to urgent status on the agenda. Prior to the occurrence of these disgraceful incidents, the Democrat MPs, on 27 March, attempted to intimidate General Sonthi, who chaired the ad hoc House committee on national reconciliation, for his act of proposing the reconciliation bill to parliament for consideration. Abhisit, a leader of the Democrat Party, justified his party's disgraceful actions by arguing that his party was ready to put aside its image and reputation for the sake of "national interest".[4]

While this parliamentary chaos was taking place, the Yellow Shirts sealed off all the entrances to the Parliament Building on 1 June, forcing an adjournment of the House session for the first reading of the reconciliation bills. The PAD then claimed victory over the Pheu Thai-led government. Surprisingly, on the same day, the Constitution Court swiftly issued an injunction to temporarily stop the Pheu Thai-dominated parliament from conducting its third and final reading of the proposed charter amendment bill until they finished considering the petitions made by several parties, including the opposition Democrat MP, concerning whether the amendment bill was in violation of section 68 of the 2007 Constitution.[5] The amendment bill was initially scheduled for a third reading on 5 June. The petitioning parties argued that this bill aimed at overriding the 2007 Constitution — which was tantamount to an act of abolishing the democratic regime of the constitutional monarchy as stipulated in section 68 of the Constitution. The first and second paragraphs of this section state that those who are aware of any attempt to overthrow the democratic regime of the constitutional monarchy or to seize power in unconstitutional ways have the right to request the Attorney General to investigate the facts, and then, if there are grounds, to submit a motion to the Constitution Court to order the cessation of such an act.

The Constitution Court cited the escalating political tension as the main reason for its swift action in suspending the third reading of the amendment bill. The court order caused quite a stir. It was criticized as an act that "overstepped its authority", "bypassed the standard procedure" set forth in section 68 of the 2007 Constitution, and "seriously violated democratic principle".[6] Although there are no punitive measures if parliament chooses to defy a suspension order, such an act of defiance, according to the Court, could reflect ill intent, as claimed by the petitioners.

What was at stake here was exactly which agency — the Constitution Court or the Office of the Attorney General (OAG) — has the right to interpret the Constitution. Those who sided with the Court, including, of course, the anti-Thaksin camp, believed that the Court had the authority to accept the petitions, while the majority of lawyers and the pro-Thaksin camp felt that the petitions had to be screened by the OAG, which is in accordance with section 68. In other words, the Court was accused of acting outside its jurisdiction. In terms of democratic principles, it is quite strange to see the line that separates the legislative and judicial power being trampled in this manner. Besides, the announcement of the OAG that the petitions were hypothetical and thus baseless dealt a heavy blow to the Court. Ironically, in May 2006, the same Constitution Court rejected a petition based on section 68 to disband the Democrat Party on the basis that a petition must be submitted to the OAG to investigate the facts prior to filing it with the Court.[7]

The row over the Constitution Court cooled down when the Speaker of the House decided to take a step back by postponing the final reading of the constitution amendment bill and the deliberation of the reconciliation bills until the next parliamentary session in August. The move not only earned him positive comments such as that this was the "right, the sensible, decision",[8] but also effectively ended the first battle of the reconciliation war. The ball was bounced back to the *ammart*, or conservative elites, to use the Red Shirts' jargon, and the Constitution Court.

It is interesting to note that the chaos in parliament over the national reconciliation bills took place at the same time that the meeting of the World Economic Forum on East Asia was being held on the other side of Bangkok. This could be seen as a kind of political vengeance for the collapse of the ASEAN-Plus-Three and East Asia Summit at Pattaya in April 2009, when the Red Shirts stormed the venue, causing the Summit to end abruptly. The incident badly embarrassed then Prime Minister Abhisit. The stories of chaos in parliament had been given more coverage by the media than the Forum meeting. Furthermore, the whole idea of this series of political manoeuvres, which were reminiscent of the situation leading to the 19 September 2006, coup, was probably to incite violence from the Red Shirts in order to provoke the security-conscious military elites to stage another coup to topple the Pheu Thai-led government. However, this time the military backed down.

The stalling of the reconciliation and the constitution amendment bills forced the Red Shirts to realize that the *ammart* and their networks had been fighting back through various independent organizations. Furthermore, on 18 May the Constitution Court disqualified the UDD core leader, Jatuporn Prompan, as an MP due to his failure to vote in the 3 July 2011 general election.[9] On 13 June, the National Anti-Corruption Commission (NACC) ruled that Deputy Prime Minister and Interior Minister Yongyuth Wichaidit was guilty of malfeasance by certifying the sale of monastic land to the developer of the Alpine golf course while he had been Deputy Interior Permanent Secretary a decade earlier. This forced Yongyuth to resign from his cabinet post in late September. On the same day, the OAG, upon the recommendation of the NACC, filed a case against Thaksin and other parties to the Supreme Court Criminal Division for Political Office Holders for approving a 9.9 billion baht loan from the state-owned Krung Thai Bank to a major real estate company despite the fact that it was categorized as a non-performing debtor by the bank. Moreover, the Office of the Ombudsman ruled that the appointment of another UDD core leader, Nattawut Saikua, as deputy agricultural minister was "ethically inappropriate". The same office kept silent when the Abhisit government appointed Kasit Piromya as foreign minister. Kasit, one of the

PAD's core leaders, was prosecuted for the forced closure of Suvarnabhumi Airport in 2008.

Strikingly, on 22 June, Constitution Court president Wasan Soypisudh told reporters that he believed the proposed constitution amendment bill might be intended to end the constitutional monarchy.[10] Here it was inappropriate for a judge to voice his views regarding a case under consideration prior to the announcement of a verdict. At the height of the controversy over which agency had the right to accept the petitions against the amendment bill, Wasan cited the English translation of section 68 of the current Constitution as a source of legitimacy. Accordingly, the UDD leadership came to the conclusion that the *ammart* had gone beyond "judicial activism" when they toppled the Samak Sundaravej and Somchai Wongsawat governments in 2008 and began acting like a "state within the state" by trying to override the authority of the elected leadership and to disrupt the functioning of the elected government.

After much wrangling among all the parties concerned, the Constitution Court finally reached its verdict on 13 July to dismiss a charge that the proposed bill to amend the Constitution was an attempt to overthrow the constitutional monarchy on the grounds that the complainants did not present enough evidence to support their claims.[11] The Court also stated that since the 2007 Constitution was endorsed by a public referendum, any attempt to draft a new one should therefore be approved in the same manner. The Court further said that section 291 of the Constitution, which parliament amended so that it could set up a new body to rewrite the charter, was meant to empower parliament to amend the charter section by section and not to draft a new one. In effect, the ruling stopped the attempt by the Pheu Thai Party to push the amendment bill through its third reading in parliament.

Although the ruling was not sufficiently clear and left room for interpretation, it helped defuse the highly anticipated renewal of political turmoil after both sides in the conflict had threatened to take action if the ruling was not in their favour. For the business sector, the verdict diminished political uncertainty and allowed the country to move forward. For the critics, the verdict served as an avenue to hand over authority unduly to the Court so that it could intervene in the charter amendment process. It set an improper precedent, namely that any future charter amendment must first be considered by the Court. While the Court made a call to respect public opinion in the form of a referendum, it showed its disrespect for the mandate of fifteen million votes that the Pheu Thai Party received in the 3 July 2011 general election in which the amendment of the

2007 Constitution was one of the key agendas of its election campaign. As for the UDD leaders, the verdict was filled with personal opinions and suggestions rather than any real legal judgement. Therefore, only the dismissal of the petition was legally binding, and the Pheu Thai Party and the Yingluck government should have gone ahead and voted for the third reading of the amendment bill. Sceptics of the Court's ruling have pointed out that the ruling as a whole had the appearance of a legal landmine through which the Pheu Thai-led government must tread carefully.

The problems with the proposed reconciliation bills and the charter amendment bill served as a wake-up call for Thaksin, the Pheu Thai Party, and the Red Shirts. Thaksin was blamed for acting too hastily. Perhaps Thaksin misinterpreted the signal sent out by the head of the *ammart*, Privy Council president and statesman General Prem Tinsulanonda. Although General Prem displayed a cosy relationship with Prime Minister Yingluck by presiding over her government dinner function, held in February for those involved in flood relief, and opened his residence for Yingluck to pay her respects to him during the Songkran New Year celebrations, these gestures did not mean that the *ammart* and their networks were totally in agreement with Thaksin's move. Indeed, what Prem accomplished was simply to cause a rift between Thaksin and the Red Shirts by showing them that Thaksin was ready to compromise with the *ammart* over the dead bodies of the Red Shirt protesters. Thaksin was quoted as saying that he did not consider General Prem "a party to the conflict".[12] This is in stark contrast to his previous position. Ironically, if Prem's posture was able to cause a rift between Thaksin and the Red Shirts, then the friendly relationship between Prime Minister Yingluck and the army chief General Prayuth Chan-ocha opened a crack in the relations between the Yellow Shirts and the army.

The Politics of Truth

There are several approaches to the politics of truth worth mentioning here. First, there is the politics of truth concerning the struggle between those who wanted to establish the whole truth about the killing of ninety-one people in the May 2010 unrest and those whose intention was to suppress the truth of this political event.[13] The Yingluck government's compensation scheme involving the payment of a huge sum of money to those who were injured and to the families of those who had died in the May violence could not stop the Red Shirts' quest for the truth. A court hearing on those who were killed in the event started in March and the verdict on the first case was made known in September. This was the case of a taxi driver named Phan Khamkong, who, according to the Court's ruling, was shot dead by troops. The Court ruled the death of Phan Kamkong a murder, paving the way for the prosecutors to investigate former Prime Minister Abhisit and his deputy Suthep for ordering the crackdown on protesters.

The release of the final report from the Truth for Reconciliation Commission of Thailand (TRCT) on the 2010 political violence in late September further complicated the issue of what the truth really was. The report blamed both the Red Shirts and the military for the violence. It also confirmed the existence of the controversial "men in black" who were involved in the violence of 10 April. While little attention was given to the role of the September 2006 coup as the root cause of the conflict, the report instead called for Thaksin to compromise for the sake of national reconciliation by ending his role in Thai politics. Thus, instead of bringing about healing, the report simply reopened old wounds. It is quite obvious that the truth in this instance would not lead to reconciliation as easily as had been expected.

Second, there is the painful truth about the nature of Thai politics in general, and of the Pheu Thai-led government in particular, as perceived by certain elements within the Red Shirts. It is painful because, after a long and arduous fight against the *ammart*, the Red Shirts have begun to realize that both Thaksin and the Yingluck government that they have supported have compromised with the *ammart* under the pretext of "national reconciliation". The Yingluck government adamantly abides by its stated intention not to concern itself with the amendment of section 112 of the Criminal Code,[14] the so-called *lèse-majesté* law, despite an outcry from the Red Shirts and other supporters of the amendment following the controversial death of Amphon Tangnoppakul, known as Ah Kong (grandfather) or "Uncle SMS", a sixty-two-year-old man imprisoned for the offence.[15] Amphon was sentenced to twenty years in prison for allegedly sending four text messages deemed insulting to the monarchy from his mobile phone to Somkiat Krongwattanasak, private secretary to the then Prime Minister Abhisit. Amphon always insisted on his innocence because he was incapable of text messaging. Amphon was poor and seriously ill, but his eight requests for bail were rejected on the ground that he posed a flight risk. In contrast, Sondhi Limthongkul, the PAD's leader, who was sentenced in February to twenty years in jail for falsifying documents to obtain loans of 1.07 billion baht from Krung Thai Bank, was granted bail.

The Yingluck government focused exclusively and hurriedly on the amendment of the 2007 Constitution and the reconciliation bills to pave the way for amnesty for Thaksin. Thaksin himself shamefully equated reconciliation with his amnesty in his telephone speech during the second anniversary to commemorate the May 2010 violence at Rajchaprosong. In his speech, Thaksin asked the Red Shirts to put unity before justice. In short, Thaksin's amnesty was more important than the loss of Red Shirt lives during the May crackdown. This example of the true nature of the relationship between Thaksin and the Yingluck government should serve as a second eye opener (*ta sawang*) among those Red Shirts who fought wholeheartedly for Thaksin.[16]

Third, there is the politics of the creation of truth. There are at least three "political" television channels in Thailand that vie for control over the manufacture of truth and consent:[17] the infamous ASTV of the Yellow Shirts, the Asia Update channel of the Red Shirts, and the Blue Sky channel of the opposition Democrat Party. Each channel systematically provides its own version of the truth to its viewers. Both sides in the conflict — the pro- and anti-Thaksin camps — have built up their respective strategic partnerships. The alliance in the pro-Thaksin camp consists of the Pheu Thai Party, the Yingluck government, and the Red Shirts as well as their strategic television channel, Asia Update, while the alliance on the anti-Thaksin side is composed of the opposition Democrat Party, the *ammart*, notably the judiciary and the military, the Yellow and the Multi-coloured Shirts, and two strategic television channels, ASTV and Blue Sky, which was established by the Democrat Party after its total defeat in the 3 July 2011 general election.

Members and supporters of each camp do not tolerate opposing views. Neither side is willing to listen to or take the time to understand the other before rebutting anything they say or propose. Each side is speaking the "truth" by creating its own distorted version of the truth. If there is some truth in their presentation, it is only a partial truth. Thus, the Red Shirts emphasized the murder of ninety-one people in the May 2010 mayhem while the Democrat Party focused on those who had burned the city. The chaos in parliament led by the Democrat Party during the debates on the reconciliation bills was seen as a disgrace by their critics, but for their supporters it was a victorious moment in the fight against the tyranny of the majority led by the Pheu Thai Party. The Pheu Thai Party talked about reconciliation and democracy by means of supporting the charter amendment and the reconciliation bills while the opposition Democrat Party regarded these bills as attempts to whitewash Thaksin.

Fourth, it is the politics of truth initiated by the Nitirat ("Law for the People") group that the *ammart* fears most. The name "Khana Nitirat" in Thai is similar to and reminiscent of the "Khana Rat" or "Khana Ratsadorn" (the People's Party), which launched a putsch to overthrow the absolute monarchy in 1932. The Khana Nitirat was formed in 2011 and comprises seven law lecturers from Thammasat University under the leadership of Associate Professor Dr Worachet Pakeerat. The group has sparked public debate on matters that the Thai people would only whisper about a few years ago. They broke a taboo and made possible debate on subjects that are both unthinkable and unsayable within the Thai context but are undeniably important to the country's future. They are thus a fearless movement that has projected an ideal image of Thai society through an act of *parrhesia* or truth-telling.[18]

The four major reforms put forth by the Nitirat are: (1) nullify all that was accomplished by the 19 September 2006 coup, which effectively destroyed democracy and the rule of law and led to the current deep political divide; (2) amend section 112 of the Criminal Code, whose legality, enforcement, and ideology are all problematic; (3) reform the judiciary and provide compensation for those who were injured and to families of those who had died following the coup; and (4) abrogate the 2007 Constitution, which was the product of the coup, and draft a new constitution. The group argues that these four points of reform could do Thailand's revered monarchical institution more good than harm.

The proposed amendment of section 112 of the Criminal Code has become the basis for a nationwide campaign by the Campaign Committee to Amend Section 112 (CCAS 112), a coalition of academics, media activists, and human rights activists, which aims to collect at least 10,000 signatures in support of the amendment to be submitted to parliament for further action. Both the Nitirat group and the CCAS 112 have faced growing harassment and threats. On the afternoon of 21 February 2012, for example, Professor Worachet was physically assaulted by two men outside the Faculty of Law at Thammasat University. The CCAS 112 has encountered various kinds of threats, ranging from verbal abuse to specific death threats. The call to address the actions and rectify all the consequences of the 2006 coup has earned the Nitirat group a reputation for being supporters of Thaksin. The call to amend section 112 itself is accused of being both un-Thai and anti-monarchy.

Finally, there is the politics of truth surrounding the nature of Thailand's revolution. Opponents of the 24 June 1932 event have long argued that it was far from constituting a revolution. Rather, it was simply a usurpation of power from King Prachadipok (Rama VII), who was about to institute democracy in Thailand. In the eyes of these people, the June 1932 event was the prototype of the modern military coup in Thailand. For supporters of the event, the 1932 incident constituted a revolution in the sense that power was transferred to the ordinary people by replacing the system of absolute monarchy with a constitutional one. In the past, debates over the true nature of the 1932 event were confined narrowly to intellectual circles. After the September 2006 coup, in which a close palace associate was implicated, there was a resurgence of interest in the 1932 incident among political activists and ordinary people, notably members of the Red Shirts. This was accompanied by an implicit gesture by the palace in support of the Yellow Shirts and of judicial activism in the aftermath of the September coup, which drove the Red Shirts to search for the true meaning of the June 1932 incident to support their quest for democracy. Furthermore, there was an effort to redesignate 24 June as Thai National Day before it was changed to 5 December, which is the birthday of King Bhumibol. A steady revival of interest in the day that marked the end of absolute monarchy and that once served as Thailand's National Day is in itself a political event par excellence.

The fact that many Red Shirts have shown interest in the event and in the Nitirat's move ostensibly demonstrates that they are leaving Thaksin behind and moving towards a broader vision of Thailand's evolution towards democracy. The meaning and origin of democracy in Thailand is now linked to the June 1932 event, and each year since the 2006 coup there has been a growing interest in the commemoration of the event. If the coup of Field Marshall Sarit Thanarath in 1957 had eclipsed the history and the memory of the 1932 event, then the September 2006 coup has invoked a fresh revival of interest in the event to the extent that it has become a matter of great importance as to who will be able to control the social memory and the meaning of the 24 June 1932 incident.

The Economy

The prolonged eurozone debt crisis, the weakening U.S. economy from the financial crisis, and the devastating flood of 2011 in Thailand all contributed to the decline of Thailand's exports in 2012. When exports dropped due to the global crisis, imports surged, contributing to the balance-of-payments deficit and thus the weakening of the baht. A rise in the cost of living and inflation due to the unstable price of oil and gas in the global market became an issue in May. When asked by reporters about the rising inflation, Prime Minister Yingluck retorted: "You're imagining it."[19] This caused quite a stir. A campaign to help curb rising consumer goods prices was launched later with the opening of government-supported cheap product outlets such as Thong Far (Blue Flag), Took Jang (Real Cheap), and Took Tang Paendin (Cheapest in the Land).

The heavy economic toll from the massive flood disaster of 2011 has prevented the Yingluck government from focusing on other crucial and longer term issues such as Thailand's strategic preparation for membership in the planned ASEAN Economic Community (AEC), which will become effective in 2015. This will put Thailand in a disadvantageous position. When united as a bloc, ASEAN will have a combined economic value of US$2.6 trillion, making it the ninth largest economy in the world. In the past, Thailand's economic growth depended largely on the exploitation of cheap labour and natural resources. When the AEC becomes effective, Thailand will need to shift its efforts to innovation and brand-building. The idea is to increase the value of its products in order to be competitive with other economies. However, the percentage of the national budget allocated to research and development is still relatively low.

The recent open-door policy in Myanmar, which encouraged Burmese workers to return home, has begun to cause a labour shortage in certain sectors of the Thai economy, which has up to now been driven by the input of millions of Burmese migrant workers. A sharp increase by the Yingluck government of the minimum daily wage to 300 baht in selected provinces failed to hold back the Burmese migrant workers. The rampant patronage system, corruption, and populist policies, all of which have stifled the economy, have been of great concern to the business community. The Thai economy has become stuck in the middle-income trap of development due mainly to populist policies and corruption. Serious reforms are needed to escape this trap.

In the eyes of the business sector, an increase in the daily minimum wage to 300 baht by the Yingluck government was just another means to siphon off private sector money to fund the government's populist measures.[20] Besides, the government's rice-pledging programme badly distorted market mechanisms because rice was sold at rates higher than market prices and at the same time undermined Thailand's competitiveness in the global market because the price of Thai rice was higher than that of its neighbours. The rice scheme also eroded incentives for Thai farmers to improve their productivity. Corruption aside, the noisy arguments against the rice-pledging scheme were a reflection of the class distinctions in Thai society. Academics, economists, politicians from the opposition camp, and urban elites all came out in force to criticize the programme, while not a single complaint was to be heard from the farmers, who were the real beneficiaries of the scheme. The continued steep decline in rice export volume and rubber prices led to a significant drop in farm-product exports. In late July, the U.S. Department of Agriculture reported that Thailand would lose its ranking as top rice exporter to India.

The government's tax rebate policy for first-time car and home buyers resulted in unexpectedly high demand for cars and homes. Three hundred and fifty billion baht have been set aside by the Yingluck government to implement massive water resource projects nationwide to permanently solve flood problems. In early October, Prime Minister Yingluck announced her government's plan to invest 2.75 trillion baht in infrastructure development, the largest investment in the country's history. The idea was to facilitate the launch of the AEC and the economic expansion of the Greater Mekong Subregion (GMS). However, most of the money would come from borrowing.[21]

On 25 July, the Bank of Thailand revised its economic growth projection downward from 6 to 5.7 per cent and export growth from 8 to 7 per cent. If the current pattern of public spending continues, then public debt will rise to about 54 per cent of the gross domestic product (GDP) in the next four years, up from about 42 per cent currently. According to the opposition party leader, the Yingluck government had accumulated almost 1 trillion baht in public debt due to excessive borrowing and policy mistakes.[22] The current and past governments have run fiscal deficits in an effort to bolster the economy in the face of the global financial crisis and the severe floods of 2011. High public debt will sink the country's economy quickly. The rice-pledging scheme side by side with the three-year debt moratorium for "good debtors" will increase public debt.

Consequently, there has been a call for an increase in direct investment in infrastructure projects, education, and research and development to support sustainable growth, while any short-term economic stimulus such as a variety of populist schemes should be avoided. It was estimated by the Thailand Development Research Institute (TDRI) that a comprehensive rights-based social welfare system could be established at the cost of around 200 to 300 billion baht a year.[23] This amount is relatively lower than the money the government has put into the populist schemes. Simply boosting the economy by giving out money in the form of populist policies without tackling the underlying structural issues such as income inequality, land reform, or education, will not lead to sustainable economic growth.

Foreign Affairs

United States-Thai relations have been somewhat strained by several incidents since the September 2006 coup. The coup itself brought Thailand into confrontation with American democratic values. The Wikileak affair revealed that in October 2008 U.S. Embassy cables indicated that Queen Sirikit had "encouraged [the] 2006 coup".[24] In December 2011, a group of royalists protested in front of the American Embassy in Bangkok, denouncing what they perceived as interference by the United States in Thailand's internal affairs.[25] Their rally was a response to a comment made by the current American Ambassador to Thailand, Kristie Kenney, concerning a harsh prosecution and lengthy jail term under the *lèse-majesté* law and the concern over freedom of expression.[26]

In June, a request by the U.S.-based National Aeronautics and Space Administration (NASA) to use Thailand's U-tapao military airbase for a climate study between August and September had been so politicized that the Yingluck government decided to halt the project by forwarding the issue to parliament for debate. This forced NASA to withdraw its request, leading to a new criticism of the government for its lack of leadership. The project was viewed by conservative elites and the opponents of the Yingluck government as having a hidden agenda, ranging from conspiracy to the infringement of Thai sovereignty. NASA had signed the deal in September 2010 with the Abhisit government. The opposition Democrat Party nonsensically accused the Yingluck government of trading access to U-tapao for an entry visa to the United States for former Prime Minister Thaksin Shinawatra. Others argued that the climate study project could be related to the U.S. military strategy to contain China's influence in Southeast Asia.

The NASA case clearly demonstrates that the conservative Thai establishment or *ammart* and their networks have increasingly grown hostile to Western, particularly American, values, which have been seen as partly responsible for the growing pressure from ordinary people like the Red Shirts for greater equality and freedom of expression. Furthermore, the *ammart* believe that the United States has been meddling in Thailand's *lèse-majesté* law as well as in Thailand's political affairs by allowing Thaksin, who had been convicted of a crime, to enter the United States in early August 2012. The NASA affair not only badly tarnished Thailand's image on the international stage but it also pointed to the seriousness of the political divide as a result of which national interest has come to be held hostage.

Trade with the rest of Indochina grew steadily until 2007 when the conflict erupted over the 4.6-square-kilometre disputed area surrounding Preah Vihear Temple between Thailand and Cambodia. Fighting broke out during 2010 and 2011 under the Abhisit-led government. Since the Pheu Thai-led government came to power, Thai-Cambodian relations have improved. Troop withdrawals from the provisional demilitarized zone (PDZ) area near the temple began exactly one year after the provisional ruling in 18 July 2011 by the International Court of Justice (ICJ). But it should not be taken for granted that violence will not erupt again as long as each side has troops stationed so close to each other.

The conflict over the disputed area had resumed when the Cambodian government applied to register the temple as a world heritage site with UNESCO in 2008 with the support of the Thai government under the premiership of the late Samak Sundaravej. The move was strongly opposed by conservatives, including the opposition Democrat Party. When the Democrat Party assumed control of the government and tried to block the Cambodian application, the Cambodian government sought the ICJ's clarification on its verdict in 1962. In that verdict, the court ruled that only the temple was under Cambodian sovereignty, leaving the sovereignty over the contested area undecided. Both countries then claimed sovereignty over the surrounding area. Although no date has yet been set for the ICJ's final ruling, the Thai-Cambodian territorial dispute will be one of the thorniest issues with which any Thai government has had to deal. If the ruling is in Cambodia's favour, the Thai government at the time of the ruling will definitely run into trouble.

The failure of ASEAN to issue a joint communiqué after its 45th Ministerial Meeting held in Cambodia, due to the South China Sea territorial waters disputes between China and some ASEAN members, reflected deep division in the regional group and the influence of China and the United States on some ASEAN countries.[27] The disputes have been fuelled by a regional power shift, with China increasingly asserting its power. As a result, immediately after his re-election, President Barack Obama made an official visit to Thailand, Myanmar, and Cambodia as part of his policy of a "rebalancing act" in Asia and the Pacific to contain China.[28]

The annual ministerial joint communiqué is as old as ASEAN itself, and the absence of one being issued was a crucial blow to ASEAN's credibility and cohesiveness in the upcoming meeting of the AEC in 2015. As a coordinating country for ASEAN-China relations, Thailand has an important role to play in this conflict. However, pressing domestic issues have prevented Thailand from playing such a role. As a result, ASEAN's ability to stand together has been put in doubt. The South China Sea dispute is indeed a key test for Thailand and for the future of Southeast Asia.

Conclusion

After half a decade of political volatility, 2012 can probably be best described as another year of uncertainty and instability for Thailand. Political conflict and southern violence remain the two defining forces for the country. Violence in the south, which escalated in July, only added to this uncertainty. The insurgents there outpaced Thai security forces in a well-publicized ambush, bombed major economic enterprises, and attacked public transport facilities. On 1 September, after a series of attacks, the insurgents put hundreds of Malaysian flags on display in the southern province of Yala. Perhaps the flags symbolized their desire to challenge Thai authority and to unite with Malaysia. In early October, business districts in Narathiwat, one of the three southernmost provinces, became ghost towns after the insurgents made violent threats against traders who opened their businesses on Friday, the Muslim day of prayer. It has been nine years since the violence in the south first broke out in early 2004, and there is no sign that it will end soon.

The Yingluck government had begun to face a new round of the anti-Thaksin protests in late October. This time the group came with a new banner called Pitak Siam or Protect Siam. It openly championed a coup and a five-year freeze on elected politicians. Its second rally in late November ended abruptly after a day of scattered violence with the police. The opposition party launched its no-confidence motion against Yingluck a day after the Pitak Siam rally ended. However, the real battle lies in the renewed attempt by the Pheu Thai government to push for the third reading of the constitution amendment bill. The charter amendment would pave the way for Thaksin's amnesty, allowing him to return home. Meanwhile the *ammart* is fully aware of this option and will fight hard to block Thaksin's move.

Indeed, the overall political situation in Thailand in 2012 went beyond the point of accommodation. Each side is waiting for the right moment to wage a total war to eradicate the other side in the conflict in order to set up its hegemony. In the process of hegemonic construction, truth and reconciliation became a means of achieving this end. The alleged plot to assassinate Thaksin and the renewed charge of Abhisit as a draft dodger helped intensify the conflict by harvesting the existing sentiments of fear, hatred and anger harboured within both sides of the political divide. The politics of truth and reconciliation had been dangerously played through the politics of fear and hatred.[29] It is thus difficult to imagine what Thai society will look like in the future when, on the one hand, people are weighed down by harsh political persecution, in which distortion and lies against political opponents have become an intrinsic part of their daily lives, while, on the other hand, the increasing use of new social media such as Facebook, Twitter, and YouTube among the Thai public has made distortion and lying much more difficult. This game of truth versus lies has increasingly become the Thai politician's worst nightmare. Distortions, lies, and hypocrisy are manufactured as well as scrutinized by social media and this will help increase the level of political consciousness and participation among the Thai public.

Notes

1. The notion of "eternal recurrence" is drawn from German philosopher Friedrich Nietzsche in his *A Nietzsche Reader*, selected and translated with an Introduction by R. J. Hollingdale (London: Penguin Books, 1977/2003), pp. 249–62.
2. A historical account of the relationship between King Bhumibol and the military is provided by Kobkua Suwannathat Pian, *Kings, Country and Constitutions: Thailand's Political Development 1932–2000* (London and New York: RoutledgeCurzon, 2003), Chapter 5, pp. 145–80.
3. "Reconciliation bid risks spawning fresh turmoil", *Bangkok Post,* 26 May 2012, p. 3. There were four proposed bills, but the most contentious version was ironically proposed by the 2006 coup leader General Sonthi Boonyaratglin, now Matubhum Party leader and MP.
4. "Unity bills given urgency", *Bangkok Post* [online], 1 June 2012.
5. "Charter vetting put on ice", *Bangkok Post*, 2 June 2012, p. 1. Sonthi Limthongkul, a core leader of the PAD, informed his Yellow Shirt demonstrators on the rally stage in front of parliament that they would hear good news from the Constitution Court *before* the Court actually issued its injunction. This is similar to the case of the Constitution Court's verdict on the dissolution of the People's Power Party in early December 2008 in which Sonthi knew the verdict in advance. This is in no way a coincidence.
6. "Charter row flounders in legal brawl", *Bangkok Post*, 9 June 2012, p. 1.
7. One of the main features of the proposed amendment bill was to amend section 291 of the current constitution, allowing for the establishment of a drafting assembly to rewrite the constitution. Since a drafting assembly had not yet been established, how could anyone tell what the new constitution would look like? Furthermore, the amendment bill prohibited any amendment regarding the chapter on the monarchy

in the current constitution that would lead to changes regarding the democratic regime of constitutional monarchy. See "Amended CDA bill passes 2nd reading", *Bangkok Post* [online], 15 May 2012, and "Second reading of constitution bill finalized", *The Nation* [online], 15 May 2012.

8. "A sensible decision by parliament president", *Bangkok Post* [online], 12 June 2012.
9. "Jatuporn banned as MP", *Bangkok Post*, 19 May 2012, p. 1, and "Court defends Jatuporn ban ruling", *Bangkok Post*, 20 May 2012, p. 3.
10. "Wasan sees plot in charter change bill", *Bangkok Post*, 23 June 2012, p. 3.
11. "Ruling set to halt charter bill push", *Bangkok Post*, 14 July 2012, p. 1.
12. "Reconciliation begins at home", *The Nation* [online], 3 May 2012.
13. An interesting discussion regarding the politics of truth is provided by Michel Foucault, *The Politics of Truth*, translated by Lysa Hochroth and Catherine Parker (Los Angeles: Semiotext(e), 2007).
14. Section 112 reads: "Whoever defames, insults or threatens the King, Queen, the Heir-apparent or the Regent, shall be punished with imprisonment for three to fifteen years". A historical discussion of the law is provided by David Streckfuss, *Truth on Trial in Thailand: Defamation, treason, and lèse majesté* (London and New York: Routledge, 2011).
15. "PM adamant she will not reform lese majeste law", *Bangkok Post*, 12 May 2012, p. 1, and "Oddities abound in Amphon's trial and jailing", *The Nation* [online], 15 May 2012.
16. The first incident, which served as an eye opener for the Red Shirts, occurred in October 2008 when Queen Sirikit presided over the funeral ceremony of one of their arch-rival Yellow Shirt PAD demonstrators, who died during the protest against the People's Power Party government, Thaksin's reincarnation of the dissolved Thai Rak Thai (TRT) Party.
17. See Edward S. Herman and Noam Chomsky, *Manufacturing Consent: The Political Economy of the Mass Media* (New York: Pantheon Books, 1988/2002).
18. See Michel Foucault, *Fearless Speech*, edited by Joseph Pearson (Los Angeles: Semiotext(e), 2001).
19. "You're imagining it, says PM", *Bangkok Post* [online], 4 May 2012.
20. "Shock over corruption, patronage, lack of reform", *Bangkok Pos*t, 14 July 2012, p. B1. The Yingluck government's populist measures include: the rice-pledging scheme, free tablet computers to first-grade students, a first-car and first-home buyers scheme, a debt moratorium for good debtors, an increase in monthly payments to the elderly, a 300 baht minimum daily wage, an energy credit card scheme to help taxi drivers cope with higher fuel prices, a 15,000 baht monthly salary for new bachelor's degree graduates, and a women's development fund.
21. "PM unveils $90 bn infrastructure plan", *Bangkok Post*, 6 October 2012. p. 1.
22. "Budget fails to target living costs, poverty: Abhisit", *The Nation* [online], 22 May 2012.

23. "How can Thailand escape the populist policies trap", *Bangkok Post*, 26 May 2012, p. 9.
24. "US embassy cables: The Queen Sirikit encouraged 2006 coup", *The Guardian*, 14 December 2010.
25. "US Embassy 'to keep out of Thai affairs'", *The Nation* [online], 17 December 2011.
26. Ambassador Kenney's comment was a reaction to the Thai court sentencing in December 2011 of the Thai-American Joe Gordon to two and a half years in jail, for translating parts of a banned book, *The King Never Smiles*, and posting them on the Internet while in the United States. This was the first time an American citizen was charged under the law and for actions committed outside Thailand. Mr Gordon was arrested in Thailand in May 2011 while making a visit to the country. He was granted a royal pardon in July 2012 and quietly left the country to prevent bilateral relations from being further strained.
27. "China, US widen Asean rifts", *Bangkok Post* [online], 27 July 2012.
28. "Obama hails Thai ties", *The Nation* [online], 19 November 2012, and Daljit Singh, "Pivoting Asia, Engaging China-American Strategy in East Asia Today", *ISEAS Perspective*, 19 October 2012.
29. "A political game played with fear, hatred and anger", *Bangkok Post* [online], 11 November 2012.

Timor-Leste

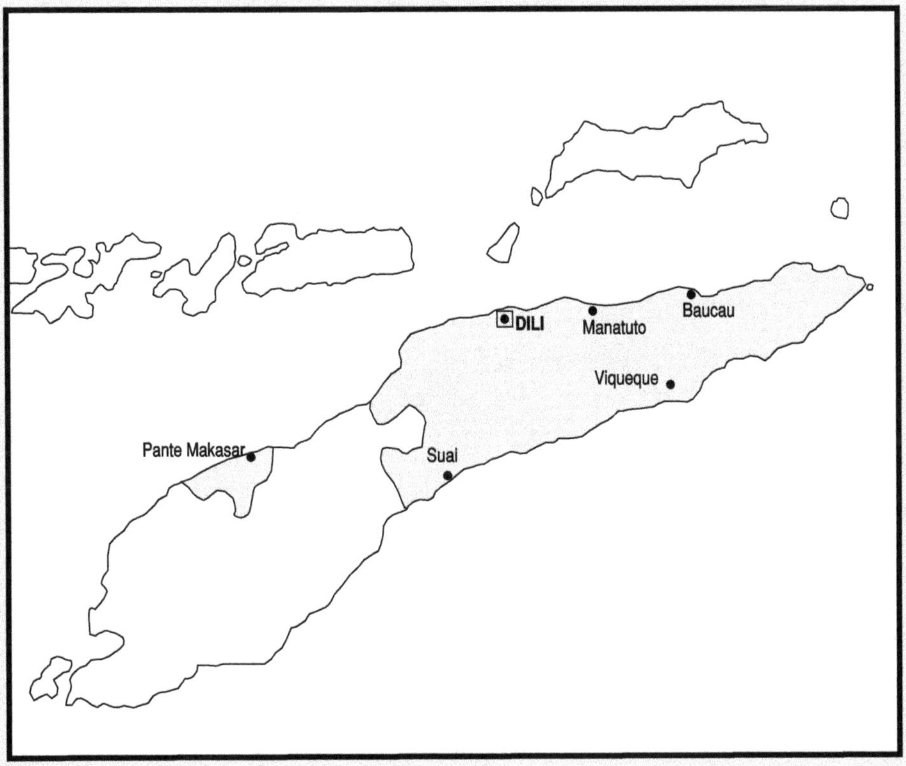

TIMOR-LESTE IN 2012
The Harsh Reality of Independence

Damien Kingsbury

Overview

In April 2012, Timor-Leste elected its third president and, not long after celebrating its tenth anniversary of independence on 22 May, elected its third government. After a tumultuous beginning, elections and anniversaries in Timor-Leste had, like the process and problems of development, started to become routine. It could be said that, ten years after independence, Timor-Leste was beginning to consolidate as a democratic state.

The reappointment of Xanana Gusmao as Timor-Leste's Prime Minister in 2012 confirmed what was becoming a "business as usual" approach to the tiny state's development. His appointment reflected a broad measure of public intention and reassured most of Timor-Leste's international partners of its continued stability. Increasingly confirmed as the power broker of Timor-Leste's politics, Gusmao's reappointment as the head of the "most voted party" as well as his role in forming a majority coalition fulfilled each of Weber's three criteria for legitimacy. He had assumed much of the mantle of traditional leadership through appeals to military leadership in combination with a *liurai*-type[1] status, which, although damaged by the rough and tumble of day-to-day politics, helped him retain considerable charismatic authority and increasingly, if sometimes problematically, helped him to construct his authority based on a rational-legal appeal to improved material conditions, public order, and state building.

The people of Timor-Leste broadly responded in kind. Many identified with appeals to pre-colonial traditions[2] and unabashed displays of military heroism which often accorded Gusmao a larger than life status and, rationally, responded

DAMIEN KINGSBURY is Director, Centre for Citizenship, Development and Human Rights, Faculty of Arts and Education, Deakin University, Melbourne.

to a series of economic and other material benefits that came from high albeit uneven flows of government spending. Gusmao was not alone in appealing to tradition, with most political leaders at times presenting themselves in the traditional *liurai* attire of *tais*,[3] a feathered *kaibauk*[4] and a *belak*[5] on the chest in recursive complimentarity, as well as a *surik*[6] without which no traditional leader would be complete. Other candidates and parties, primarily Fretilin, were less successful in their charismatic campaigns and instead appealed mainly to a rational-legal framework based on sustainable economic development. Timor-Leste was establishing a political style that marked it as being in transition to more or less conventional democratic politics but, after Portuguese colonialism, Indonesian repression and international modernism, one that is also deeply imbued with a series of local identifiers.

Economics, Politics, and Security

Timor-Leste's transition through the electoral period of 2012 towards the drawdown of UN presence and the complete withdrawal of international security forces raised three key sets of interconnected issues. These three issues were the status of its economic development, the embedding of its political processes, and the country's increasing sense of stability.

Timor-Leste's economic development over 2012 also continued to reflect, in line with the reappointment of Gusmao as Prime Minister, "business as usual". The newly elected government continued to endorse the country's Strategic Development Plan (SDP) first presented in July 2011 and continued with high levels of government spending, notably on infrastructure — deriving overwhelmingly from the country's Petroleum Fund. As of mid-2012, the Petroleum Fund was capitalized at US$10.2 billion, with an estimated sustainable rate of withdrawal of 3 per cent.[7] The Parliamentary Majority Alliance (AMP) government's budget of US$1,736.4 billion (of which US$33 million was in borrowings)[8] carried forward under the newly elected government. This expenditure exceeded the sustainable drawdown of Timor-Leste's capital reserves by approximately five times. Of the budgetary allocation, US$746 million was directed towards infrastructure development, US$200 million for the capitalization of the Timor-Leste Investment Company, and US$52 million for Decentralization Development Programs I and II. Of the government's budget, approximately 92 per cent was sourced from the Petroleum Fund, with the government in turn providing the overwhelming source of capital for economic growth.

This expenditure was justified by Prime Minister Gusmao on the basis of "policies integrated in 2012 concern[ing] the long-term sustainable development of the Nation".[9] He said: "The implementation of the SDP entails the need for considerable investment, at least during the first five years of execution". However, in terms of ease of investment and doing business, the International Finance Corporation ranked Timor-Leste 168 of 183 countries, improving by one position but overall ranking very poorly as a place in which to do business.[10] In particular, Timor-Leste was rated worst in the world for registering property, enforcing contracts, and resolving insolvency. This assessment does not augur well for "long-term sustainable development".

Gusmao continued: "Still, we know that making the dreams and aspirations of our people come true is an investment with a return that cannot be expressed in words."[11] Comments such as these led some observers to note that Timor-Leste's government had not established a clear connection between the government's expenditure and cost recovery, reflecting a lack of a detailed plan for how infrastructure investment would specifically build the economy.[12]

The three biggest projects identified under the SDP were road building, national electrification, and the establishment of the Tasi Mane southwest petroleum project. Of the three, the US$20 million road building project was perhaps the most critical, with the country's road system having fallen into serious disrepair since 1999, impacting not just general movement and transportation but also access to markets and government services. After a troubled start, the national electrification programme, intended to "stimulate economic growth in line with the SDP",[13] was rolled out throughout 2012, gradually reaching more remote villages.

The Tasi Mane plant was the government's most ambitious project. The plan was for the development of a series of interlinked liquefied natural gas processing facilities and resupply bases on Timor-Leste's southwest coast, to take advantage of the development of the Greater Sunrise liquefied natural gas field located in the Timor Sea about 100 kilometres southeast off Timor-Leste's south coast. The Tasi Mane project is intended to kick-start industrial development around a petrochemical industry in Timor-Leste.

There was however, at the time of writing, disagreement with the development partner, Woodside Petroleum, over the location of this processing plant. Woodside Petroleum proposed that it float at the upstream Greater Sunrise site in the Timor Sea. Objections to onshore processing at Tasi Mane cited the lack of existing infrastructure in Timor-Leste and the need to build a gas pipeline across the 3,300-metre-deep Timor Trough in addition to the estimated $5 billion required for the onshore development. Should the project proceed, it was expected to pump US$13 billion dollars into Timor-Leste's Petroleum Fund.[14] However, following the 2012 elections, Prime Minister Gusmao reconfirmed Timor-Leste's insistence on onshore processing. If an agreement between the government and Woodside is not reached by February 2013, the existing lease agreement is scheduled to lapse, with Timor-Leste saying that it would seek a new development partner agreeable to its onshore processing plan.

Timor-Leste's proven oil reserves were at just over 550 million barrels, placing it about mid-way among oil-producing countries but with a relatively strong population to oil reserve ratio. Apart from oil, Timor-Leste's exports were around US$10 million a year, mostly in coffee while its imports exceeded US$200 million.[15]

One of the key criticisms of the government's spending programme, beyond the question of its sustainability, was what was referred to as the "resources curse". The "resources curse" commonly refers to countries that have strong resource-based economies, implying a relatively high level of wealth, but suffer from the paradox of low economic and human development. In Timor-Leste, the term was used to describe the tendency towards a lack of adequate oversight of state spending leading to high-level corruption, high levels of waste, and beggaring other aspects of economic development.

In particular, Timor-Leste's government continued its practice of awarding government contracts without open tendering, sometimes to companies owned or with substantial shareholdings by family members of government ministers, well into 2012. In the first months of the previous AMP government, this practice could have been seen as a reasonable response to urgent development needs set against limited tenderer capacity. However, by 2012 it was looking much more like nepotism, if not outright corruption. It was instructive that the recently established Anti-Corruption Commission (CAC) was, in June, instrumental in having then Minister for Justice, Lucia Lobato, sentenced to five years in prison for the "misadministration of funds", while actively pursuing investigations into two other former ministers. Timor-Leste's corruption ranking on the Transparency International Corruption Perception Index deteriorated in 2011 from 125 to 143 on the scale of corrupt countries, with the openness of its budget process being classed as "minimal".[16] According to a CAC household survey of corruption, "more than half of the interviewees perceive that the government has a sincere desire and will to combat corruption, even though an almost equal number think corruption exists in most government institutions".[17]

High levels of cash flowing through the economy had a declining impact on prices, with the mid-2012 inflation rate running at just under 11 per cent,[18] down from 15 per cent in mid-2011. Areas outside the capital, Dili, were less affected by inflation, reflecting more limited flow of money beyond the capital.

Broad human development indicators continued to improve in Timor-Leste, if unevenly, with per capita GDP rising to over US$3,000, but with mean incomes being closer to US$730. Poverty also remained high, if declining slightly, at 37 per cent of the population.[19] A report by the UN Special Rapporteur on Human Rights also highlighted the extent of continued extreme poverty in Timor-Leste.[20]

There was more development in Dili, while many in Timor-Leste's rural areas saw only modest improvement in their lives. The UN Special Rapporteur on extreme poverty estimated that a majority of the 75 per cent of Timorese living in rural areas were "entrenched in inter-generational cycles of poverty",[21] and that some 58 per cent of children suffered from chronic malnutrition, with almost half of all children under five underweight for their age (a problem that had historically afflicted Timorese children). The same report claimed that income inequality had "risen significantly", with particularly stark gaps between Dili and rural areas.

Despite a growing annual budget, just 11.5 per cent of GDP was dedicated to health, while the 16.8 per cent on education contributed to a school enrolment rate of just under 70 per cent.[22] Overall literacy remained problematic; the literacy rate for those aged fifteen and above stood at 50 per cent, and declined with increased age (thus reflecting educational exclusion under both the Portuguese and Indonesian administrations). On average, human development indicators in Timor-Leste had improved, especially in the areas of infant and maternal mortality, which had been cut by half over the decade. However, after a quick improvement after 2007 (probably due to increased government handouts), the rate of improvement had slowed and had remained uneven.

Political Development

In 2012, Timor-Leste went to elections for the third time in its history. Its first elections were held under UN administration and the two following elections were held when it was an independent state. With one transition of prime ministership, three transitions of presidency, and a peaceful election in 2012, it has been suggested that Timor-Leste has cast off its troubled and sometimes violent history and consolidated itself as a democratic state.

Post-independence states are often established with democratic credentials, but almost as often abandon them under the weight of conflicting priorities set against limited capacity. The literature on democratic failure highlights how low levels of economic development and high levels of insecurity are commonly found in, and linked to, the collapse of democratic models.[23] This was almost the case in Timor-Leste in 2006.

As a result of simmering political animosities, limited state capacity and increasingly rigid responses by the then Fretilin government set against high social expectations and the qualified success of the UN's first full state-creation programme, Timor-Leste suffered the beginning of an almost textbook democratic collapse in 2006. In what has been characterized as a politico-military crisis,[24] it is generally agreed that, had there not been international intervention, the country would likely have descended into full-scale civil war.

Despite technically successful, if tense, elections in 2007, the consequent change of government led to another round of violence and the continued displacement of around 15 per cent of the population. Matters came to a head in February 2008 when renegade soldiers shot and critically wounded President Jose Ramos-Horta. The widespread shock at his shooting and the subsequent windfall from rising oil prices (which funds the Timor-Leste government and much of the country) allowed the new AMP government to embark on a major stabilization programme. The AMP government, under the charismatic leadership of Prime Minister Xanana Gusmao and a coalition government built around his party, the Council for Timorese National Reconstruction (CNRT), saw increasing stability and security across Timor-Leste and improvements across a range of human development indicators.

Despite the unevenness of Timor-Leste's development and questions about sustainability and growing corruption, Timor-Leste returned to the polls in 2012 in what have been universally regarded as peaceful, free, and fair elections.[25] Gusmao returned as Prime Minister at the helm of a stronger CNRT-led government.

At one level, Timor-Leste has fulfilled many of the technical criteria for democratic consolidation: free, fair, and peaceful elections; political transition; continuing strong voter turnout and, in 2012, with one exception, broad acceptance of the electoral outcome.

However, democratic outcomes are not determined as if by fate and Timor-Leste continues to face many pressing challenges, some of which will increase, including unsustainable population growth, a potentially dwindling Petroleum Fund and limited alternative economic development.

As was noted, internal security across Timor-Leste continued to improve over 2012, with one notable exception. Indeed, for an election year, there were very few reports of violence or destruction, with the principal incidents during the election period being rocks thrown by Fretilin supporters at the home of presidential candidate (and later, President) Taur Matan Ruak, seven houses being burned down, and one person killed in the long-troubled town of Uatulari in Viqueque district. The pre-election period was calm and, as the campaigning period approached, while there was considerable public debate, political rallies were otherwise quiet and generally smaller, especially compared to the rallies of the 2007 elections.[26]

The first round of the presidential elections, on 17 March, saw twelve candidates compete for the largely ceremonial position, with the Timorese Social Democratic Association's (ASDT) presidential candidate Xavier do Amaral dying just eleven days before the first electoral round. Incumbent President Jose Ramos-Horta decided in February to also run again, after vacillating throughout 2011. However, by the time he announced his decision to run, support from CNRT, which had helped him win the 2007 election, had already shifted to former defence chief and nominally independent Taur Matan Ruak. With Xanana Gusmao campaigning heavily on his behalf, Ruak polled second, gaining just under 26 per cent of the vote, after Fretilin's Francisco "Lu Olo" Guterres, who polled just under 29 per cent of the vote. Ramos-Horta came third, with 17.4 per cent, just ahead of the Democratic Party's Fernando "Lasama" de Araujo's 17.3 per cent.

The two leading presidential contenders, Ruak and Lu Olo, went into the second presidential round on 16 April: Lu Olo's vote share increased to just under 39 per cent of total votes while Ruak polled more than 61 per cent, emerging as a clear winner. Two factors shaped the elections. The first factor was that, as in 2007, Xanana Gusmao's personal support appeared to determine who would win the presidential poll. The second factor was that Fretilin's primary vote appeared to be stuck at around the 30 per cent mark which, when translated into voter preferences, indicated the continuation of strong anti-Fretilin sentiments. Voter turnout in the 2012 presidential elections fell to 73 per cent from 78 per cent in 2007 — although "eligible voters" included a portion of voters who had since died but had not been removed from the rolls, and this brought the participation rate up to 80 per cent.

In all, the peaceful character of the presidential elections augured well for the more important parliamentary elections and helped set the stage for the end of the United Nations Mission in Timor-Leste (UNMIT) and the withdrawal of peacekeepers. It was in this context that Timor-Leste commemorated its tenth anniversary of independence on 22 May. Almost everyone, from the UN Secretary-General Ban Ki Moon, U.S. Secretary of State Hillary Clinton and public commentators, to Timor-Leste's own political leaders emphasized Timor-Leste's positive achievements. Timor-Leste went to the parliamentary elections riding on this broadly "glass half full" mood.

Perhaps the only real oddity of the parliamentary elections was that former President Jose Ramos-Horta campaigned on behalf of ASDT and PD. In the case of ASDT, Ramos-Horta — not a member of ASDT — appeared on banners with that party's founder, the late Xavier do Amaral. The general view was that Ramos-Horta wanted to bring ASDT and PD together as a third force in Timor-Leste's politics and strike a deal with Fretilin based on Fretilin's leader, Mari Alkatiri, agreeing not to run for the prime ministership. It was thought that Ramos-Horta would then put himself forward for that position (ministers, including the Prime Minister, are able but not required to sit in parliament). However, following the death of do Amaral, the son of a traditional *liurai* (regional ruler), the party was divided over who would inherit control. As a consequence, ASDT's vote collapsed to 1.8 per cent, while PD agreed to join CNRT two weeks before the ballot. Ramos-Horta's last shot at political leadership had been fired, and missed.

The parliamentary elections, although more animated than the presidential ones, were also peaceful. Fretilin polled just under 30 per cent but CNRT did better than anticipated — its vote share increased by 50 per cent from its 2007 standing to 36.6 per cent. It was widely held that CNRT's total votes would reflect that of its supported presidential candidate, Ruak, who polled 26 per cent in the first presidential round. As it transpired, Ruak was significantly less popular than the party that backed him (his final vote seeming to reflect an "anyone but Fretilin" sentiment). PD's vote share also remained relatively consistent, polling at just over 10 per cent, while the 2007 Fretilin breakaway party, Frenti Mudanca, only just managed to cross the 3 per cent threshold. Of the twenty-one parties that contested the election, seventeen did not meet the 3 per cent threshold required to secure a seat in parliament;

KHUNTO, a party based on Timor-Leste's street gangs, missed the cut-off by a mere 0.03 per cent.

The outcome of the vote could be seen as rationalizing support around key parties. However, it did also mean that around 20 per cent of Timor-Leste's voters, who voted for parties that did not cross the 3 per cent threshold, were left without any political representation in parliament. Importantly, too, this meant that the effective allocation of seats to those parties sitting in parliament was proportionately increased, with CNRT taking thirty of the sixty-six seats, Fretilin twenty-five, PD eight, and Frenti Mudanca two. Despite Fretilin's leaders telling their party faithful that they expected to be included in government and some others, such as Ramos-Horta and the bishop of Dili, Alberto Ricardo, calling for a "government of national inclusion",[27] it was never expected that CNRT would accommodate its political opponents in such a way. The subsequent CNRT national conference on 16 July voted to form a government with PD and Frenti Mudanca in what was to be called the Government Coalition Bloc (BGK, or Bloku Governu Koligasaun).

The calm surrounding the election period was suddenly shattered on the evening of the announcement of the BGK government, when Fretilin members rioted in Dili, Baucau and Viqueque. Rioters set up roadblocks of burning tyres, burned or otherwise damaged sixty-three cars, including four police cars in Viqueque, and burned down seven houses and the Viqueque police station. The police killed one person at Hera, which is to the east of Dili. Many others were injured, including five police officers.[28]

Fretilin leaders attributed the outbreak of violence to intemperate comments made by CNRT members at their national conference, which had been televised live and viewed by Fretilin members at the party's headquarters. However, other observers also attributed the angry response to Fretilin's frustration at not being included in the new government. The rioting was quickly controlled by police and normality was restored within days.

As Fretilin began contemplating another five years in opposition, the BGK parties negotiated the allocation of ministries and, within three weeks, agreed on a core Cabinet of seventeen ministers together with an expanded vice-ministry and more secretaries of state, bringing the total of Cabinet positions to fifty-three. The announcement of the Cabinet led to two sets of criticism, mostly along partisan lines, that the new Cabinet had three sets of siblings and that the enlarged Cabinet reflected pay-offs for support rather than a reflection of individual competencies.[29] While there appeared to be some truth to the claim that the Cabinet reflected the need to keep supporters happy, a number of previous coalition ministers were dropped.

Gusmao had nominated Maria Alves as Defence Minister but the nomination was rejected by President Ruak on the grounds that she was "not suitable".[30] This was despite the requirement of the President to appoint ministers "following" the advice of the Prime Minister.[31] Alves rejected an offer to head another ministry and the post of Defence Minister was instead allocated to former intelligence chief, Cirilo Christopher.

International Relations

Timor-Leste's foreign relations are characterized by leveraging the small size of its geographic and diplomatic position. For a tiny country, Timor-Leste exercises more influence than many larger states. While Timor-Leste's history and positioning within the Indonesian archipelago underlies its influence — and in 1975, its vulnerability — it also means that a number of countries seek to shape that influence. Timor-Leste has increasingly balanced these competing interests; Indonesia, Australia, Portugal (and other Lusophone states) and, increasingly, China and the United States.

Indonesia and Timor-Leste have yet to resolve outstanding border demarcation issues, at Memo, near Maliana and in the Oecussi enclave within West Timor where localized disputes at Pasabe[32] and Citrana had occurred. Bilateral relations between the two states were otherwise cordial and increasingly close, with Timor-Leste considering having some of its armed forces train and engage in peacekeeping operations with Indonesian armed forces.[33]

Timor-Leste's relations with Australia remained positive, if at times qualified. Australia remained Timor-Leste's largest aid donor (US$127 million in 2012–13), provided the bulk of peacekeeping troops and retained strong civil society relations, notably through community to community "friendship" groups. However, Australia was also viewed as placing its own national interests above those of Timor-Leste's, notably in relation to continued Timorese dissatisfaction with the placement of the Timor Sea boundary and the ongoing dispute with the Australian-based company, Woodside Petroleum.

Timor-Leste's growing relationship with China reflected the latter's "soft power" push into a number of small states. China provides uniforms for the country's small military, brings in medical teams and police, trains public servants and farmers, and invites students and official delegations to Beijing. China's ambassador to East Timor, Tian Guangfeng, said China "would like to make joint efforts with Timor-Leste to further strengthen friendly cooperation in all fields, and embrace an even brighter future for the relations between China and Timor-Leste".[34]

After constructing a number of key buildings as a key part of its aid programme, in 2012 China shifted its focus to supporting Timor-Leste's infrastructure development. "Our relations with the People's Republic of China are excellent", said President Taur Matan Ruak when visiting Macao. "Cooperation between our governments has been intense and fruitful,"[35] he said.

China's increasing interest in Timor-Leste piqued the interest of the United States in particular, which responded by mounting a series of naval visits to East Timor, of hospital ships doing pro bono medical work and of "floating city" aircraft carriers. The rotation of U.S. Marines through Darwin which began in 2012 was a further outcome of this attention. Through the United States Agency for International Development (USAID), the United States provides US$12.4 million (2012) in bilateral aid, particularly in the areas of good governance and democratization.

As a small country trying not to be dominated by any one of its major bilateral partners, Timor-Leste is set to continue its close relationship with China. By doing so, it will have a useful counterweight to Australia, and to the United States, who are also asserting their own regional strategic and economic interests.

Timor-Leste's other major bilateral relationship is with Portugal and, through it, also with the Community of Portuguese Language Countries (CPLP), which notably includes Brazil. Portugal's worsening financial position has meant that its bilateral aid to Timor-Leste in 2012 has been reduced.[36] Portugal, however, retained a close relationship with Timor-Leste, for example through integrating Timorese troops into Portuguese peacekeeping forces in Lebanon, as well as through ongoing support for Portuguese language teaching.

Timor-Leste also continued its enthusiastic embrace of multilateral forums, in particular its active pursuit of joining the Association of Southeast Asian Nations (ASEAN), with the active support of Indonesia. However, ASEAN has remained less enthusiastic about accepting Timor-Leste, partly on the grounds that Timor-Leste might struggle to maintain offices in each of the ASEAN states as required but also because, as a fragile state, Timor-Leste might test ASEAN's principle of non-interference in the affairs of member countries.[37] More successfully, Timor-Leste continued to lead the "g7+" group of the least developed countries, which was established in 2009 in response to perceived inadequate and inappropriate international approaches to the poorest countries.[38]

By mutual agreement, the UNMIT was due to conclude at the end of 2012, to be replaced by a much smaller office, with some 1,200 UN police also withdrawing. The Australian-led International Stabilization Force was also due to withdraw by the end of 2012, leaving behind Australia's smaller Defence Cooperation Program training team. There was consideration in 2012 that the Timor-Leste government might request, and pay for, a contingent of Portugal's Republican National Guard to remain to enhance local security.

While Timor-Leste was very active in engaging in international relations, realistically seeing this as its best opportunity for maintaining independence and development, there was also growing tension within Timor-Leste, both officially and unofficially, towards many in the international community. There remained considerable public anger over the lack of accountability for human rights abuses during the Indonesian occupation; Portugal and the Portuguese language was unpopular in some areas (notably in the west of the country);[39] there was widespread discontent, especially in Dili, towards the influx of Chinese workers, many of whom stayed beyond their contract brief; Australia was, as noted, seen as self-interested; and the United States was widely viewed as having overarching imperial ambitions. But more than anything else, there was a widespread sense in Timor-Leste, especially within its government, that what were perceived as the patronizing views of the international community on issues of good governance, transparency, development and sustainability were unwanted. In the years leading up to the 2012 elections, political leaders expressed increasingly pointed observations that Timor-Leste was a sovereign state that no longer needed or desired a high level of external involvement in its affairs. Public attacks on the United Nations Development Programme (UNDP), for example, reflected growing impatience within government circles for the departure of international state-building forces.

Conclusion

The big question over Timor-Leste moving towards being entirely responsible for its own affairs was whether it would manage them in a way that would not lead to a new breakdown. Given the substantively different and broadly improved circumstances, Timor-Leste was widely expected to avoid another major crisis. Since 2006, Timor-Leste has had a further six years in which to rebuild and consolidate its state institutions, its economy is growing alongside government spending and hence many development indicators continued to improve. The government also appeared more responsive to and engaged with the concerns of its constituents. This echoed the outcome of the 2012 elections, which was widely deemed to reflect considerable disaffection towards Mari Alkatiri as a leader, but considerable support for Xanana Gusmao.

Less positively, Timor-Leste still had widespread low levels of development and a growing sense of development inequity, continuing high unemployment and a growing population of youth for whom there appeared little prospect of jobs. While state institutional capacity continued to improve, it was from a low base and did not extend far from the capital. The police force was perhaps better trained than it had been in 2006 but remained similarly inclined to brutality. There was also the question of the extent of the impact of the UN drawdown on local employment, with 989 local staff directly employed and thousands more working in related service industries,[40] expected to lose their jobs. The withdrawal of approximately 2,000 international staff, who contribute 7.4 per cent of non-oil GDP,[41] was expected to impact on wider economic activity. If there was a silver lining in this otherwise foreboding cloud, it was that the two-track economy that had dominated Timor-Leste since the return of the UN in 1999 was likely to narrow, with a positive impact on the cost of living for many Timorese, notably in Dili, where 69 per cent of UNMIT staff were located,[42] but also in other larger towns.

There was little doubt that Timor-Leste's leaders felt confident about taking on the challenges of running their country with less international assistance. Indeed, as noted, many were impatient to be rid of what some saw as a neo-colonial presence. But even with a relatively high level of international assistance, Timor-Leste had shown itself to be vulnerable to many of the problems that can befall newly independent developing states. It had also demonstrated that while it was increasingly adept at spending its oil-based income, it was less adept at longer term, detailed and sustainable planning.

In all, 2012 was a particularly important year for Timor-Leste as it consolidated its political system, got on with the complicated business of development and, finally, said goodbye to much of the international presence that had helped steer it through the preceding half a dozen years and, with a brief interregnum, for some years before that. As Timor-Leste looks to the future, it faces three possible scenarios, the first and most optimistic of which is that all its development plans will work out, within a couple of decades it will join the ranks of middle income countries and that it will enjoy peace and increasing prosperity. The second scenario is that few if any development plans will work out as anticipated, poverty will remain widespread and worsen in line with population growth and this may lead to continuing political instability and renewed international assistance.

The third and most likely scenario is, however, that Timor-Leste will exit from 2012 to face a future somewhere in between these two extremes, hoping for much but perhaps achieving somewhat less. Timor-Leste travelled through 2012 putting in place many of the prerequisites for a sound future. There were, however, many indications throughout the year that it would need to perform at a higher level than in the past, particularly in terms of detailed planning and creating greater equity, if it wishes to see this broadly sound base built upon.

Notes

1. *A liurai* is a traditional local "king", lit: "earth lord".
2. Notably, Gusmao's recognition of the *lulic* (sacred) helped secure support for his preferred presidential candidate in the enclave of Oeccusi.
3. Woven cloth similar to *ikat* of the archipelago's southeastern island chain.
4. Crescent-shaped metal head-dress representing a stylized new moon: female, passive, cool.
5. Disc, symbolizing the sun: male, active, hot.
6. Traditional short sword.
7. Petroleum Fund of Timor-Leste, "Quarterly Report", Vol. 8, Issue XXI, pp. 2, 6.
8. Timor-Leste State Budget 2012 Overview, p. 14.
9. Ibid.
10. International Finance Corporation/World Bank, "Ease of Doing Business: Timor-Leste 2012".
11. Ibid., p. 15.
12. Despite the government's Strategic Development Plan, observations of these type were common enough, but in particular reflected the views of two individuals who were both close to the budgetary process, who cannot be named here for obvious reasons.
13. State Budget Overview, p. 33.
14. "Woodside expects E Timor to buckle over gas field", ABC News, 7 May 2010.
15. These figures were broadly accurate, but not exact as the official trade figure ran well behind the year in question.
16. Transparency International Corruption By Country: Timor-Leste.
17. Anti-Corruption Commission, Timor-Leste, Corruption Perception Survey 2011, p. 10.

18. Ministry of Finance, Timor-Leste, Consumer Price Index, June Quarter 2012.
19. UNDP Human Development Indicators, Country Profile: Timor-Leste, 2012.
20. Magdelela Carmon, "Report of the Special Rapporteur on extreme poverty and human rights", Mission to Timor-Leste, Human Rights Council, United Nations General Assembly, New York, 24 May 2012.
21. UN News Centre, "Not All Timorese Benefiting from Economic Gains, UN Human Rights Expert Says", 18 November 2011 <http://www.un.org/apps/news/story.asp?NewsID=40437 &Cr=timor&Cr1=> (accessed 16 August 2012).
22. UN Human Development Indicators, Country Profile: Timor-Leste, 2012.
23. For example, see D. Kaufmann, A. Kraay, and M. Mastruzzi, "Political Stability and Absence of Violence", in Worldwide Governance Indicators <http://info.worldbank.org/governance/wgi/index.asp> (accessed 5 November 2011); P. Collier and N. Sambanis, *Understanding Civil War, Vol. 1, Africa* (Washington, D.C.: World Bank, 2007); P. Collier and N. Sambanis, *Understanding Civil War, Vol. 2, Europe, Central Asia and Other Regions* (Washington, D.C.: World Bank, 2007); *Wars, Guns and Votes: Democracy in Dangerous Places* (New York: Harper, 2009); P. Collier, L. Elliot, H. Hegre, A. Hoeffler, M. Reynal-Querol, and N. Sambanis, *Breaking the Conflict Trap: Civil War and Development Policy* (Washington, D.C. and Oxford: World Bank and Oxford University Press, 2003).
24. M. Leach, and D. Kingsbury, "Introduction", in *The Politics of Timor-Leste* (Ithaca: Cornell University Press, 2012).
25. All election observer reports agreed on this point.
26. Based on the author's observation of rallies at both sets of elections as an accredited election observer.
27. M. Bachelard, and M. Lopez, "East Timor considers rainbow government", *Canberra Times*, 10 July 2012.
28. Timor Newsline, "One person killed during Monday's violence: PNTL Commander", 18 July 2012; Radio Timor-Leste, "More violence as PNTL and UN Police cars destroyed in Uatulari", 20 July 2012.
29. *Tempo Seminal*, "East Timorese Fifth Government: An Oligarchy", 6 August 2012.
30. *Jornal Timor Post*, "Taur Estuda Estrutura Kintu Governu: "Kestiaona Ministru Defeza", 7 August 2012.
31. Section 86 H, Constitution of the Democratic Republic of Timor-Leste.
32. See, for example, Albertus Rehi, "Villagers clash over border construction project", *UCA News*, 2 August 2012.
33. *DiaroNacional*, "TNI ready to work together with F-FDTL in peacekeeping force", 26 March 2012, p. 13; *Suara Timor Lorosae*, "Gusmao participates in defence dialogue in Jakarta", 26 Match 2012, p. 1; see also Edward Ress, "A decade after independence, East Timor's surprising best friend? Indonesia", *Christian Science Monitor*, 23 May 2012.

34. Tia Guangfeng, "A Perfect Example of Good-neighborly and Amicable Relationship", Embassy of the People's Republic of China in Timor-Leste, 15 May 2012.
35. Ibid.
36. According to Timor-Leste's Aid Management System, due to Portugal's budget being revised, the amount of Portuguese aid to Timor-Leste in 2012 was unclear at the time of writing.
37. Luke Hunt, "Timor-Leste's ASEAN Play", *The Diplomat*, 18 February 2012.
38. See Simon Fenby, "The G7+ Group of Fragile States: Towards Better International Engagement and Accountability in Aid Delivery to Fragile Nations", in *Rethinking Development*, edited by Damien Kingsubry (London: Palgrave, 2012).
39. Based on discussions with individuals in Bobonaro district.
40. UNMIT 2012, Joint Transition Plan, p. 30.
41. Ibid.
42. Ibid.

Vietnam

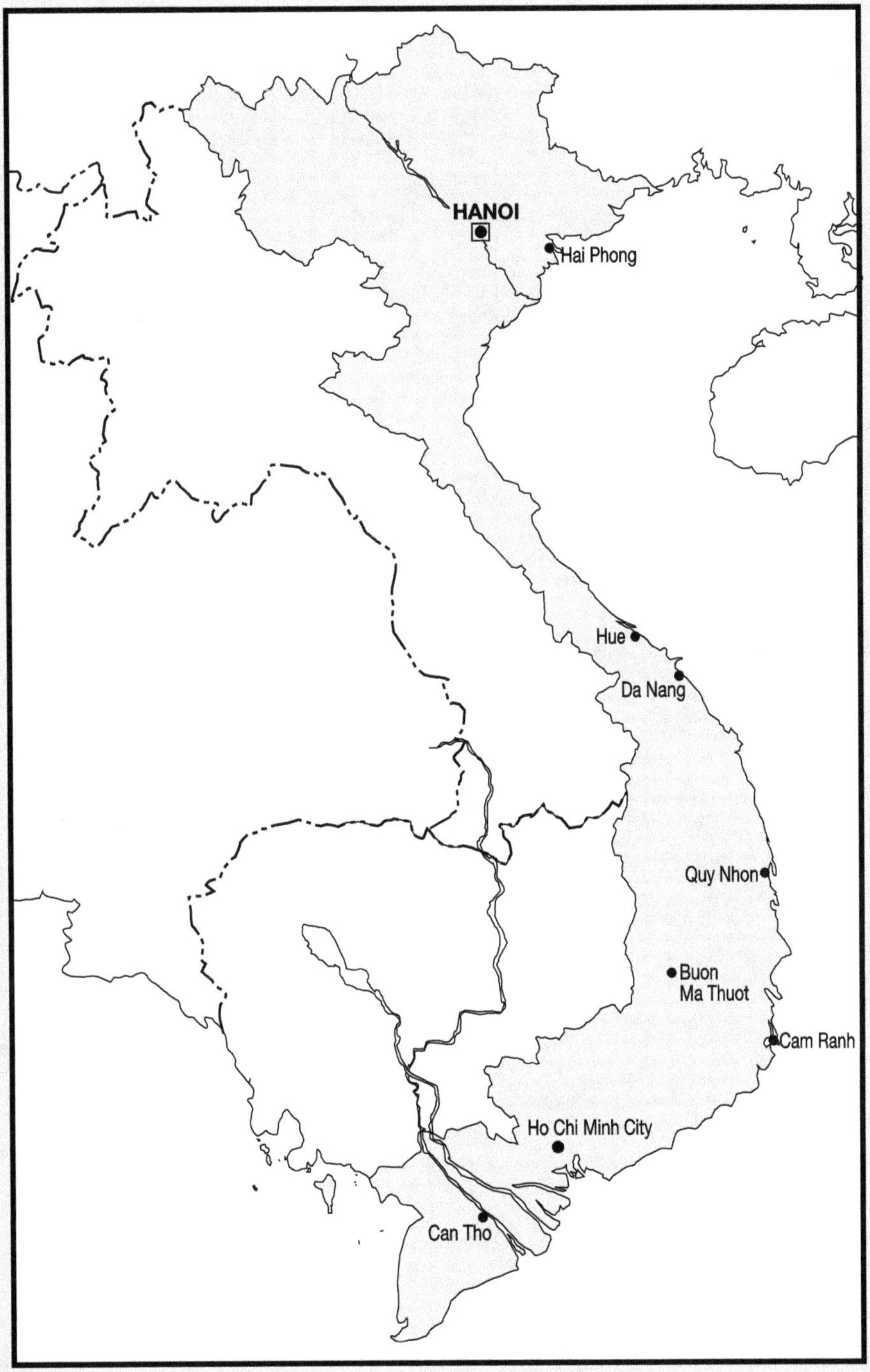

HANOI
Hai Phong
Hue
Da Nang
Quy Nhon
Buon Ma Thuot
Cam Ranh
Ho Chi Minh City
Can Tho

VIETNAM IN 2012
A Rent-Seeking State on the Verge of a Crisis

Alexander L. Vuving

After the passage of twenty-six years from the launch in 1986 of *doi moi*, Vietnam's large-scale reform programme, the single most important feature of the country's domestic politics that stands out today is the rise and crisis of a rent-seeking state. The marriage of the communist regime with the capitalist economy in Vietnam's reform era has given rise to a new type of state that is similar to the classical communist state in form but different in substance. The ethos of the classical communist state, which governed Vietnam prior to the reform era, was to transform society into one that is imbued with socialist values. By contrast, the ethos of the rent-seeking state, which administers Vietnam today, is to create barriers and extract rents from society. Both types of state rule society in an authoritarian way but each is guided by a different spirit.

As Vietnam's communist regime tries to survive by adopting some elements of capitalism while retaining most of its authoritarianism, rent-seekers have gradually become the dominant force in the Vietnamese body politic, thereby quietly changing the nature of the state they occupy. Rent-seeking finds fertile ground in Vietnam, where the state owns all the land, controls all the press, and is accountable to none but itself. A natural tendency in every authoritarian regime, rent-seeking is kept at bay when the state is imbued with strong patriotic sentiments or when the state is dependent on a liberal world outside for survival. These conditions existed in Japan, South Korea, Taiwan, and Singapore, as do they in China, helping these countries to achieve high growth over several decades. Contrary to the conventional wisdom, similar conditions

ALEXANDER L. VUVING is Associate Professor at the Asia-Pacific Center for Security Studies, Honolulu, Hawaii, United States.

have largely been absent in post-Cold War Vietnam. Vietnam entered the post-Cold War era with the belief that the key to the survival of the communist regime is friendship with communist China. Since 1989, unlike the Chinese Communist Party, which made patriotic education a key element of its survival kit, the Vietnam Communist Party (VCP) has suppressed patriotic sentiments because they tend to take an anti-China direction. Without the check provided by patriotism and the pressure to comply with a liberal order, rent-seeking has conquered the commanding heights of Vietnamese politics and economy.

The hegemony of the rent-seekers implies the crisis of their state, however. As rent-seekers live on what society pays to overcome the barriers they create, their dominance leads to a large reduction of productivity and growth and a strong resentment of perceived unfairness. Vietnam's rent-seekers reached the apex of their hegemony in 2007, when Prime Minister Nguyen Tan Dung, a leading rent-seeker, obtained primacy in the Vietnamese collective leadership. He was given a largely free hand to appoint the members of the government and the bosses of the state-owned conglomerates. With these powers, the prime minister became even more powerful than the VCP general secretary, who was by statute the supreme leader in the communist state. The rent-seekers' hegemony soon threw the country off balance. In early 2008, months ahead of the global financial turmoil that started the same year, Vietnam fell into a period of economic volatility and slowdown that would last for years. The year 2012 marked a dramatic milestone on Vietnam's road to a major crisis. This essay chronicles the year's most important events and spotlights the key dynamics of Vietnam's economy, politics, and foreign relations. As will be seen, these dynamics strongly suggest the advent of a severe political, economic, and national security crisis that can rival the one that ravaged the country in the 1980s.

A Clogged Economy Whose Rescue is Thwarted by Rent-Seeking

In 2012 Vietnam's economy continued to improve on the macroeconomic front, apparently as a result of the stabilization measures announced in 2011. Foreign trade posted the first export surplus since 1993. With exports increasing by 18 per cent, Vietnam recorded the highest rate of export growth in East Asia. The trade surplus and a robust flow of remittances, which partly reflected high interest rates, have helped Vietnam to report a record surplus of 2.7 per cent in current account balance. This in turn has contributed to the improvement in the balance of payments situation and augmented the stock of foreign exchange reserves. By year's end, Vietnam's foreign exchange reserves were estimated to reach US$23 billion, an increase of US$14 billion from the previous year and a return to the highest level recorded historically in 2008. Meanwhile, year-on-year inflation fell to 9.21 per cent from 18.58 per cent in the previous year.[1]

These gains, however, face serious downside risks. Vietnam's foreign exchange reserves were sufficient for only 2.3 months of imports, an indication of the economy's high vulnerability. They were considerably low compared with China's 22.4 months, Thailand's 8.7 months, Indonesia's 7.2 months, and South Korea's 7.1 months. The replenishment of the foreign exchange reserves was financed by the central bank pumping domestic currency worth about US$10 billion. The fact that this large amount had little impact on inflation was seen by experts as an indication of an ominous lack of domestic demand, which was one of the major factors responsible for meagre growth.[2] In 2012 Vietnam's economy grew by a mere 5 per cent, slower than even the worst case scenario (5.2–5.5 per cent) envisioned by the National Financial Supervisory Commission at the year's start. It was the lowest growth rate since 1999.[3] It reflected the fact that an unusually large number of enterprises were closed, liquidated, or temporarily suspended operations in 2012. In addition, many of the remaining enterprises had to reduce capacity by 30–50 per cent. The number of closures and liquidations in the past two years — 55,000 in 2012 and 49,000 in 2011—made up half of the total number of closures and liquidations in the past twenty years. It was estimated that one-third of the enterprises had left the market while most of the remaining two-thirds operated at a loss.[4]

The roots of the problems can be traced back in large part to the rent-seeking state. Economists identified four major structural impediments that clogged the economy — high interest rates, a gridlock in the real estate market, a large amount of bad debts, and high taxes and fees. A mundane example that illustrates how the rent-seeking state contributed to the problem is that at the same time as the government announced it would cut taxes, its various agencies increased fees.[5] Another, far from mundane, example is the case of the transportation firm Mai Linh. The country's largest private taxi company and a success story in the last decade, Mai Linh defaulted in 2012 on debts worth 500 billion dong (US$24 million). The firm had borrowed at interest rates higher than the official rate by 5–10 percentage points. One must question why this apparently reputable company had to accept such high rates, when the government successively lowered the interest rates and issued a "rescue package" worth 29 trillion dong (US$1.4 billion) during the year. As the journalist Dao Tuan noted, "this question can only be answered by [the central bank's] Governor Nguyen Van Binh."[6] The lion's share of the bad debts resulted from corruption in the state-owned conglomerates, which received preferential treatment because of ideological bias and personal ties. In April, for instance, the State Inspectorate reported that wrongdoing at Petro Vietnam and Song Da Corp. had cost the state US$874 million and US$512 million, respectively. The biggest corruption scandal of the year involved Vinalines, the largest state-owned shipping and port operator in the country. Reports by the State Inspectorate revealed that mismanagement had caused a total debt of more than 43 trillion dong (US$2 billion) at Vinalines, which defaulted on five loans worth more than 23 trillion dong (US$1.1 billion). The state-run giant had spent 23 trillion dong to purchase seventy-three foreign vessels, most of which were second-hand, incurring a huge expense for repair and maintenance.[7]

It has become a widely held consensus that the Vietnamese economy needs structural reforms in numerous areas. Under pressure from the public, the government prioritized three key areas for restructuring — banks, state-owned enterprises, and public investment. However, despite government pronouncements, restructuring was either delayed or heavily influenced by the parochial interests of shadowy rent-seeking networks. Behind every major measure by the government in the name of stabilization and restructuring there lurked the spectre of rent-seeking. Besides the corruption scandals involving the state-owned conglomerates, a ban on gold trade and the restructuring of the private sector, two of the most important changes that occurred in 2012, best illustrate this phenomenon.

The government set up a state monopoly over gold bullion traded in the market. A government decree (No. 24, in effect from 25 May 2012) prohibited seven activities, including using gold bars as a medium of payment, processing jewellery gold or trading bullion without a licence from Vietnam's central bank, and conducting other gold-related business without the approval of the relevant authority. The ban was officially explained in terms of stabilizing the gold market and making the precious metal more productive. It was also thought to be aimed at reducing inflation and the trade deficit. Gold has a special place in Vietnamese investment portfolios. It often plays a key role in hedging property transactions and provides a safe haven for savings. Vietnam is one of the world's largest gold consumers. A key element of the government's gold policy is the designation of the Saigon Jewelry Co. (SJC) as the only body allowed to verify the quality and authenticity of gold. This monopoly allowed SJC to collect fees on transactions involving gold while denying this to gold previously produced by other companies. The policy caused big losses to the population and created a feeling of insecurity. Contrary to the government's stated intent, the ban actually destabilized the gold market. Gold prices were spiralling and turmoil reigned in the market.[8] Needless to say, the new monopoly is a big beneficiary of the new policy.

The restructuring in the private sector during 2012 resulted in acquisitions, mergers, and leadership changes at several of the country's largest private banks and industrial firms. Remarkably, many of these deals occurred under dubious conditions. The takeover of Bianfishco, one of the country's largest seafood processors, by SHBank is one prominent example. But perhaps the most important of all such deals during 2012 is the takeover of Sacombank, the country's largest private bank by charter capital and the sixth largest commercial bank by assets with a market value of US$7 billion. Early in the year, a group of unknown investors led by Eximbank, Vietnam's seventh largest bank, claimed to hold more than 51 per cent of Sacombank's stock and demanded the control of the board. Some of these investors had acquired their Sacombank shares illegally, but the stock market watchdog, the State Securities Commission, imposed fines for their transactions only after the outsiders had successfully taken control of the bank in late May. Following this management shake-up, Sacombanks's new board was dominated by four new members from Southern Bank, a small private lender that had run out of cash and cash equivalents to meet the demands of depositors and borrowers, and two from Eximbank. By early November, Sacombank chairman and founder Dang Van Thanh was forced to unload most of his holdings and subsequently resigned from the board. The new Sacombank chairman was Pham Huu Phu, who represented Eximbank's stake.[9] The takeover of Sacombank was not just hostile; it bordered on the criminal. In a letter publicized by the newspaper *Bao ve Phap luat* of the Supreme People's Procuracy, Thanh complained that the Sacombank board had dismissed him as the board's chairman without his consent when he was held by the police for interrogation. In addition to questioning the legality of the police interrogation, he also raised concerns over the central bank's inspection of his bank and the authorities' accusations that he and his family members had committed wrongdoing causing a loss of thousands of billions of dong.[10] These questions, and other puzzles like how the acquirers of Sacombank were able to obtain such a large amount of money for the takeover, remained either unaddressed or inadequately answered by the authorities.

The veil of secrecy was partly lifted by the blog Quan Lam Bao (Officials Doing Journalism), which was probably informed by knowledgeable officials working in the government. Started on the day of the first round of takeover at Sacombank, Quan Lam Bao reported that a loan package authorized by Central Bank Governor Nguyen Van Binh had rescued Southern Bank from liquidity loss and enabled its owner Tram Be to take over Sacombank. A large amount of the monies the acquirers used to buy Sacombank's shares was raised through multiple borrowings in the interbank market. The three Eximbank officials who held major stakes at Sacombank were only front men for the actual acquirers, who were identified by the blog as Tram Be, Nguyen Duc Kien, and Nguyen Thanh Phuong. Kien was a well-known multimillionaire and former senior executive of Asia Commercial Bank (ACB), the largest private bank in the country, Be an illiterate businessman, and Phuong none other than the daughter of Prime Minister Nguyen Tan Dung. Quan Lam Bao further argued that in the past year there emerged two dominant "interest groups" (*nhóm lợi ích*) that attempted to control the entire financial-economic system of the country. The group that was seeking control of the banking sector included Kien, Be, Phuong, and Governor Binh. The other group included Phuong, Binh, and two other businessmen with close ties to them — Techcombank Chairman Ho Hung Anh and Masan Group Chairman Nguyen Dang Quang.[11]

The Near-Split of an Elite That Worships Stability

The key feature of Vietnam's elite politics in 2012 was the clash between an anti-corruption coalition led by VCP General Secretary Nguyen Phu Trong and a rent-seeking group headed by Prime Minister Nguyen Tan Dung. Many observers argued that the infighting within Vietnam's ruling elite was a struggle for domination that would have little impact on the country's overall policy. Others asserted that this was no more than a personal duel between the prime minister and his archrival, President Truong Tan Sang. These views ignore, however, the larger political, economic, and historical context in which the power struggle unfolded and without which the events could hardly be understood. The single most important feature of that context is the rise and crisis of the rent-seeking state in Vietnam. After more than two decades of a symbiosis of communism and capitalism, it is widely recognized that the state is in a legitimacy crisis and that the central cause of this crisis is corruption. Although rent-seekers have become the dominant current in Vietnamese politics, they have yet to unite in an effective coalition. Moreover, other currents such as the conservatives, who are anti-Western in domestic and foreign policy; the reformers, who promote economic and political modernization; and the moderates, who stand in the middle of the road between the conservatives and the reformers, remain major forces in the ruling elite.

Against this background, Nguyen Phu Trong, a middle-of-the-roader untainted by corruption, was elected VCP chief at the party's eleventh congress in early 2011. The choice of Trong as the party boss helped to both polish the party's image and maintain a delicate balance among the contending factions and policy currents. In the run-up to the congress, Trong was favoured by the major rent-seeking factions over Ho Duc Viet, then head of the VCP Central Organization Department and a strong candidate for the party chief post, because unlike Viet, who went head-on against what he perceived as corruption, Trong had always been a man of compromise. Viet's vehement opposition to the plans to get the sons of then VCP chief Nong Duc Manh, a corrupt anti-Westerner, and Premier Dung into the new party central committee eventually cost him the job.[12]

Like other VCP chiefs, Trong owes his position not just to a special arrangement among the party factions, but more importantly for the long run, to some larger tendencies in the ruling elite. The hegemony of the rent-seekers has helped to create a rainbow coalition consisting of moderates, reformers, and conservatives. Different groups with different final goals are united in this broad-range coalition for the common aim of fighting corruption. The dominant bloc in the coalition are party survivalists — moderates like Trong and conservatives whose final aim is to maintain the VCP's power — but reformers, whose ultimate goal is to modernize the country and make it strong and rich (*dân giàu nước mạnh*), also form a substantial part of this coalition.[13] When party chief, under pressure from party elders and the impact of the Arab Spring, Trong was determined to clean the party of corruption. Echoing a growing chorus, he repeatedly warned that "corruption is threatening the survival of the Party." His main objective was to prevent popular revolt against the party by correcting officials' corrupt behaviour. His goal was not to introduce reform as such but to maintain stability.

At the fourth plenum of the VCP Eleventh Central Committee in December 2011, Trong launched a major campaign to "rectify the Party" (*chỉnh đốn Đảng*). Faithful to a long-held VCP tradition, he chose the practice of "criticism and self-criticism" as the campaign's main approach. Learning from the failure of the previous anti-corruption measures, which were often criticized as "bathing without washing the head" (a phrase that former VCP chief Le Kha Phieu helped to popularize), Trong emphasized that the new campaign should implement criticism and self-criticism from the top down.[14] Unlike most other rectification measures by the party, this one was no mere rhetoric. Indeed, if successful, an anti-corruption campaign focused on the top leadership would only strengthen the position of Trong and his core allies in the Politburo because they were relatively clean from corruption.

As the campaign was concentrated on the top leadership, its main target was Prime Minister Dung, who was responsible for the big corruption scandals — the Vinashin and Vinalines fiascos, to name just the most well-known ones — that had both hugely tarnished the party's reputation and greatly reduced the state's treasure. Dung was not an easy target, however. Sitting on the Politburo since 1996 and having been a deputy minister of public security, the head of the VCP Central Economics Department, the governor of the central bank, and the permanent deputy prime minister prior to becoming the prime minister in 2006, Dung had built a vast network of allies with access to key resources. Extremely pragmatic, daring, and determined, he skilfully took advantage of the reformers' hope for a leader fearless of change, the conservatives' preference for a leader tough on any opposition, and the party-state's unlimited power, to consolidate his position. Besides his networks and skills, Dung had yet another powerful asset — the party leadership's extreme fear of instability. The battle between Trong's anti-corruption coalition and Dung's rent-seeking group was one in which the former's pet idea — stability — was taken hostage by the latter.[15]

The tide of the battle moved during 2012 like a see-saw, which showed no clear winner. Law enforcement was one of the central theatres of this battle. On 17 May, the former boss of the scandal-ridden Vinalines Duong Chi Dung successfully fled before the police came to arrest him. Dung had been promoted by Transportation Minister Dinh La Thang to head of the Vietnam Maritime Administration in February and had close ties to Vice-Minister for Public Security Pham Quy Ngo and Prime Minister Nguyen Tan Dung. He was only captured in early September after hiding in his native Hai Phong. The successful escape of Duong Chi Dung suggested complicity in sections of the police force.[16] The arrest on 20 August of Nguyen Duc Kien, the multi-millionaire thought to be a mastermind behind the recent taking over of the banking sector, was more successful. According to the blog Cau Nhat Tan (Nhat Tan Bridge), Premier Dung was not informed about the order to arrest this businessman, who had close ties to his family, until a few hours prior to the event. The plan was directly supervised by Minister for Public Security Tran

Dai Quang and sanctioned by party chief Trong. None of the vice-ministers for public security, including Dung's allies Pham Quy Ngo and To Lam, was informed about the plan.[17] In the following months, both camps launched attacks and counter-attacks, which resulted, among others, in the detention and interrogation, as well as the blocking of attempted arrests, of several senior executives of large private banks and enterprises.

The clash between General Secretary Trong's anti-corruption coalition and Prime Minister Dung's rent-seeking group was embedded in a larger battle that spread over various fronts and involved a myriad of participants. The two camps appeared to be more or less self-organized loose galaxies without a central hub of command. A key front in this larger battle was the social media. Perhaps the biggest event on this front in 2012 was the appearance of the blog Quan Lam Bao. Focusing on murky ties between big businesses, members of the prime minister's family and senior government officials, and accusing them of greed, cronyism, and mismanagement, the blog quickly became one of the country's most-visited websites. The daily number of the site's visitors from Vietnam surged from around 6,000 to nearly 31,000 on the day after Nguyen Duc Kien's arrest, which Quan Lam Bao was the first to report, and stayed above 30,000 over the following months despite a ban (from 12 September) by the prime minister.

On the central front of high politics, the anti-corruption coalition made limited advances while the rent-seeking group struck back vigorously. The Trong camp scored its first major success when the fifth plenum of the VCP Central Committee in mid-May decided to transfer the Central Anti-Corruption Steering Committee from under the prime minister to under the party chief and reinstall the Central Department for Internal Political Affairs to support this committee.[18] However, at the sixth Central Committee plenum (1–15 October), Dung successfully prevented decisive action by his opponents. Central to the meeting's agenda was what in effect amounted to a no-confidence vote against him. In a manoeuvre to cut short the Dung camp's preparations, the meeting was convened two weeks earlier than planned. According to the blog Cau Nhat Tan, several Central Committee members were given less than 24 hours' advance notice about the change.[19] But the Trong camp made a fatal mistake when scheduling the discussion of Dung's censure at the middle of the two-week long meeting, giving the Dung camp plenty of time to influence the Central Committee members. At this meeting the Central Committee admitted big mistakes in preventing and remedying corruption. It also decided to revive the Central Economics Department to check and watch over the economic management of the government. However, when it came to Dung's case, the Central Committee rejected the Politburo's proposal to discipline the Politburo as a collective and Dung as an individual, who was referred to anonymously as "a comrade member of the Politburo" in the plenum's communiqué.[20]

Towards the year's end, the tide of the contest started to reverse. A new National Assembly resolution passed in November required a confidence vote annually on every official elected by the National Assembly. Starting from February 2013, this new mechanism would subject the prime minister and all members of the cabinet, the state president, and the National Assembly chair, among other officials, to annual review. The National Assembly also amended the Anti-Corruption Law and removed the stipulation that the prime minister be the chairman of the Central Anti-Corruption Steering Committee, paving the way for the party chief to take over the committee.[21] In December, the position of the anti-corruption camp was considerably strengthened with the promotion of Public Security Minister Quang to four-star general and the appointment of Da Nang party boss Nguyen Ba Thanh and Finance Minister Vuong Dinh Hue as heads of the new Central Departments of Internal Political Affairs and Economics, respectively. Thanh is, as a Western investor observed, "the nearest Vietnam has to a Lee Kuan Yew."[22] An enlightened strongman and an outspoken critic of Premier Dung and his acolytes, he is regarded as the best Vietnam has to counter the prime minister.[23]

The outcome of the sixth plenum reflects a delicate balance of power between the anti-corruption coalition and the rent-seekers. In the Politburo, the former can easily secure the votes of at least six of the fourteen members, including party chief Trong, State President Sang, Public Security Minister Quang, Chairman of the party's Central Inspection Commission Ngo Van Du, Hanoi party boss Pham Quang Nghi, and Vice-Prime Minister Nguyen Xuan Phuc. The five rent-seekers in the Politburo — Prime Minister Dung, National Assembly chair Nguyen Sinh Hung, Central Organization Committee chair To Huy Rua, Central Propaganda Committee chair Dinh The Huynh, and Ho Chi Minh City party boss Le Thanh Hai — do not form a unified coalition. A reverse configuration exists in the Central Committee. According to the blog Bo Cau Den (Black Dove), 129 of the 175 Central Committee members (nearly 74 per cent) voted against the Politburo's proposal to discipline Premier Dung.[24] This bizarre situation poses an important puzzle about current Vietnamese politics. Why does the Politburo, despite being elected by and from among the Central Committee members, not reflect the general make-up of its constituents? While forming the majority in the Central Committee, rent-seekers are in the minority in the Politburo. This can be explained by the fact that although rent-seekers are birds of the same feather, they work to the benefit of their own clique and as a species they do not always flock together. Besides, rent-seekers are by nature more inclined than conservatives, reformers, and moderates to commit corruption. True, corrupt officials are more likely to be promoted in the rent-seeking state. But as corruption is still officially public enemy number one, rent-seekers' higher vulnerability to corruption charges also reduces their chance to get to the top tiers of public offices.

Yawning Gap Between Rulers and Ruled

The year 2012 saw the gap between the state and society in Vietnam continue to widen. Capturing a widespread feeling in the country, President Sang acknowledged in an October 2012 meeting with voters that "the population is tremendously indignant" (*lòng dân đang bất bình ghê gớm*).[25] The most burning issues were land seizure, official corruption, and the China threat in the South China Sea.[26] An indication of the indignation was a growing tide of protest and resistance in various forms. The brutality with which the authorities cracked down on opposition also seemed to increase.

Most of the clashes between the state and the population involved illegal government land grabs. According to a National Assembly report, roughly 70 per cent of the petitions lodged by the citizens were related to land disputes.[27] In his review of the year, the popular blogger Truong Duy Nhat selected the *dân oan* as the person of the year.[28] Coined in the late 1990s to refer to petitioners who are unjustly treated by the government, the word *dân oan* is mostly associated with farmers or residents whose land is illegally repossessed by the state. Two of the numerous land grabs in 2012 aroused sustained debate among the public.

The first took place on 5 January in the district of Tien Lang of Hai Phong. The farmer Doan Van Vuon and his brothers ambushed security forces with homemade landmines and guns in a bid to stop local officials from taking their farm. The farm was on land reclaimed from the sea and developed by Vuon and his family for decades. More than 100 police officers and troops were deployed to attack the farmers and destroy their property. The attack was praised by the Hai Phong police chief as an "excellent joint combat" by the police, the military, and the border guards, which resulted in a "beautiful battle". The action sparked outrage among the public. Vuon quickly became a national hero. Even former President Le Duc Anh weighed in, deploring the use of the military in law enforcement and showing sympathy towards Vuon. In an unprecedented manner, the media was allowed to go far beyond the usual limits. Under pressure from various directions, Premier Dung was forced to acknowledge the illegality of the seizure and ask local authorities to return the land to the farmers. This government response turned out to be the exception that proves the rule, however. The Doan brothers stayed in jail. Despite the prime minister's request for a reduction of the sentence, local authorities upheld the charge of murder against them. The prosecution of local officials was equally unfair. The responsibility for the illegal land grab was put on an official who actually opposed the plan. The real culprits were either left out or charged with minor offences.[29]

The second land grab that caused sustained debate involved the Ecopark project in the district of Van Giang in Hung Yen province. According to witnesses, more than 2,000 police officers and unidentified men not wearing uniforms were deployed on 24 April to disperse about 2,000 villagers defending their land. Video footage posted on YouTube showed mobs of policemen brutally beating bystanders, some of whom were identified as journalists from the state-owned broadcaster Voice of Vietnam. Unlike the Tien Lang incident, the media was not given free rein to cover the Van Giang episode. It was reported in social media that the daughter of Premier Dung was one of the Ecopark developers.[30]

The land seizure incidents sparked a nationwide debate over official corruption, the role of the government in land disputes, and the pros and cons of state ownership of land. Most experts argued that state ownership of land and government involvement in setting land prices were the key sources of official corruption and popular indignation.[31] Despite a growing call for reform, the party opted for the status quo. Both the fifth and sixth VCP Central Committee Plenums re-emphasized that "all land comes under the ownership of the entire people and is uniformly administered by the state as the representative of the landowner" (*đất đai thuộc sở hữu toàn dân do Nhà nước là đại diện chủ sở hữu và thống nhất quản lý*). The sixth plenum added that direct negotiation over the transfer of land-use right and the prices between the incoming developer and the present user of land is not allowed.[32]

Frustration with the party-state over corruption dominated voters' meetings with party leaders. Responding to the popular anger, VCP chief Trong stressed prudence while President Sang urged courage in fighting against corruption. Both leaders acknowledged that official corruption had become a powerful trend and warned that it might cause the demise of the party.[33] Meanwhile, the party-state's commitment to combat corruption appeared to be mere lip service, when a harsh sentence was meted out to the journalist Hoang Khuong, who uncovered a corruption case by employing illicit but effective methods.[34] Continuing a trend that started a few years ago, the year 2012 saw more public intellectuals protest the government's abuse of power and bad governance. In sum, while a small section in the party-state stepped up the fight against corruption, the state as a whole continued in practice to define its interests in opposition to those of the population, alienating both the populace and the intelligentsia.

Ambiguous Measures to an Unambiguous Threat

The single most important feature in the realm of Vietnam's foreign policy in the last five years is the rise of the South China Sea dispute to the top of the country's national security and foreign policy concerns. For most of the two decades that followed the end of the Cold War, Vietnam did not face any major threats to its physical security. Although anti-Westerners and particularly the military leadership constantly called for vigilance against a possible U.S. invasion of Vietnam, this was rarely perceived as an imminent threat.[35] The surge of Chinese assertiveness in the last few years has substantially changed Vietnam's perception of its security environment. By 2012, the country's leaders were no longer uncertain about China's ambitions in the South China Sea. Even the military, whose leadership is one of the most pro-China groups in the Vietnamese government, has come to the conclusion that Beijing is determined to take over the South China Sea, including the Spratly Islands and a vast area within Vietnam's exclusive economic zone (EEZ). Speaking in September to visiting overseas Vietnamese, the head of the Military Education and Information Department, Major General Nguyen Thanh Tuan, emphasized: "We should not be ambiguous and lose vigilance about China's scheme to take exclusive control of the East Sea [South China Sea]."[36]

Intriguingly, Vietnam's response to this now unambiguous threat remains anything but unambiguous. It includes efforts to get third parties involved but also efforts to exclude them. It contains measures to solidify Vietnam's position vis-à-vis China but also measures that undercut it. This ambiguous policy reflects the China dilemma of the VCP state: At the same time as China presents an imminent threat to Vietnam's territorial integrity it also holds a key promise to Hanoi's regime survival.

Seeking strategic partnerships and security cooperation with global and regional players is a main thrust of post-Cold War Vietnamese foreign policy. During a visit by President Sang to Russia in late July, Vietnam and Russia formally elevated their eleven-year old strategic partnership to "comprehensive strategic partnership".[37] With this new epithet, Russia is now ranked on par with China, Vietnam's "comprehensive cooperative strategic partner", and above Vietnam's other strategic partners. In September, party chief Trong paid a high-profile visit to Singapore, his first to a non-communist country as VCP general secretary. The two countries pledged to sign, in 2013, a Strategic Partnership Agreement, the first between Vietnam and an ASEAN state and the first among Vietnam's strategic partnerships that is sanctioned by a formal agreement rather than a joint statement. During Trong's meeting with the chairperson of Singapore's ruling People's Action Party (PAP), the two leaders also talked about a "strategic partnership" between the VCP and the PAP.[38] In December, at the second joint cabinet meeting between Thailand and Vietnam, Prime Ministers Yingluck Shinawatra and Nguyen Tan Dung followed suit with plans aiming towards the Thai-Vietnamese strategic partnership.[39] In August, Vietnam and Australia agreed to upgrade their bilateral Strategic Dialogue to an Annual Defense Ministers' Dialogue.[40] Remarkably, Vietnam's other strategic dialogues are held at the vice-ministerial level, whereas Australia is not even a formal strategic partner. The year 2012 marked the first defence strategic dialogues between Vietnam and South Korea (in February) and Japan (in November).

Continuing a trend that started in 2009, the South China Sea issues remained a dominant theme in Vietnam's foreign affairs during 2012. On 21 June Vietnam passed a domestic Maritime Law to give legal bases to its activities in the South China Sea. The law reaffirmed Vietnam's sovereignty over the contested Paracel and Spratly Islands. Vietnamese leaders such as party chief Trong lauded the adoption of the law as a "victory".[41] It was indeed a victory over the fear within the Vietnamese leadership of Chinese retaliation. The passage of Vietnam's Maritime Law had been delayed for several years due to Chinese pressure.[42] Not surprisingly, China reacted angrily to what it perceived as Vietnam's insolence. On 25 June the China National Offshore Oil Corporation (CNOOC) announced that it would open to bidding nine oil and gas blocks that lay entirely within the 200 nautical mile EEZ that Vietnam is allowed under the UN Convention on the Law of the Sea (UNCLOS). During 2012 Vietnam's patience and determination continued to be tested by numerous incidents related to disputes with China over the South China Sea. In one incident, Hanoi refused to stamp the new Chinese passports that showed most of the South China Sea as Chinese territory, issuing the visitors a separate visa.[43] In another incident, Hanoi delayed publication of news about the cutting of a Vietnamese state-owned ship's oil exploration cables by Chinese vessels for three days until a meeting between VCP chief Trong and a senior Chinese Communist

Party official had concluded.[44] These and other perceived aggressive acts by China were the triggers of four anti-China protests in Hanoi and Ho Chi Minh City during 2012, on 1, 8, and 22 July, and 9 December. The Vietnamese party-state did not confine itself to clamping down on the protests and stepping up harassment of the protesters. After the fourth protest, the VCP Central Propaganda Department punished those journalists in the state-owned media who it claimed had added fuel to the fire by using "incorrect" words such as "cutting" the cables instead of "causing" them to break.[45]

Since 2009, gathering international support for the Vietnamese cause in the South China Sea has become a main element of Vietnam's foreign policy. At the ASEAN Ministerial Meeting in Phnom Penh in July, Vietnam brought up the issue of Chinese encroachment into the Vietnamese EEZ. However, a disagreement with Cambodia over the inclusion of that issue (and a stand-off between China and the Philippines over the Scarborough Shoal) in the final statement of the meeting blocked the issuance of that statement, causing a blow to ASEAN's reputation and the Cambodia-Vietnam relationship. Being in a weak position to compete with China for influence over the small neighbour, Hanoi responded softly. Not only did it refrain from criticizing Phnom Penh publicly, but it continued to curry favour with the latter through economic largesse and other shows of friendship. A week after the Phnom Penh debacle, Hanoi gave visiting Cambodian dignitary Heng Samrin a warm reception, expressed its support for Cambodia's bid for a non-permanent seat in the UN Security Council, reminded its guests of Vietnam's role in Cambodia's national salvation, and gave the Cambodian leader a present that featured a map of Vietnam.[46] Between CNOOC's announcement in June that it would tender for nine oil blocks within Vietnam's EEZ and the ASEAN Ministerial Meeting and ASEAN Regional Forum in July, Hanoi dispatched Vice-Prime Minister Nguyen Xuan Phuc to Japan and National Assembly Chairman Nguyen Sinh Hung to Laos, both to strengthen bilateral ties and to seek support for its view on the South China Sea. While Japan showed great sympathy for Vietnam's predicament, Laos remained lukewarm. The year 2012 saw numerous exchanges of senior leaders between Hanoi and Vientiane as the two countries celebrated the thirty-fifth anniversary of their mutual defence treaty. Meanwhile, Vietnam continued to court its neighbour, Cambodia.

Still, the strongest support for Vietnam against the threat to its territorial integrity in the South China Sea came not from its only treaty ally Laos but from India, the United States, Japan, and Russia. On 10 July 2012 in Hanoi, U.S. Secretary of State Hillary Clinton gave one of the strongest statements of public support that Hanoi had ever received from a foreign country on the South China Sea. She said: "The United States greatly appreciates Vietnam's contributions to a collaborative, diplomatic resolution of disputes and a reduction of tensions in the South China Sea."[47] To further demonstrate America's endorsement of close ties with Vietnam, Clinton invited VCP General Secretary Trong to visit the United States, preferably in 2013, something that was unimaginable just a few years ago. The invitation was, however, not made public. Clinton's visit followed a symbolic visit by U.S. Secretary of Defense Leon Panetta in early June, which included a stop in Cam Ranh Bay, the most coveted strategic harbour on the South China Sea. Standing on the U.S. Navy cargo ship Richard Byrd, which docked there for repair, Panetta said: "Access for United States naval ships into this facility is a key component of this relationship [with Vietnam] and we see a tremendous potential here for the future … It is very important that we be able to protect key maritime rights for all nations in the South China Sea and elsewhere."[48] Also in Hanoi, on 14 July, Japanese Foreign Minister Koichiro Gemba said that his country was willing to help Vietnam bolster its coastal patrol capabilities.[49] On 3 December, just as Vietnam accused Chinese boats of sabotaging an oil and gas exploration operation, Indian Navy chief Admiral D.K. Joshi told journalists that, while India was not a territorial claimant in the South China Sea, it was prepared to act, if necessary, to protect its maritime and economic interests in the region.[50] Besides India, America, and Japan, Russia was another major power that sided with Vietnam in the maritime dispute over the latter's EEZ by backing its companies in joint exploration with Vietnam in areas also claimed by China.

While trying to make advance by inches, Vietnam resisted offers to progress by miles. The U.S. proposal of a strategic partnership, which would lift the U.S. arms embargo and open up other big opportunities, was greeted tepidly. While modernizers and moderates were more or less enthusiastic about the proposal, rent-seekers were indifferent, and anti-Westerners remained hostile to it. Washington's offer came with one string attached — Hanoi should improve its human rights record. Instead, as if in calculated defiance, the human rights situation in Vietnam has deteriorated further.

Conclusion

In an audio tape posted on the popular blog Ba Sam in December 2012, a propagandist with the Vietnamese military, Senior Colonel Tran Dang Thanh, is lecturing to leaders of universities and colleges in Hanoi. The military officer has authority because "national defence and security education" has been made compulsory and a necessary condition for promotion in the government in the years following the collapse of communism in Eastern Europe. Like patriotic education in post-1989 China, national defence and security education is a key tool of indoctrination in post-1989 Vietnam.

While reflecting the views of the anti-Westerners, Thanh's presentation reveals some of the key ideas guiding current Vietnamese politics and foreign policy. He says that despite China's ambition to put the South China Sea under its exclusive control and the United States' support for Vietnam in the South China Sea dispute, China has shared grains of rice and clothes and guns with Vietnam to enable the latter to defeat the French and Americans, whereas the United States is trying to change the communist regime through peaceful evolution. The United States, Thanh emphasizes, has never been and will never be truly benevolent to Vietnam. To make the implication blunt: China is an enemy of the country but it is a friend of the regime; the United States is a friend of the country but it is an enemy of the regime; and the regime takes precedence over the country. Thanh informs his audience that there are three things Vietnam cannot afford to lose. The first is sovereignty and right of sovereignty, the second a peaceful environment, and the third the Sino-Vietnamese friendship. Acknowledging that the requirements for the first and the second contradict each other, he stresses that the highest priority is given to a peaceful environment.[51]

These objectives-cum-self-limitations reflect the dire predicaments Vietnam's communist regime is facing. To some extent, these predicaments are the result of the rise of a rent-seeking state that is built on an anti-Western national identity. The rent-seeking state has massively reduced economic productivity, political legitimacy, and international opportunity. The elite response to this crisis has been the clash between rent-seekers and an anti-corruption coalition. Unfortunately, this struggle is unable to resolve the crisis. As a result, the crisis will worsen until a different solution is found. In the meantime, Vietnam is heading towards more turbulent times in economics, politics, and foreign affairs.

Notes

The author wishes to thank Amratpreet Kaur Sidhu, Daljit Singh, and Don Keyser for their valuable comments. The views expressed here are the author's own.

1. Deepak Mishra and Viet Tuan Dinh, *Taking Stock: An Update on Vietnam's Recent Economic Development* (Washington, D.C.: The World Bank, 2012); General Statistics Office of Vietnam, "Tình hình kinh tế xã hội năm 2012" [Socio-economic Situation

in 2012], 24 December 2012; "Kiều hối sẽ đạt 10 tỉ USD" [Oversea Remittance Will Reach US$10 Billion], *Người Lao Động*, 16 November 2012.

2. Mishra and Dinh, *Taking Stock*; "Vì sao lạm phát không tăng mạnh" [Why Inflation Is Not Rising Rapidly], *Thời báo Kinh tế Sài Gòn*, 16 December 2012.
3. General Statistics Office, "Tình hình kinh tế xã hội năm 2012"; "Ba kịch bản tăng trưởng kinh tế Việt Nam năm 2012" [Three Scenarios of Economic Growth for 2012], *Tuổi Trẻ*, 10 January 2012.
4. "Doanh nghiệp chưa bao giờ chết nhiều như 2 năm qua" [Never Before Have So Many Enterprises Died as in the Last Two Years], *VnExpress*, 5 November 2012; "Bà Phạm Chi Lan: Niềm tin sụt giảm, doanh nghiệp không dám đầu tư, không dám vay tiền" [Madame Pham Chi Lan: With Trust Decreasing, Enterprises Do Not Dare to Invest and Borrow], *TTVN*, 30 November 2012; "Doanh nghiệp đang … chết" [Firms Are … Dying], *Người Lao Động*,11 December 2012.
5. Ibid.
6. Dao Tuan, "Mai Linh: Tự tử và bức tử" [Mai Linh: Suicide and Forced to Die], 28 December 2012 <http://daotuanddk.wordpress.com/2012/12/28/mai-linh-tu-tu-va-buc-tu/>.
7. "PetroVietnam Causes $874mln State Budget Loss", *TuoiTre*, 6 April 2012; "Wrongdoings at Song Da Corp Cost State $512mln", *TuoiTre*, 2 April 2012; "Inspectors Find Many Wrongdoings at Vinalines", *TuoiTre*, 5 May 2012; "Vinalines Is $2bln in Debt: Report", *TuoiTre*, 15 June 2012; "Vinalines Wastes Money on Ineffective Ports", *TuoiTre*, 21 May 2012.
8. "Central Bank Wants Unofficial Gold Bullion Trade Banned", *Thanh Nien*, 4 March 2011; "Vietnam to Reintroduce Gold Trading to Cool Spiralling Prices", *Bullion Street*, 7 October 2011; "Vietnam: Ban on Gold as Medium of Exchange", *Global Legal Monitor*, 18 April 2012; "Lãng phí do độc quyền vàng miếng" [Waste Because of Bullion Monopoly], *Thanh Niên*, 19 June 2012; "Đừng để dân đem vàng về cất" [Don't Cause the People to Store Their Gold at Home], *Thanh Niên*, 30 November 2012; "Hàng nghìn tiệm vàng sắp bị xóa sổ" [Thousands of Gold Stores Will Soon Be Eliminated], *VnExpress*, 29 December 2012.
9. "ACB, Eximbank, Sacombank sẽ là người một nhà?" [Will ACB, Eximbank, and Sacombank Be of the Same House?], *Sài Gòn Tiếp Thị*, 10 February 2012; "Sacombank's Operation Remains Normal: SBV", *Tuoi Tre*, 23 February 2012; "Vietnam's Stock Regulator Takes Flak for Oversight", *Thanh Nien News*, 2 July 2012; Manh Ha, "Ai đang nhảy vào Sacombank, Eximbank?" [Who Are Intruding on Sacombank and Eximbank?], *Vietnam Economic Forum*, 6 November 2012.
10. "Có đúng thủ tục tố tụng?" [Is It in Accordance with the Prosecution Procedures?], *Bảo vệ Pháp luật*, 19 November 2012 <http://baobaovephapluat.vn/don-ban-doc/201211/Co-dung-thu-tuc-to-tung-2205189/>.
11. Quan Làm Báo, "Nhóm lợi ích & mưu đồ thâu tóm tài chính tiền đến chính trị" [Interest Groups and the Plot to Take Control the Country's Finance and Then

Politics], 7 June 2012 <http://quanlambao.blogspot.com/2012/06/bai-4-nhom-loi-ich-muu-o-thau-tom-tai.html>; Quan Làm Báo, "Trò chơi của hai bố già Anh & Quang" [The Game of Two Godfathers Anh and Quang], 26 June 2012 <http://quanlambao.blogspot.com/2012/06/tro-choi-cua-bo-gia-anh-quang.html>.

12. This and other details in this section are based on author's conversations with well-informed Vietnamese, who wish to remain anonymous, during 2010–12.
13. I thank Amratpreet Kaur Sidhu for suggesting the term "party survivalists".
14. "Phát biểu của Tổng bí thư bế mạc Hội nghị Trung ương 4 khóa XI" [Closing Remarks by the General Secretary at the Fourth Plenum of the Eleventh Central Committee], *VOV online*, 31 December 2011 <http://vov.vn/Chinh-tri/Phat-bieu-cua-Tong-Bi-thu-be-mac-Hoi-nghi-Trung-uong-4-khoa-XI/195969.vov>.
15. Alexander L. Vuving, "Vietnam's Search for Stability", *Diplomat*, 26 October 2012 <http://thediplomat.com/asean-beat/2012/10/25/vietnams-paradoxical-search-for-stability/>.
16. Quan Làm Báo, "Ai tiết lộ thông tin để Dương Chí Dũng trốn thoát" [Who Leaked Information to Help Duong Chi Dung to Escape], 14 June 2012 <http://quanlambao.blogspot.com/2012/06/ai-tiet-lo-thong-tin-e-duong-chi-dung.html>; "Dương Chí Dũng đã bị bắt" [Duong Chi Dung Has Been Caught], *Tuổi Trẻ*, 5 September 2012; "Bắt phó phòng công an xã tiếp tay cho Dương Chí Dũng bỏ trốn" [Deputy Chief of Commune Police Who Helped Duong Chi Dung to Flee Is Arrested], *Dân Trí*, 26 December 2012.
17. Cầu Nhật Tân, "Kế hoạch bắt Nguyễn Đức Kiên được Bộ trưởng CA giữ tuyệt mật" [The Plan to Arrest Nguyen Duc Kien Was Kept Top Secret by the Minister of Public Security], 21 August 2012 <http://caunhattan.wordpress.com/2012/08/21/bat-nguyen-duc-kien-duoc-bo-truong-ca-giu-tuyet-mat/>.
18. "Thông báo Hội nghị lần thứ 5 BCH TW Đảng khóa XI" [Communique of the Fifth Plenum of the Eleventh Central Committee of the Party], Vietnam News Agency, 15 May 2012.
19. Cầu Nhật Tân, "Hội nghị TƯ6 đã khai mạc sáng nay trong đường đột và bất ngờ" [In a Surprise Move, the Sixth Central Committee Plenum Was Opened This Morning], 1 October 2012 <http://caunhattan.wordpress.com/2012/10/01/cuc-nong-hoi-nghi-tu6-da-bat-ngo-khai-mac-sang-nay/>.
20. "Thông báo Hội nghị lần thứ 6 Ban chấp hành Trung ương Đảng khóa XI" [Communique of the Sixth Plenum of the Eleventh Central Committee of the Party], Vietnam News Agency, 15 October 2012.
21. "Bỏ phiếu tín nhiệm Chủ tịch nước, Thủ tướng từ 2013" [Confidence Vote on State President and Prime Minister from 2013], Vietnam News Agency, 21 November 2012; "Nhiều điểm mới trong Luật Phòng chống tham nhũng sửa đổi" [Several New Points in the Revised Anti-Graft Law], *Tiền Phong*, 23 November 2012.
22. Ben Bland, "Vietnam: Danang's Masterly Mayor", *Financial Times*, Beyond BRICS blog, 8 February 2011.

23. Ba Sàm, "Tin thứ Bảy, 29-12-2012" [Saturday News, 29 December 2012], 29 December 2012 <http://anhbasam.wordpress.com/2012/12/29/tin-thu-bay-29-12-2012/>.
24. According to Bồ Câu Đen, five members who spoke out at the plenum to support a censure of Dũng were Phú Thọ province party boss Nguyễn Doãn Khánh, Vice-Chairman of the National Assembly Huỳnh Ngọc Sơn, General Secretary of the Fatherland Front Vũ Trọng Kim, Hanoi party boss Nghị, and An Giang province party boss Phan Văn Sáu. Those who came out in support of Dung included Deputy Head of the Central Organization Department Nguyễn Tuấn Khanh, Defence Minister Phùng Quang Thanh, Vice-Minister for Defence and Navy Commander Nguyễn Văn Hiến, and Vice-Minister for Public Security Tô Lâm. Bồ Câu Đen, "Quyết định bỏ phiếu ủng hộ Thủ tướng Nguyễn Tấn Dũng diễn ra như thế nào?" [How Was the Decision to Vote in Support of Prime Minister Nguyen Tan Dung Made?], 15 October 2012. Defence Minister Thanh had reportedly been a strong proponent of the proposal to discipline Dung at a Politburo meeting just two weeks earlier. Regardless of the validity of these reports, there must be a large number of the Central Committee members who were ambiguous about this divisive issue.
25. "Thực hiện NQ Trung ương 4: Còn nhiều việc phải làm" [Implementing the Fourth Plenum Resolution: Many Tasks Remain to Be Done], *Tuổi Trẻ*, 18 October 2012.
26. "Chống tham nhũng không được thì mất lòng tin của dân" [Failure to Fight Corruption Will Cause Loss of the People's Trust], *VietNamNet*, 29 June 2012.
27. "QH 'bắt mạch' căn bệnh trầm kha về đất đai" [National Assembly "Diagnoses" the Land Problems], *Pháp Luật Việt Nam*, 7 November 2012.
28. Truong Duy Nhat, "Nhân vật của năm 2012: dân oan giữ đất" [Person of the Year 2012: Land Defending Petitioners], 20 December 2012 <http://www.truongduynhat.vn/nhan-vat-cua-nam-2012-dan-oan-giu-dat/>.
29. "Giám đốc CA Hải Phòng: 'Bất ngờ với vụ nổ súng ở Tiên Lãng'" [Superintendent of the Haiphong Police: "Surprised by the Shooting in Tien Lang"], *VnMedia*, 8 January 2012; "Đất ông Vươn lấn biển bị coi là đất lấn chiếm?" [Land Reclaimed from the Sea by Mr Vuon Considered Encroachment], *Đất Việt*, 13 January 2012; "Đoàn Văn Vươn đã vi phạm pháp luật, nhưng…" [Doan Van Vuon Violated the Law, But…], *VietNamNet*, 13 January 2012; "Vietnam Farmer a Hero after Shootout with Police," Associated Press, 10 February 2012; "Thủ tướng kết luận cưỡng chế đất ở Tiên Lãng là trái luật" [Prime Minister Concluded That the Enforced Repossession of Land in Tien Lang Is Against the Law], *Tiền Phong*, 10 February 2012; "Chính quyền sai toàn diện trong vụ Tiên Lãng" [Authorities Totally Wrong in the Tien Lang Case], *VnExpress*, 10 February 2012; "Vụ cưỡng chế đất ở Tiên Lãng: sai luật – trái đạo lý" [The Enforced Repossession of Land in Tien Lang: Illegal and Immoral], *Tuổi Trẻ*, 11 February, 2012; "Xét xử vụ Đoàn Văn Vươn trước tháng 6" [The Doan Van Vuon Case to Be Tried Before June], *VnExpress*, 11 April 2012; "Vụ Tiên Lãng: Gia đình ông Vươn không trách ông Khanh" [The Tien Lang Case: Mr Vuon's Family Doesn't Blame Mr Khanh], *Người Lao Động*, 24 October 2012;

Minh Diện, "Lại là ông Khanh à?" [Still Mr Khanh?], Bùi Văn Bồng Blog, 24 October 2012; "Vụ hủy hoại tài sản tại đầm ông Đoàn Văn Vươn: Đề nghị truy tố 4 người" [The Case of Property Destruction at Mr Doan Van Vuon's Farm: Four Individuals to Be Prosecuted], *Người Lao Động*, 17 December 2012; "Đề nghị truy tố ông Vươn tội giết người" [Mr Vuon Charged with Murder], *Tuổi Trẻ*, 29 December 2012; "Đủ căn cứ để khởi tố chủ tịch huyện Tiên Lãng" [Enough Evidence to Prosecute the Chairman of Tien Lang District], *Tiền Phong*, 29 December 2012.

30. "Security Forces Seize Land from Vietnam Villagers", Reuters, 24 April 2012; "Twenty Held after Mass Protest", Radio Free Asia, 25 April 2012; Lê Trần, "'Nguyễn Tấn Dũng, Nguyễn Thanh Phượng va Ecopark' — một bài viết xuyên tạc" [Nguyen Tan Dung, Nguyen Thanh Phuong va Ecopark: A Distorting Article], nguyentandung.org, 26 April 2012.
31. "'Không sửa luật đất đai, sẽ còn nhiều vụ Tiên Lãng'" [There Will Be Many Tien Langs If the Land Law Is Not Revised], *VnExpress*, 16 February 2012; "Sửa Luật Đất đai: Cần đổi mới từ… ban soạn thảo?" [Revising the Land Law: Need for Reform from … within the Draft Committee], *VnEconomy*, 9 October 2012; "'Dự thảo Luật Đất đai chưa đi trúng yêu cầu thực tế'" [Draft Land Law Has Not Met the Demand from Reality], *VnExpress*, 10 October 2012; "Dự thảo Luật Đất Đai gây thất vọng lớn" [Draft Land Law Causes Large Disappointment], Radio Free Asia, 12 October 2012.
32. "Một số kết quả Hội nghị Trung ương 5, khoá XI" [Some Results of the Fifth Plenum of the Eleventh Central Committee], *Tạp chi Tuyên giáo*, 28 June 2012; "Phát biểu của Tổng Bí thư bế mạc Hội nghị TƯ 6" [Closing Remarks by the General Secretary at the Sixth Central Committee Plenum], *VietNamNet*, 15 October 2012.
33. "Chủ tịch nước muốn cử tri nói thẳng 'dù mất lòng'" [President Wants Voters to Speak out "Even If It Causes Resentment"], *VietNamNet*, 25 June 2012; "Chống tham nhũng không được thì mất lòng tin của dân" [Failure to Fight Corruption Will Cause Loss of the People's Trust], *VietNamNet*, 29 June 2012; "'TƯ 6 cơ bản đạt yêu cầu nhưng chưa phải là xong'" [Sixth Plenum Basically Met Expectation but Not Yet a Done Thing], *VietNamNet*, 16 October 2012; "Thực hiện Nghị quyết T.Ư 4 chưa đến bước cuối cùng" [Fourth Plenum Resolution Has Not Come to the Final Step], *Tiền Phong*, 17 October 2012; "Chủ tịch nước: Sợ trù úm thì đất nước ra sao?" [State President: How the Country Will Be If Its People Fear of Unfair Treatment], *VietNamNet*, 17 October 2012; "Không kỷ luật không có nghĩa là không có khuyết điểm" [No Censure Doesn't Mean No Errors], *Lao Động*, 18 October 2012; "'Bỏ phiếu vì cái ghế, chế độ sẽ suy vong'" ["Vote for the Seat, Regime Will Die"], *VietNamNet*, 26 November 2012; "Toàn dân đang bàn việc nước" [The Entire People Are Debating National Affairs], *Tuổi Trẻ*, 2 December 2012; "Tổng Bí thư: Cảnh tỉnh những người quên nguy cơ với nước, với Đảng" [General Secretary: A Warning to Those Who Forget the Threat to the Country and the Party], *Tiền Phong*, 2 December 2012; "Tổng bí thư: Bước đầu phải nhóm lò lên..." [General Secretary:

The First Step Is to Ignite the Light...], *VietNamNet*, 3 December 2012; "Thủ tướng: Dồn lực lượng giữ bằng được biển đảo" [Prime Minister: Accumulate Forces to Keep Sea and Islands], *VietNamNet*, 4 December 2012.

34. "Hoàng Khương bị tuyên y án sơ thẩm" [Hoang Khuong's Verdict Not Changed], *Tuổi Trẻ*, 28 December 2012.
35. A recent warning of a possible U.S. invasion of Vietnam can be found in a December 2012 article by Defence Minister Thanh. Phùng Quang Thanh, "Chiến thắng 'Hà Nội - Điện Biên Phủ trên không' và những bài học cần phát huy trong sự nghiệp bảo vệ Tổ quốc hiện nay" [The Victorious Battle of "Hanoi-Dien Bien Phu in the Air" and the Lessons to Be Brought into Full Play in the Current Cause of Defending the Fatherland], *Tạp chi Quốc phòng Toàn dân* (December 2012).
36. "Chủ quyền của Việt Nam là bất khả xâm phạm" [Vietnam's Sovereignty Is Inviolable], *Infonet*, 29 September 2012 <http://infonet.vn/Utilities/PrintView.aspx?ID=29350>.
37. "Tuyên bố chung về tăng cường quan hệ Việt-Nga" [Joint Statement on Strengthening Vietnam-Russia Relations], *Đất Việt*, 28 July 2012; "Việt-Nga tuyên bố về quan hệ đối tác chiến lược toàn diện" [Vietnam and Russia Declare Comprehensive Strategic Partnership], *Đất Việt*, 28 July 2012; "Thông điệp gần gũi, tin cậy và trách nhiệm từ Xô-tri" [A Message of Closeness, Trust, and Responsibility from Sochi], *Quân đội nhân dân*, 28 July 2012.
38. "Tuyên bố báo chí về chuyến thăm của Tổng Bí thư" [Press Statement on the General Secretary's Visit], Vietnam News Agency, 12 September 2012; "Tổng bí thư hội kiến chủ tịch đảng PAP của Singapore" [General Secretary Met Singapore's PAP Chairman], Vietnam News Agency, 13 September 2012.
39. "Việt Nam - Thái Lan hướng tới quan hệ đối tác chiến lược" [Vietnam and Thailand to Move toward a Strategic Partnership], *Thời báo Kinh tế Sài Gòn*, 27 October 2012.
40. Minister for Defence Stephen Smith, "Minister for Defence Completes Visit to Vietnam", 31 August 2012 <http://www.minister.defence.gov.au/2012/08/31/minister-for-defence-stephen-smith-minister-for-defence-completes-visit-to-vietnam/>; "Việt Nam — Ô-xtrây-li-a đẩy mạnh hợp tác quốc phòng" [Vietnam and Australia Step up Defense Cooperation], *Quân đội nhân dân*, 29 August 2012.
41. "Chống tham nhũng không được thì mất lòng tin của dân" [Failure to Fight Corruption Will Cause Loss of the People's Trust], *VietNamNet*, 29 June 2012.
42. An instance of China's telling Vietnam not to adopt the Maritime Law is captured in a Vietnamese military intelligence report leaked to the social media. "Tài liệu đặc biệt: Nội dung giao thiệp của Bộ ngoại giao Trung Quốc ngày 19.4.2012 với Đại sứ Việt Nam tại Bắc Kinh" [Special Document: Exchange between China's Ministry of Foreign Affairs and Vietnamese Ambassador in Beijing on 19 April 2012], *Dân Làm Báo*, 1 June 2012 <http://danlambaovn.blogspot.com/2012/05/noi-dung-giao-thiep-cua-bo-ngoai-giao.html>.

43. "Không đóng dấu vào hộ chiếu có 'đường lưỡi bò'" [No Stamps on Passports Featuring the "Cow's Tongue"], *Thanh Niên*, 25 November 2012.
44. "Việt Nam phản đối Trung Quốc làm đứt cáp tàu Bình Minh 02" [Vietnam Protests China for Causing the Binh Minh 02's Cable Cut], *VnExpress*, 4 December 2012; "Tổng Bí thư tiếp Đoàn đại biểu Đảng CS Trung Quốc" [General Secretary Hosts Chinese Communist Party Delegation], Vienam News Agency, 2 December 2012.
45. Ba Sàm, "Giao ban Báo chí, thứ Ba 11-12-2012" [Press Review and Instruction, Tuesday, 11 December 2012], 16 December 2012 <http://anhbasam.wordpress.com/2012/12/16/1476-giao-ban-bao-chi-thu-ba-11-12-2012/>.
46. "VN muốn Campuchia vào Hội đồng Bảo an" [Vietnam Wants Cambodia in the Security Council], BBC Vietnamese, 26 July 2012; "Bộ trưởng Bộ Công an Trần Đại Quang thăm và làm việc tại Campuchia" [Minister of Public Security Tran Dai Quang Visits and Works in Cambodia], *Công An Nhân Dân*, 15 August 2012.
47. Hillary Rodham Clinton, "Remarks with Foreign Minister Pham Binh Minh after Their Meeting," Hanoi, 10 July 2012 <http://www.state.gov/secretary/rm/2012/07/194766.htm>.
48. "Panetta Wants More Access to Vietnam Harbor", Associated Press, 3 June 2012.
49. "Japan Supports Vietnam Coastal Defense", Kyodo, 14 July 2012.
50. "Indian Navy Ready to Deploy to South China Sea as Tensions Climb", Reuters, 3 December 2012; "We'll Send Force to Protect Our Interests in South China Sea, Says Navy Chief", *The Hindu*, 3 December 2012.
51. Ba Sàm, "Đại tá Trần Đăng Thanh giảng về Biển Đông cho lãnh đạo các trường Đại học" [Senior Colonel Tran Dang Thanh Lectures on the East Sea to Leaders of Universities], 19 December 2012 <http://anhbasam.wordpress.com/2012/12/19/1481-dai-ta-tran-dang-thanh-giang-ve-bien-dong-cho-lanh-dao-cac-truong-dai-hoc/>.

NAVIGATING THE CRISIS
The VCP's Efforts to Restructure the Economy and Fight Corruption

Le Hong Hiep

Introduction

This chapter focuses on the Vietnam Communist Party's (VCP) efforts, especially in 2012, to promote its political legitimacy. In particular, the chapter will analyse Vietnam's recent endeavours in restructuring the economy and intensifying its fight against corruption. These two measures have been adopted by the VCP as a major part of its wider response to the perceived decline in its performance-based legitimacy due to the country's enduring socio-economic difficulties over the past few years. The chapter will argue that although both the economic restructuring and the fight against corruption have achieved certain progress, the actual results still leave much to be desired mainly because of the VCP's unwillingness to embrace radical measures to reform the economy and to make its fight against corruption truly effective. As a result, although the two measures tend to help the VCP gain more popular support in the short term, whether or not they are sufficient to significantly improve the VCP's political legitimacy in the long run is still unclear.

The chapter is divided into four sections. The first section analyses the rationale behind the VCP's twin efforts by providing a background of Vietnam's socio-economic and political conditions in recent years. The second

---

LE HONG HIEP is a Lecturer at the Faculty of International Relations, College of Social Sciences and Humanities, Vietnam National University, Ho Chi Minh City, and is currently a PhD candidate at the University of New South Wales, Australian Defence Force Academy, Canberra.

and third sections will discuss recent developments around Vietnam's economic restructuring and its intensified fight against corruption, respectively. Finally, the chapter will offer some analysis of the implications of the VCP's above mentioned efforts for the country's future economic and political outlook.

A Crisis within a Crisis

After the 1997–98 Asian financial crisis, Vietnam's economy entered a second wave of growth before the country was hit by the 2008 financial crisis and the subsequent global economic recession. While the average annual growth rate for the period of 2000–07 reached 7.6 per cent, that for the 2008–11 period stood modestly at only 6 per cent.[1] Vietnam's economic slowdown has been accompanied by high inflation with the average Consumer Price Index (CPI) increasing by 14.3 per cent annually from 2008 to 2011. High inflation has offset the positive effects of the already modest economic growth and lowered living standards of almost the entire population, especially wage earners and the poor. It has also led the government to tighten its monetary policy, causing the benchmark interest rate of the country to reach as high as 14 per cent in 2008.

Increased borrowing costs, coupled with shrinking demand from both domestic and foreign markets, caused production to shrink and forced thousands of businesses into bankruptcy.[2] For example, according to a report in the *Saigon Times*, 48,700 out of more than 400,000 businesses in Vietnam went bankrupt or ceased operations in the first nine months of 2011.[3] The harsh economic conditions, together with poor management, have also brought some large state-owned economic groups and general corporations (GCs)[4] such as Vinashin to the verge of bankruptcy. At the same time, sluggish economic conditions and widespread bankruptcy among businesses have led to mounting bad debts throughout the banking system. In June 2012, the governor of State Bank of Vietnam (SBV) Nguyen Van Binh admitted before the National Assembly (NA) that bad debts might have reached 10 per cent of the whole banking system's total gross loans,[5] triggering speculation that Vietnam may have to seek an IMF bailout.[6]

Despite certain improvements in the macroeconomic conditions in 2012, experts believe that Vietnam's economic prospects will remain cloudy at least until the end of 2013.[7] The country's sluggish economic performance has added to the growing tension within Vietnam's political system as the government of Prime Minister Nguyen Tan Dung has come under heavy criticism for flawed economic policy and poor management, especially regarding state-owned enterprises (SOEs). PM Dung was elected by the NA for a second tenure in August 2011 when the economy was still in a bad shape. In the first tenure, his ambition to accelerate Vietnam's economic growth following the country's accession to the World Trade Organization (WTO) in 2007 was soon dampened by the outbreak of the global financial crisis and the economic recession in 2008. However, adverse global economic conditions have not been the only factors accounting for the country's poor economic performance. In particular, inefficient state-owned economic groups and GCs which experienced unprecedented yet unsustainable expansion, thanks to the government's intention to rely on them to drive growth, also played an important part.[8] The de facto bankruptcy of Vinashin as well as the poor performance of large SOEs such as Vinalines was timely evidence for critics of Mr Dung to call into question the credibility and efficacy of his cabinet's economic management policies, especially regarding SOEs.

Meanwhile, widespread and enduring corruption is yet another factor that undermines not only the credibility of Mr Dung's administration but also the legitimacy of the whole VCP regime. While corruption is rampant, the number of cases exposed and prosecuted is still limited. For example, according to a report by Government Inspector-General Huynh Phong Tranh before the NA Standing Committee, only 106 cases involving 409 defendants were tried in courts of different levels from 1 October 2010 to 30 July 2011. The report also estimated that from August 2010 to July 2011 corrupt officials caused losses of 11.4 trillion dong (US$550 million) to the state budget, of which only 300 billion dong had been recovered.[9] The number of cases uncovered as well as losses is, however, just a tip of the iceberg. A report in 2010 by Towards Transparency, a local anti-corruption NGO, shows that 62 per cent of Vietnamese ordinary urban citizens surveyed perceived corruption in the country to be getting worse, and 18 per cent said it stayed the same.[10] Further, in 2011, Vietnam was ranked 112 out of 182 countries surveyed in the expert-polled Corruption Perception Index of Transparency International.[11] Widespread corruption has also impeded the government's efforts to implement reforms and improve the country's economic performance. Corruption, for example, contributes to the decline in ranking for Vietnam on the World Economic Forum's Global Competitiveness Report for two consecutive years. In 2012, Vietnam was ranked 75 out of 144 countries surveyed, down 16 spots from its standing in 2010. Out of eight Southeast Asian nations presented in the report, Vietnam now only ranks ahead of Cambodia in terms of competitiveness.[12]

Although persistent corruption is not new to Vietnam, it has presented itself as a more serious problem to the VCP regime in recent times when anaemic economic growth tends to put the VCP's performance-based legitimacy under mounting pressure. Since *doi moi* was adopted in 1986, socio-economic performance has become the single most important source of legitimacy for the VCP rule.[13] As long as the country's economic growth remains robust and the people's living standards keep rising, other problems, including corruption, are likely to stay outside the public spotlight and remain less significant as a political challenge to the Party's rule. However, as the economy experiences prolonged slumps and the people's living standards start to deteriorate, wide-spread corruption tends to add to the people's growing frustration towards the regime and threatens to plunge the Party into a legitimacy crisis. Therefore, facing economic difficulties since 2009, the VCP would not only have to make every effort to improve the country's economic performance, but also to pay more attention to fighting corruption.

It is against this background that economic restructuring and stepping up the fight against corruption have emerged as two major items on the VCP's agenda. After more than two decades of easy growth from a low base, Vietnam's economy has exposed certain weaknesses that can prevent the country from maintaining strong and sustainable development. Restructuring the economy therefore becomes an urgent task before its weaknesses puts a further drag on the country's economic growth. At the same time, intensifying the fight against corruption not only reinforces the VCP's efforts to restructure the economy as corrupt officials may obstruct the restructuring process if it hurts their interests, but also serves as a temporary recourse for buttressing the legitimacy of VCP rule in case the economic structuring fails to achieve expected outcomes.

Restructuring the Economy

In the wake of the 2008 global financial crisis and economic recession, the need to restructure the economy towards greater efficiency and sustainability was raised first by the Ministry of Planning and Investment (MPI) in early 2009. In November 2009, the Central Institute for Economic Management (CIEM), a think-tank under the MPI, released a report on economic restructuring that proposed seven key measures to enhance the efficiency of the economy.[14]

However, it was not until almost two years later that the VCP Central Committee (VCPCC) adopted a resolution on the issue at its third plenum in October 2011. The resolution decided that restructuring the economy as well as moving towards a more efficient growth model was an urgent task for Vietnam in the next five years. It also identified three key areas that the restructuring efforts needed to focus on: public (i.e. state-funded) investment, SOEs, and the financial market.[15] While reflecting the VCP's continuous efforts to promote the country's economic performance as a foundation of its legitimacy, the resolution also showed that the Party perceived the economic difficulties to be acute and that serious reforms needed to be made.

As a political document of the Party, however, the resolution needed to be translated into specific policies for the government to implement. Accordingly, the MPI finally submitted a draft blueprint for economic structuring to the NA Standing Committee in April 2012 for its initial review. One month later, a refined version was officially presented to the NA at its third session. The economic restructuring's overall objective as identified by the thirty-nine-page document is to improve the economy's efficiency, productivity and competitiveness, thereby moving the country's economic growth model from that based on investment, resource- and labour-intensive industries to a more sustainable one driven by technological innovation and high productivity. To implement this overall objective in the long run, the blueprint outlined twelve groups of measures. These can be summarized as follows:

1. Improving the quality of development planning;
2. Restructuring the financial market and stabilizing macroeconomic conditions;
3. Restructuring and enhancing the efficiency of public investment;
4. Restructuring SOEs and improving the quality of private and foreign-invested enterprises;
5. Improving market institutions and the business environment to encourage and improve the efficiency of investments;
6. Reforming incentive schemes to attract and direct private and foreign investments towards industries and products of high priority;[16]
7. Implementing programmes for synchronously developing industries and products of high priority with a view to increasing their technological and domestic inputs, thereby enhancing their competitiveness;
8. Restructuring regional economies to best exploit each region's advantages;
9. Modernizing and enhancing the efficiency and productivity of agricultural production;

10. Improving the quality of the workforce;
11. Developing science and technology; and
12. Effectively solving social and environmental problems.

The document was criticized on a number of counts when it was submitted to the NA. For a start, the measures proposed by the blueprint were viewed as not specific enough. In response, the MPI stated that the blueprint only provided general directions, and ministries would have to follow up by working out specific measures to implement the blueprint regarding fields under their portfolio. More importantly, the blueprint was criticized for failing to estimate the costs associated with the implementation of proposed measures. While acknowledging the issue, the MPI, however, cited the lack of time in preparing the blueprint to justify its failure to detail the costs. In the end, after much discussion, on 8 June, the NA decided neither to ratify nor to adopt a resolution on the blueprint. Instead, it just provided the comments and left the government to modify and approve the blueprint accordingly.

Long before the blueprint was submitted to the NA for comments, the Vietnamese government, however, had identified public investment, SOEs, and the banking system as three key areas that the restructuring needed to focus on. These areas, therefore, have been the focus of Vietnam's economic restructuring in 2012.

In the area of public investment, restructuring efforts have been aimed at gradually reducing public investment by encouraging more investment from the non-state and foreign-invested sectors, and improving the efficiency of public investment projects, especially infrastructure building ones. In this connection, recent efforts to restructure public investment have shown mixed results. For example, although public investment's proportion of the economy's total investment decreased from 38.9 per cent in 2011 to 37.2 per cent by September 2012, it increased by 10.4 per cent in absolute terms.[17] This reflects the fact that even though public investment has long been playing an important role in promoting Vietnam's state-led economic development, it is not easy for the government to cut it down overnight without hurting GDP growth. Therefore, enhancing the efficiency of public investment projects, especially through improved legal framework governing public investment, is more essential. However, Vietnam made little progress in this regard in 2012. For example, the draft Law on Public Investment, which was scheduled to be submitted for deliberation at the NA in October 2012 and passed in May 2013, has failed to meet its deadlines. Consequently, the long-expected law will not be passed before the end of 2013 at the earliest. As the law contains important provisions to enhance the efficiency of public investment, such as ensuring officials' accountability and improving coordination between different levels of authorities regarding public investment projects, its delayed enactment will undoubtedly impede Vietnam's economic restructuring process.

Similarly, progress in the restructuring of SOEs has largely been slower than expected. In July 2012, PM Dung approved the blueprint for restructuring SOEs for the period of 2011–15.[18] Before that, all state-owned economic groups and GCs were required to submit their restructuring plan to the government for approval by the end of March 2012. However, by August, only fifty-three out of more than a hundred economic groups and GCs had submitted their plans, of which only nine had been approved by the relevant authorities.[19] In addition, following the near bankruptcy of Vinashin, which was partly caused by Vinashin's reckless investments into non-core businesses, one of the government's key requirements for the restructuring of SOEs has been their divestment of non-core businesses. However, the divestment process has been slow mainly due to concerns about capital loss, given the recent unfavourable market conditions.

Meanwhile, in a response to criticisms about the hasty and ill-conceived establishment of state-owned economic groups, PM Nguyen Tan Dung decided in early October 2012 to dissolve the Vietnam Industry Construction Group (VNIC) and the Housing and Urban Development Group (HUD), bringing the number of state-owned groups down from thirteen to eleven.[20] Chair of the Government Office Vu Duc Dam also confirmed the government's objective was to maintain only five to seven state-owned groups in essential sectors, with remaining groups in non-essential sectors being equitized in the coming years.[21] Meanwhile, in an attempt to better supervise the government's economic policies, including those regarding SOEs, the VCPCC decided at its sixth plenum in October to re-establish the Party's Central Department of Economic Affairs, which was abolished in 2007.[22]

Vietnam's restructuring of SOEs has been undertaken in close connection with its restructuring of the banking system. By the end of 2011, the total debt of Vietnam's state-owned economic groups and corporations reached 1,292 trillion dong (US$62.2 billion),[23] of which 200 trillion dong (US$9.5 billion) was bad debt, accounting for about 70 per cent of the bad debt of the whole banking system.[24] Apparently, improving the performance of SOEs may help reduce the banking system's bad debts, but only in the long run. In order to improve the country's economic performance in the immediate future, Vietnam needs more radical measures to remove as quickly as possible the banking system's accumulating bad debts that have been blocking the flow of credit within the economy.

However, little of significance has been achieved so far. In June 2012, when SBV Governor Nguyen Van Binh admitted that bad debts might have reached 10 per cent of the whole banking system's total gross loans, he also revealed the SBV's plan to establish a company to buy bad debts from commercial banks. The SBV, however, did not specify how the company would operate or from where it would acquire the charter capital of 100 trillion dong (US$4.8 billion), especially when the idea of using state budget to finance the company had been rejected.[25] In late October, the SBV stated that it would formally submit its blueprint for setting up the company to the government on 15 November for its initial review. As the blueprint will be further scrutinized before going to the Politburo for final approval, it is unlikely that such a company will be established in the near future. Against this backdrop, there was a speculation in September that Vietnam might need to seek an IMF bailout to solve its bad debt problem. However, citing Vietnam's improving macroeconomic conditions, the SBV later dismissed this possibility.

Although removing the bad debt burden is an urgent task for the SBV in the short run, making the banking system stronger and healthier has been its more important objective in the long run. Towards this end, the SBV's blueprint for restructuring credit institutions was approved by the Prime Minister in March 2012. One of the key measures proposed by the blueprint was to merge weak banks or let them be acquired by stronger ones. Accordingly, a merger was carried out in August 2012 between HabuBank and Saigon-Hanoi Bank (SHB), the second in two years.[26] In a press conference in late October, the SBV confirmed that four more weak banks, namely GP Bank, TrustBank, Western Bank and NaviBank, would have to be restructured.[27] Therefore, more mergers and acquisitions are likely to occur in Vietnam's banking sector in the coming months.

In addition, measures to better enforce rules and regulations in the banking sector were also adopted. In August 2012, Nguyen Duc Kien, one of the founders of Asia Commercial Bank (ACB), was arrested and prosecuted for conducting illegal businesses, fraud, and deliberate wrong-doing against state regulations. The arrest of Kien was followed by the resignation and prosecution of five other executives of the ACB, including its chairman and former Minister for Planning and Investment Tran Xuan Gia. In addition, the SBV also sent strong message against "interest groups" who wish to manipulate the banking system to their advantage. On 7 October 2012, SBV governor Nguyen Van Binh revealed in a television interview that there are banks which are illegally controlled by a small number of shareholders/groups of shareholders. These shareholders, through their illegal manipulation, manage to acquire up to 70 to 90 per cent of the banks' total loans, threatening to destabilize the whole banking system when such loans turn into bad debts. Identifying these groups as the most significant force resisting the restructuring of the banking system, he confirmed the government's determination in fighting these groups to make the banking system stronger and healthier.[28]

In sum, although Vietnam's recent efforts to restructure the economy have achieved certain positive results, the overall progress is not as fast as many people expected. The main reason is that the restructuring is still in its very initial phase and it takes time for major changes to come. In addition, most of the measures proposed for the restructuring are not radical enough to bring about breakthroughs in the country's economic conditions in the short term. Therefore, whether Vietnam's economic structuring is successful or not still remains to be seen, at least in the coming two to three years. In the meantime, the VCP's performance-based legitimacy continues to come under mounting pressure. It is against this background that the Party decided to step up its fight against corruption as an additional measure to boost popular support for the Party.

Fighting Corruption

Vietnam's recent efforts to step up its fight against corruption started with the fourth plenum of the VCPCC (eleventh tenure) in late December 2011. The plenum adopted Resolution No. 12 on party building which aimed to make the Party cleaner and stronger, and to strengthen the people's confidence in the Party.[29] The Resolution identified the moral decay, loss of ideological faith and corruption among a large segment of party members, including high-ranking officials, as the main problems which led to the people's declining confidence in the Party and threatened the regime's survival. The Resolution accordingly launched a campaign of criticism and self-criticism throughout the whole Party as an essential step to warn Party members against committing corrupt practices. The campaign started from the highest echelons, with Politburo members spending twelve days in August conducting their criticism and self-criticism, followed by party members of lower levels.[30] General Secretary Nguyen Phu

Trong, who devised and led the campaign, declared that his goal was to turn criticism and self-criticism into frequent activities among party members.

The most significant evidence of the VCP's determination to step up its fight against corruption, however, was the fifth plenum of the VCPCC which took place in May 2012. One of the key items on the plenum's agenda was to discuss how to "strengthen the Party's leadership in fighting corruption and wastefulness".[31] The plenum, while acknowledging that some progress had been made since the VCPCC's Resolution No. 4 in 2006,[32] also stressed that the fight against corruption had largely fallen short of the Party's expectations. The plenum therefore adopted a series of measures to make the anti-corruption efforts more effective.

Although most of the measures have been more or less similar to those embraced by Resolution No. 4, the plenum did take a number of new initiatives.[33] For example, it decided to remove the Central Steering Committee on Anti-Corruption (CSCAC) from the government's portfolio and put it under the direction of the Politburo, which tends to make CSCAC more powerful and independent of the executive branch. Accordingly, the former national office of CSCAC headed by PM Nguyen Tan Dung will be abolished and replaced by the VCP's Central Department of Internal Affairs, which is going to be re-established. The move could be seen as the VCP's attempt to both make its fight against corruption more effective and to reduce the scope of power of PM Dung, who has been said to wield too much power and to be responsible for the country's sluggish economy and widespread corruption in SOEs.

The plenum also called for the improvement of the legal and institutional framework to deal with corruption, especially in highly corruption-prone areas. Accordingly, the revised Law on Anti-Corruption was passed at the fourth session of the NA in November 2012. The revised law not only reflects changes in CSCAC's modus operandi, but also embraces stronger and more feasible provisions regarding, for example, government officials' accountability, responsibility to publicly disclose personal assets, the people's and the media's right to access information, and mechanisms to protect whistleblowers. A number of laws related to corruption fighting, such as the revised Law on Thrift Practices and Anti-Wastefulness, Law on Public Investment, Law on Public Procurement, and Revised Land Law, have also been put on the agenda of the NA and are likely to be passed in its forthcoming sessions. In another attempt to hold high-ranking officials accountable for, among other things, corruption within agencies under their portfolios, the NA also passed at its fourth session a resolution that establishes policies and procedures for casting votes of confidence on key post holders elected or approved by the NA and People's Councils.

The VCP's efforts to step up its fight against corruption in 2012, however, have not brought about the desired effects. In its annual report on anti-corruption submitted to the NA, the Government Inspectorate, the main anti-corruption agency in Vietnam, admitted that corruption is still rampant, with a low number of corruption cases uncovered and prosecuted. In reviewing the report, the NA Judicial Committee pointed out that while the investigation and prosecution of many major corruption cases are prolonged, in certain cases the corruption charges against defendants are dropped and replaced by less serious charges, such as "deliberate wrong-doing against state regulations". It is noteworthy that in the two scandals related to Vinashin and Vinalines, dozens of the two corporations' executives have been prosecuted, but not for corruption.[34]

In sum, there is evidence that the VCP has recently stepped up its fight against corruption, which is best illustrated by the VCPCC's fifth plenum in May 2012. The Party's strengthened political will to fight corruption has also been translated into specific actions to improve the legal and institutional framework to fight corruption, as showcased by the transfer of the CSCAC into the Politburo's portfolio and the revision of the Law on Anti-Corruption. However, whether these measures will be more effective or not has been unclear so far.

Implications for Vietnam's Economic and Political Outlook

Both the economic restructuring and the intensified fight against corruption that Vietnam has been pursuing so far will undoubtedly have significant implications for the country's future economic and political outlook.

The outcomes of the economic restructuring will obviously impact Vietnam's economic performance in the coming years, and thus the VCP's performance-based legitimacy. The most critical question is whether the restructuring will be successful in fixing the country's economic problems. In explaining Vietnam's economic turmoil over the past few years, the authorities have repeatedly referred to the global economic recession as a major cause. However, even when the recession is over, there's little ground to believe that Vietnam's economy will recover robustly. Overdependence on public investment as a source of growth; a weak and opaque banking system; favouring inefficient SOEs at the expense of non-state sectors; or tolerating corruption or dealing with it only half-heartedly — all these will continue to make Vietnam's economic performance vulnerable and unsustainable in the long run. Among these problems, the VCP's reliance on SOEs as the most important driving force in its envisioned socialist-oriented market economy seems to be the most challenging one to fix.

In fact, inefficient SOEs, especially large economic groups and GCs, have been lying at the heart of Vietnam's economic problems. These SOEs undertake most of the government's inefficient public investments, account for a large part of the banking system's bad debts, and are the place where corruption and wastefulness are raging. Nevertheless, the VCP is unwilling to stop favouring them. There are a number of reasons for this. First, while the Party believes SOEs are the key foundation for the country's transition to a socialist economy, the government considers them an essential tool to regulate macroeconomic conditions. Second, and more importantly, the SOEs have formed an integral part of the VCP's power structure. SOEs provide a place for the Party's unofficial patronage network to exist and thrive. In such a network, Party's high-ranking officials can command a certain level of influence on their subordinates by appointing them into leading positions in SOEs, while these subordinates may have to return such favours by offering political loyalty or even financial benefits to their patrons. In addition, if the army and the internal security forces are the Party's right hand, it is the SOEs which form its left hand. Without an adequate control of the economy through these SOEs, the Party will find itself in an uncomfortable position to maintain its rule and exercise its power effectively. Ironically, the VCP's policy regarding SOEs may backfire. If these SOEs do not manage to become more transparent and competitive, they may eventually curtail the success of Vietnam's economic restructuring and impair the Party's performance-based legitimacy in the future.

Similarly, the VCP has shown a political will to fight corruption, but political will is not everything that counts. In addition to the VCP's determination, whether or not Vietnam will be successful in suppressing corruption still largely depends on the effectiveness of the law enforcement system, especially the corruption fighting agencies. The efficacy of the law enforcement system, however, is closely related to the nature of Vietnam's political system. In a single-party system, the independence of the judiciary and of law enforcement agencies, key requirements for effectively fighting corruption, is hard to guarantee. In addition, the media and the civil society, which can contribute to the exposure of corruption, cannot work effectively due to their lack of independence and restrained scope of operation. Against this background, the VCP will have few options to make its fight against corruption truly effective. For example, the VCP's decision to put the CSCAC under the Politburo, though testifying to the Party's determination to step up its fight against corruption, may turn out to be merely a symbolical move. After all, it is difficult for the Party to eliminate and punish its own corrupt members, especially when they form the upper hierarchy of the Party. Furthermore, the move also makes Vietnam's political system less transparent and less efficient because it strengthens the Party's administrative and law enforcement powers at the expense of the government's law enforcing agencies.

If the Party wants to make its fight against corruption more effective, it may have to consider more radical measures in the future. The question is how radical the Party can afford to be? As maintaining its unchallenged rule remains the Party's top priority, it is almost impossible for it to adopt radical measures like making the judicial system independent, liberalizing the media, or allowing the establishment of opposition parties. Consequently, the Party is facing a paradox in that weak efforts to fight corruption will be detrimental to the Party's rule, but radical measures that are truly effective may also backfire by undermining the Party's monopoly of power. Therefore, as long as the current political situation in Vietnam holds, one may be excused for expecting that corruption will likely remain enduring and pervasive despite the VCP's efforts to prevent it from undermining the Party's legitimacy to rule.

Conclusion

Vietnam has recently sought to restructure the economy and step up the fight against corruption against the background of the declining legitimacy of VCP rule due to widespread corruption and serious economic difficulties over the past few years. The economic restructuring has focused primarily on improving the efficiency of public investment, enhancing the performance of SOEs, and strengthening the banking system. Meanwhile, efforts to step up the fight against corruption have resulted in some positive moves to upgrade the country's legal and institutional anti-corruption framework.

Although the economic restructuring has witnessed some progress, the results still leave much to be desired. The restructuring is still in its very initial stage and it may take time for significant results to materialize. However, the fact that the VCP continues to attach importance to SOEs as the core driving force of the economy shows that the restructuring will probably remain incomplete and that the Party will be unwilling to embrace radical economic reforms that may threaten the Party's rule in the long run. Similarly, although the Party recognizes the need to step up its fight against corruption to gain the people's confidence, it has limited options to make the fight effective. The nature of Vietnam's one-party system has in one way or another made the endurance and pervasiveness of corruption hard to tackle without radical political reforms, from which the VCP has always shied away. Therefore, although the VCP's economic restructuring and intensified fight against corruption tend to help it gain more popular support in the short run, whether or not the two measures are sufficient to help maintain and strengthen the VCP's rule over the longer term without more political reforms remains to be seen.

Notes

The author would like to thank Professor Carlyle A. Thayer for his helpful comments on an earlier draft of the chapter.

1. World Bank, "Vietnam Country Metadata (in Excel)", retrieved 20 November 2012 from <http://api.worldbank.org/datafiles/VNM_Country_MetaData_en_EXCEL.xls>.
2. In May 2011, loan interest remained as high as 25 per cent per annum.
3. *Saigon Times*, "Ước tính 40% số doanh nghiệp vừa và nhỏ đã phá sản" [An Estimated 40 percent of Small and Medium-Sized Enterprises Have Gone Bankrupt], 9 November 2011 <http://www.thesaigontimes.vn/Home/doanhnghiep/quantri/65348/>.
4. State-owned economic groups (*Tập đoàn kinh tế*) and general corporations (GCs, or *Tổng Công ty*) form the most important and largest force of Vietnam's SOEs. In 1994, the prime minister's Decisions No. 90 and No. 91 form two types of GCs, known as GC 90 and GC 91, by grouping together a number of SOEs of similar or related businesses. According to the decisions, each GC 90 must have at least five voluntary members and a minimum legal capital of 100 billion dong, while GC 91 must have at least seven members and a minimum capital of 1,000 billion dong. Since 2005, Vietnam has also been experimenting with upgrading a number of large GCs 90 and 91 to the status of economic groups. The major difference between GCs and groups rests with their model of operation. As GCs were formed simply by grouping SOEs together, they are loosely organized and in most of the cases, member companies still maintain their relative independence of the GCs. Meanwhile groups are formed by GCs, which now become the parent companies, plus subsidiaries or associate companies in which they invest. The parent companies' investments enable them to exert a certain level of control over subsidiaries and associate companies, thereby facilitating corporate management within the groups. By early 2012, Vietnam had thirteen state-owned groups and nearly a hundred GCs.

5. VnExpress, "Thống đốc Ngân hàng sẽ giải trình về nợ xấu" [State Bank Governor Will Account for Non-Performing Loans], 16 July 2012 <http://vnexpress.net/gl/kinh-doanh/2012/07/thong-doc-ngan-hang-se-giai-trinh-ve-no-xau/>. In the fourth session of the NA in November, however, Binh updated that bad debts amounted to 8.82 per cent of the banking system's total gross loans.
6. Bloomberg, "Vietnam Risks Biggest East Asia IMF Rescue Since 1990s: Economy", 6 September 2012 <http://www.bloomberg.com/news/2012-09-06/vietnam-risks-biggest-east-asia-imf-rescue-since-1990s>.
7. VnExpress, "Kinh tế Việt Nam còn xấu đến hết năm 2013" ['Vietnam's economy remains pessimistic until end of 2013], 22 September 2012 <http://vnexpress.net/gl/kinh-doanh/2012/09/kinh-te-viet-nam-con-xau-den-het-nam-2013/>.
8. State-owned enterprises have been identified by the VCP as the country's "leading" economic actors, meanwhile under PM Dung's administration, state-owned groups have been expected to become the "iron fists" (*quả đấm thép*) and "red big-brothers" (*anh cả đỏ*) of the economy.
9. Dan Viet, "Tham nhũng gây thiệt hại 11.400 tỷ đồng" [Corruption causes losses of VND 11.4 trillion], 16 October 2011 <http://danviet.vn/61790p1c24/tham-nhung-gay-thiet-hai-11400-ty-dong.htm>.
10. Mireille Razafindrakoto, François Roubaud, and Matthieu Salomon, "Global Corruption Barometer 2010: Vietnam Country Analysis of the Views and Experiences of Urban Citizens" <http://archive.transparency.org/content/download/66652/1068775>, September 2011.
11. Transparency International, "Corruption Perceptions Index 2011" <http://cpi.transparency.org/cpi2011/results/>.
12. Klaus Schwab, ed., *The Global Competitiveness Report 2012–2013* (Geneva: World Economic Forum, 2012).
13. See, for example, Le Hong Hiep, "Performance-based Legitimacy: The Case of the Communist Party of Vietnam and Doi Moi", *Contemporary Southeast Asia* 34, no. 2 (2012): 145–72.
14. These seven proposals include: (1) Stabilizing macroeconomic condition; (2) Improving the quality of policy-making and implementation; (3) Enhancing the efficiency of government investment; (4) Reforming SOEs; (5) Encouraging private investment, balancing between investment in exports and domestic consumption; and redirecting FDI towards more value-added projects; (6) Modernizing agricultural production; and (7) Supporting the development of small and medium-sized enterprises. See VnExpress, "7 đề xuất tái cơ cấu kinh tế Việt Nam" [Seven proposals for restructuring Vietnam's economy], 23 November 2009 <http://vnexpress.net/gl/kinh-doanh/2009/11/3ba15f1e/>.
15. VnEconomy, "Trung ương Đảng quyết định tái cơ cấu nền kinh tế" [The Party Central Committee decides to restructure the economy], 10 October 2011 <http://

vneconomy.vn/20111010090152106P0C9920/trung-uong-dang-quyet-dinh-tai-co-cau-nen-kinh-te.htm>.

16. The blueprint proposes seven industries of high priority, namely metallurgy, petrochemistry, shipbuilding and manufacturing of transport vehicles, electronics, renewable energy and green industries, logistics, and tourism.
17. General Statistics Office, "Tình hình kinh tế-xã hội 9 tháng năm 2012" [Socio-economic situation in the first nine months of 2012], 27 September 2012 <http://www.gso.gov.vn/default.aspx?tabid=403&idmid=2&ItemID=13263>
18. For a summary of the blueprint (in Vietnamese), see VnEconomy, "Thủ tướng phê duyệt đề án tái cơ cấu doanh nghiệp nhà nước" [PM approves blueprint for restructuring SOEs], 20 July 2012 <http://vneconomy.vn/20120720092549746P0C9920/thu-tuong-phe-duyet-de-an-tai-co-cau-doanh-nghiep-nha-nuoc.htm>.
19. Government Web Portal, "53 tập đoàn, tổng công ty đã xây dựng đề án tái cơ cấu" [53 groups, GCs have finished restructuring plans], 5 October 2012 <http://baodientu.chinhphu.vn/Home/53-tap-doan-tong-cong-ty-da-xay-dung-de-an-tai-co-cau/201210/150754.vgp>.
20. These eleven groups include: PetroVietnam, Petrolimex, Electricity of Vietnam (EVN), Vietnam Posts and Telecommunications Group (VNPT), Vietnam Rubber Group (VRG), Viettel, Vietnam National Chemical Group (Vinachem), Bao Viet Holdings (BVH), Vietnam National Coal — Mineral Industries Holding Corporation Limited (Vinacomin), Vietnam Shipbuilding Industry Group (Vinashin), and Vietnam National Textile and Garment Group (Vinatex).
21. Dan Tri, "Chỉ giữ lại 5-7 Tập đoàn kinh tế nhà nước chủ đạo" [Government to Keep Only 5–7 essential state-owned economic groups], 6 September 2012 <http://dantri.com.vn/c728/s728-637689/chi-giu-lai-5-7-tap-doan-kinh-te-nha-nuoc-chu-dao.htm>.
22. Vietnam News Agency, "Thông báo Hội nghị lần 6 BCH Trung ương Đảng XI" [Communique of the VCPCC's fifth plenum (11th tenure)], 15 October 2012 <http://www.vietnamplus.vn/Home/Thong-bao-Hoi-nghi-lan-6-BCH-Trung-uong-Dang-XI/201210/163652.vnplus>.
23. The average debt/equity ratio of these groups and corporations was 1.77, with thirty of them having the ratio of greater than 3. As these groups and corporations had not been "equitized" and could not mobilize capital through the stock market, they had to rely on bank loans to expand business. Consequently, they had difficulties in paying off their debts, which kept growing, when the government increased interest rates in recent years to rein in inflation. See VnEconomy, "Tổng nợ của tập đoàn, tổng công ty nhà nước là bao nhiêu?" [How much is the total debt of state-owned groups and corporations?], 16 November 2012 <http://doanhnhan.vneconomy.vn/20121115073522550P0C5/tong-no-cua-tap-doan-tong-cong-ty-nha-nuoc-la-bao-nhieu.htm>.

24. Saigon Times, "Nợ xấu của DNNN tới 200.000 tỉ đồng" [SOE's bad debt reaches 200 trillion dongs], 30 September 2012 <http://www.thesaigontimes.vn/Home/doanhnghiep/quantri/84286/>.
25. Vietnamnet, "Tiền đâu lập công ty mua bán nợ xấu?" [Where to get the money for financing the debt buying company?], 14 June 2012 <http://tuanvietnam.vietnamnet.vn/2012-06-14-tien-dau-lap-cong-ty-mua-ban-no-xau->.
26. The first happened in December 2011 between Ficombank, TinNghiaBank, and Saigon Commercial Bank.
27. Vietnamnet, "Điểm mặt các ngân hàng sắp tái cơ cấu" [Information on banks to be restructured], 29 October 2012 <http://vietnamnet.vn/vn/kinh-te/94593/diem-mat-cac-ngan-hang-sap-tai-co-cau.html>.
28. VnExpress, "Thống đốc tuyên chiến với lợi ích nhóm ngân hàng" [Governor declares war on banking interest groups], 8 October 2012 <http://ebank.vnexpress.net/gl/ebank/tin-tuc/2012/10/thong-doc-tuyen-chien-voi-loi-ich-nhom-ngan-hang/>.
29. Full text of the Resolution (in Vietnamese) can be found at Government web portal, "Nghị quyết Hội nghị Trung ương 4: Một số vấn đề cấp bách về xây dựng Đảng hiện nay" [Resolution of VCPCC's fourth Plenum: Some current urgent matters regarding Party building], 17 January 2012 <http://baodientu.chinhphu.vn/Home/Nghi-quyet-Hoi-nghi-Trung-uong-4-Mot-so-van-de-cap-bach-ve-xay-dung-Dang-hien-nay/20121/125067.vgp>.
30. The criticism and self-criticism results of Politburo members formed the most important agenda item of the VCPCC's sixth plenum which took place in October. There were speculations prior to the plenum that PM Dung might be removed from his office, which finally did not happen. See Alexander Vuving's chapter in this volume for more information on the sixth plenum.
31. For a press communiqué of the plenum (in Vietnamese), see Dan Tri, "Thông báo Hội nghị lần thứ 5 BCH TW Đảng khóa XI" [Communique of the VCPCC's fifth plenum (11th tenure)], 15 May 2012 <http://dantri.com.vn/c20/s20-596217/thong-bao-hoi-nghi-lan-thu-5-bch-tw-dang-khoa-xi.htm>.
32. The Resolution No. 4 of the VCPCC's third Plenum (10th tenure) in 2006 addresses the Party's leadership in fighting corruption. Full text of Resolution No. 4 (in Vietnamese) is available at <http://www.ubmttq.hochiminhcity.gov.vn/WEB/data/news/2006/9/809/nghiquyetBCHTW%20ve%20chong%20tham%20nhung.doc>.
33. For a list of the measures (in Vietnamese), see Ha Noi Moi, "Kết luận Hội nghị Trung ương 5 (khóa XI) về tăng cường sự lãnh đạo của Đảng đối với công tác phòng, chống tham nhũng, lãng phí" [Conclusion of VCPCC's Fifth Plenum (11th tenure] on strengthening the Party's leadership in the prevention of and fight against corruption and wastefulness], 15 June 2012 <http://hanoimoi.com.vn/newsdetail/Chinh-tri/550492/ket-luan-hoi-nghi-trung-uong-5-khoa-xi-ve-tang-

cuong-su-lanh-dao-cua-%C4%91ang-doi-voi-cong-tac-phong-chong-tham-nhung-lang-phi.htm>.

34. Voice of Vietnam, "Công tác phòng chống tham nhũng 2012: Giơ cao, đánh khẽ?" [Corruption fighting in 2012: Just slaps on the wrist?], 21 September 2012 <http://vovgiaothong.vn/doi-thoai-voi-cong-luan/2012/09/cong-tac-phong-chong-tham-nhung-2012-gio-cao-danh-khe/>.